Founders of Modern Political
and Social Thought

Mill

D1610868

FOUNDERS OF
MODERN POLITICAL AND
SOCIAL THOUGHT

SERIES EDITOR
Mark Philp
Oriel College, Oxford

The *Founders* series presents critical examinations of the work of major political philosophers and social theorists, assessing both their initial contribution and their continuing relevance to politics and society. Each volume provides a clear, accessible, historically informed account of a thinker's work, focusing on a reassessment of the central ideas and arguments. The series encourages scholars and students to link their study of classic texts to current debates in political philosophy and social theory.

Published in the series:

JOHN FINNIS: *Aquinas*
GIANFRANCO POGGI: *Durkheim*
MAURIZIO VIROLI: *Machiavelli*
CHERYL WELCH: *De Tocqueville*
MALCOLM SCHOFIELD: *Plato*
JOSHUA COHEN: *Rousseau*

MILL

Founders of Modern Political and Social Thought

Frederick Rosen

OXFORD
UNIVERSITY PRESS

OXFORD

UNIVERSITY PRESS

Great Clarendon Street, Oxford, OX2 6DP,
United Kingdom

Oxford University Press is a department of the University of Oxford.
It furthers the University's objective of excellence in research, scholarship,
and education by publishing worldwide. Oxford is a registered trade mark of
Oxford University Press in the UK and in certain other countries

© Frederick Rosen 2013

The moral rights of the author have been asserted

First Edition published in 2013

Impression: 1

British Library Cataloguing in Publication Data

Data available

ISBN 978-0-19-927105-4 (hbk)
978-0-19-927106-1 (pbk)

Printed in Great Britain by
MPG Books Group, Bodmin and King's Lynn

For Maria

Preface

This study of John Stuart Mill's philosophy and social and political thought begins with a brief consideration of his conception of truth and what I have called a 'Socratic moment'. This starting point is important for understanding Mill's method in philosophy as well as in ethics and practical politics. The book then follows Mill through discussions of politics, ethics, economics, and social science to more detailed analyses of topics such as democracy, liberty, liberalism, psychology, active character, religion (including the religion of humanity), 'civil, or social liberty', property, co-operation, socialism, justice, equality, despotism, and the status of women.

I have tried to release Mill from numerous stale arguments and debates in an attempt to establish a more rounded view of his ideas as well as to capture the turmoil that surrounded his intellectual and personal life. Although Mill was occasionally mistaken in his conjectures and conclusions, once his larger aims and ambitions are taken into consideration, he was usually clear, consistent, creative, and deserving of his high reputation as a philosopher during the nineteenth century and today.

This book could not have been written without the unique resource of *The Collected Works of John Stuart Mill*, which challenges the student of Mill to understand his thought as a coherent whole. The size and uncompromising complexity of J. M. Robson's elegant edition not only serves as an important tool but also can terrify the scholar, as one realizes how much remains unexplored, even, as in my case, after eight years of dedicated research. I thank both Mill and Robson for providing a unique opportunity to enter into a relatively unexplored world of imagination and understanding.

All of the chapters have been written for this book, though several have appeared earlier as articles. An earlier version of Chapter 2, entitled 'J. S. Mill on Truth, Liberty, and Democracy', is now in the process of publication (with permission from Oxford University Press), in J. Elkins and A. Norris (eds.), *Truth and Democracy* (Philadelphia: University of Pennsylvania Press, 2012). A French translation of the chapter has also been published: 'Vérité, Liberté, et Démocratie chez John Stuart Mill', in M. Bozzo-Rey and E. Dardenne (eds.), *Deux siècles d'utilitarisme* (Rennes: Presses

Universitaires de Rennes, 2011). I am grateful to Malik Bozzo-Rey for translating the text.

Chapter 3 has been published as 'The Method of Reform: J. S. Mill's Encounter with Bentham and Coleridge', in N. Urbinati and A. Zakaras (eds.), *J. S. Mill's Political Thought: A Bicentennial Reassessment* (Cambridge: Cambridge University Press, 2007). My thanks to the editors and publisher for permission to reprint the essay here. Part of an earlier version of Chapter 4 was published as 'John Stuart Mill's Science of Politics', *Politeia*, 24/90 (2008), 7–19 (special issue on *Utilitarianism: Historical Theories and Contemporary Debates*, ed. G. Pellegrino); in Italian as 'Il caratere, "l'etologia" e la politica in John Stuart Mill', *Revista di filosofia*, 99 (2008), 397–419 (translation by G. Pellegrino); in French as 'La Science politique de John Stuart Mill', *Revue d'études benthamiennes, Numèro special John Stuart Mill*, 4 (Paris: Centre Bentham, 2008), pp. 121–33 (http://bentham.free.fr) (translated by E. de Champs); in Spanish as 'La Ciencia de la Política de John Stuart Mill', in Josefa Dolores Ruiz Resa (ed.), *John Stuart Mill y la Democracia del Siglo XXI* (Madrid: Dykinson, 2006), 191–210 (translated by Manuel Escamilla). Here again, I am grateful to the translators, editors, and publishers.

I have received assistance and advice over many years from colleagues and friends, a few of whom I am happy to acknowledge here: Daisuke Arie, Richard Bourke, Malik Bozzo-Rey, José de Brito y Sousa, D. G. Brown, J. H. Burns, Emmanuelle de Champs, Gregory Claeys, the late Maurice Cranston, Roger Crisp, Kyriakos Demetriou, Manuel Escamilla, Yasunori Fukagai, Angus Gowland, Kristopher Grint, Marco Guidi, Esperanza Guisan, Knud Haakonssen, Ofir Haivry, Hans Hansen, Paul Kelly, Ellen Kennedy, Eugenio Lecaldano, Michael Levin, David Lewisohn, David Lieberman, Peter Momtchiloff, James Moore, Peter Nicholson, Kevin O'Rourke, Gianfranco Pellegrino, Mark Philp, Michael Quinn, D. D. Raphael, Jonathan Riley, Ann and the late J. M. Robson, Philip Schofield, Huei-Chun Su, José Tasset, Georgios Varouxakis, David Weinstein, Cheryl Welch, Richard Whatmore, Geraint Williams, Donald Winch, and an anonymous reviewer for Oxford University Press. Special thanks are due to Mark Philp for reading the whole of the text and making numerous suggestions for improvement. Thanks are also due to Peter Nicholson for reading several chapters, making numerous corrections, and suggesting new aspects of Mill's thought to explore. Georgios Varouxakis has been very helpful on many aspects of the book, but particularly in encouraging me to examine Mill on character, including his use of the idea of national character. Kyriakos Demetriou has generously shared his work on the Platonic roots of modern utilitarianism, particularly, Grote and Mill. I have benefited greatly from Jonathan Riley's research on Mill and especially his understanding of the role of Mill's *Principles of Political Economy* in many aspects of his thought. Of course, I remain wholly responsible for the arguments developed here.

I wish to thank my family, Maria, Greg, Alex, Georgina, and Polly, for giving me time and space to carry on the research over such a long period of time. I dedicate the book to my wife, Maria, who combines an understanding of Mill's theory of psychology with a professional expertise in the field of psychiatry. She has also provided support and encouragement which has enabled me to continue on a very long and hard journey. In addition, Alex Rosen provided assistance in computing without which this book might easily have been lost in cyberspace. As with my other publications, parts of the book were written in the Dartmoor village of Peter Tavy. I am particularly indebted to the late James and Gillian Hacker, and to the whole Collins family (John, Graham, Angela, Sylvia, and Julia), for support and encouragement. Thanks are also due to Edward Dodd and his family for many acts of kindness including the loan of a few sheep to cut the grass.

The following abbreviations have been employed. *CW* followed by the volume number in roman numerals refers to *The Collected Works of John Stuart Mill*, 33 vols. (Mill 1963–91). The following works are most often mentioned:

i. *Autobiography*
ii–iii. *Principles of Political Economy*
v. 'Chapters on Socialism'
vii–viii. *System of Logic*
ix. *An Examination of Sir William Hamilton's Philosophy*
x. 'Bentham', 'Coleridge', *Utilitarianism, Auguste Comte and Positivism: Three Essays on Religion*
xi. 'Whately's Elements of Logic', 'Grote's History of Greece', 'Grote's Plato', 'Grote's Aristotle', 'Bain's Psychology'
xii–xiii. *The Early Letters 1812–1848*
xiv–xvii. *The Later Letters 1849–1873*
xviii. 'De Tocqueville on Democracy in America' I and II, *On Liberty*

xix. *Considerations on Representative Government*

xxi. *The Subjection of Women*, 'The Enfranchisement of Women', 'The Negro Question', *Inaugural Address Delivered to the University of St Andrews*

xxxi. Mill's notes on James Mill's *Analysis of the Phenomena of the Human Mind*

xxxii. *Additional Letters*

Other references may be fairly easily identified from the text itself.

CG (Comte 1973–90) refers to Auguste Comte's correspondence (*Correspondance générale et confessions*, 8 vols., ed. P. E. de Berrêdo Carneiro, P. Arnaud, P. Arbousse-Bastide, and Angèle Kremer Marietti (Paris: École des Hautes Études en Sciences Sociales and Vrin, 1973–90)).

Frederick Rosen
University College London
December 2011

Contents

II The Spell of Comte

III *Principles of Political Economy*

1

Introduction

This book is a study of the social and political philosophy of John Stuart Mill (1806–73) and is intended to provide a new interpretation of many of his ideas.[1] Unlike my last book on classical utilitarianism (Rosen 2003a), which concentrated on the development of the idea of utility in Western philosophy, this study ranges more widely over Mill's thought including such themes as the status of women, co-operation, socialism, despotism, liberty, equality, justice, Christianity and other religions, phrenology, logic, psychology, ethology (the science of character), and truth, to name a few.

1. *The Structure of the Argument*

Most students begin and end their study of Mill's ideas by reading *On Liberty* (1859), *Utilitarianism* (1861), and *Considerations on Representative Government* (1861), and wonder why their experience is relatively unsatisfactory. These three works do not fit neatly together, and they do not deal with numerous issues concerned with liberty, moral philosophy, and government with which philosophers and political theorists are now concerned. The reason for this state of affairs is that the students are reading a narrow group of essays and are reading them in the wrong way. The problem is a complex one. To approach Mill mainly through the three works just mentioned tends to cut the reader off from the main currents of his thought, as developed in his two great works, the *System of Logic, Ratiocinative and Inductive* (1843) and *Principles of Political Economy* (1848). Mill scholars have been aware of this problem for many decades and have reacted in various ways, mainly through interpretation to fill in what seems missing in the three texts, or using extracts from the *Logic* and *Principles* to supplement the arguments presented in these texts. This tendency has had at least two consequences.

First, the topics that we suppose *On Liberty*, *Utilitarianism*, and the *Considerations* are meant to highlight (e.g. liberty, justice, utility, liberalism, and democracy) turn out not to be addressed in any coherent way, thereby liberating an army of scholars to attempt to do Mill's work for him. As a result, debates over such issues as the connections between liberty and utility, liberty and justice, and justice and utility, Mill's account of political institutions and democracy, the different versions of utility (act, rule, virtue, etc.), and different versions of hedonism have become the staple diet of most discussions of Mill's ethical, social, and political thought. But these discussions simply underline the fact that the three texts mainly studied in lectures and tutorials throughout the world cannot themselves provide satisfactory accounts of the topics under consideration.

Second, the insights that one might legitimately seek in Mill's thought, such as a deeper understanding of his idea of liberty, if obtained from a different perspective, are obscured by this wealth of commentary. Modern commentary may go to the heart of key issues in recent moral and political philosophy from a Millian perspective, but they do not necessarily go to the heart of Mill's thought. One object of this book is to provide a different and more rounded view of Mill's thought. This interpretation will not only highlight different texts, such as those concerned with truth, ethology, and religion, to name a few, but will also provide a different way of interpreting Mill's ideas. For example, greater attention will be paid to Mill's rhetoric and ways of presenting arguments which fit in well with his writings on logical and practical topics.

In the following paragraphs I set out what I think is central to Mill's philosophical, sociological, and historical project. I do so in bold—perhaps even bald—terms so that readers can have a secure understanding of the position that the rest of the book will seek to extend, deepen, and further clarify. I then sketch the way in which the book addresses the different components of this, in my view, more subtle and more complex and faithful understanding of Mill's intellectual project.

Mill's philosophy is centred on the sciences of psychology and character (ethology). Ethology is a science of the development of the manifold elements of human character and an associated understanding of the components of human flourishing. This science is central to Mill's *Logic*, and while it is clear that Mill's confidence in being able fully to establish this on a scientific basis did wane over his lifetime, he retained the view that this was the central point of philosophical endeavour—to understand the processes, the interactions between individual personality and external forces that lead to the fuller development and flourishing of individual capacities and abilities, above all, the development of 'active character' in society. Active character concerns a capacity for reflection, questioning, and self-examination on the part of individuals—a capacity to make one's beliefs and commitments one's own, rather than inheriting them and abiding by them passively—and in the process to make one's life and one's commitments one's own—to become a self-directing agent rather than a brute merely responding to internal or external stimuli.

It is the concern with ethology that is at the heart of Mill's approach and it is this that animates his reflections on liberty, the subjection of women, political economy, and so on. It is not opposed to concerns with utility, since Mill remains committed in broad terms to a modern version of Epicureanism—seeing in the development of active character the key to the fuller enrichment of human capacities for pleasure and flourishing.

Mill did not claim to be in possession of the truth about character formation. That is the subject of the science of ethology and is a matter for ongoing scientific investigation. Indeed, we need to acknowledge the depth of Mill's belief in the importance of the Socratic questioning of claims to knowledge. It is in the pursuit of scientific truth through ethology and guided by logic that we come to a deeper and more sophisticated account of the relations between aspects of individual psychology and the social and moral world, but that endeavour is ongoing, open-ended, and permanently subject to revision. This understanding provides the tools to assist us in eliciting and sustaining liberty (rather than thinking of liberty as itself the crucial instrument for the emergence of truth). Moreover, critical inquiry is a necessary condition for the development of active character, without which people are capable only of coarser pleasures passively received. Psychology and ethology do not and cannot, however, set the *goal* of activity—they are sciences of causes and effects, the former inductive, the latter deductive. What is needed in addition to these sciences is an account of the appropriate end which this science can then help to secure. The 'art of life'—the very brief final chapter of the *Logic*—makes it clear that this is something separate from the science of ethology.

The art proposes to itself the end to be attained, defines the end, and hands it over to the science. The science receives it, considers it as a phenomenon or effect to be studied, and having investigated its causes and conditions, sends it back to the art with a theorem of the combinations of circumstances by which it could be produced. Art then examines these combinations of circumstances, and according as any of them are or are not in human power, pronounces the end attainable or not. . . . Art concludes that the performance of these actions is desirable, and finding it also practicable, converts the theorem into a rule or precept. (*CW* viii. 944)

Every art has one first principle, or general major premise, not borrowed from science; that which enunciates the object aimed at, and affirms it to be a desirable object. (*CW* viii. 949)

It is in this section that Mill argues that 'the general principle to which all rules of conduct ought to conform, and the test by which they should be tried, is that of conduciveness to the happiness of mankind: or rather, of all sentient beings; in other words, that the promotion of happiness is the ultimate principle of Teleology' (*CW* viii. 951). Moreover, the art of life is important only for setting the ultimate end—happiness. Its work is then done. For each science (like ethology) there is a distinct art, and the art related to ethology is not itself the art of life, but education. Progress and Improvement depend on what the teachers in one generation pass on to the students who come to power in the next generation.

In *On Liberty* it seems clear that Mill is not setting out what is optimal for the securing of happiness in terms of social and political arrangements—with happiness acting as a determinate criterion against which particular proposals can be measured. His position seems to be: that happiness is the end set by the art of life, and that we need to examine the complex set of issues (in a scientific manner) that allows us to generalize about conditions that lead to the development and sustaining of active character in society. We seek that because we recognize it as a necessary component of happiness. It is not sufficient: active character will in and of itself produce change between generations (which Mill refers to as progress) but it does not necessarily produce improvement. For that science and truth are additional conditions. But two features of Mill's position should be emphasized: first, that the content of happiness is not especially determinate—it is not a principle that exists as a standard against which we can measure sets of relationships in detail—allowing us to make maximizing calculations. It is an end, the content of which is open to further and deeper exploration, that evolves over time and changes as our understandings change. It is a horizon that both expands but also constantly recedes as we approach it—much as a criterion of a full and worthwhile life is—becoming richer and more open-ended. The science of ethology has to do the work to develop generalizations about what relationships, arrangements, and conditions will enhance such a broad goal, but part of what it is doing is to discover and articulate components of human flourishing. However, such flourishing should not be understood as a static condition—its components and elements are not fixed but change over time, responding to the interaction between facts of human psychology and facts about the social and political orders in which individuals participate.

If Mill seems curiously blind to the philosophical issues about the maximization of happiness and its place in *On Liberty*, which have obsessed his critics over the last forty years, this is because he never saw himself as trying to answer their questions, but was himself driven by a different and broader set of questions, in which the principle of utility is simply one, highly abstract, rather indeterminate, and historically developing component. This means that, in so far as we want to follow the spirit of Mill's enterprise, we should be approaching *On Liberty* (and many of his other essays) as an attempt to explore the causal conditions, within the (often rapidly changing) social and political orders of the West, for the development of active character and the associated evolving possibilities for human flourishing in the widest possible sense. For Mill there is no single concrete standard, no one universal character to which we all tend. Instead, there are laws and generalizations concerning the formation of character—and we can study the way in which character is shaped, constrained, or enhanced by the institutions and practices of our time. But these will change, new horizons will develop, and the purpose of this science is to try to identify these emerging possibilities and to advance proposals for their protection and defence, with a view to maintaining the active and developing character of humankind. In our discussion of these possibilities we will be concerned that people are in the most general sense happier, but our grasp of what that involves will also be developing. Moreover, active character should not be understood as a matter of having the liberty to get closer to the truth, so much as a critical enterprise by which we can doubt and question our beliefs and commitments. In doing so we open up our own conduct to change and experiment. We can then reverse the tendency of social conformity and the power of opinion to eradicate our independence of thought and action, *thereby* enhancing the liberty of society as a whole. We cannot say that doing so will make each one of us happier—we can say that we can only understand happiness in terms of the development and exercise of human powers and that such a society realizes such a condition more fully than one that closes down inquiry and self-exploration and development. But the standard of evaluation is soft, not hard—we feel our way, with the help that science can give us, through experiment and activity, and in doing so we undertake an exploration, individually and collectively, of our character as agents and of the flourishing (or happiness) we are capable of attaining. Rather than following Bentham who starts with the art and deduces institutions that will (he thinks) realize it—concluding that if you want happiness, you have to have representative democracy every-where—Mill places his emphasis on the sciences. As the sciences progress, the institutions that might develop from them will appear gradually and change often, and will not be the same in all countries.

This accounts for Mill's willingness to set a telos—and his unwill-ingness to say very much determinate about it. He is not being inconsistent between *Utilitarianism* and *On Liberty*—he is looking at different things, whose relationship is extremely complex and unfolding. So much so that we cannot reduce the principles and the complex discussion of social relations and the force of opinion in *On Liberty* to the principle of utility, any more than we can say that *On Liberty* has no reference to the standard of utility. But the relationship between the art of life on the one hand, and the subor-dinate art of education and the ends it sets for the sciences of psychology and ethology is simply not going to have the direct and deductive character that so many modern interpretations assume. By resisting their readings, and trying to do justice to the project that Mill set himself, we can gain a much fuller appreciation of the distinctive character of the complex body of writings that Mill produced, and may also gain a more enlarged and richer sense of the kind of activity that we, as philosophers, political theorists, and historians of the present ought to be engaged in.

II. *Outline of the Book*

In embarking on this study of Mill's moral and political thought, it will be clear that the starting point must be the *Logic,* but no full account of Mill's writings on philosophy will be attempted here. In part, this has already been achieved by a number of excellent scholars (see e.g. Jackson 1941; Kubitz 1932; Ryan 1987; Scarre 1989; and Skorupski 1989, to name a few). The book concentrates on Mill's social and political thought, but does so from the perspective of Mill, the philosopher, as this is the way Mill conceived his own role. To approach Mill as a philosopher, without examining all of his philosophical texts in detail, may invite criticism. But this approach will enable one to bring to light the deeper foundations of his moral and political thought, which are often overlooked in studies of Mill's philosophy.

The starting point for the book is the remark of Alexander Bain (1818–1903) that Mill's creative energy was mainly confined to two works, the *Logic* and the *Principles* (Bain 1882: 91).[2] As we shall see, many of Mill's later writings were derived from these two earlier major works. This book adopts Bain's important perspective, with Part I based on themes from the *Logic* and Part III on themes from the *Principles.* Part II concentrates on the elaborate correspondence between Mill and Auguste Comte (1798–1857) which consists of eighty-nine letters written between 1841 and 1847, and forms an important bridge between the two works just mentioned.[3] In this correspondence we see Mill formulate his views on the sciences relevant to society with which the *Logic* is concerned. We also see him turning away from Comte to embrace political economy and, additionally, to return to some of the ideas of Jeremy Bentham (1748–1832). Positively and negatively, Comte played a crucial role in the evolution of Mill's social and political thought. Unfortunately, much of the critical discussion by commentators concentrates on Mill's views in *Auguste Comte and Positivism* (1865) and uses the correspondence in a supporting role to supplement and explain the later published work. The correspondence is the masterpiece, which is supplemented, often in a misleading fashion, by the published essay (see below, Chapters 5 and 6). The correspondence often reads like a Platonic dialogue with the two interlocutors asserting and replying in a carefully constructed literary work, all the more remarkable for being composed by two different authors and with neither for the most part keeping copies of their own letters.

The prominence given here to the Mill–Comte correspondence and the recognition of the importance of Comte in Mill's thought will require some further explanation. It is arguable that Comte's importance does not extend much beyond book 6 of the *Logic* concerned with social science where most of the explicit references to Comte seem to occur. If so, his importance to Mill and the *Logic* would appear to be far less than suggested here. It is true, for example, that Mill's study of induction in book 3 of the *Logic* is not directly dependent on Comte. Nevertheless, Comte's views on the nature of science and the relationship between science and art are relevant to the whole of Mill's *Logic*. His account of the historical nature of ideas is also important. Their shared views on religion have a direct effect on Mill's conception of the purpose of logic and the importance of empirical truth. In addition, the importance of Comte's positivism, itself, to Mill's understanding of logic and philosophy is an important theme in the *Logic* and elsewhere.

The book concludes with a lengthy study of Mill's *The Subjection of Women* (1869) which is examined as a work on liberty and despotism. This object enables one to draw together many of the themes discussed in the earlier chapters and focus them on practical applications in the context of oppression in society. The *Subjection* has traditionally been an underrated and poorly studied work. Its fairly recent adoption by feminists as an important text has made it more widely known and studied, though this development has removed it somewhat from the contexts developed in this book. I have tended to read the *Subjection* as Mill's great work on despotism in society.

In the chapters that make up the book numerous themes in Mill's thought are considered. All of them, however, are placed under the rubric of the *Logic, Principles*, and the correspondence with Comte, even though many other works by Mill and his colleagues are discussed, including the familiar *On Liberty* (see Chapters 2, 4, 6, and 7 below), *Utilitarianism* (see Chapters 11 and 13 below), and *Considerations on Representative Government* (see Chapters 2, 3, and 4 below). In the brief summary of the chapters that follows, this additional and important dimension to the book will become apparent.

Chapter 2, the first of three chapters based on the *Logic*, begins with Mill's belief in the importance of logic to the discovery of truth.

In his view logic became a master science, even a 'sovereign judge' of numerous issues from logic and science to those of social science, ethics, politics, and economics. Mill also attempted to draw into his conception of logic the Aristotelian traditions of the syllogism and the study of fallacies, modern inductive logic, and most important of all, a negative, dialectical approach that drew on the work of Plato's early Socratic dialogues. The chapter challenges the commonplace interpretation of Mill on truth which places its emphasis on freedom of expression as the means of achieving truth. I argue that Mill never believed that freedom of expression alone would lead to truth, and contend that it is not liberty that assists the emergence of truth, but the pursuit of truth through logic that assists the emergence of liberty. Nonetheless, freedom of expression plays an important role in keeping truth alive by allowing one to pursue the truth and communicate it to others. It is also contended that for every person there is a 'Socratic moment' when to recognize one's ignorance allows one to pursue the truth. To possess liberty without such a 'moment' leads mainly to an endless pursuit of variety and novelty, as entertainment, or, even worse, to a dogmatism that substitutes for truth.

The chapter next attempts to apply Mill's ideas about truth and liberty of expression to his understanding of liberty and democracy in *On Liberty* and *Considerations on Representative Government*. If the Socratic elenchus is the key to his views on truth, the democracy of Periclean Athens is treated as embodying his ideal political society in so far as the public realm unusually allowed liberty to flourish in the private sphere. Drawing on George Grote's *History of Greece* (1846–56), Mill regarded Athens in this period as superior to all modern states, including modern democracies (which, after all, threatened the individual with the tyranny of the majority) in the liberty allowed and encouraged in private and public life. That Socrates was put to death in Athens at this time did not seem to diminish Mill's praise of Athens. After all, Socrates was accepted and flourished there for seventy years.

The foundation of Mill's idea of representative government was based on the diffusion of the Socratic elenchus throughout society, via the negative and critical dialectic. The key to this diffusion is the cultivation of active character, which belongs to the science of ethology and works mainly indirectly in politics in opposing the 'pedantocracy' that Mill associated with the form of despotism he believed existed in China and elsewhere at the time. The chapter concludes with a first discussion of the much-debated problem of Mill's status as a liberal. Here again, it is argued that a concern for truth and its diffusion in society is a key component of Mill's view of society and its reformation.

In Chapter 3 I turn from a consideration of logic in general to Mill's conception of the logic of social and political science. My starting point, however, is not the *Logic* itself but what I have called Mill's 'method of reform'. In the preface to the *Considerations* Mill used the opposition between liberals and conservatives to show how opposed and apparently irreconcilable positions might nonetheless be reconciled and major reform achieved in politics. To see how Mill introduced this move from irreconcilable opposition to reconciliation and progressive politics, I first examine how he rejected the Benthamite approach in the 1830s with the creation of philosophic radicalism. This discussion provides the background for understanding Mill's essays, 'Bentham' (1838) and 'Coleridge' (1840) in which he worked out (probably for the first time) the important use of contraries (as opposed to contradictories) for social and political progress. The development of these ideas and Mill's personal involvement with John Sterling (1806–44) and other Coleridgeans, like F. D. Maurice (1805–72), begins with Mill's dispute with Sterling (over Bentham's philosophy) in the London Debating Society in 1829.

Mill's new 'method of reform' was also grounded in several respects in the *Logic* itself. Here, he rejected what he called the Benthamite 'geometric method' in politics and replaced it with the 'Inverse Deductive, or Historical Method', inspired by both Coleridge and Comte. That Mill appeared to reject Bentham's method is shown to be somewhat curious. Mill did not simply replace Bentham with Coleridge and/or Comte. The historical method he adopted was dependent on the sciences of psychology and ethology, derived from the 'school' of Locke and Bentham, and revived by James Mill's psychology. Mill's approach to method in social science was thus fairly complex, as he attempted to identify polarities of thought that defined the transition from the eighteenth to the nineteenth centuries and sought to show how contrary positions could be reconciled to achieve improvement in thought and in practical politics.

Chapter 4 begins with Mill's critique of the traditional notion of a science of politics that focused on constitutions, conceived in the abstract, e.g. monarchy, aristocracy, and democracy. Although Mill was aware of T. B. Macaulay's (1800–59) critique of his father's essay, 'Government', and the subsequent debate (see Lively and Rees 1978), he looked elsewhere for the deeper foundations of the study of politics in the science of character or ethology. The importance of this science and its relationship to an art of politics are explored, as are key differences between Bentham and Mill on the connection between art and science generally. Also considered is Mill's conception of 'political ethology'—that branch of social science which, when created, would replace or improve the general study of constitutional forms with a more 'scientific' exploration of political societies. For Mill, political ethology was the study of the character and education of the people in society and the causes of its institutions.

The chapter then explores further the idea of ethology by questioning the ascription to Mill of the label 'public moralist', when such a notion obscures Mill's own conception of his role as mainly that of a logician, and as one who thought of himself as developing a scientific theory. That scientific theory is briefly examined in terms of the legacy from Bentham and James Mill. A final issue raised in the chapter deals with the question of whether or not Mill abandoned or minimized the importance of ethology in his thought after the publication of the *Logic*. In rejecting these alternatives, I begin by following Ball's position regarding Mill on ethology (see Ball 2000: 25–48; 2010: 35–56) and then deviate from it in some important ways to stress the significance of ethology as a science linking psychology to social science. The role Mill gave to ethology did not diminish during his lifetime, though he became increasingly aware that he was unable to undertake the task of establishing it as a science.

Having set out the foundations of Mill's approach, as developed in the *Logic*, we return in the final part of the chapter to the *Considerations*, where Mill declared (in apparent conflict with the argument in the *Logic*) that representative government was 'the ideally best form of government' (see *CW* xix. 399). In sorting out Mill's contention and showing that there is no contradiction between the *Considerations* and the earlier *Logic*, I uncover one of the main themes of 'active' as opposed to 'passive' character. The development of this distinction allowed Mill to establish a very different approach to politics through the cultivation of active character in society. In *On Liberty* we see this manifested in the study of the individual as embedded in society, as a social being, apart from the traditional institutions of government.

The chapters that constitute Part II of the book are concerned with the importance of Comte more generally in Mill's thought. Chapter 5 consists of a study of the Mill–Comte correspondence as a distinct literary work. It was written by the two philosophers over a number of years without any obvious intention to produce a single work. It forms a distinct text, because of the unusual interaction between Comte and Mill. It brings to mind the form of the Platonic dialogue, except the 'triumph' of Mill's Socrates is not orchestrated by Comte's 'Plato'. We also see Mill's *Logic* in a new light. The correspondence reveals Mill's diffidence about his own work and a willingness to regard the *Logic* as a temporary production, suiting English character at the time, and subordinate to Comte's major works that defined the new science of positivism. Furthermore, we learn from the correspondence that the *Logic* was not mainly intended to provide the methodological 'common ground' where the 'partisans of Hartley and of Reid, of Locke and of Kant, may meet and join hands' (*CW* vii. 14). Mill's strategy in writing and publishing the work related more to a battlefield for defeating German or ontological philosophy whose roots in England in philosophy and theology had an important effect not only on philosophy but also on the creation of obstacles to social and political reform.

The chapter also explores the circumstances behind Mill's decisions to abandon his proposed treatise on ethology and to turn to political economy. In part, due to the numerous differences between the two philosophers, once Mill published the *Logic*, he seemed less in need of participating in Comte's movement. His taking up political economy gave him an intellectual project that need not be actively related to Comte's work and, additionally, enabled him to return to his roots in Bentham's and his father's thought.

In examining the dialogue itself the chapter considers the motives of the two correspondents for sustaining it. The belief that it was based on friendship or 'their game of mutual admiration' (Pickering 2009: ii. 70) is rejected and replaced by an interpretation that sees them seeking agreement but for different objects. Comte believed that agreement from Mill represented proof of the truth of his system, while Mill believed that Comte's system enabled him to defeat an intellectual enemy he called variously 'intuitive', 'German', 'ontological', and 'transcendental'.

In Chapter 6 our attention turns to *Auguste Comte and Positivism*, a late work, in which we see Mill as a mature philosopher. Mill also provided in this work a thorough critique of aspects of Comte's thought without any specific reference to the correspondence. In this chapter, however, Mill's essay will be interpreted in light of the correspondence rather than the correspondence being used selectively to interpret *Auguste Comte and Positivism*. Mill's essay was written in two parts, with the first covering the period when Mill was a disciple, and the second, the later period, when Mill had rejected Comte's absurdities. If Mill admittedly had overly praised Comte in the *Logic* he thought that he could redress the balance in this essay. The tone is more critical, but with regard to the correspondence, some important changes also appear.

For example, Mill never insisted in the correspondence (as he did in *Auguste Comte and Positivism*) that the *Logic* should be held up to assess the validity of Comte's philosophy. During the correspondence Mill only sought agreement on a number of issues in order to establish his role as a disciple, while in *Auguste Comte and Positivism* he criticized Comte's failure in logic to appreciate induction or to realize the importance of the Aristotelian syllogism. A related theme in their correspondence concerned Comte's practice of 'cerebral hygiene', in which he abstained from reading books, learned journals, and newspapers to live at the highest level of generalization and with the purest feelings, and which Mill accepted in the correspondence (as it was part of Comte's life at the time). Although Comte briefly suspended cerebral hygiene in order to read Mill's *Logic*, Mill soon knew that the practice left Comte on the edge of madness. Mill placed his discussion of cerebral hygiene in the second part of *Auguste Comte and Positivism*, implying that Comte did not practise it in the earlier period, when they corresponded, and Mill seemed devoted to this 'superior' philosopher. Thus, Mill used *Auguste Comte and Positivism* to defend himself against being seen to accept the views of a man who was possibly insane.

An important aspect of *Auguste Comte and Positivism* is Mill's attempt to show how his political ideas (particularly, his views on liberty and liberalism) both differed from, yet were related to Comte's positive philosophy. Contrary to Comte, Mill adhered to elements of 'metaphysical' politics, associated with the Enlightenment consisting of revolutionary, radical, liberal, free-thinking, sceptical, and critical views. He also believed that Comte had rejected these doctrines (nearly all associated with liberty in some form), but had failed to establish positivist sciences of ethics and politics to replace them. In working out these ideas in relation to ethics, he connected Comte's doctrine to extreme Calvinism (see also Rosen 2003*a*: 203ff.), which he rejected, and his own views to Epicureanism, which provided an important space in its ethics for the cultivation of liberty.

With Chapter 7 we begin a series of five chapters which are based on Mill's second great published work, the *Principles of Political Economy*. As I have suggested, the *Principles* represents the beginning of Mill's break with Comte and 'return' to Bentham. This chapter is concerned with the theme of liberty and with the connection between the discussion of liberty in the *Principles* and that in the later *On Liberty*. I start with Mill's definition and elucidation of what he called at the beginning of *On Liberty*, 'Civil, or Social Liberty' (*CW* xviii. 217). Despite Mill's statement that he was concerned with 'one very simple principle' (*CW* xviii. 223), he actually started with two principles: civil liberty and social liberty. Civil liberty was most associated with the tradition of Locke and Bentham, while the 'social' in social liberty might in part have been taken from Comte. The chapter then explores Mill's approach to civil liberty in terms of security, an idea he derived from Bentham. Bentham's idea consisted of individual freedom of action, protected by law and government, so long as one did not harm others. However, Mill discussed 'security' in the *Principles* differently, as he distinguished between protection *by* government and protection *against* government. If Bentham emphasized protection by government (which enabled the individual to enlarge one's freedom), Mill emphasized freedom, even within an 'unsettled and turbulent' society, which was based on active character, with the society itself sufficiently free to encourage the cultivation of active character. Mill thus seemed to minimize a key aspect of Bentham's emphasis on the security of persons and property, that achieved by law and government.

Mill developed a different idea of liberty in the *Principles*, which he depicted in terms of a circle around every human being. The circle of liberty was intended to reduce what he called 'authoritative' intervention by government, while allowing the development of non-authoritative intervention. He conceived of this formulation by reconciling two contradictory opinions regarding laissez-faire: that government should be free to intervene in any circumstance that intervention was considered useful; and that the sphere of government should be severely limited to the protection of person and property from force and fraud. In developing his distinction Mill could envisage an expanded role for government in society in a way that would not interfere with free agency and the free flow of active character. Furthermore, this freedom, and not the institutions of representative democracy, was the main security against political slavery.

The chapter concludes by returning to *On Liberty* and applying the insights gained from the study of liberty in the *Principles*. I begin by suggesting that in *On Liberty* the phrase 'Civil, or Social Liberty' was not meant to depict civil and social liberty as two different conceptions of liberty, as Mill made clear a few lines further on in referring to 'one very simple principle'. Nor did he see civil and social liberty as synonymous terms. Furthermore, it is argued that the conception of liberty that appears in the circle of liberty in the *Principles* is best spelt out in the final chapter of *On Liberty* titled 'Applications'. We see here how Mill used the notions of authoritative and non-authoritative intervention to reveal the dimensions of the circle of liberty. We also see the importance Mill gave to social liberty.

Chapters 8 and 9 are concerned with Mill's intellectual journey to socialism. If civil liberty leads to representative democracy (in so far as the people can secure their lives and property by choosing and rejecting their rulers), social liberty leads to an unusual form of socialism. The first section in Chapter 8 is concerned with the legacy of Alexis de Tocqueville (1805–59) in Mill's journey. This legacy is more problematic than first appears, and has been discussed by both Mill and Tocqueville scholars. What becomes clear is that Tocqueville's legacy for Mill is more one of pointing out the dangers of democracy than its benefits. His influence might be seen in Mill's acceptance of a modified version of democracy in the *Considerations* (see Chapters 3 and 4). However, if Tocqueville alerted Mill to the dangers of the 'tyranny of the majority', he did not assist Mill directly on the journey to socialism. But perhaps he provided Mill with an additional reason to undertake such a journey.

Contrary to the Benthamite radicals, Mill believed that representative democracy did not provide the political liberty and security that was claimed for it. Not only was there the danger of the tyranny of the majority, but also Mill did not believe that representative democracy would end the conflicts between rich and poor or capital and labour that so divided modern European societies. The only way to end such conflicts would be the acceptance and institution of co-operation in society, based on the idea of social liberty. To advance the cause of co-operation, Mill turned to his conception of active character. The cultivation of active character came from the people themselves and allowed them to develop and exercise their 'active energies' in ways that included 'labour, contrivance, judgment, self-control', etc. (see *CW* iii. 943). Where a people usually looked to government to solve their problems, their faculties were only half-developed. The exercise of active character meant people doing things for themselves. Mill was not advancing here a conception of civic virtue; his emphasis was on laissez-faire and even his conception of compulsory education (as made clear in Chapter 7) was fully compatible with social liberty.

Of greatest importance to Mill was the condition of the working classes. He opposed restrictions on trade unions and the prohibition of strikes, so long as no compulsion was used to force workers to join a union and engage in strikes. Mill sought through the cultivation of active character 'the elevation of the character and condition of the entire body' of the working class (*CW* iii. 931). This transformation was to be achieved through the development of co-operation. In this respect he supported the co-operative and trade union movements, not for the sake of gaining political power, or as a prelude to violent revolution or to create state socialism. His object was to enhance social liberty throughout society and, particularly, among the ordinary workers. The way forward to achieving this end was through the adoption of co-operation and, additionally, the removal of legal restrictions on freedom of expression.

Chapter 9 examines the final steps in the journey to socialism undertaken by Mill and Harriet Mill (1807–58). It concentrates on two chapters in the *Principles*, one concerned with the 'stationary state' (*CW* iii. 752–7), and the other, with the probable future of the working classes (*CW* iii. 758–96). The material on the stationary state belonged to the realm of economic dynamics, and was used to challenge the views of economists who envisaged the end of economic development in terms of an end to prosperity and the presence of a 'pinched and stinted' condition for the masses (*CW* iii. 752–3). For Mill, however, the stationary state represented a beginning, a starting point for a major improvement in existing conditions. Leaving less developed countries to concentrate on increasing production, he wanted more advanced countries to move away from this goal. With the encouragement of prudential restraints on the increase of population plus limits on inheritance, Mill looked forward to a condition in society where the working class was relatively well-paid and prosperous, and no one could amass a fortune beyond what could be earned in a lifetime. Those who did not have to engage in hard labour were also free to cultivate 'the graces of life' (*CW* iii. 755).

In Mill's view most economists were wrong to see the end of a highly competitive and growing economy as a sorry state of affairs, when it presented excellent opportunities for both individual human development and the improvement of society. In this respect the use of co-operative institutions to develop socialism became highly important. Mill began his discussion of the future of the labouring classes by utilizing what I have called his 'method of reform', in which he stated two contrary doctrines and then reconciled them in the direction of reform. The first doctrine was called the theory of dependence and security, in which the rich were to look after, educate, and give morality and religion to the poor. Mill insisted that this condition had in fact never existed, but it had a seductive influence in Mill's day, as a powerful and attractive model of care and protection. The second contrary was called the theory of self-dependence. Once the working classes acquired the skills to read and write, which had begun with the Reformation, their dependence on the rich for instruction and religion would end, and they could then look after themselves. Mill was clearly on the side of self-dependence, but he did not wholly reject the doctrine of dependence. He turned to this doctrine for one ingredient that his theory needed: deference. The principle of self-dependence would require deference—to institutions as well as to individuals—if reform was to take place. The theory of dependence also provided evidence to suggest that other values, such as those linked to association and co-operation, which were beyond narrow economic ones, could flourish in daily life.

Mill developed the idea that co-operative associations could end the unsatisfactory situation that required the individual either to work for a master or to work for oneself. He admired the ideas of workers' associations developed in the theories of Robert Owen (1771–1858) and Louis Blanc (1811–82) and the practice of the co-operatives developed in France following the revolution of 1848. He believed that properly established and run workers' co-operatives could advance the values associated with active character and social liberty among the working classes. Mill's admiration of the co-operatives did not diminish even though many of them, like the Manufacturing Society of Rochdale, were transformed into joint stock companies as they became successful. However, he realized that these former co-operatives could not compete with individual capitalists, as they would quickly lose their capacity for innovation and taking risks.

Mill's journey to socialism also ran into difficulty from some socialist theories and institutions. Many socialists rejected piece-work and most other forms of competition as an economic evil. Mill defended competition here, in *On Liberty*, and in the 'Chapters on Socialism' as a way of raising wages, developing character, and avoiding indolence among workers.

The focus of Chapter 10 is on Mill's posthumously published 'Chapters on Socialism' (1879) (*CW* v. 703–53), but it also utilizes the earlier discussion of property in the *Principles* (*CW* ii. 199–234). The immediate context of the 'Chapters' was the passage of the new Reform Act of 1867. For Mill, the Act gave power and influence for the first time in Britain to those who lived on weekly wages and who would have had little incentive to uphold the existing inequalities of property. The 'Chapters' might also be considered a first draft of a contribution to the scientific study of politics, which emphasized the state of the working classes and an appreciation of different strands of socialist and communist thought. It might be considered 'scientific', because it took into account British national character and various psychological factors such as the motivation to perform arduous and repetitive tasks. Mill also expressed some urgency regarding his topic. He believed that approximately a generation was available for reconciliation between those seeking and opposing change to enable Britain to avoid bloodshed, if not civil war.

To understand Mill's arguments in the 'Chapters', I return to the discussion of property in the earlier *Principles*. Mill's starting point was the frank acknowledgement that the existing laws and practices for the ownership and control of property were wholly accidental and unrelated to any principles of justice and utility. All that recommended existing property arrangements was the fear that chaos would follow any major change.

The main alternative would appear to be a system of communism, based on equality of property and reward as a principle of justice, but Mill did not reach this conclusion. He believed that a comparison between an ideal system of social justice, based on equality, and the existing property system was misleading, and he could envisage an ideal form of individual property rights that could rival a communist system with regard to wealth and poverty and avoid the chaos of the transition from one form to the other. He also believed that there were other values, like liberty, that were as important as social justice.

In addition, Mill pointed out how within socialist theories there were conflicting views concerning equality and justice. For example, equal distribution had been replaced in some systems by piecework, even though such a change (which Mill approved) gave more to those already favoured by nature and education. In examining a number of other theories and practices from St-Simonism, Fourierism, and Owenism to the Jesuits in Paraguay, he found numerous principles and practices that did not aspire to equality. Furthermore, those which approached equality in distribution were in danger of being disregarded because they set standards that were too high. As they might need to utilize force to achieve equality, they were in danger of denying liberty. Such equality, though representing the highest standard of justice, was a flawed companion for liberty, and pointed to important difficulties within the notion of distributive justice that I shall consider in Chapter 11.

In carefully comparing the merits and deficiencies of socialism versus capitalism, taking into account the natural indolence of workers as well as national character, Mill began to develop a way of dealing with the current irreconcilable camps regarding the ownership of property and the realistic possibilities of socialist schemes. He rejected the view of those who upheld traditional rights to property, however obtained, as a 'natural right'. He also rejected the position of those who advocated immediate revolution and the public ownership of the means of production. He looked first to a general consensus that the adoption of socialism in Britain in some form within a generation was nearly inevitable. Within this context he tried to reconcile capitalism in Britain as it was, on the one hand, with the doctrine of socialism, on the other. Having ruled out immediate revolution, he focused on the moral and intellectual issues raised within the alternative versions of socialism to see which of them might be reconciled with a change for the better within the existing system of property.

Chapter 11 returns to the problem of distributive justice, which we have already found to be difficult to understand and apply. We were left with the problem that the most exalted claims for justice were far beyond human application. I turn here for enlightenment to the well-known account of justice in *Utilitarianism*, and to a notion of justice linked with liberty as security. Such security of persons, property, and expectations, as a principle of justice, also leads to Mill's discussion of rights. The two references to distributive justice in *Utilitarianism* raise questions that are similar to those raised in Chapter 10. These deal with the relationship between justice and equality, the application of principles of justice to practice in light of the sciences of psychology and national character, and the role of liberty in such an application. Recent commentators on Mill have found his idea of justice a topic worthy of study, and usually approach it via a consequentialist theory, or by an abstract theory that clarifies notions of equality, desert, fairness, and impartiality in relation to some ideal concept of justice. I emphasize the extent to which Mill took another path and sought to develop an account of justice with minimal content, utilizing the sciences of psychology and ethology to determine actual distributions.

If, as we shall see, consequentialism cannot set forth a theory of justice, and a theory of justice must be related to the ethology of different societies at different times, it is clear that no single formulation of distributive justice can be applied universally, except, perhaps, a formal notion of justice concerned with equal things for equal people. Such a formulation might lead to equality or inequality, but would mainly be part of a principle of rationality in the logic of the sciences. The belief in individual liberty and widespread opposition to violent revolution, as principles of British national character, constitute limits to the introduction of strict equality in Britain. National character might change and perceptions of justice might also change, and hence, as Mill freely admitted, new notions of liberty and justice could emerge through education and changes in public opinion.

Is it possible to say that Mill was a socialist? In the concluding section I begin with the passage from the *Autobiography* (*CW* i. 239) where he referred to Harriet Mill and himself as socialists. After considering those who believe that there is no clear answer to this question and those who believe that there is, I provide an answer by again criticizing the view that Mill was a public moralist and might be expected to take a stand and provide a clear answer to such an issue. Mill was a philosopher and logician, who worked within the sciences of psychology and ethology, examined all sides of issues, and provided less categorical answers to questions such as that concerned with his belief in socialism. If he could answer the question to a degree, it was because he understood psychology and national character. The chapter concludes with a quotation from Sidgwick who, in my opinion, correctly grasped Mill's position.

Chapter 12 builds on a distinction Mill made in a letter to Comte between religion on the one hand and God on the other. Mill wrote that he had unusually, for Britain, never believed in God (see *CW* xiii. 560). But Mill was not opposed to some forms of religion, and developed the idea of a religion of humanity. In their correspondence we find Mill remarkably frank concerning his reticence about discussing religion in his publications and, indeed, his avoidance, wherever possible, of any reference to religion. We see here how Mill's sensitivity to English national character allowed him to support Comte's publications in France but to oppose their translation and publication in English. Even the much-admired *Cours* suffered in this respect. This position should not be interpreted in terms of some kind of opposition by Mill to freedom of expression or freedom of religion, but it might be seen as advancing a form of self-censorship with regard to free expression. This apparent difference between Comte and Mill was largely ascribed by Mill not to a difference in doctrine but to necessary adjustments in relation to national character.

Two doctrines that Mill adopted from Comte were discussed by Mill in *Auguste Comte and Positivism*: the separation of spiritual and temporal powers and the religion of humanity. The first enabled Mill to reject utopian doctrines involving the rule of philosophers or a clerisy. But Mill was also critical of Comte's creation of a spiritual despotism by giving so much unchecked power in the realm of education to a few philosophers, and his creation of a temporal despotism by his failure to establish institutional checks on temporal power.

In adopting the idea of the religion of humanity Mill seemed to be setting a marker rather than developing a practical policy intended to be applied. Nevertheless, he seriously supported the idea of a religion without God. He developed the logical conditions for such a religion, involving a 'creed', an inward sense of duty, and a sentiment that gave authority to the creed. He then argued (through an analogy with Thomas Carlyle's (1795–1881) notion of the 'infinite nature of duty') that Comte had put together the ingredients for a genuine religion.

At the very point where Mill was extolling Comte's view of religion as genuine in logical terms he turned to criticize Comte for his denial of individual liberty, and used the arguments of *On Liberty* to reveal flaws in Comte's conception of moral duty. Mill also linked morality with a version of Epicureanism, and generally provided an argument in favour of a religion of humanity that was distinct from and opposed to that of Comte. In a concluding section the views of Mill scholars who either applaud Mill for developing a liberalism more sympathetic and open to religion or criticize him for using the religion of humanity to develop a 'proselytizing liberalism' and a 'narrow and intolerant creed' (see Knights 1978: 141, quoting from Cowling 1963) are briefly considered.

Chapter 13 on *The Subjection of Women* (1869) has a special role to play in this book. I have chosen to study the *Subjection* as an important late work of Mill in which he drew on and brought together the main themes of his social and political philosophy. In this sense the chapter provides both a conclusion to the book and a test of the coherence of Mill's thought. It confirms the arguments developed in the earlier chapters and reveals how Mill could apply his ideas to an important theme. This theme is that of despotism, and, together with liberty, was a theme in Mill's thought from his earliest writings. In dealing with despotism in the *Subjection*, Mill brought together numerous themes that he developed first in the *Logic*, *Principles*, and other writings. In the various sections of this chapter, we again encounter his 'method of reform' in forming and reconciling contraries to avoid stalemate in society due to sharply opposed opinions. We see his 'Socratic' method and explore this to reject Hamburger's belief (1999: 203) that Mill's method (his 'rhetoric') was meant to disguise, conceal, equivocate, and mislead. We encounter another dimension of Mill's account of the relationship between the eighteenth and nineteenth centuries as a struggle between a reliance on reason on the one hand and instinct (or feeling) on the other, and see his emphasis on reason as a reaffirmation of his return to the Enlightenment views of his father and Bentham. In emphasizing that women were in a condition of slavery, he invoked and rejected the position of Carlyle who had justified the condition of African slaves in terms of the 'old law of the strongest', taking one back to a very old argument first uttered by Thrasymachus in Plato's *Republic*. Mill also referred to ancient Greek societies, which thought themselves to be free in spite of the practice of domestic slavery. He believed that the enslavement of women in otherwise free modern societies followed a similar pattern. In addition, he emphasized the importance of discussing the status of women in these so-called free societies in stark terms of slavery, oppression, and despotism rather than in the language of Victorian sentimentality and religiosity. He did not confine his attention to legal enslavement, but showed how women's character in all aspects of social and domestic life was affected. If the end to legal enslavement through the reform of the institutions of marriage and related property arrangements might be the first step towards liberation, it was only the first step, as women should be free to break out from the restraints imposed on their character to end despotism in the family and in social life.

Mill returned to numerous themes discussed in this book, from ethology to religion, from the relationship between liberty, justice, and equality to the role of utility in understanding the future. These discussions hopefully reaffirm the interpretation made of Mill's thought in the earlier chapters and establish the application of his ideas in an important field of thought and action. In this sense there is no need to summarize further what is already a summary of his ideas.

III. *Intellectual Contexts*

One dimension of this study is a fuller appreciation of how important Bentham was to Mill on a number of different levels. It is suggested here that one cannot understand Mill's ideas in detail or some of Mill's major changes of direction without a careful study of Bentham. Bentham's thought thus forms one of the major contexts for understanding Mill.

Another context for understanding Mill's thought was his complex relationship with Comte. Mill felt that he could not complete his *Logic* without Comte having completed the *Cours de philosophie positive* (1830–42) and was even tempted to devote his time to a translation of the *Cours* rather than to the completion of his own masterpiece. The *Principles* reflects Mill moving away from Comte and returning to the tradition of political economy and to the philosophical ideas of Bentham and the Enlightenment. As Comte had earlier adopted and then rejected the tradition of political economy in favour of positivism, he had no inclination to return to it.

A third context is provided by the younger colleague and disciple, Alexander Bain, whose connection with Mill is depicted here in terms of their intertwined relationship in the fields of logic and psychology. Bain assisted Mill in writing and revising numerous editions of the *Logic* and even wrote a work on logic of his own that can be read as a commentary on Mill's earlier work (see Bain

1870). Mill was closely involved in Bain's two works on psychology, *The Senses and the Intellect* (1855), and *The Emotions and the Will* (1859), as well as the critique of phrenology (as a way of studying character) (Bain 1861). The two also worked together on the second edition of James Mill's *Analysis of the Phenomena of the Human Mind* (1869) for which Mill wrote extensive notes (see *CW* xxxi. 95–253).

There are, of course, many other figures who played important roles in Mill's life and thought, including James Mill (1773–1836), Harriet Taylor Mill, George Grote (1794–1871), Alexis de Tocqueville, Thomas Carlyle, John Sterling, to name a few, and these figures are studied here in various chapters. But Bain, Bentham, and Comte were more than influential colleagues. Their presence, their writings, and, above all, their ideas provide a framework for grasping the essence of Mill's social and political thought. Harriet Taylor Mill and James Mill also form useful contexts for understanding Mill. There is no doubting Harriet Mill's importance and influence in Mill's life, but it seems clear that, as to the originality of his ideas, she was less important than one might expect from Mill's own pronouncements and from those of some commentators.[4] The context provided by James Mill is more difficult to ascertain and might well require a book on its own to work out.[5] As we shall see, Mill tended to exaggerate the importance of his father and to criticize Bentham when the object of his criticisms might well have been James Mill.

IV. *Mill Today*

This new reading of Mill does not fit into any recent major category, say, of traditional or revisionist interpretation.[6] Nor does it engage with the army of rule, act, consequentialist, and hedonist utilitarians, except in so far as it places Mill in the modern Epicurean tradition in which he usually placed himself (see also Rosen 2003*a*: 15–28, 166–84). Nevertheless, it is claimed that this new view of Mill's thought more accurately reflects the movement of his ideas during his lifetime. But what is the relevance of Mill today and how does this book address present concerns? Mill's legacy in philosophy and social thought is particularly rich, and he not only addressed numerous traditions in these fields but also put his mark on them. Each chapter in the book, even those on seemingly obscure topics, deals with a problem or problems of current interest, even if in a slightly different form.

If one considers phrenology, for example, the views of Mill and Bain remain relevant to numerous claims by scientists today that they have discovered the origin of various character traits in the gene structure or through brain imaging. In so far as they claim causal connections between these physical attributes and, say, creativity or criminality, they are following in the footsteps of the phrenologists and omitting psychological and acquired character traits that are not so amenable to simple causal explanations. To take another example, Mill's account of a science of politics in rejecting the importance of constitutional forms, like monarchy, aristocracy, and democracy, and relying on the state of 'active character' to assess a country's progress as a modern state, would never lead him to support the imposition of 'regime change' on a country like Iraq in the hope of creating a modern democracy.

In a third example, it is clear that Mill's idea of the circle of liberty could not be linked simply with capitalism and the minimal state, or with revolution and state socialism. He recommended a different way forward, which might be called large-state liberalism based on co-operative foundations and laissez-faire. But he always viewed political change as best achieved gradually. Fourth, in the material on religion Mill clearly would reject the claims of multiculturalism to legitimacy and authority in modern societies. He does this while accepting some progressive elements in Christianity, but rejects what he calls the rigidity and backwardness of 'Islamism' and 'Brahminism'. But all religions are seen as potentially changeable, depending on numerous factors that make up national character. One crucial test for Mill, as it remains today, is the status of women in religion and society and their aspiration to achieve equality with men in a framework of liberty. No cultural or religious practice that opposes this aspiration should be encouraged in a modern society.

A final example is Mill's belief that continually increasing economic growth may not be the key to happiness in society. In his study of the 'stationary state' Mill argues with great skill and cogency that the emphasis on constant economic growth leads to destructive competition, a failure to utilize the creative energies of the higher classes, and increased impoverishment of the lower classes. At this time of economic recession, if not depression, Mill offers an alternative to our condition that need not condemn a generation to unemployment, impoverishment, and unhappiness.

It might be argued that Mill's views are relevant to our problems today, but that we can understand the problems he addressed better by studying more recent authors. Why read Mill when one can read Barry on multiculturalism, Williams on truth and liberalism, Skorupski on liberty of expression, or any number of feminists on women's liberation? The knowledge that these issues were addressed more than 150 years ago may not be sufficient to lead students today to undertake a considerable amount of reading. In addition, one should also call attention to some mistakes and failures by Mill in his approach to these and other topics. He may have addressed issues that are still important today, but did he not also make mistakes that might discredit his analysis? For example, in looking to developments in the future, a vital part of his utilitarianism, he seemed to ignore the possibility of a major war in Europe, such as the First World War. He tended to think that wars by advanced societies in the future would mainly be limited to struggles over colonies and fought in these distant countries. This false belief might well have influenced his optimism regarding the possible existence of the stationary state, as it ignored the need for economic growth, technological progress, and funds to fight such wars. In the mean time, the moral aspirations of the stationary state, set forth as a realistic alternative, might have to be recast as a utopian vision. Of course, one might reply in Mill's favour that he was not a 'public moralist', as some have claimed, and his ability to see into the future was severely limited. Such mistakes are more acceptable for a logician who was looking at the pros and cons of progress and improvement in relation to growth in the economy.

We can easily acknowledge that Mill could be mistaken. In addition, at times he is not easy to understand due to the long sentences containing numerous qualifications that occasionally lead him to conclusions that seem at variance with his original assertions. But we shall discover a great deal in his thought. The depth and breadth of his philosophy was unequalled in his lifetime, even though he credited others more than himself for many of his insights. He possessed a dialectical skill in argument that rivalled that of Plato's dialogues. His 'method of reform' led to a unique moderation in his political thought, combining an emphasis on stability with a context of progressive change. His published essays contain layer upon layer of discourse, combining reason and feeling, and each layer has a life of its own, informing the others. Mill can start with a commonplace problem and take the careful reader in directions one might not think possible, while ostensibly concerned with the pros and cons of the commonplace problem. Who would not want to study Mill today? The real question is whether or not we have lost the capacity to understand him. This book at least addresses this issue.

I

System of Logic

2

A Socratic Moment: Truth, Liberty, and Democracy

In common political debate a belief in absolute values is often opposed to relativism. Those who uphold the importance of 'truth' in politics are usually on the side of the absolutists, and relativism tends to attract sceptics who deny that truth has much to do with politics or morality. John Stuart Mill was an unusual philosopher in adopting a historically based (and hence relativist) system of ethics and politics, a strong belief in individual liberty, and, at the same time, a robust commitment to truth.

This commitment was developed primarily, though by no means exclusively, in his major work, the *System of Logic* (1843) (*CW* vii, viii), and remained relevant to numerous works concerned with ethics and politics. Before turning to the *Logic*, however, we shall first consider a passage from Bernard Williams's *Truth and Truthfulness*, which brings out in an interesting way a common misinterpretation of Mill this chapter is meant to challenge. According to Williams:

Democracy (in its modern, constitutional, forms) is valued, to an important extent in the name of liberty.... The appeal to liberty comes in stronger and weaker versions. The minimal version insists merely that government should permit maximum freedom (compatible with other goods, especially others' freedom), and that to deny people information and the right to spread information both violates liberty directly, in particular the freedom of speech, and devalues liberty in other areas, since effective action requires knowledge. A stronger version of the appeal calls, as J. S. Mill did, on the value of individuals' exercising and developing their powers. Both versions of the appeal to liberty raise an important question: how far are we concerned with liberty (above all, the freedom of speech), and how far are we concerned with truth? The standard liberal assumption is that the two objectives go together, and to some extent this is true. Self-development has been understood as development in the light of the truth, and liberties do get their point, in good part, from the possibility of effective action, which implies true information. However, it does not follow that all liberty, and specifically the freedom of speech, is necessarily helpful to the spread of the truth. We cannot take for granted Mill's optimistic conclusion that maximal freedom of speech must assist the emergence of truth in what has come to be called 'a market-place of ideas'.

(Williams 2002: 211–12)

This lengthy but helpful passage attempts to relate truth, liberty, and democracy with reference to Mill's thought and with reference to the commitment of liberalism generally to freedom of speech. Nevertheless, one may ask, does this fairly commonplace criticism of Mill embrace the whole of Mill's approach? Did Mill believe, as Williams seems to suggest, that maximum freedom of speech 'must assist' the emergence of truth? This view omits the emphasis Mill placed on logic, for it is logic that assists the discovery of truth, and liberty that simply, though importantly, keeps truth alive. Mill defined logic as 'the science which treats of the operations of the human understanding in the pursuit of truth' (CW vii. 6).[1] Such a science might change from place to place or from age to age, but logic, though also evolving, as a rational science, remains committed to the discovery of truth.

1. *Truth and Logic*

It is important to appreciate the novelty of Mill's approach to logic and to truth in an age when great strides were being made to free logic from the scholastic tradition that in the early nineteenth century was still firmly entrenched in English universities.[2] For Mill, there was considerable merit in the scholastic tradition, based on Aristotelian philosophy, but its study had become repetitive and lacklustre. Nevertheless, modern philosophy, from Locke onwards, tended to reject the tradition and concentrated mainly on psychology and language, and in the process minimized the importance of traditional logic (see Locke 1975: 671). For Locke, for example, traditional logic seemed to generate useless disputes of little practical benefit to society (see Locke 1975: 495).

In Richard Whately's *Elements of Logic* (1826) an attempt was made to revitalize the study of logic at Oxford by restating Aristotelian logic in a new context, using fresh examples and without the burdensome baggage of scholasticism (see Whately 1975). This context might be described as Coleridgean, as early versions of both the *Elements of Logic* and its companion, *Elements of Rhetoric*, first appeared in the *Encyclopædia Metropolitana*, a work inspired by Coleridge to advance progressive views which could be seen as emerging out of traditional thought and institutions (see *Encyclopædia Metropolitana* 1845: i. 1–43, 193–240, 241–303).

Mill was an enthusiastic reviewer of Whately's book on logic,[3] and his review represented his first major essay in this field (*CW* xi. 1–35). Among the ideas and arguments to which Mill was drawn was Whately's defence of the syllogism, which was considered important both as part of traditional logic and for the discovery of truth (see *CW* xi. 33). The whole thrust of modern philosophy and science was to dismiss the syllogism as irrelevant to the pursuit of truth, as the conclusion (e.g. Socrates is mortal) was considered already present in the premise (e.g. all men are mortal). The rejection of Aristotelianism by modern philosophers usually included the dismissal of the syllogism almost in passing, in favour of an emphasis on induction. Francis Bacon was generally credited with initiating this shift in focus to investigating nature by means of induction. Mill, however, argued that Bacon did not reject the syllogism, but simply criticized the scholastic philosophers in the Aristotelian tradition for being poor investigators of nature, that is to say, for neglecting inductive logic (see *CW* xi. 12ff.). Mill then proceeded to argue that the syllogism enabled one to discover new truths, even though these truths were implicit in the premises of the syllogism. He pointed to numerous fields, from geometry to mechanics, where the syllogism had been used to discover new truths. In the *Logic* Mill also retained the syllogism and created a new theory of inductive logic. In addition, he developed features of Aristotelian thought, such as the theory of logical fallacies, in which he adopted the traditional fallacies and then expanded the whole genre in a novel and striking manner (see Rosen 2006: 121–47; Hansen 1997).

In the *Logic*, as in the early essay on Whately, we have seen that Mill took the view that logic was concerned with the pursuit of truth. He acknowledged that many writers on logic believed that it was wholly concerned with an art of reasoning or thinking (see *CW* vii. 4–5). For Mill, no such art could stand alone, as all arts were connected with various sciences, and logic had to be regarded as a science as well as an art. This science, like all others, had to aim at truth, in this case, universally true laws of thought and reasoning.

We might gain some insight into Mill's emphasis on truth in logic by considering those whom he regarded as his opponents. In the *Autobiography* he referred to the *Logic* as providing 'a text-book of the opposite doctrine' to the 'German, or à priori view [early draft: "German, or ontological view"] of human knowledge and of the knowing faculties' (*CW* i. 232–3). Mill's doctrine, in contrast, 'derives all knowledge from experience, and all moral and intellectual qualities principally from the direction given to the associations'. Mill's opposition to the 'German, or à priori view' was deeply felt. He went on to declare:

The notion that truths external to the mind may be known by intuition or consciousness, independently of observation and experience, is, I am persuaded, in these times, the great intellectual support of false doctrines and bad institutions. By the aid of this theory, every inveterate belief and every intense feeling, of which the origin is not remembered, is enabled to dispense with the obligation of justifying itself by reason, and is erected into its own all-sufficient voucher and justification. There never was such an instrument devised for consecrating all deep seated prejudices. And the chief strength of this false philosophy in morals, politics, and religion, lies in the appeal which it is accustomed to make to the evidence of mathematics and of the cognate branches of physical science. (*CW* i. 233)

Mill clearly believed that the task of the *Logic* was to oppose this doctrine and even 'to expel' it from mathematics and the physical sciences through his own system of logic. In the *Logic*, however, he was far less combative. Logic, he declared, was 'common ground on which the partisans of Hartley and of Reid, of Locke and of Kant, may meet and join hands' (*CW* vii. 14). Doubtless, there would be disputes between the successors of these figures, but such disputes could be resolved. Even metaphysics needed to use the tools of logic to deal with the themes which fell within the scope of its enquiries. When metaphysics proceeded, like other sciences, to require evidence to establish a position, it was forced to draw inferences from evidence. To accomplish this, 'logic becomes the sovereign judge' as to whether the inferences were properly grounded or whether or not other inferences should be considered (*CW* vii. 14).

For logic to become 'the sovereign judge', however, it had to base itself on truth. Other philosophers were prepared to recognize the importance of logic, but in their view its province was limited to that of achieving consistency in argument rather than truth. Mill ascribed this view to Henry Mansel and, particularly, to Sir William Hamilton, who either held that logic had no concern with truth or that it was subordinate to other studies or sciences which did have these concerns. Mill called their conceptions of logic formal logic (see *CW* ix. 367), which consisted mainly of syllogistic logic that considered only the consistency of arguments from premises to conclusions. It rejected the possibility of a general theory of evidence, which Bacon had envisaged (see *CW* ix. 368). For Hamilton, each science contained its own criterion of truth, and he denied that there could be some general theory of evidence applicable to all enquiries (see *CW* ix. 369).

Mill did not reject formal logic or what he called at times the logic of consistency (see *CW* vii. 208). He regarded it as a small, though important, part of the logic of truth. He also pointed out that the study of the logic of truth, which rivalled in complexity and difficulty the study of mathematics and many sciences, would be open to and attract only a few superior minds in any generation. Formal logic, however, was separable from logic as a whole and could be introduced into education at a much lower level. It aimed at removing obstacles to the attainment of truth by functioning in a negative manner and pointing out fallacies and inconsistencies (see *CW* ix. 370). Formal logic thus retained its connection with truth, though it could be taught, as it was, almost as sporting exercises.

In his essay on education, the *Inaugural Address Delivered to the University of St Andrews* (1867), Mill restated these ideas in a new context. Here we again find the emphasis on logic as being concerned with truth ('Logic lays down the general principles and laws of the search after truth') and closely related to mathematics and physics (*CW* xxi. 238). He also distinguished between ratiocinative and inductive logic, with the former 'already carried to a high degree of perfection by Aristotle', and the latter, more difficult, requiring a knowledge of the inductive sciences. All logic is praised, including ratiocinative logic, roughly equivalent to what he had earlier called formal logic. But in this work on education he dwelt more on this aspect of logic and its importance in society. Discovering and pointing out error is mainly a negative function designed 'not so much to teach us to go right, as to keep us from going wrong' (*CW*

xxi. 238). 'Logic,' he continued, 'is the great disperser of hazy and confused thinking: it clears up the fogs which hide us from our own ignorance, and make us believe that we understand a subject when we do not.' For those who disparaged school logic, he wrote: 'take the trouble to learn it. You will easily do so in a few weeks, and you will see whether it is of no use to you in making your mind clear, and keeping you from stumbling in the dark over the most outrageous fallacies' (*CW* xxi. 239).

II. *Socrates*

These allusions to keeping one from going wrong, curing ignorance, and preventing one from stumbling in the dark lead us to the importance of Plato's Socrates in Mill's account of logic. Although most discussions of the history of scholastic logic include Aristotle and Thomism, one seldom finds many of Mill's contemporaries (or ours) going back to Socrates. Yet Mill's logic is almost unique in its being grounded in an understanding of the Socratic elenchus.[4] He wrote in the early draft of the *Autobiography* that 'the Socratic method . . . is unsurpassed as a discipline for abstract thought on the most difficult subjects. Nothing in modern life and education, in the smallest degree supplies its place' (*CW* i. 24). Even as a boy, the Socratic method 'took such hold on me that it became part of my own mind; and I have ever felt myself, beyond any modern that I know of except my father and perhaps even beyond him, a pupil of Plato, and cast in the mould of his dialectics' (*CW* i. 24).

Mill did not refer to the Plato of the transcendent forms, but to Plato's Socrates in the early dialogues where a negative dialectic revealed the ignorance of the most confident and learned of his interlocutors. Mill was strongly impressed by Plato's picture in the *Gorgias* and *Republic* 'of the solitary and despised position of the philosopher in every existing society, and the universal impression against him, as at best an useless person, but more frequently an eminently wicked one' (*CW* xi. 399).[5] He adopted George Grote's arguments that, while Plato might have despised the Sophists, because they were more concerned with appearances than with reality, and took money for their services, they were not the real enemy. The real corruptors of the young were not the Sophists, but society itself:

their families, their associates, all whom they see and converse with, the applauses and hootings of the public assembly, the sentences of the court of justice. These are what pervert young men, by holding up to them a false standard of good and evil, and giving an entirely wrong direction to their desires. As for the Sophists, they merely repeat the people's own opinions. (*CW* xi. 400)

Mill not only adopted Grote's view of the importance of the Sophists to public debate and the role of Socrates in this debate, but in a review of Grote's posthumously published study of Aristotle, he acknowledged the importance of Aristotle's *Sophistical Refutations* in the development of an important aspect of logic and in the pursuit of truth. Even though Aristotle's work was a study of the art of arguing for victory rather than for truth, Mill saw nothing wrong with such public debates so long as they took place within established rules. Furthermore, he believed that Aristotle regarded such exercises in dialectical argument to be valuable in the pursuit of truth. Quoting from Grote, Mill gave three reasons for this belief (*CW* xi. 508). First, the debates constituted a kind of mental exercise that was valuable and stimulating. Second, the debates put one in touch with the ordinary opinions held by other members of society. Third, such dialectical debate influenced science and philosophy, encouraging one to look at both sides of questions and to determine which answers were true and which were false. Mill believed that Aristotle's method in dialectical argument 'was greatly in advance not only of his own time, but of ours':

His general advice for exercise and practice in Dialectic is admirably adapted to the training of one's own mind for the pursuit of truth. 'You ought to test every thesis by first assuming it to be true, then assuming it to be false, and following out the consequences on both sides.' This was already the practice of the Eleatic dialecticians, as we see in the *Parmenides*. (*CW* xi. 508)

In Mill's view Aristotle's account of dialectic also took one directly back to the Socratic elenchus.

III. *Socrates and Liberty of Thought and Discussion*

One of the most striking arguments in *On Liberty* (1859), in which Socrates was invoked, arose from Mill's defence of liberty of expression (see O'Rourke 2001). Mill was concerned with the lack of attention paid to truth in the way most people, even those who were willing to entertain dissenting opinions, formed their views and enforced them on others. He noted that they tended to be diffident about their own opinions and were happy to accept those held by 'the world', or by that part of the world with which they came into contact. Few were troubled by the fact that this acquiescence in the views of others led to a kind of relativism, as opinions differed in various parts of the world—'the same causes...make him a Churchman in London...[and] a Buddhist or a Confucian in Pekin—and in different ages, (*CW* xviii. 230).

The legal or popular enforcement of these opinions involved an assumption of infallibility, and it is worth noting that such an assumption went hand in hand with what might be called an indifference to truth. The deaths of Socrates and Jesus were terrible events to which we look back with horror. But Mill believed that those who carried out these crimes were not evil people but were 'men who possessed in a full...measure, the religious, moral, and patriotic feelings of their time and people: the very kind of men who, in all times, our own included, have every chance of passing through life blameless and respected' (*CW* xviii. 236). What was missing with these 'ordinary' people was a serious concern for the truth, which initially involved a recognition that they might not know the truth and hence could not act with any infallible certainty. According to Mill, for people to act on the basis of their opinions with regard to truth, they should accept, as a condition of doing so, a complete liberty of challenging their opinions (see *CW* xviii. 231ff.). This condition should apply whether or not the received opinions were false or true. If they were false, then freedom of expression would enable people to have access to the truth. If they were true, Mill believed that freedom of expression would enable the truths to be living truths and not dead dogmas. Received truths were regarded by Mill as particularly dangerous. They lulled the mind into a passive acceptance and almost a vacancy of understanding where the truth was forgotten and never reconsidered. In some cases, he argued, accepted doctrines remained 'outside the mind, incrusting and petrifying it against all other influences addressed to the higher parts of our nature' (*CW* xviii. 248).

Mill's approach to truth was a crucial part of his doctrine of freedom of expression. His admiration of Socrates was as much due to Socrates' insistence on the search for truth as on whatever truths Socrates might have uncovered in his searches. Nevertheless, Mill was never optimistic that truth would prevail over error; after all,

Socrates and Jesus died for truth (*CW* xviii. 235–6). On the one hand he could write:

for, on any matter not self-evident, there are ninety-nine persons totally incapable of judging it, for one who is capable; and the capacity of the hundredth person is only comparative; for the majority of the eminent men of every past generation held many opinions now known to be erroneous, and did or approved numerous things which no one will now justify. (*CW* xviii. 231)

Just following this pessimistic view of the human condition, Mill posed a different question, which seems somewhat at odds with his view of ninety-nine of a hundred persons, and, strikingly, provided an answer apparently at odds with it:

Why is it, then, that there is on the whole a preponderance among mankind of rational opinions and rational conduct? If there really is this preponderance—which there might be unless human affairs are, and have always been, in an almost desperate state—it is owing to a quality of the human mind, the source of everything respectable in man either as an intellectual or as a moral being, namely that his errors are corrigible. (*CW* xviii. 231)

Mill's sudden ascription of rationality in mankind reveals an important duality in *On Liberty* and in his thought generally. On the one hand, the great thinker must be free to follow his intellect wherever it led. The person who thought for oneself and did not give up was superior to those who held only opinions, some possibly true and others possibly false, due to an indifference to the truth. But, as we have seen, Mill was not satisfied only to provide liberty of thought and discussion or liberty generally for a few great people:

Not that it is solely, or chiefly, to form great thinkers, that freedom of thinking is required. On the contrary, it is as much and even more indispensable, to enable average human beings to attain the mental stature which they are capable of. There have been, and may again be, great individual thinkers, in a general atmosphere of mental slavery. But there never has been, nor ever will be, in that atmosphere an intellectually active people. (*CW* xviii. 243)

Mill's argument regarding 'an intellectually active people' takes us back to the *Logic* and to the Socratic dimension in numerous other works. The study of elementary logic and, particularly, the study of logical fallacies reveal a Socratic dimension to this intellectual activity. It is within the grasp of most people to question the opinions they have accepted and, with an understanding of the elements of logic and argument, discover their ignorance and its significance. With freedom of expression it is also within their grasp to look for truth and to keep truth alive, so long as they retain this knowledge of their ignorance and the belief that their errors are corrigible.

Mill was also restating in this context his distinction in the *Logic* between formal logic or the logic of consistency and the logic of truth. The former was an important part of the latter, and could play a significant role in the great Socratic enterprise of making people aware of their own ignorance and the need to pursue and maintain truth. In opposition to the view set forth by Williams, quoted above, we can see that for Mill it is not liberty that assists the emergence of truth, but the pursuit of truth (even if confined to the recognition of one's ignorance) that assists the emergence of liberty. For each person there is potentially a Socratic moment when an acknowledgement of ignorance allows one to pursue truth. This pursuit then requires liberty of thought and discussion to be successful. To possess liberty without a Socratic moment leads nowhere, except perhaps to an endless pursuit of variety and novelty, as entertainment, or even worse, substitutes for truth.

IV. *Democracy*

It is well known that Mill was highly ambivalent about the virtues of modern democracy and, like Tocqueville, was critical and fearful of the tyranny of the majority. But, despite his fears regarding democracy, he became a strong admirer of ancient Athenian democracy as depicted in Pericles' famous funeral oration (see Urbinati 2002: 14ff.; Riley 2007: 221–49).

Prior to Grote's magisterial *History of Greece* there were few champions of ancient Athenian democracy, which, after all, had condemned Socrates, who remained a major hero of the Victorian period and, additionally, was known as a critic of democracy (see Demetriou 1999: 118ff., 125, 230–43; 2011). Most historians of Greece followed Plato, Aristotle, Xenophon, Lysias and Isocrates, and favoured Sparta over Periclean Athens (see Demetriou 1999: 119–23), as did philosophers like Rousseau (see Cranston 1968: 17). It is important to appreciate the significance of Grote's history of Greece for Mill's thought.[6] Grote referred to the emphasis Pericles placed on liberty of thought and action not only from legal restraints but also 'from practical intolerance between man and man, and tyranny of the majority over individual dissenters in taste and pursuit' (Grote 1940: vi. 181). In a remarkable passage

Grote elevated Periclean Athens above all modern states, including modern democracies, in the liberty it granted to individuals. For Grote, Pericles' funeral speech both encouraged a wide diversity of tastes and sentiments and reflected this encouragement within Athenian democracy.[7]

Grote was well aware that his praise of Periclean Athens required him to provide an account of the life and death of Socrates that was compatible with it. Just as with Mill, Socrates was a philosophical hero for Grote, and both emphasized the significance for later thought of Socrates' negative method (see Demetriou 1999: 229ff.). Grote had also corrected the general opinion of the Sophists as corrupt and subversive (Grote 1940: viii. 312–59), and he did not hesitate to link Socrates with the best (particularly those who encouraged liberty of thought and discussion) among the Sophists (see Demetriou 1999: 231ff.; 1996: 36–50). As for the Athenian condemnation of Socrates, he wrote:

In any other government of Greece, as well as in the Platonic Republic, Sokrates would have been quickly arrested in his career, even if not severely punished; in Athens, he was allowed to talk and teach publicly for twenty-five or thirty years, and then condemned when an old man. Of these two applications of the same mischievous principle, assuredly the latter is at once the more moderate and less noxious. (Grote 1940: ix. 87)

Mill accepted this new version of Greek history with enthusiasm (see *CW* xxiv. 867–75, 1084–8; xxv. 1121–8, 1128–34, 1157–64). He twice reprinted the passage on Pericles that Grote had written (as well as quoting at length from Pericles' funeral oration as it appeared in Thucydides), and referred to the passage as a valuable contribution to a 'vital question of social morals' (*CW* xi. 319–20; xxv. 1129–31). He wrote:

In the greatest Greek commonwealth, as described by its most distinguished citizen [Pericles], the public interest was held of paramount obligation in all things which concerned it; but, with that part of the conduct of individuals which concerned only themselves, public opinion did not interfere: while in the ethical practice of the moderns, this is exactly reversed, and no one is required by opinion to pay any regard to the public, except by conducting his own private concerns in conformity to its expectations. (*CW* xi. 319)

In most modern European states vigorous self-assertion on the public stage was not encouraged. Not only was submission and obedience the norm in public life, but Mill also noted the tendency for individuals to conform in private life to the expectations of society. By emphasizing the example of Periclean Athens, Mill was first pointing to the importance of a free and vigorous public sphere in which there was full debate of ethical and political issues. This public sphere then enabled the private sphere to be free as well, in so far as it was left to its own devices.

Mill was mainly concerned here with the public sphere of modern societies in which the tyranny of the majority in its 'collective mediocrity' had begun to assume power (*CW* xviii. 268ff.). He found this majority, however powerful in limiting liberty, nonetheless passive and susceptible to being led by others. He particularly criticized Carlyle's idea of hero-worship and believed that Carlyle's 'strong man of genius' would undoubtedly be corrupted in the process of exercising power (*CW* xviii. 269). Mill sought instead a society that embraced individual liberty and allowed and encouraged individuality to flourish, as did Athens with its acceptance of Socrates for seventy years. Mill wanted to oppose the 'tyranny of opinion' in his own society by the encouragement of eccentricity. As he wrote:

Eccentricity has always abounded when and where strength of character has abounded; and the amount of eccentricity in a society has generally been proportional to the amount of genius, mental vigour, and moral courage which it contained. That so few now dare to be eccentric marks the chief danger of the time. (*CW* xviii. 269)

The cultivation of individuality thus depended on individuals of strong character and genius daring to be eccentric, but to dare to be eccentric depended in turn on a public sphere that encouraged such eccentricity to develop. Without the Periclean perspective Mill believed that the cultivation of eccentricity would seriously diminish and, with it, the existence of liberty throughout society.

As we have seen, Mill's conception of Periclean democracy encouraged liberty in both the public and private spheres. But to say that Mill's conception of democracy was based on liberty is to state only half (or even less than half) of the story. Let us contrast Mill with Bentham, whose theory of constitutional democracy was well known to Mill and, on some important issues, was rejected by him (see Rosen 1983: 183–99). Bentham (who tended to write of representative *democracy* rather than simply of representative *government*, as Mill did) believed that his theory of constitutional democracy was based on liberty. The liberty that was relevant here was civil liberty, where the law prevented others from interfering in one's life and activities, and one should be free to think and act freely so long as one did not harm others. Bentham came to believe that civil liberty could not establish the security an individual required without constitutional liberty, because it could not on its own secure the individual from the corruption and tyranny exercised by government itself. The only way to establish constitutional liberty, as an extension of civil liberty, was to provide institutions to remove from power those rulers who threatened it. This was to be achieved by representative democracy, including a widespread and equal suffrage, the use of the secret ballot, and freedom of expression (see Rosen 1992: 25ff.; see also Chapter 8 below).

It is worth noting that Bentham was as concerned with truth as was Mill. He wrote extensively on logic and on evidence (see Bentham 1827; 1838–43: viii. 193–293), but his theory of democracy was based on liberty rather than truth. A well-run representative democracy would, of course, give those dedicated to the search for truth the liberty to do so, and government officials were to be educated in their fields of expertise, but democracy would not be based on some attempt to embody the pursuit and representation of truth in its very institutions.

Mill's idea of representative government was entirely different, and was based on a diffusion of the Socratic elenchus, via the negative and critical dialectic, throughout society. This diffusion took various kinds of active character in the population and directed them towards establishing and sustaining representative institutions (see Chapter 4 below). For Mill, human beings were for the most part active beings, but unless their critical faculties were awakened, they tended to accept the prevailing opinions of their societies, nations, and generations. A growing knowledge of one's ignorance could first crack the shell that enclosed the human mind in received opinion. Liberating the individual mind to question such opinions and to challenge the utility of established institutions in turn encouraged active character in families, societies, and governments. Mill believed that in most societies the level of such development of active character was not sufficient to create and maintain representative government. In a few, like Britain and the United States, it was. Thus, Socratic self-awareness of ignorance, plus a psychological disposition to be active, plus the development of active character could lead to representative democracy and the institutions that might support it, like the open ballot.

It is possible to argue, as Williams seems to do, that Mill is nonetheless basing democracy on a different notion of liberty from that employed by Bentham and the earlier generation of radicals. Williams depicts this liberty in terms of 'individuals exercising and developing their powers', but he then finds it inadequate to believe that freedom of speech will deliver the truth involved in the exercise of human powers. I have already suggested that for Mill it is not liberty that assists in the emergence of truth, but truth, via the Socratic dialectic, that assists the emergence of liberty. Furthermore, this truth-based liberty works only indirectly in politics, as it is mainly confined to the cultivation of active character in society. It is important to note that, unlike philosophers such as Aristotle and Montesquieu, Mill did not develop a typology of political constitutions. Following Comte, he looked to a historically based social science, which was also founded on 'the progressiveness of the human race' and 'generally adopted by the most advanced thinkers on the Continent' (CW viii. 914). It differed from the 'chemical or experimental' approaches he associated with Macaulay and the 'geometrical mode' he linked with Bentham. He depicted this progress and the tendency towards progressiveness as follows:

[T]here is a progressive change both in the character of the human race, and in their outward circumstances so far as moulded by themselves: that in each successive age the principal phenomena of society are different from what they were in the age preceding, and still more different from any previous age: the periods which most distinctly mark these successive changes being intervals of one generation, during which a new set of human beings have been educated, have grown up from childhood, and taken possession of society. (CW viii. 914)

Mill's idea of the progressiveness of the human race formed the basis of the laws of human nature (understood through 'ethology' and psychology), and while they suggest that there might be not simply change in society, but change for the better, Mill was anxious to distinguish progress and progressiveness from improvement. If the theory of progress was in part derived from Comte's historically based social science, the idea and importance of improvement was taken from Bentham. As Mill wrote in the *Autobiography* (CW i. 71): 'And the vista of improvement which he [Bentham] did open was sufficiently large and brilliant to light up my life, as well as to give a definite shape to my aspirations'. Mill insisted that improvement might not follow from progress, though he expressed a belief that there was a 'general tendency' towards 'a better and happier state' via improvement (*CW* viii. 913–14). Mill's social science thus assumed that societies were both progressive and capable of improvement. The details of this improvement would be unique to the society under consideration, and Mill's emphasis on national character reflects this focus (see Varouxakis 1998: 375–91; 2002a; see also Chapter 4 below). Active character in turn may or may not develop into democratic political institutions so that Mill's emphasis on the development of the individual's powers may not lead to democracy at all.

In *On Liberty* Mill did not dwell on politics to any extent, as he was concerned with liberty in society. At the end of the essay, however, he referred to a form of government for which he had earlier coined the term 'pedantocracy' (see Riley 1998a: 144; Urbinati 2002: 55ff.; Riley 2007: 221ff.).[8] In an early letter to Comte, Mill had written:

The majority of an educated class is perhaps less disposed than any other class to allow itself be led by the most developed and intelligent people they meet; and as this majority cannot be composed of great thinkers, but simply of scholars or scientists without true originality, there could result only what one sees in China, that is to say, a pedantocracy (*pédantocratie*). (*CW* xiii. 502)

The context of Mill's remark was his acceptance of Comte's arguments for the separation of the spiritual and temporal powers which would prevent some kind of rule by philosophers or educated bureaucrats in a Platonic, St-Simonian, or other utopian form of rule by intellectuals.[9] For Mill, the allusion to pedantocracy in *On Liberty* was closely connected with his estimation of the kind of bureaucratic regime existing in China where virtually all liberty was extinguished (see *CW* xviii. 308). As he wrote elsewhere:

yet if the lettered and cultivated class, embodied and disciplined under a central organ, could become in Europe, what it is in China, the Government—unchecked by any power residing in the mass of citizens, and permitted to assume a parental tutelage over all operations of life—the result would probably be a darker despotism, one more opposed to improvement, than even the military monarchies and aristocracies have in fact proved. (*CW* xx. 270; see Knights 1978: 169)

He also referred to this kind of rule as 'a perfection of despotism' (*CW* xx. 274). In *On Liberty* itself, he evoked the Chinese mandarin who was 'as much the tool and creature of a despotism as the humblest cultivator' (*CW* xviii. 308). This material in *On Liberty* was concerned with the extent to which government interference might assist with the development of individual liberty in society. As Collini has pointed out, this discussion might easily be confused (and was confused) with a debate over individualism versus collectivism (Collini 1989: pp. xvi–xvii). But Mill was arguing here, more profoundly, perhaps, that rule by an educated elite, even a liberal elite, apparently in favour of helping people to possess and enjoy liberty, might easily degenerate into despotic rule. For this very reason we would do well not to seek 'improvement' through government but through the maintenance of groups of educated people outside government able and willing to criticize and challenge the ruling bureaucracy.

For Mill in *On Liberty* the opposing term to pedantocracy, if he possessed a constitutional typology, might be Athenian democracy under Pericles. The key feature of this form of rule was less its commitment to democracy, and more its commitment to a private space in which the Socratic elenchus and its cultivation could take root. It is possible to see the *Considerations on Representative Government* as an attempt to establish modern liberal democracy on the foundations of Athenian democracy (see Riley 2007: 221ff.), but such a view abstracts the regime from the context, on which Mill insisted, of particular societies evolving historically. The *Considerations* was clearly written for Britain in the 1860s, and despite ingenious attempts to see in it some relevance to later politics and other societies, Mill's doctrine, unlike that of *On Liberty*, has resisted most attempts at reincarnation. Perhaps, as I argue in Chapter 3, the *Considerations* is linked more with a 'method of reform' than with a typology of constitutions, as a way to bring together liberals and conservatives to pursue reform in an ideologically divided society.

v. *Liberalism*

The status of Mill as a liberal, and what kind of liberal he was, has been hotly debated over the last fifty years. Alan Ryan has written of *On Liberty*: '*That* it is a liberal manifesto is clear beyond doubt; *What* the liberalism is that it defends and *how* it defends it remain matters of controversy' (Ryan 1998: 497).[10] Ryan's point is undoubtedly true, and Mill's *On Liberty* is deeply embedded in current debates about liberty as well as in the history of liberalism.[11] Nevertheless, one might easily argue that how Mill saw himself as a liberal in its nineteenth-century context and how we see Mill today are considerably different, because liberalism itself has evolved. But Mill is as much part of the evolution as its historical source, and his ideas appear and reappear in numerous contexts. The passage from Williams, to which we have returned on several occasions, almost innocently ascribes to Mill a view to which Mill himself might not have subscribed. I have emphasized Mill's concern with truth, not just in the *Logic*, but in *On Liberty* as well. In a letter to Alexander Bain, written in 1859 just after the publication of *On Liberty*, Mill rejected Bain's interpretation of his position and emphasized the importance of truth:

The 'Liberty' has produced an effect on you which it was never intended to produce if it has made you think that we ought not to attempt to convert the world. I meant nothing of the kind, & hold that we ought to convert all we can. We *must* be satisfied with keeping alive the sacred fire in a few minds when we are unable to do more—but the notion of an intellectual aristocracy of *lumières* while the rest of the world remains in darkness fulfils none of my aspirations—& the effect I aim at by the book is, on the contrary, to make the many more accessible to all truth by making them more open minded.

(*CW* xv. 631)

Mill continued by asserting that only in the matter of religion was he not prepared to convert the world to all of his views but only 'really superior intellects & characters'. As for the rest, he would prefer 'to improve their religion than to destroy it', which might occur if his views were fully revealed at that time (*CW* xv. 631; see also Chapter 12 below).

The 'sacred fire' to which Mill and Bain are dedicated is that of truth, and liberty of thought and discussion is a way of extending a concern for truth to a wider group in society. Mill's reservations regarding religion are not reservations about freedom of worship, but about the extent to which people generally in Britain were prepared in the 1850s to have their deepest views on religion challenged by Mill. Mill had clearly hoped that one day he would be able to reveal the truth to all, that is to say, that British society would be able to put his position regarding truth and religion to good use and not merely react negatively against Mill himself (cf. Capaldi 2004: 346ff.).

At the outset of this chapter it was noted that, while Mill was a relativist, he held to the importance of truth in society and for the individual. This adherence to truth did not mean that truths concerning the individual and society could not change from time to time and from place to place. On the contrary, unless this change took place, stagnation in science and politics might occur. A commitment to truth also embodied a belief that there were new truths to discover, that natural and social science evolved, and improvement in all aspects of human life and understanding was possible. Nevertheless, to favour liberty without any concern for truth (as some liberals might argue today) would not make much sense to Mill. The foundation of his liberalism, as we have seen, is in logic, but it is fair to acknowledge that he regarded some developments in logic to be as great a threat to the pursuit of truth as its apparent disregard by later liberals. For the logic Mill favoured was one inspired by the Socratic elenchus and even in his lifetime this approach was threatened by highly technical work in mathematical aspects of logic (see Rosen 2010: 67–83). When Mill began writing on logic, he found that it had been dismissed by many as irrelevant to truth and the same may be said nowadays, though for different reasons. To appreciate Mill's liberalism requires us, almost as archaeologists, to recover the Socratic dimension to his logic and to show its connection with liberty in numerous areas of ethics and politics.

3

The Method of Reform: Mill's Encounter with Bentham and Coleridge

In the preface to *Considerations on Representative Government* Mill addressed his work to those Liberals and Conservatives who, in recent debates on parliamentary reform, seemed 'to have lost confidence in the political creeds which they nominally profess' (*CW* xix. 373). He noted that, while this loss of confidence seemed to have taken place, no better creed had presented itself to either side. We thus encounter in the two creeds two opposing views without any obvious means of reconciliation or moving to a better doctrine or doctrines or to parliamentary reform. Nevertheless, Mill held out for a better doctrine—not a compromise between the two, but another perspective 'which, in virtue of its superior comprehensiveness, might be adopted by either Liberal or Conservative without renouncing anything which he really feels to be valuable in his own creed' (*CW* xix. 373).

Mill's starting point of addressing opposing views and looking for ways of reconciling them from a different perspective is not simply a rhetorical flourish. The roots of his method might be found in the consideration of opposing views characteristic of the Socratic elenchus. Here, in the *Considerations* we also find echoes of Mill's approach in the famous essays on 'Bentham' (1838) and 'Coleridge'

(1840), beginning with contrary doctrines forming an opposition which Mill then overcomes. Although it would be wrong to see these remarks in the *Considerations* as a simple restatement of views taken in these earlier essays, the arguments seem to presuppose the essays as well as the development of his political thought prior to their composition.[1] By examining these earlier works, we shall be able to understand more clearly Mill's approach to government and particularly to its reform and the continuing significance of the method of reform for ethics and politics generally.

In this chapter I hope to provide a brief survey of some aspects of Mill's early political thought, as it culminated in the essays on Bentham and Coleridge. From this material it is hoped that we might see how Mill developed these and related ideas in book 6 of the *Logic* and there established the foundations of a social science, which has great relevance for a method of reform. I shall then examine the *Considerations* in relation to this method and the wider significance of the method for political reform.

1. *Philosophic Radicalism*

Although Mill's earliest political writings are now readily available in the *Collected Works,* for this chapter I shall concentrate on his reaction to the ideas of Bentham and James Mill for the starting point of the evolution of his political thought. Prior to the 1830s, if Mill did not always agree with Bentham and his father, most of his topics and arguments followed in the radical tradition in which he was carefully nurtured. This tradition favoured liberty in numerous fields, from freedom from religious persecution to freedom of speech and action, including the freedom to own property and exchange it. In international relations it was hoped that free trade might lead to a more pacific world. In politics radical thought favoured the accountability of rulers to the ruled through representative government, based on the secret ballot, near-universal suffrage, and equal electoral districts. It stressed the importance of public opinion, a free press, and widespread publicity to enhance accountability in government. In education radical thought favoured the extension of provision to the middle and lower classes, the cultivation of higher pleasures through education, and the replacement of a classical and religious curriculum by one more firmly rooted in the modern secular world.

For various reasons, some psychological and others political, the young Mill felt trapped and even stifled either by his inheritance or by those from whom he inherited his views. His creation of 'philosophic radicalism' and his involvement with the *London and Westminster Review* in the 1830s represented attempts to develop a new perspective. In the *Autobiography* he wrote that he was pursuing two objects:

One was to free philosophic radicalism from the reproach of sectarian Benthamism. I desired, while retaining the precision of expression, the definiteness of meaning, the contempt of declamatory phrases and vague generalities, which were so honorably characteristic both of Bentham and of my father, to give a wider basis and a more free and genial character to Radical speculations; to shew that there was a Radical philosophy, better and more complete than Bentham's, while recognizing and incorporating all of Bentham's which is permanently valuable. In this first object I, to a certain extent, succeeded.

(*CW* i. 221)

The second object was the attempt to reinvigorate radical politics, which, he admitted, was for the most part a failure (*CW* i. 221–3). In fact, one can argue that Mill's essays on Bentham and Coleridge are the culmination of this attempt to free philosophic radicalism from what he has called 'sectarian Benthamism', and, additionally, to recognize his failure to advance radical politics in this period just after the success of the Reform Bill. The two essays are also closely related to the *Logic*, which Mill was writing at this time, and hence reflect further a turning away from practical politics.

But what was philosophic radicalism?[2] When Mill used the term, he referred to a small group of radicals in parliament following the passage of the Reform Bill (see *CW* vi. 191, 212) who attempted, but not always successfully, to advance the cause of reform, men such as George Grote, John Arthur Roebuck, Charles Buller, and Sir William Molesworth. Mill sought to support and lead this group through his editorship of the *London and Westminster Review* (see Thomas 1979: 1ff., 199ff.). When he discussed various kinds of radicals, he distinguished four groups who differed from the philosophic radicals. The first were the 'historic radicals' who believed in popular institutions as the inheritance of Englishmen transmitted to modern Britain from 'the Saxons or the barons of Runnymeade'. The second, 'metaphysical radicals', believed in democracy based on 'unreal' philosophical abstractions such as natural liberty or natural rights. The third, 'radicals of occasion and circumstance', opposed the government over particular issues and at particular times, and the fourth, 'radicals of position', were radicals simply because they were not lords. The philosophic radicals 'are those who in politics observe the common practice of philosophers—that is, who, when they are discussing means, begin by considering the end, and when they desire to produce effects, think of causes' (*CW* vi. 353).

What is curious about this depiction of philosophic radicalism is that neither Bentham nor James Mill would find it alien to their approaches to politics. Nor would their views be incorporated in the other four categories. Furthermore, Mill distinguished philosophic radicalism by its philosophical method and not by particular proposals for institutional reform. There is no reference here to such radical proposals as universal suffrage, the secret ballot, or constitutional reform (abolition of second chamber, monarchy, etc.). It is as if Mill expected radical reformers to be reinvigorated, not by particular proposals for reform, but by a new philosophical method for politics, which was nonetheless derived from and related to the utilitarianism he inherited from his father and Bentham.

II. *The Critique of Bentham*

To understand Mill's position we might begin with his efforts to distinguish his views from those of Bentham. In 'Remarks on Bentham's Philosophy', published as an appendix to Bulwer's *England and the English* (1833) he made his first substantial attempt to consider both the favourable and unfavourable sides of Bentham's doctrines 'considered as a complete philosophy' (*CW* i. 207). For Mill, Bentham's achievements could be compared favourably with those of Francis Bacon. But Bentham went beyond Bacon: while Bacon prophesied a science, Bentham actually created one. Bentham was the first 'to deduce all the secondary and intermediate principles of law, by direct and systematic inference from the one great axiom or principle of general utility'. He was also praised for his 'first, and perhaps the grandest achievement'—his discrediting of technical systems in law. Law ceased to be a mystery and became a matter of 'practical business, wherein means were to be adapted to ends, as in any of the other arts of life'. 'To have accomplished this', Mill continued, 'supposing him to have done nothing else, is to have equalled the glory of the greatest scientific benefactors of the human race' (*CW* x. 10).

Mill mainly concentrated on Bentham's contributions to the civil and penal branches of the law and to judicial evidence and procedure. He curiously omitted numerous important fields, such as constitutional law, logic, codification, and writings on liberty, such as *Defence of Usury*, which was much discussed in the 1820s (see Bentham 1952–4 (1787): i. 123–94). He mainly criticized Bentham as a moral philosopher. In his view, Bentham neglected character in his ethics, and particularly in the chapters on motives and dispositions in *An Introduction to the Principles of Morals and Legislation* (see Bentham 1996 (1789): 96–142; *CW* x. 8–9). Bentham and his followers, he believed, emphasized the consequences of actions alone and 'rejected all contemplation of the action in its general bearings upon the entire moral being of the agent' (*CW* x. 8).

We should note that Mill ignored those aspects of Bentham's philosophy which might have formed a reply, such as, for example, Bentham's account of dispositions as a theory of virtue (see Bentham 1996 (1789): 3, 125ff.). But Mill sought a more earnest and uplifting morality (see Rosen 2003a: 29–57). He criticized Bentham for using the language of interests, when such a language tended to be understood as purely self-regarding interest (see *CW* x. 14). Bentham's philosophy provided no moral message and uplifting theme:

Upon those who *need* to be strengthened and upheld by a really inspired moralist—such a moralist as Socrates, or Plato, or (speaking humanly and not theologically) as Christ; the effect of such writings as Mr. Bentham's ... must either be hopeless despondency and gloom, or a reckless giving themselves up to a life of that miserable self-seeking, which they are there taught to regard as inherent in their original and unalterable nature. (*CW* x. 16)

In addition, Mill continued, 'by the promulgation of such views of human nature, and by a general tone of thought and expression perfectly in harmony with them, I conceive Mr. Bentham's writings to have done and to be doing very serious evil' (*CW* x. 15).

If Mill sought a new philosophical method to be applied to politics, he also wanted to infuse it with the spirit of the 'inspired moralist', a Socrates, Plato, or Jesus. His criticisms of Bentham's failure to inspire as a moralist remind one of numerous writings in the seventeenth and eighteenth centuries where Epicurean philosophy, also based on self-interest, was criticized by traditional theologians and moralists for similar self-serving tendencies (see Rosen 2003a: 15–28). But his depiction of philosophic radicalism, as we have seen, did not carry with it such moralistic overtones, as it simply concentrated on relating means to ends and causes to effects. Nor did his later writings on logic and philosophy. One exception is *Utilitarianism*, where Mill attempted to establish an approach to utilitarian philosophy which was based on pleasure, pain, and utility, but which could favourably accommodate a dissatisfied Socrates as opposed to a satisfied pig. But here we see Mill acknowledging the views of his real and imaginary critics, and answering them by showing how utilitarianism could accommodate the inspired moralist (see Hansen 2005). In this sense Mill's approach was not only that of a traditional moralist but also that of a rhetorician who appreciated that utilitarianism could not succeed unless it captured the imagination and moral sensibility of a wider circle of people than would ever be attracted to Bentham's philosophy.

To focus here on Mill's rhetoric is not to deny his sincerity, his moral feeling, or his desire to see people awakened to an inner life that leads to self-understanding, fulfilment, and happiness (see Donner 1991). Nor would one want to diminish the personal importance that Mill gave to reaching out beyond what he called 'sectarian Benthamism'. In the essays on Bentham and Coleridge we shall see his attempt to use Coleridge's thought to reach out from the thought of Bentham, and to signal the importance of a new approach to ethics and politics on a theoretical, if not immediately on a practical plane.

III. *John Sterling and the Coleridgeans*

Many of the themes first developed in 'Remarks on Bentham's Philosophy' were considered again in 'Bentham' and 'Coleridge'. Although the essay on Bentham was ostensibly a review of the early volumes of the edition of Bentham's *Works*, edited by John Bowring, the two essays were conceived from the outset as being related to each other (*CW* x. 76, 77–8).

We might wonder why Mill chose in the first place to write on Bentham and Coleridge as 'the two great seminal minds of England in their age' (*CW* x. 77; see Bain 1882: 56; cf. Colmer 1976: p. lxxii). When one considers his critique of Bentham in numerous spheres, and the fact that Coleridge was known more as a literary figure than as either a philosopher or a contributor to political ideas (cf. Morrow 1990: 164; Snyder 1929), his choice of these two figures is somewhat problematic. It is important to emphasize that Mill was confining his attention to England, and hence eighteenth-century philosophers from Scotland, like David Hume and Adam Smith, who were the greatest of the age, were apparently excluded. Furthermore, both Bentham and Coleridge were introduced as 'closet-students', secluded 'by circumstances and character, from the business and intercourse of the world', and whose ideas were treated by those engaged in public life 'with feelings akin to contempt' (*CW* x. 77). Such a depiction, with obvious Socratic overtones, was intended to place both Bentham and Coleridge in a very distinct and special category of thinker, largely created by Mill himself, in which ideas combined philosophical depth and originality with an important practical bearing on ethics and politics. Thus, he could refer to them both in vaguely political terms as progressive and conservative thinkers, and, additionally, call them progressive and conservative *philosophers*.

Robson has commented that 'the roots of Mill's comparison of Bentham and Coleridge in the opening pages of his essay on the latter, probably go back to arguments with Coleridgeans in the London Debating Society' (see *CW* x, p. cxxi). One might take this observation further by pointing to the significance of one particular member of the London Debating Society, the Coleridgean John Sterling, and the fact that throughout Mill's surviving correspondence, virtually every reference to Coleridge occurs in letters to or about Sterling.

Sterling (an exact contemporary of Mill) is not well known today, but until his early death in 1844, he had a profound personal impact on Mill's life (perhaps overshadowed only by his relationships with his father and Harriet Taylor) (see Capaldi 2004: 76–7). Just before Sterling's death, Mill wrote to him: 'I shall never think of you but as one of the noblest, & quite the most loveable of all men I have known or ever look to know' and earlier in the same letter, he wrote: 'the remembrance of your friendship will be a precious possession to me as long as I remain here' (*CW* xiii. 635). What we know of their friendship comes mainly from Mill. In the *Autobiography* Mill depicted the arrival of the two Coleridgeans, Sterling and F. D. Maurice, in the London Debating Society as presenting the view of 'a second Liberal and even Radical party, on totally different grounds from Benthamism and vehemently opposed to it' (*CW* i. 133). They developed within the Society the doctrines associated with what Mill called the European reaction of the nineteenth century against the thought that predominated in the eighteenth century. The debates of the Society were unusual in being based at the same time on philosophical principles and intense, direct confrontation between the debating parties. The debates clearly meant more to Mill than intellectual victory, as he began to develop his feelings as well as his intellect in these very personal confrontations. Even though Sterling did not possess the intellectual stature of Mill, as we have seen, Mill was strongly attracted by his warmth as a person and his capacity for friendship.

According to Mill, in 1829 Sterling made a 'violent and unfair attack' on Mill's mainly Benthamite political philosophy to which Mill delivered a sharp response, leading to Sterling's resignation from the Society, and, subsequently, to his own (CW i. 162). Although it is not possible to reconstruct Sterling's attack, we can obtain some hints from Mill's reply (see CW xxvi. 443–53). Sterling seems to have accused Bentham of advocating immorality or, at least, of advancing a doctrine that would have the effect of increasing immorality generally in society, presumably by being concerned with the external consequences of actions rather than with the internal cultivation of virtue. Mill responded by arguing that an emphasis on the internal cultivation of virtue alone would only serve as a cover for the vilest selfishness and a failure to concern oneself with the welfare of others. Mill thought that Sterling had made two errors. First, he failed to see that most philosophers, including Stoics and Epicureans, those who followed Kant and those who followed Locke, possessed moral virtue 'very considerably above the average of ordinary men' (CW xxvi. 445n.). Second, Sterling had changed his position regarding reform. Where previously his view had been compatible with that of Bentham (in pursuing the same ends but for different reasons), he now seemed to oppose reform generally and particularly that connected with the ballot.

After Sterling left the Society, Mill successfully attempted to re-establish their friendship. His letter to Sterling, written on 15 April 1829, is surely one of the most remarkable letters Mill wrote (CW xii. 28–30). Sterling's friendship meant more to Mill than that of any other man, not only because of the affection he felt towards him, but also because of the differences between them. For Mill, the friendship 'appears to me peculiarly adapted to the wants of my own mind; since I know no person who possesses more, of what I have not, than yourself, nor is this inconsistent with my believing you to be deficient in some of the very few things which I have' (CW xii. 29). What did Mill believe that Sterling possessed that he lacked? He was probably referring to Sterling's unique position to help remedy Mill's intense feelings of loneliness and isolation by virtue of the fact that

Sterling did not belong to the political circle inhabited by his father and Bentham (both of whom were still alive at this time).

In the *Autobiography* Mill wrote:

He and I started from intellectual points almost as wide apart as the poles, but the distance between us was always diminishing: if I made steps towards some of his opinions, he, during his short life, was constantly approximating more and more to several of mine: and if he had lived, and had health and vigour to prosecute his ever assiduous self-culture, there is no knowing how much further this spontaneous assimilation might have proceeded. (*CW* i. 163)

In addition to Mill's emphasis on his friendship with Sterling starting at opposite poles, a distinctive feature of the essays on 'Bentham' and 'Coleridge' was Mill's employment of the image of polar opposites, and in a letter to Sterling, Mill wrote that the article on Coleridge served 'as a counter-pole to the one on Bentham' (*CW* xiii. 405). These opposing poles of thought could be moved or overcome in at least two ways. In 1831 he wrote to Sterling:

I once heard Maurice say... that almost all differences of opinion when analysed, were differences of method. But if so, he who can throw most light on the subject of method, will do most to forward that alliance among the most advanced intellects & characters of the age, which is the only definite object I ever have in literature or philosophy so far as I have any *general* object at all. *Argal*, I have put down upon paper a great many of my ideas on logic, & shall in time bring forth a treatise... (*CW* xii. 79)

Thus, one way of overcoming these dividing polarities was to explore them philosophically with the emphasis on method, and one might look to Mill's work on logic to see how Benthamite radicals and progressive Coleridgeans might come closer together. The second way of moving or even overcoming these opposing poles lay in seeing the task of intellect or philosophy as exploring 'the pros and cons of every question'—a position Mill ascribed to Wordsworth, and which he contrasted with that of the radicals and utilitarians (*CW* xii. 81). This is a theme emphasized in a number of Mill's ethical and political writings (see O'Rourke 2001: 42ff.).

iv. *Method in the Social Sciences*

If we examine Mill's treatment of moral and social theory in the *Logic*, we can see how he used a philosophical method first, to criticize what he called 'the Bentham school', and, secondly, to extend his view of the logic of social science by incorporating elements derived initially from his reading of Coleridge and interaction with the Coleridgeans.[3] In book 6 of the *Logic* Mill considered the methods of social science and rejected what he called 'the Geometrical, or Abstract method' (*CW* viii. 887–94). After dismissing Hobbes' attempts to base the foundation of government solely on the emotion of fear and the use of the doctrine of the original contract falsely by reasoning in a circle, Mill turned to the most remarkable and important example, that of 'the interest-philosophy of the Bentham school'. According to Mill, like Hobbes, the Bentham school used a single doctrine, in this case, self-interest, as the basis of its theory of government. Hence, due to the emphasis on self-interest, the school focused on the establishment of the accountability of rulers to the ruled through representative government and other means to minimize the corrupting tendency of this aspect of human nature. Mill, however, believed that this view of accountability as the essence of the problem of government was misleading, as it was based on the false premise of universal self-interest. In ringing Coleridgean tones, he declared:

But I insist only on what is true of all rulers, viz., that the character and course of their actions is largely influenced (independently of personal calculation) by the habitual sentiments and feelings, the general modes of thinking and acting, which prevail throughout the community of which they are members; as well as by the feelings, habits, and modes of thought which characterize the particular class in that community to which they themselves belong. And no one will understand or be able to decipher their system of conduct, who does not take all these things into account. (*CW* viii. 891)

Much of this rejection of the self-interest principle can be found in the earlier 'Bentham' and 'Coleridge', as well as in Sterling's critique of Bentham. What is important here is Mill's argument that the Bentham school was mistaken due to its 'unscientific' method in attempting to apply the model of geometry to politics. While he granted that the theory was important in the political struggle for parliamentary reform in focusing attention on representation, it possessed no claim to truth beyond this historical moment in practical politics.

There are two main difficulties with the use of what Mill called the geometric method in politics. First, as we have seen in the cases of Hobbes and the Bentham school, those who employed it tended to fix on a single cause to explain the whole of politics and political morality. Mill insisted that whatever deductions were set forth to explain events in society, they must proceed, not from one or a few causes, but 'considering each effect as (what it really is) an aggregate result of many causes, operating sometimes through the same, sometimes through different mental agencies, or laws of human nature' (*CW* viii. 894). Rather than attempting to trace out a few causes and effects in the complex worlds of ethics and politics, Mill looked to more complex natural sciences, like astronomy and mechanics, to provide better models for social science (see Ryan 1987: 133ff.). Second, Mill seemed to reject a science of society based on universal principles. This does not mean that the psychological theory and the science of ethology supposedly deduced from it were not based on universal principles of human nature and the formation of character. But the pattern of causation determining behaviour in society was complex and changed over time. Human agency and morality became part of historical tradition, and politics at one particular moment depended on a different pattern of causation than at another moment.

This relativism provides some insight into Mill's choice of Bentham and Coleridge, not as the two greatest thinkers ever, but as the two who had the greatest impact at a particular time in relation to a particular field of thought. Furthermore, Mill used them to understand society from a perspective that had no claim to truth beyond the period in which the essays were written. Mill admitted in the *Autobiography* (*CW* i. 225–7; see x, p. cxxi) that his essay on Coleridge was written to enlarge and improve the thinking of Radicals and Liberals at that time. That is the perspective from which it must be initially understood, even though Mill touched on numerous philosophical and literary problems, which transcended this fairly narrow perspective.[4]

Furthermore, Mill must have realized, for example, that, for Bentham, all actions, even those in politics, were not based on self-interest. Bentham's theory could accommodate most of the traditional virtues and at the level of motivation, sympathy and benevolence could be as powerful as more self-serving motives. His idea of self-interest was also more complex than Mill seemed to appreciate. At one level a healthy self-regard was essential for survival. If Adam's regard was only for Eve, and Eve's only care was for Adam, in Bentham's view, both would have perished (and presumably the human race) within twelve months (Bentham 1983*b* (1830): 119). At another level, Bentham regarded the 'constant and arduous task as of every moralist, so of every legislator who deserves to be so' as to 'increase ... the influence of sympathy at the expense of that of self-regard, and of sympathy for the greater number at the expense of sympathy of the lesser number' (Bentham 1983b (1830): 119). This could be achieved by education on the one hand and law on the other. We are educated within the family and society to deepen and extend our fellow feelings and make them habitual so as to increase happiness generally for others and for ourselves. The laws can also guide us towards the same ends in establishing duties, for example, to pay taxes to defend society, build hospitals, schools, roads, and bridges, and look after the poor and needy.

It is true that Bentham argued that in devising institutions of government one must assume that a person would attempt to advance 'his own private and personal interest ... at the expense of the public interest' unless prevented from doing so by institutions or morality (Bentham 1983b (1830): 119). But such an assumption has for its object the prevention of corruption and the advancement of happiness and is not simply a theory of self-interest. For Bentham, most rulers *appeared* to act as if they were ruling in the interests of the ruled, and most of the ruled seemed devoted to their rulers, even to the point of ignoring self-interest, for example, in cheerfully going to war (placing their lives at risk) in support of their rulers' plans and ambitions. But he ascribed such actions to what in modern times we might call 'false consciousness'. A good deal of his political theory was devoted to an explanation of how this false consciousness originated and persisted in societies, affecting politics, religion, language, and even feelings. An understanding of interests, both self-regarding and other-regarding, beneath the façade of ordinary politics is an important part of Bentham's approach and crucial for an understanding of its scientific character.

Another important element in Bentham's political theory, which was not based on self-regarding or other-regarding interest, was that of public opinion. At one point he depicted public opinion as a body of law emanating from the people and on a par with the so-called Common Law. In depicting its role in government, he wrote:

To the pernicious exercise of the power of government it is the only check; to the beneficial, an indispensable supplement. Able rulers lead it; prudent rulers lead or follow it; foolish rulers disregard it. Even at the present stage in the career of civilization, its dictates coincide, on most points, with those of the *greatest happiness principle*; on some, however, it still deviates from them: but, as its deviations have all along been less and less numerous, and less wide, sooner or later they will cease to be discernible; aberration will vanish, coincidence will be complete.   (Bentham 1983*b* (1830): 36)

All members of a given society and, indeed, all of those in the world who took an interest in that society belonged to what Bentham called its public opinion tribunal. Its object was to advance human happiness through writings, attendance at public meetings, serving on juries, and even by popular demonstrations and uprisings. Public opinion had a critical function in society, as well as one of gathering and disseminating information. Through the encouragement of obedience and disobedience the public opinion tribunal also performed an 'executive function' in rewarding and punishing rulers.

Although Bentham was not original in basing government ultimately on public opinion, he was original in making public opinion the engine of reform (see Rosen 1983: 19–40). Mill ignored this important aspect of Bentham's theory, perhaps because he grew increasingly wary of public opinion and feared its potential power in the tyranny of the majority. But neglecting this most important element in Bentham's theory led Mill to present a misleading account of Bentham's political ideas in his writings on Bentham, including book 6 of the *Logic*. It is clear that Mill was using Bentham at a particular time and place and for his own purposes.

If Mill's own approach also rested partly on Coleridgean foundations, what were those foundations? Consider, for example, Mill's discussion of polarities, particularly, in the essays on Bentham and Coleridge. Coleridge, himself, though using a slightly different terminology, employed the idea of opposites to explain a number of his ideas. In expounding the ideas of 'permanence' and 'progressiveness' as opposites, he referred to them as being like the positive and negative poles of a magnet—'opposite powers are always of the same kind, and tend to union, either by equipoise or by a common product' and they 'suppose and require each other' (Coleridge 1972 (1830): 16n.). Elsewhere, he referred to 'Property' and 'Nationalty' as opposites: 'correspondent and reciprocally supporting, counterweights, of the commonwealth; the existence of the one being the condition, and the perfecting, of the rightfulness of the other' (Coleridge 1972 (1830): 26). Similarly, in expounding the idea of the Christian church in the context of opposing forces and institutions, Coleridge used the metaphor of opposite banks of the same stream and words like 'counter-balance' and 'contra-position' (Coleridge 1972 (1830): 100).

Mill developed this imagery and mode of argument at the beginning of 'Coleridge', as he brought Bentham and Coleridge together as 'completing counterparts'. They were in Mill's terminology 'contraries'—'the things which are farthest from one another in the same kind'. The two men contributed to awaken the spirit of philosophy, and while they never interacted, they defined English philosophy at this time (CW x. 120–1). One cannot approximate the truth simply by adding Bentham's and Coleridge's philosophies together, but their combination requires, in Robson's view, 'careful analysis and comparison, with the aim of revealing limitations of experience and errors of generalization' (Robson 1968: 192).

In the *Logic* Mill adopted a new approach to understanding society, taken partly from Auguste Comte, which he called the 'Inverse Deductive, or Historical Method'. In explicating this approach, he declared that the object was to discover 'the causes which produce, and the phenomena which characterize, States of Society generally' (CW viii. 911). By a state of society (also called a state of civilization) he meant:

the degree of knowledge, and of intellectual and moral culture, existing in the community, and in every class of it; the state of industry, of wealth and its distribution; the habitual occupations of the community; their division into classes, and the relations of those classes to one another; the common beliefs which they entertain on all the subjects most important to mankind, and the degree of assurance with which those beliefs are held; their tastes, and the character and degree of their aesthetic development; their form of government, and the more important of their laws and customs. (CW viii. 911–12)

The state of society at any given time must be understood in terms of what he called 'the progressiveness of the human race'. This idea, he believed, should not be confused with a tendency towards improvement and increased happiness in society. This element of progressiveness provided a 'theorem' of social science on which a predictive science of society might be based. He depicted this theorem as follows:

there is a progressive change both in the character of the human race, and in their outward circumstances so far as moulded by themselves: that in each successive age the principal phenomena of society are different from what they were in the age preceding, and still more different from any previous age: the periods which most distinctly mark these successive changes being intervals of one generation, during which a new set of human beings have been educated, have grown up from childhood, and taken possession of society. (CW viii. 914)

The theorem of the progressiveness of the human race had led some thinkers, particularly those on the continent, to study history to discover the 'law of progress' and thereby predict future events. Mill rejected this approach as never forming a science of society as its laws were simply empirical generalizations, often erroneous ones, and not verified by psychological and ethological laws. But he did not abandon this general approach. He first distinguished, following Comte, between social statics, which investigated stability in society, and social dynamics, which was concerned with progress and succession. In illustrating the nature of social statics, he quoted at length from his own essay on Coleridge (*CW* viii. 921–4) to illustrate how one might identify certain requisites in every society, which maintained 'collective existence' (*CW* viii. 920). Although these requisites were only empirical laws, some of them 'are found to follow with so much probability from general laws of human nature, that the consilience of the two processes raises the evidence to proof and the generalizations to the rank of scientific truths' (*CW* viii. 920). The passage from Coleridge mentioned three requisites for stability: (*a*) a system of education which established 'a restraining discipline' in society; (*b*) a feeling of allegiance or loyalty to settled aspects of society or to people or to common gods; and (*c*) a strong and active principle of cohesion in society—not based on nationalism—but a principle of sympathy which united members of a given society.

Besides the intrinsic value of Mill's discussion, the effect of this material was to use part of the essay on Coleridge to undermine, if not dismiss, Bentham's approach to government. For Bentham, representative democracy could be shown to be the best form of government and universally applicable to all societies in placing the rulers under the control of the ruled. The only condition necessary for its success was that the people desired such a government for themselves and developed the habits of obedience to maintain it. For Mill, no form of government could be universally applicable to all societies. Societies must first have developed a number of principles of stability and cohesion, and forms of government depended on the character and continuity of these principles.

Mill's account of social dynamics followed in a similar vein as that of social statics, except that social dynamics was concerned with the explanation of changes in social conditions. In the history of societies one found 'general tendencies', and he noted, as examples, that as societies progressed, mental qualities tended to prevail over physical ones and that an industrial spirit tended to prevail over a military spirit. In combining the static with the dynamic view of society, Mill hoped to develop scientific laws concerned with the development of human societies. Yet, such a process, even as Mill outlined it, seemed a difficult, if not impossible, task due to the complexity of the data to which such a science must be related and from which it was ultimately derived.

Mill then turned to what he called the 'predominant, and almost paramount', of the agents of social progress, 'intellectual activity' or 'the speculative faculties of mankind' (CW viii. 926). Although he accepted that only a few individuals gave a major role to intellect in their lives, he nonetheless claimed that 'its influence is the main determining cause of the social progress' (CW viii. 926). All other changes were dependent on them. He illustrated this view by pointing first to the force for improvement in the conditions of life in the desire for increased material comfort. Such a desire, however, could only be realized by the knowledge that was possessed at a given time. Furthermore, as the strongest propensities in human nature were those of a selfish nature, social existence required the discipline which established a common set of opinions and which upheld the social union. Thus, Mill argued, 'the state of speculative faculties' determined the social and political state of the society in the same way that they determined the physical conditions of life (CW viii. 926). He then asserted:

Every considerable change historically known to us in the condition of any portion of mankind, when not brought about by external force, has been preceded by a change, of proportional extent, in the state of their knowledge, or in their prevalent beliefs. (CW viii. 926–7)

Mill believed that every advance in civilization was based on a prior advance in knowledge. He pointed to the way a succession of religions, from polytheism to Judaism to Christianity and to Protestantism, followed by the critical philosophy of the Enlightenment and the positive sciences related to it, had changed society in each successive period. He rejected the view that philosophy and science were changed by developments in the material conditions of life. Thus, speculation, though often confined to a few, determined the development of society as a whole unless conditions were such (e.g. the breakdown of society) that no progress was possible.

Mill's methodology of social science was also related to his accounts of Bentham and Coleridge. He chose the two greatest thinkers of the age, who were 'closet philosophers', but whose influence on the generation which moved forward from the eighteenth to the nineteenth century implied a rejection of the view that the industrial revolution or productive forces alone determined the character of society. Mill, himself, thought that progress in social science required the rejection of the geometrical method of Bentham and his father and its replacement by the historical method of Comte, which he also associated with Coleridge. But he did not simply replace one with the other, as the historical school was wholly dependent on the sciences of psychology and ethology, which were ultimately derived from the school of Locke and Bentham, as revised by his father's work in psychology. And the revival of associationist psychology was stimulated by the critique of modern eighteenth-century empiricism by those in the 'Germano-Coleridgean' school. Thus, Mill's approach to social science reflected his attempts to identify these polarities of thought in Bentham and Coleridge and to show how they might be reconciled and used to advance new thinking in this field.

v. *The* Considerations *and the Method of Reform*

What can Mill's encounter with Bentham and Coleridge as well as the development of his ideas in the *Logic* teach us about a method of reform? To answer this question we might look briefly at the *Considerations* to see how the ideas became part of a more general theory of government. Although Mill did not develop a major category that might be called 'method of reform', he would presumably place the task of political reform under the category of Art (see *CW* viii. 943–52). With an end defined in utilitarian terms as one of increasing happiness, issues concerned with the institutions best suited to realize this end would be discussed with an eye to replacing those which produced unhappiness or failed to produce sufficient happiness with those which advanced the greatest happiness of the members of a given society. But Mill did not proceed in this fashion.

He began the *Considerations* with 'two conflicting theories' concerning political institutions (*CW* xix. 374). The first saw government as a practical art of adjusting means to ends. Institutions were chosen to realize these ends and the people were stirred to demand the creation of the institutions. Practitioners of the art looked upon a constitution, he wrote, 'as they would upon a steam plough, or a threshing machine', as a series of mechanisms for producing good government (*CW* xix. 374). The second theory saw the development of institutions as a spontaneous development and not a matter of choice. One simply learned about them and adapted oneself to work with them. Political institutions were then regarded as an 'organic growth' from the people and 'a product of their habits, instincts, and unconscious wants and desires, scarcely at all of their deliberate purposes' (*CW* xix. 375).

Mill's starting point for these two conflicting theories should not be assumed to be the same starting point for the essays on Bentham and Coleridge, and the two theories cannot be assumed to be those of Bentham and Coleridge. The two conflicting theories seem closer to the general views Mill ascribed to Liberals and Conservatives in the preface to the *Considerations*, and they are prevented by these positions from joining together to adopt an agenda of reform. Mill challenged the Conservative position more than the Liberal one, but in important ways, he challenged both. He sought to show that the views expressed by both of these theories could not lead to or sustain good government, because one excluded the other and without general support from both reform was not possible.

Mill was clearly on the side of reform and he set forth a view of opposing positions which were not hostile to reform, and which could be reconciled to achieve radical reform. In this first chapter Mill thus moved deftly from two conflicting theories, which contradicted each other, to two opposed theories, which were merely contraries and which, together in this qualified form, could accept a series of arguments that supported the reform of existing institutions. In this manner Mill was roughly following the method of reform he devised for the essays on Bentham and Coleridge, even though the circumstances of its employment were considerably different. He insisted that political institutions were constructed by human beings and within limits were open to choice. But these limits included three conditions: (*a*) the people must be willing to accept or not to oppose the institutions; (*b*) they must be willing to maintain the institutions; and (*c*) they must be willing and able to take steps for the institutions to realize their purposes. Thus, although political institutions were a matter of human artifice, the reformer was constrained by what the people were willing to adopt and sustain. To this extent, the reformer was reconciled with the 'new' conservative who, while accepting the role of human endeavour in building institutions, did not agree that a society was free to accept or reject any institution that one wished and at any time one pleased.

Mill also added a further ingredient in this reconciliation of contrary positions. He rejected the older conservative view that political institutions were determined by social circumstances, by insisting on the role of intelligence in the construction and adoption of institutions. He employed examples of enlightened reform in the past to support this view of the importance of intelligence. Such a view did not accept that institutions were a matter of free choice, but rather a matter of intelligent and rational choice. This element not only assisted in the reconciliation of the two contrary views, but also alerted the reader to Mill's position in the *Logic* regarding social science as mainly a matter of the way the ideas of one generation determined the institutions of the next.

We see in this opening chapter Mill's method of reform taking a longer view of the development of institutions than that taken by earlier radicals and drawing in conservatives who were not wholly opposed to intelligent change and reform. Yet, the issues he proposed to discuss within this framework were issues of radical reform. Let us see very briefly how he proceeded to combine these various views.

In the next chapter Mill considered, not the best form of government, but the objects or functions of government, which this best form was designed to achieve. He began with two provisos, which were taken from the *Logic*. First, the functions of government could not be fixed, as they differed in different states of society; and second, the character of a government could be understood only by looking beyond the sphere of government institutions to take into account the well-being of society as well as the nature of government itself. In the ensuing discussion Mill critically invoked both Coleridge and Bentham, not to accept or reject aspects of their political thought, but to transform them. He took up Coleridge's famous distinction between permanence and progression in society reflecting the landed and mercantile interests, which, in Coleridge's view, should be balanced. Mill argued that the distinction was a false one as progression was not possible without permanence and that these were not opposites (see *CW* xix. 385). Thus, one of Coleridge's own famous contraries was reconciled in a brief argument which showed that they need not be contraries at all. Order and permanence were also removed from the province of a particular section of society and made part of progression in both its psychological and institutional contexts. When Mill referred to Bentham in this chapter, he adopted Bentham's idea of aptitude and its different components (moral, intellectual, and active), but he then applied it to the people generally, while Bentham applied it only to those holding public office (see *CW* xix. 390). But however Mill used Bentham and Coleridge in the *Considerations*, the important point is that he carried forward the distinct legacy of the method of reform he developed fully for the first time in the essays on Bentham and Coleridge.

According to Robson, the influence of Coleridge on Mill was mainly confined to the 1830s, and the essay on Coleridge was 'less a criticism of Coleridge, or a reassessment of Bentham, than a declaration of assured and well-founded independence' (Robson 1968: 76). Robson's comment is partly true, though the influence of the essays on Bentham and Coleridge surely extended throughout his life. Mill's starting point for reform was not the identification of means to established ends, as he found in Bentham, but, as in Coleridge's thought, the initial identification of contradictory views that constituted obstacles to reform, which were then transformed into contraries and reconciled in a distinctive way to advance reform. One might argue that Mill's use of contraries for this purpose was simply part of a rhetoric of politics, employed in drawing in the enemies and encouraging the friends of reform. But the method of reform had deeper foundations and objects. It allowed Mill more easily to emphasize that reform must be adapted to particular times and the means devised to achieve given ends could not be assumed to apply universally. Thus, a particular reform, like the introduction of the ballot, might have to be secret at some points and open at others in the development of a society. Mill believed that we could not simply assume, as did earlier radicals, that the secret ballot was universally valid as an important means to prevent corruption and establish good government through a system of representation, because such a view did not take into account the new factor in emerging democracies of the tyranny of the majority. But whatever the outcome, Mill's method looked beyond the traditional radical arsenal, which was based on the assumption of a tight means–ends conception of the art of government.

Furthermore, Mill's method of reform started with the preparation of the people to receive and support ongoing reform. It began with the ideas of intelligent elites in one generation who then prepared the minds of the people generally to see the merits of reform and progress in particular institutions and practices. Although Bentham's radicalism was intended to lead to gradual reform rather than to revolution, Mill's method itself ensured that successful reform had to be gradual by its very nature, in that the ideas which could establish and support such reform had first to develop in society. That is to say, the new institutions had to be preceded by the understanding of the institutions and their acceptance by members of society. Otherwise, the politics of reform would become an empty and futile rhetoric meeting determined opposition from those who, rightly or wrongly, felt that they had much to lose from whatever reforms were proposed.

Mill's *Considerations* has always lacked the appeal and popularity of *On Liberty* and even *Utilitarianism*. To some, it seems eccentric in its advocacy of such proposals as plural voting, the open rather than the secret ballot, and the scheme of proportional representation originally devised by Thomas Hare. To others, it seems remarkably conservative in relation to the earlier radicalism of Bentham and many of his followers.[5] It is no wonder that Bentham's star as a *reformer* has outshone that of Mill, except perhaps in the sphere of liberty. But this examination of Mill's radicalism reveals a different method of reform than is commonly found by commentators, one based initially on his personal encounter with the Coleridgeans in the London Debating Society in the 1820s, developed in the essays on Bentham and Coleridge, and refined in book 6 of the *Logic*.

When Dennis Thompson discusses Mill's theory of government, with its two principles of participation and competence, he fails to embed this discussion into Mill's method of reform (see Thompson 1976; see also Ten 1998: 374ff.). This failure leads him to write of Mill's theory of democracy as if competence and participation are important aspects of Mill's conception of the end of government and are combined to advance this end. But Mill himself rejects the idea of an ideal form of government that can stand apart from society. As we shall see in Chapter 4, Mill turned away from traditional discussions of forms of government in order to emphasize the method of reform through the transforming power of intellect in society. Thompson deals with some aspects of this problem under the heading of a theory of development, which draws on the *Logic*, but not on Mill's essays, 'Bentham' and 'Coleridge' (see Thompson 1976: 136ff.).

One consequence of Thompson's approach is that he dismisses earlier views that suggested that Mill was never a democrat (see Thompson 1976: 4). He does so partly because his theory requires that democracy serves as the overarching end. The opposing thesis, as, for example, developed by J. H. Burns, concludes that, although Mill's political thought was consistent throughout his life, he never adopted 'the viewpoint of a democrat' (Burns 1969: 328; cf. Robson 1968: 224). In my opinion Burns, rather than Thompson, has a better understanding of Mill's position, insofar as Mill's attitude towards democracy is much less enthusiastic than Bentham's a generation earlier. But even Burns's conclusion needs qualification. What makes Mill consistent in his political thought from the 1830s to the *Considerations* is his commitment to a method of reform, derived from the early philosophic radicalism, which matures into the doctrine of the *Considerations*. While Burns is correct in stating that Mill never adopted the viewpoint of a democrat, he might have added that there is nothing in Mill's method of reform that prevents him from doing so and, at another point, rejecting it.

What makes democracy an end to be sought through reform is the willingness of the people to accept and support a particular version. This version must be adapted to that society in a way that does not destroy numerous other constituents of happiness to which that society aspires. In other words, as Mill works out clearly in the *Logic*, the theory of government is subordinate to social science generally. This is not to deny, as Mill states in the *Autobiography*, that the *Considerations* consists of an exposition of 'the best form of a popular constitution' and that this requires a 'general theory of government' (*CW* i. 265). But Mill's discussion would be seriously deficient if his method of reform were not recognized as an essential ingredient of such an exposition and, particularly, of the theory itself. To focus simply on the pros and cons of particular institutions as the best means to increase happiness would be somewhat similar to taking Marx's comments on a future communist state as a fully developed theory of government. For Mill, one needs to understand how society works at a given time, and use the method of reconciling opposing views to see what reforms are possible. Reform then becomes a process of adapting means to ends by human effort and artifice and persuading other members of society to see the matter in this fashion. Without such a method it is arguable that Mill's theory of government becomes idle speculation, at best a form of utopian thought, and without much relevance to practical politics. The method of reform, as worked out in the *Considerations*, and as explored in 'Bentham' and 'Coleridge' and book 6 of the *Logic*, can still raise the major questions of any given age, even if the practical solutions might have to await a later stage in the evolution of particular societies.

4

Psychology, Character, National Character, and the Science of Politics

1. *The Science of Ethology*

We turn now from the role of logic and truth generally in Mill's thought to the way Mill's *Logic* approached morality, society, and politics. My object in this chapter is to explore some aspects of Mill's approach to social and political science with an emphasis on the significance of character or 'ethology' in this science. This exploration is then followed by an account of how he applied the logical arguments concerning character to his conception of 'the ideally best form of government' in the *Considerations*. At one point he wrote:

[T]here can be no separate Science of Government.... All questions respecting the tendencies of forms of government must stand part of the general science of society, not of any separate branch of it. (*CW* viii. 906)

For the student of J. S. Mill's political theory, this categorical denial that government can be the subject of a separate science might be unsettling.[1] The historian of political thought might be dismayed to discover that the traditional study of forms of government, 'from Plato to Bentham', seems no longer relevant to an understanding of politics (see *CW* viii. 876n.).

In the *Logic* Mill presented a highly critical account of the current state of political science. He compared the study of politics to that of medicine 'before physiology and natural history began to be cultivated as branches of general knowledge' (*CW* viii. 875), and wrote:

Students in politics thus attempted to study the pathology and therapeutics of the social body, before they had laid the necessary foundation in its physiology; to cure disease without understanding the laws of health. And the result was such as it must always be when persons, even of ability, attempt to deal with the complex questions of a science before its simpler and more elementary truths have been established. (*CW* viii. 876)

Mill particularly criticized those who eschewed the careful study of 'universal sequences' in politics, but proceeded to develop 'universal precepts'—based on the application of one form of government to every society and at all times. He thought that this kind of reasoning brought the subject into disrepute and made little sense even in terms of the analogy with medicine. 'No one now supposes it possible,' he wrote, 'that one remedy can cure all diseases or even the same disease in all constitutions and habits of body' (*CW* viii. 877).

Many commentators use Mill's experience of the critique of James Mill's *Essay on Government* by T. B. Macaulay in 1829 and the subsequent debate for the source of his interest in this topic (see Lively and Rees 1978; Ryan 1987: 133ff.; Skorupski 1989: 269ff.). Eventually, his own position was based on the rejection of both the 'chemical' or experimental approach of Macaulay and the 'geometrical' method of what he called 'the Bentham school' (see *CW* vii, pp. liv–lv; viii. 879–94). In the *Autobiography* Mill clearly regarded his rejection of both of these views as providing an important context for the main chapters of book 6 of the *Logic* (*CW* i. 167–9).[2]

Although Mill was obviously influenced by this debate, the debate itself might not have provided the deeper foundations for his treatment of politics.[3] These foundations were also set out in book 6 of the *Logic*, and the most important were concerned with psychology and character. In Mill's theory the study of character became the science of ethology, which he described as follows:

A science is thus formed, to which I would propose to give the name of Ethology, or the Science of Character; from *ethos*, a word more nearly corresponding to the term 'character' as I here use it, than any other word in the same language. The name is perhaps etymologically applicable to the entire science of our mental and moral nature; but if, as is usual and convenient, we employ the name Psychology for the science of the elementary laws of mind, Ethology will serve for the ulterior science which determines the kind of character produced in conformity to those general laws, by any set of circumstances, physical and moral. According to this definition, Ethology is the science which corresponds to the art of education; in the widest sense of the term, including the formation of national or collective character as well as individual. (*CW* viii. 869)

Let us briefly consider several themes raised in this passage. First, there is no doubting the standing and importance that Mill gave to the science of ethology. In numerous passages he proclaimed its importance: 'this science of Ethology may be called the Exact Science of Human Nature'; or Ethology is 'the immediate foundation of Social Science' (*CW* viii. 870, 907). But however such statements established the significance of ethology, they should be juxtaposed to the fact, as he admitted, that ethology, as a science, 'is still to be created' (*CW* viii. 872–3). As Mill put it, 'a science of Ethology, founded on the laws of Psychology, is therefore possible; though little has yet been done, and that little not at all systematically, towards forming it' (*CW* viii. 873). Robson (1998: 363) refers to Mill as possibly 'the first and only ethologist' to suggest that not only did Mill discover this science and give it pride of place in his science of society, but he never developed it, and apparently neither did anyone else.[4]

Second, Mill located ethology in relation to psychology, and the task of psychology was to establish the laws of the mind. Mind, for Mill, was not reducible to matter and its laws were discoverable through observation and experiment. He linked psychology with the theory of association developed by his father and by Bain's *The Senses and the Intellect* (1855) and *The Emotions and the Will* (1859), and Herbert Spencer's *The Principles of Psychology* (1855) (see *CW* viii. 853n.). Mill's close relationship with Bain from 1842 to his death formed the main conduit for the development of Mill's ideas on psychology and ethology. If psychology was 'a science of observation and experiment', ethology was treated as a deductive science. Ethology traced the operations of the laws of the mind 'in complex combinations of circumstances' (*CW* viii. 870). 'In other words', Mill wrote, 'Ethology, the deductive science, is a system of corollaries from Psychology, the experimental science' (*CW* viii. 872). In reaching this position Mill provided an extensive critique of Bacon's conception of *axiomata media* by arguing that such valuable principles could be established by deduction as well as by induction. Bacon was wrong, he believed, in holding that induction proceeded from the lowest to middle principles and then to the highest principles, and Bacon left no room for the discovery of new principles by deduction. Mill said that Bacon made this mistake by not having any acquaintance with deductive sciences like mechanics, astronomy, optics, and acoustics (*CW* viii. 870–1).

Third, ethology, Mill claimed, was the science that was related to the art of education. Just how the science (ethology) and the art (education) were related was not clearly spelt out, though Mill used the distinction between art and science to advance some important points in the *Logic*. For example, when he criticized the so-called 'geometrical' method of 'the Bentham school', he referred to their 'fundamental error' in treating an art as if it was a science and believing one could have a deductive art (*CW* viii. 889). Such an error, Mill maintained, was not due to ignorance of the distinction between an art and a science, but supposedly to do with the way that distinction was employed.

For Bentham, art had priority over science, and determined which sciences or which aspects of any given science would form the knowledge the art put to use.[5] The medical art, for example, might draw on numerous sciences, e.g. anatomy, physiology, biology, chemistry, physics, etc., but only on those aspects of these sciences that served the art. Similarly, the political art might draw on numerous sciences and arts, from ethics to statistics, or from economics to law. The important task for the practitioner of the art was to identify the ends the art was to serve and then to develop or draw on the sciences to advance the art. Hence, the art and science of politics would draw on a range of other arts and sciences and serve human happiness by means of principles taken from these other spheres.

At times, Mill seemed close to Bentham. He too insisted on the close connection between art and science, though he clearly gave priority to science over art. His criticism of 'the Bentham school' was partly on this point. Mill mainly treated science (and the use of induction and deduction) in the *Logic*, though he did not neglect art, as is obvious in the brief, though important, final chapter of the *Logic* (*CW* viii. 943ff.). As Mill wrote:

The art proposes to itself an end to be attained, defines the end, and hands it over to the science. The science receives it, considers it as a phenomenon or effect to be studied, and having investigated its causes and conditions, sends it back to art with a theorem of the combinations of circumstances by which it could be produced. Art then examines these combinations of circumstances, and according as any of them are or are not in human power, pronounces the end attainable or not. The only one of the premises, therefore, which Art supplies, is the original major premise, which asserts that the attainment of the given end is desirable. Science then lends to Art the proposition (obtained by a series of inductions or of deductions) that the performance of certain actions will attain the end. From these premises Art concludes that the performance of these actions is desirable, and finding it also practicable, converts the theorem into a rule or precept.   (CW viii. 944–5)

Mill then proceeded to make the important point that, unless the whole operation of science was completed, the rules of an art could not be established. For even if one discovered a process of cause and effect within a science, the relevant art could not depend upon it, as there might be further negative conditions which prevented the effect from being realized (see CW viii. 945). Mill thus gave a some-what limited status to the various arts, particularly those in the social sciences, like ethics and politics, because of the constantly pressing need to return to and revise the science.

Mill criticized the idea that practical maxims could be deduced within an art like politics, which then could have a scientific bearing on the understanding or prescription of conduct. What status, there-fore, could be given to Bentham's maxim (from which much of his constitutional theory followed: see Bentham 1983b; Rosen 1983) that whatever qualities rulers might possess, we must assume that they in fact ruled in their own interests and constitutional systems should be devised to reduce the deleterious effects of this tendency? For Bentham, the fact of self-interest supported the political art, that is to say, the political art drew on and used this scientific fact. Mill would argue that, if the self-interest principle was a cause of political action, it was only one of numerous causes operating in politics. Rulers also acted on the basis of 'habitual sentiments and feelings, the general modes of thinking and acting, which prevail throughout the community of which they are members; as well as by the feel-ings, habits, and modes of thought which characterize the particular class in that community to which they themselves belong' (CW viii. 891). No science of politics could ignore these and numerous other causes of actions by rulers. Furthermore, one could not reach the self-interest principle by treating politics as an art. For Mill, numer-ous causes, besides self-interest, were means to advance happiness. To give self-interest this exalted status within an art would be to ignore the role of generous and selfless actions by politicians and the role generally of character in politics. Such generous and selfless actions could also not be simply reduced to self-interest. Such a reduction would diminish the importance of character.

From Mill's point of view Bentham had not paid sufficient attention to the distinction between a science and an art and the appropriate realms of each. As Mill put it, 'the grounds, then, of every rule of art, are to be found in the theorems of science' (CW viii. 947). What remained for art, then, was simply the definition of the end, or what he called teleology. Each art had a single first principle or 'general major premise', which was not taken from science, and which affirmed that the object was a desirable one. For example, the 'hygienic' art aimed at the preservation of health; the medical art, the cure of disease (CW viii. 949).

In this book considerable emphasis will be placed on Mill's reversal of the art-and-science paradigm developed by Bentham. What counted for Mill were the sciences, and the focus of the Logic is on understanding in a critical way the process of establishing all of the sciences from hypotheses to proof. Only the brief final chapter of the Logic, added in the third edition of 1851, almost as an afterthought, is devoted to the arts.

Mill's preoccupation with the development of the sciences was fairly commonplace among philosophers and scientists in numerous disciplines. The classification and the naming of the various sciences seemed more important at the time than is the case today.[6] In the nineteenth century new sciences were in the process of being discovered and old ones reformulated or discarded. At issue were the work and careers of numerous scientists and institutions (e.g. consider the threat to botany and zoology as sciences from the classification of genera and species by Darwinian science, i.e. biology which seemed to accept that no such classifications could be permanently established). But just as important was the undermining of literal Christianity by the truths established by science. For example, geology was challenging the time span of the Creation, and the accounts of numerous biblical chronologies and stories were being shown to be incompatible with science and history. As we shall see, Mill recognized that these sciences were probably more important than theological argument to undermining the strength of religious views. As science expanded and accepted the supremacy of logic, the grip of religion in numerous fields was forced to retreat. Mill reflected and encouraged these developments.

Art was given a lower status in the relationship between science and art. The moral and political arts would have to be constantly revised as psychology, ethology, and social science became established and developed. Nevertheless, contemporary moral philosophers seem to take a different view of Mill's position. Wendy Donner writes: 'John Stuart Mill's moral philosophy has a structure at its foundation that he articulates in *A System of Logic* and other writings. The architecture of his theory is organized on the basis of the Art of Life' (Donner 2011: 146). Like other moral philosophers, Donner seems to ignore the connection between art and science in this context, even though some moral philosophers can accept that the discussion of the 'art of life' grew out of Mill's distinction between art and science (see Eggleston *et al.* 2011: 3). What they tend to miss is an understanding of the role of morality within the context of the three sciences, psychology, ethology, and social science (and undoubtedly others).

The new emphasis on Mill's art of life in moral philosophy today has been skilfully chronicled in a recent essay by David Weinstein (2011: 44–70). He charts what he regards as an inconsistent understanding of Mill's views from Mill's own lifetime to the present day, as attempts have been made to reconcile Kantian rules with utilitarian calculation. In so far as the art of life is interpreted as leading to an emphasis on security, freedom, and rights, Weinstein challenges those who 'always' 'interpret Mill as holding these rights absolutely sacrosanct' (Weinstein 2011: 56). From the perspective of changing and improving sciences, such a position would be impossible to maintain, and clearly Mill did not do so. While moral rights and justice can be given a priority within a utilitarian morality and scholars may rightly regard them as relatively permanent, they must inevitably change as the sciences of psychology, ethology, and social science change.

ii. *Ethology between Psychology and Education*

For Mill, ethology, or 'the science of the formation of character', was located in the *Logic* between the science of psychology on the one hand and social science on the other. Ethology was also the science that corresponded to the art of education. As we have seen, psychology was mainly an inductive science, and ethology was primarily deductive and extended psychological truths into the realm of character and what Mill called 'national character' (*CW* viii. 861, 869).

According to Collini, though Mill and Matthew Arnold were critics of 'Victorian moralism', they shared the assumptions concerning character that pervaded Victorian thought (Collini 1991: 100–2; see also Carlisle 1998: 146; Jones 1992: 288–9). What were these assumptions? For Collini, they consisted of 'self-restraint, perseverance, strenuous effort, courage in the face of adversity' and an emphasis on doing one's duty (Collini 1991: 100). He particularly found these qualities in the writings of Samuel Smiles (Collini 1991: 100–1). For Collini's thesis to be valid, it is necessary to see Mill as a Victorian moralist of one form or another. But Mill was not a moralist in sharing the assumptions that Collini ascribes to this period. He was engaged in another activity altogether, which might be called logic or science,[7] and which might or might not have had echoes in Victorian public morality.

Mill's project has another well-known pedigree that should be stressed here. In its rejection of Aristotelian logic, modern philosophers turned to psychology to explore the basis of human understanding, action, and character. The obvious source for much later speculation was John Locke's *Essay Concerning Human Understanding*, and the traditions of discourse to which Locke's work contributed were at the heart of the Enlightenment and its legacy. To understand Mill's use of this legacy, which combined psychology and logic, we might explore briefly the two writers on whom Mill drew in his attempt to relate psychology to character: Bentham and his father, James Mill.

At the beginning of *Chrestomathia* (meaning 'useful learning') Bentham devoted a section to the general advantages that might be derived from education over and above those benefits from instruction in particular subjects and according to the distinct educational methods he proposed to employ. Besides affording the educated person 'a proportionable share of general respect', Bentham listed four 'securities' that education provided. The first was security against ennui—the condition of him who, for want of something in prospect that would afford him pleasure, knows not what to do with himself, a 'malady' he found among the idle rich and particularly among men of business who succumbed to it in retirement (Bentham 1983a (1817): 19 and table I). For Bentham, ennui was a serious condition, akin perhaps to depression, and could lead to decline and even death. In *An Introduction to the Principles of Morals and Legislation* he mentioned ennui in the context of a person suffering pain from the absence of 'all kinds of pleasure whatsoever' (Bentham 1996 (1789): 47n.), and in *Chrestomathia* he quoted at length from an obituary of John Beardmore Esq., a highly successful, self-made businessman who at his retirement seemed to possess numerous sources of pleasure and few of pain. Beardmore had many talents in business, was full of anecdotes on numerous topics, and enjoyed singing 'easy songs'. 'He was', wrote the obituarist, 'a "true-born Englishman"'.[8]

Despite much effort by Beardmore ennui set in and, as the obituarist put it, 'a train of evils ensued, comprising loss of appetite, nervous affections, debility mental and corporeal, despondency, sleeplessness, decay of nature, difficulty of respiration, weariness, pain and death'. As a 'true-born Englishman' Beardmore apparently eschewed education, the one activity Bentham thought might have saved him. What drew Bentham to this account of John Beardmore was not the moralistic (though sympathetic) tone of the obituary, but his belief that the cultivation of the art of education could improve the psychological condition of those being educated, and save them from the debilitating and even fatal condition of ennui.[9]

The second security that education provided was against what he called 'inordinate sensuality'. With excessive indulgence in sensual pleasures leading to satiety and then to the incurable ennui, education, for Bentham, could lead to the moderation of the pursuit of sensual pleasures in favour of what might be called, in a post-Millian world, 'higher pleasures'. As Bentham put it, 'the greater the variety of the shapes in which pleasures of an intellectual nature are made to present themselves to view, and consequently the greater the degree of success and perfection with which the mind is prepared for the reception of intellectual pleasures, the greater the chance afforded of security from the pains by which sensual pleasures are encompassed' (Bentham 1983a (1817): 23).[10]

The third security afforded by education was, for Bentham, that against idleness and mischievousness. The vacant mind provided neither pleasures nor pains nor any expectations of them. Ennui then set in and the mind sought pleasures to avoid the intense pain of ennui. These pleasures could be of the self-regarding, social, or dissocial kind. The pursuit of self-regarding pleasures tended to lead to sensuality and the problems just discussed. The cultivation would be generally beneficial, but, according to Bentham, was 'the least natural' (Bentham 1983a (1817): 24). The pursuit of dissocial pleasures (those obtained by mischief-making) was often accompanied by the pleasures of malevolence. Bentham emphasized two sorts: direct malevolence and a more indirect form that arose from a vacant mind. The latter was particularly related to a love of sport and among children such sport could lead to malevolence and cruelty. In calling for education to moderate such malevolence, Bentham might be seen to have anticipated Mill's famous call for experiments in living, if not more.[11] The final security afforded by education was for what Bentham called 'admission into, and agreeable intercourse with, good company, *i.e.*, company in or from which, present and harmless pleasure, or future profit or security, or both, may be obtained' (Bentham 1983*a* (1817): 25).

Bentham's discussion of the advantages of education continued for a number of pages, and provided the framework for the treatise on education that followed. We can see how his depiction of the art of education drew on an anterior knowledge of physiology and psychology, all of which were grounded on feelings of pleasure and pain. We can also see that, while alluding to character at several points, these allusions were mainly encompassed within psychological categories and were not part of a separate or even a distinct science of character.

Following his earlier criticisms of the 'Bentham school' in the *Logic* and elsewhere (see *CW* viii. 889ff.), Mill, while accepting the general orientation of Bentham, placed his emphasis on the sciences rather than on the arts. He could see that, without fully developed sciences of psychology and ethology, an art of education, as formulated by Bentham, could be simplistic in omitting elements from science that would determine the precepts governing the art. From Mill's point of view, Bentham's treatment of ennui or the vacant mind could pay too much attention to these particular ideas and underestimate, for example, the role of history and culture in education. The art of education, as depicted by Bentham, might not deal with numerous problems, because the sciences on which it drew were simply incomplete. Bentham might be seen to have served up for Mill only an agenda which Mill sought to explore, criticize, and thoroughly revise.

James Mill also followed Bentham's emphasis on the art of education as a way of increasing happiness. He might have influenced J. S. Mill even more by directly highlighting the importance of character and the circumstances governing its improvement (see J. Mill 1992 (1824): 139, 174ff., 193; 1813: 93–119, esp. 97). After all, J. S. Mill had in his early writings on Bentham criticized him severely for neglecting character and also national character (see *CW* x. 8–9, 99, 105).

James Mill's important work in associationist psychology was the second immediate source for Mill's conception of psychology and possibly ethology (see J. Mill 1869). In the *Autobiography* he wrote:

In psychology, his [James Mill's] fundamental doctrine was the formation of all human character by circumstances, through the universal Principle of

Association, and the consequent unlimited possibility of improving the moral and intellectual conditions of mankind by education. Of all his doctrines none was more important than this, or needs more to be insisted on: unfortunately there is none which is more contradictory to the prevailing tendencies of speculation, both in his time and since. (CW i. 109–11)

In this passage Mill seemed to recognize that his father's associationist psychology was not an accepted part of Victorian public morality or in the mainstream of academic or scientific scholarship. Nevertheless, he placed great emphasis on it as a science and as forming the foundation of social science. Mill acknowledged a long tradition of associationist psychology, with its origins in the writings of Hobbes and Locke (with a distant nod to Aristotle as the ancient ancestor), in the work of David Hartley and John Gay, Joseph Priestley, Erasmus Darwin, and more ambivalently, Thomas Brown (CW xxxi. 97–9). James Mill was considered by his son as 'the reviver and second founder' of the doctrine: 'When the literary and philosophical history of this century comes to be written as it deserves to be, very few are the names figuring in it to whom as high a place will be awarded as to James Mill' (CW xxxi. 99). Following James Mill, major advances were made, as we have seen, by Bain in *The Senses and the Intellect* and *The Emotions and the Will* (Bain 1855, 1859). In the opening sentence of his review of these volumes for the *Edinburgh Review* in 1859, Mill declared somewhat uncharacteristically: 'The sceptre of psychology has decidedly returned to this island' (CW xi. 341). In the review and in a financial guarantee of £100 he and Grote agreed with Parker, the publisher, for *The Emotions and the Will*, Mill strongly supported Bain's work as highly valuable and as a continuation of that of his father.[12] Mill's final foray (according to Robson (CW xxxi, p. xix), 'one of his last literary projects') into associationist psychology was the production in 1869 of the new edition of the *Analysis* (see J. Mill 1869). Mill's contribution was substantial and included several hundred pages (see CW xxxi. 95–253) of notes and extensive comments on his father's text, as well as an informative preface to the new edition.

III. *Ethology in the* Logic

As one surveys the editions of the *Analysis*, the psychological works of Bain and Spencer, and other works of Mill such as *An Examination of Sir William Hamilton's Philosophy* (1865) (CW xi), one cannot help but note that there are very few references to character and none (so far as I have determined) to ethology as a science, although some of the moral ideas which are discussed almost cry out for some sort of grounding in this new science. Although this neglect of ethology by Mill and his colleagues might be seen as evidence that he had abandoned the whole project of constructing a science of ethology (i.e. discovering its foundations and general laws), there might be another reason for this apparent neglect. This is that ethology belongs, as a science, neither to psychology nor to metaphysics, but more precisely to logic.

Let us begin to understand this thesis by first ascertaining the status Mill gave to ethology in the *Logic*. Psychology, or what he called the 'Science of Mind' (*CW* viii. 851), was initially part of a science of human nature. Mill compared this science with astronomy and tidology (the science that treats of the tides) and asserted that the science of human nature was like astronomy used to be (prior to recent advances) and like tidology was at the present time. 'The phenomena with which this science is conversant', Mill wrote, 'being the thoughts, feelings, and actions of human beings, it would have attained the ideal perfection of a science if it enabled us to foretell how an individual would think, feel, or act, throughout life, with the same certainty with which astronomy enables us to predict the places and occultations of the heavenly bodies' (*CW* viii. 846).

Mill admitted that psychology had not even begun to attain this high ideal of a predictive science. At best, much of psychology consisted of 'empirical laws', collected a posteriori, and without much predictive value. Associationist psychology, it seemed, had made great strides in showing how the mind worked, beginning with sense impressions from external sources and leading to an account of voluntary actions. Nevertheless, its predictive value was highly limited, in part due to the influence of what Mill called the 'German school of metaphysical speculation' and deeply flawed thinkers like Auguste Comte (see *CW* viii. 859).

For the most part, when attempting to predict how human beings would act in certain circumstances, one was forced to rely on 'empirical laws', which had little of value in them as 'scientific truths' (*CW* viii. 862). Mill used as an example the proposition that the character of the old was to be cautious and that of the young, impetuous. Nevertheless, the causal factor (if there was one) was not age (leading to increased caution), but experiences of life that tended to produce distrust and fear. An old man who had never had such experiences might well be tempestuous, and a young man who had such experiences might be highly cautious. As Mill put it, 'the really scientific truths, then, are not these empirical laws, but the causal laws which explain them' (*CW* viii. 862).

Empirical laws, for Mill, were valuable (reflecting 'the common wisdom of common life': *CW* viii. 864) and often had predictive value when applied in similar cases (e.g. the old are in fact often cautious and the young, more impetuous). But when they were applied to different societies or to different generations in the same society, they often failed to possess scientific (i.e. predictive) value. Mill concluded this discussion by asserting that 'mankind have not one universal character, but there exist universal laws of the Formation of Character' (*CW* viii. 864). He then went on to sketch out what the science of ethology (devoted to the discovery and explanation of the laws of the formation of character) would consist of, namely, that it was meant to be a deductive rather than an experimental science and that character could change as part of the science, as, for example, with respect to increasing equality between men and women leading to changes in the character of both.

In asserting that human beings did not have one universal character, but that there were universal laws governing the formation of character, Mill was extending his critique of Bentham's and his father's limited application of psychology to character and society. Ethology stood logically between psychology and social science, preventing empirically based psychological principles from forming the basis of social science. The psychological categories of self-regarding and other-regarding, as applied to the account of representative government by Bentham and James Mill (though differently), limited the psychological facts that underpinned the theory. Rulers were assumed to rule in their own interests and needed to be curbed by a representative system.

Mill's treatment of representative government in the *Considerations*, as we shall see, proceeded on an entirely different account of character in politics. His belief that some societies were not sufficiently advanced to adopt representative government successfully reflected the laws of the formation of character, in opposition to his father and Bentham. For Bentham, any country might adopt representative government. Ethology was thus created by Mill to solve a logical problem in relating psychology, and particularly associationist psychology, to social science and to education. If it was never established as a predictive science, it enabled Mill to assert that the thesis that mankind shared universal psychological principles, on which a science of government might be established, was false. We are not here concerned with whether or not Mill was correct in making this assertion, but with the fact that ethology existed for Mill as a principle of logic to correct earlier accounts developed by Bentham and James Mill, but along a path first carved out by his father.

IV. *Did Mill Abandon Ethology?*

The standard view of Mill's work on ethology, usually taken from Bain's biography of Mill, was that he planned to follow the *Logic* with a major work on social science with ethology forming the core of such a treatise. According to Bain, Mill soon found himself unable to complete such a work, and he turned instead in 1845 to work on political economy (see Bain 1882: 78–9, 84; 1904: 159, 164). But Mill himself never lost interest in ethology. In a letter to Bain, written in 1859, when he had completed *On Liberty* and was in the process of writing *Utilitarianism*, he responded positively to Bain's proposed book on phrenology and character by stating that 'I expect to learn a good deal from it & to be helped by it in anything I may hereafter write on Ethology—a subject I have long wished to take up, at least in the form of Essays, but have never felt myself sufficiently prepared' (*CW* xv. 645). Mill might have assisted posterity by explaining what would constitute sufficient preparation, but clearly, if Mill turned away from a major study of ethology in the early 1840s, he did not reject its significance as a concept in the late 1850s and 1860s.

Commentators on Mill on ethology have developed differing interpretations based on this and related material. Capaldi, for example, argues that while Mill turned to Comte for a philosophy of history, he adopted ethology to keep faith with his father's associationist psychology and to extend it into the realm of social science (Capaldi 1973; 2004: 167–8). According to Capaldi, Mill failed to recognize that ethology and associationist psychology, in their ambitions to achieve 'complete explanation', were incompatible with the 'radically free dialectic' of *On Liberty*. Once he did, he abandoned any attempt to construct a science of ethology (Capaldi 2004: 175, 177–8). For Capaldi, therefore, Mill's failure to create the science of ethology is interpreted as a vindication of his ultimate commitment to liberty and autonomy.

Ball has rejected the commonly held view that Mill abandoned ethology, and asserts that while Mill never wrote a treatise on ethology, he wrote four works which are 'tied together by their common ethological concerns' (Ball 2000: 27). These are the *Autobiography*, *The Subjection of Women*, *Considerations on Representative Government*, and *On Liberty*. According to Ball, the *Autobiography* and *The Subjection of Women* are concerned with 'the deformation and potential reformation' of character of a single person in the former and half of the human race in the latter. The *Considerations* deals with civic education, that is to say, the formation of civic character, and *On Liberty* is devoted to the formation of strong individual character (Ball 2000: 27). 'Without ever having written a systematic treatise on Ethology', Mill has, for Ball, 'contributed extensively and memorably to the science of character-formation' (Ball 2000: 27).

There is much to recommend in Ball's version of Mill's involvement with ethology. Ball's work confirms the thesis that it does not follow from Mill's failure to establish a science of ethology that he abandoned it. Indeed, the letter to Bain, quoted above, suggests that his interest in ethology persisted even at the time he was writing *On Liberty*. Furthermore, if Mill had changed his mind on ethology in a major way, he might have been expected to call attention to these changes in later editions of the *Logic*.

As for Capaldi's thesis regarding Mill's failure to develop a science of ethology, he seems to have confounded a problem in logic with political and possibly metaphysical ideas. I have argued that Mill created ethology to modify the way his father and Bentham used psychology in the service of the political art. Mill extended the role of science and seemed to reduce the power of the art. Capaldi, however, sees Mill's ethology as simply a continuation of James Mill's associationist psychology. Furthermore, Capaldi takes the creation of a social science based on ethology as denying individual liberty through the denial of free will. But Mill himself insisted that determinism in philosophy was perfectly compatible with individual liberty (as did most philosophers in the tradition from Hobbes and Locke to Mill). Capaldi's fear that a 'coherent hierarchical structure' in the human sciences might lead to authoritarian rule by experts in these sciences fails to capture Mill's aspirations for ethology and finds no echo in Mill's own thought.

v. *Political Ethology*

Let us now return to Mill's conception of the study of politics and government and consider its foundations. We have already examined the importance that Mill gave to psychology and ethology and their relationship to each other. We have also seen why Mill criticized the methods of 'the Bentham school'. Given his conception of a science and the relationship between art and science, it remains for us to sketch out how Mill believed that a science of society might be discovered or constructed.

Although Mill believed that social science or sociology was an a priori science, based on deductions, he regarded such a science as too complex to rest, like geometry, on a few theorems that operated everywhere and at all times. Not only was the material complex, but it was also difficult to obtain much material from society that was suitable for predictions. Such knowledge, however, would be sufficient to ascertain which tendencies would be beneficial and which would be injurious to society, even though it might not lead to predictions, universally true at all times and in all societies or even at different times in the same society (see *CW* viii. 898–9). As Mill put it:

The deductive science of society will not lay down a theorem, asserting in a universal manner the effect of any cause; but will rather teach us how to frame the proper theorem for the circumstances of any given case. It will not give the laws of society in general, but the means of determining the phenomena of any given society from the particular elements or data of that society. (*CW* viii. 899–900)

Mill focused on one of the 'separate departments' of social science that held 'a more comprehensive and commanding character than any of the other branches' (*CW* viii. 905). He called this branch 'Political Ethology: ... or the theory of the causes which determine the type of character belonging to a people or to an age' (*CW* viii. 905). He placed great emphasis on political ethology in social science, particularly, in relation to the development of forms of government and the character of rulers.[13] Instead of seeing particular regimes as determined by discrete principles (as in Montesquieu's honour in monarchy and fear in despotism) or as determining the character of society as a whole (as in Aristotle's oligarchy, democracy, or tyranny), Mill regarded political ethology as the character and education of the people in society, and as the cause of the nature of its institutions.

vi. *Representative Government and Its Foundations*

If there could be no separate science of government apart from a general science of society, and if the traditional study of forms of government was without much significance, what did Mill mean when he declared in the *Considerations* that representative government was 'the ideally best form of government' (*CW* xix. 399)? Could not representative government, like monarchy and aristocracy, fit into a traditional typology of constitutions and be the subject of independent study? At the beginning of chapter 3 of the *Considerations* in the comparison between an enlightened despotic monarch (and other forms of despotic rule) on the one hand and representative government on the other, Mill gave the impression that he was developing such a typology. Nevertheless, the argument of the whole chapter was carefully constructed to elucidate his ideas of character and national character. Put simply, Mill followed the pattern sketched out in the *Logic* to establish representative government as 'the ideally best form of government' both as a consequence of his analysis of character and in terms of the consequences of representative government for the development of character. It is clear from the *Considerations* that Mill's commitment to ethology never faded, even though he did not write a systematic treatise on the subject. Let us consider his arguments for representative government in light of this inheritance from the *Logic*.

When Mill explored the foundations of popular government, he argued that the superiority of this form of government was based on two principles which were of 'universal truth and applicability as any general propositions . . . can be . . . respecting human affairs' (*CW* xix. 404). The first, called the 'self-protecting principle', was depicted as follows: 'the rights and interests of every or any person are only secure from being disregarded, when the person interested is himself able, and habitually disposed to stand up for them'. The second, the 'self-dependent principle', was: 'the general prosperity attains a greater height, and is more widely diffused, in proportion to the amount and variety of the personal energies enlisted in promoting it' (*CW* xix. 404). Note that Mill did not say (initially at least) that self-dependence and self-protection were among the main consequences of a system of representative government. The establishment of representative government itself depended on the truth of the two principles and their implementation.

But how did Mill establish the truth of the principles? He referred to the first of them as 'one of those elementary maxims of prudence, which every person, capable of conducting his own affairs, implicitly acts upon, wherever he himself is interested' (CW xix. 404). Such maxims, one supposes, are established empirically. We know from experience that we should be self-protective and self-dependent. Mill then provided a deduction, based on these principles, for the estimation of the merits of free and unfree states existing at the same time. The two principles lead one to favour free states over unfree states, and he compared ancient Greek cities with Persian satrapies; the Italian republics and free towns of Flanders and Germany with feudal monarchies that existed at the time; and Switzerland, Holland, and England with Austria and pre-revolutionary France. 'Through the joint influence of these two principles,' he wrote, 'all free communities have both been more exempt from social injustice and crime, and have attained more brilliant prosperity, than any others' (CW xix. 406).

Although Mill might be able to establish that free governments embodied the two principles more fully than states that did not value freedom, his argument thus far was more limited than might be initially thought. For he developed an argument for free government but not necessarily for popular government, except insofar as the latter was simply an extension of the former.[14] But if Mill was going to list England, for example, and other free states as embodying his two principles, he could not then claim that this was an argument for popular government. It might be arguable that popular government merely involved an extension of the suffrage in a free government, but such an argument in Mill's context might easily be questioned. For example, those who have favoured the establishment of representative democracy on the two principles of self-protection and self-dependence (as Bentham, for example, did) would not entertain the desirability of abandoning the secret ballot or the possibility of introducing communism (as Mill did: see CW xix. 404–5, 488ff.). They would consider both as violations of the principle of self-protection of persons and property.

Mill was aware that he needed another argument to establish his main proposition regarding popular government. He turned now to the structure worked out in the Logic to develop an argument regarding ethology or character, which would enable him to establish his thesis. Implicit in the way he presented the two principles was an assumption that an active character was superior to a passive one.

After all, the interested person must be 'able, and habitually disposed' to stand up for his or her rights, and one's 'personal energies' must be actively devoted to making the system work. Nevertheless, these assumptions are not the same as the blanket proposition that an active character was superior to a passive one.[15]

For his main argument Mill started with categories of mental excellence taken from Bentham (i.e. intellectual, practical, and moral). He then developed a lengthy and complex argument against a position he admitted was shared 'as the commonplaces of moralists, and the general sympathies of mankind' (CW xix. 407). It was analogous to the argument he developed against despotism at the beginning of the chapter, where support for a benevolent despotic monarch was considered a commonplace belief (CW xix. 399). But, as a fundamental position, the belief that, for example, a clear distinction could be drawn between active and passive character and that the one was wholly superior to the other would not be easy to sustain.

Mill began in his usual manner by first setting out the virtues of the opposing position. While energetic people were admired, he admitted that those of a passive character were usually preferred. Passive neighbours, he granted, increased our sense of security and did not obstruct us in our various activities. 'A contented character,' he wrote, was considered 'not a dangerous rival' (CW xix. 407). Having stated this opposing view, Mill then asserted without qualification: 'yet nothing is more certain, than that improvement in human affairs is wholly the work of uncontented characters; and, moreover, that it is much easier for the active mind to acquire the virtue of patience, than for a passive one to assume those of energy' (CW xix. 407).

He began to establish his position by first turning to intellectual excellence, which he found wholly on the side of 'active effort'. 'Enterprise, the desire to keep moving, to be trying and accomplishing new things for our own benefit or that of others', he wrote, 'is the parent even of speculative, and much more of practical, talent' (CW xix. 407). On the other side, he claimed that there was little to recommend. The intellect of the passive character stopped 'at amusement, or at simple contemplation'. It failed to determine truth and to apply it to practice and contented itself with dreaming dreams; it could create nothing more than 'the mystical metaphysics of the Pythagoreans or the Vedas' (CW xix. 407). In practical affairs the impact of the passive character was even worse. There was no struggle to discover and learn, which in turn promoted the welfare of the individual as well as the community.

Before turning to moral excellence, we might consider briefly the significance of Mill's argument thus far. First, he has made a somewhat artificial (though admittedly clear) distinction between these two types of character, when, in fact, one might argue that active and passive character were more intertwined than he granted. He eventually had to face this problem. Second, the distinction between active and passive character blurred or covered over another distinction which had been important for his argument. This distinction was between the self-interested person as opposed to the person who considered (and acted for) the welfare of the whole community. Active character seemed to benefit oneself as well as the whole community. Although Mill stated this view tentatively, he made it part of his position.[16]

When he considered moral excellence, he first admitted that there might be room for doubt as to the superiority of the active over the passive personality. This doubt did not, he emphasized, arise from Christianity or other religions with their emphasis on submission to the divine will. In a somewhat odd statement he wrote that, while Christianity and other religions inculcated this and related ideas, 'it is the prerogative of Christianity, as regards this and many other perversions, that it is able to throw them off' (*CW* xix. 407). Granted, there were other, more active forms of Christianity, and Mill might simply be saying that Christians could easily choose among these. But why refer to passivity in religion in terms of a 'perversion'? Surely, the structures of prayer and appeals to divine grace, the idea of acceptance implicit in the crucifixion, and the patient hope of eternal life are fundamental to Christianity and might be considered to have passive as well as active elements. These doctrines cannot be regarded as 'perversions' and simply thrown off. But Mill could not accept the view, as indicated above, that active and passive character existed together and the good life consisted of their being brought into harmony, particularly, within a Christian context. He thus simply dismissed any strong argument from this Christian position, because his argument regarding popular government required that active and passive character be distinct and separate.

However, Mill did not dwell on Christianity, but turned instead to develop his main argument that contentment (as a moral virtue) depended on active rather than passive character. In a society where enterprise and exertion were favoured, those who failed to achieve their goals accepted the result, while those who were passive and devoted no energy to such achievements were either 'incessantly grumbling' or 'overflowing with envy and ill-will' with regard to more active and contented members of society (CW xix. 408). For Mill, therefore, the sort of passivity that was often praised as a virtue, i.e. as contentment, was corrupted within a passive character by the influence of envy. Having established this argument with regard to character (or ethology), he then declared in a proposition almost mathematical in its precision that it could be extended to national character: 'in proportion as success in life is seen or believed to be the fruit of fatality or accident and not of exertion, in that same ratio does envy develope itself as a point of national character' (CW xix. 408).

He proceeded to argue that the oriental character highlighted envy, and this was followed by a similar presence in southern Europeans, particularly the Spanish and French. Among 'Anglo-Saxons' (presumably the British and Americans), there was the least envy. However, this exposition of national character, presented as a deduction from character itself, is not without its problems. First, the rigid distinction between active and passive character in the individual cannot be easily transferred to national character. In national character there must inevitably be a mixture of active and passive individual characters in the society, and this mixture would mask the fact that such a mixture did not occur in Mill's argument concerning individual character. In other words, one might be able to accept what Mill asserted regarding national character in societies, but reject the initial rigid distinction between active and passive character on which it was based. If so, Mill seemed to be committing an elementary fallacy in the way he based national character on a different account of character. Second, Mill needed to exclude some forms of apparent contentment from his conception of active character. He granted that in all societies there was genuine contentment, where individuals neither desired nor sought what they did not possess (CW xix. 409). But this sort of contentment seemed to differ from the kind he ascribed to active character, where one was moved by such desires, but did not feel envious, largely because of active character. Mill dealt with this anomaly by suggesting that the numbers of such contented persons were small and spread across all societies. For the most part, however, what appeared to be contentment was 'real discontent, combined with indolence or self-indulgence, which, while taking no legitimate means of raising itself, delights in bringing others down to its own level' (CW xix. 409). Furthermore, another apparent form of contentment, where there was no ambition to advance the good of one's country, society, neighbourhood, or even one's own moral excellence, was dismissed as not being a virtue at all, but exhibiting 'unmanliness and want of spirit' (*CW* xix. 409). Mill then redefined contentment:

The content which we approve, is an ability to do cheerfully without what cannot be had, a just appreciation of the comparative value of different objects of desire, and a willing renunciation of the less when incompatible with the greater. These, however, are excellences more natural to the character, in proportion as it is actively engaged in the attempt to improve its own or some other lot. (*CW* xix. 409)

After developing this argument further, Mill was then led to conclude not only that the 'active, self-helping character' was 'intrinsically' the best, but that it incorporated all that was excellent in the passive type (*CW* xix. 409). He then considered the criticism that active character in England and America often led to an expenditure of energy on objects that were not admirable. Even where this criticism might be true, he argued, the energies of active character might easily be redirected, and such active character was far superior to the 'inactivity, unaspiringness, absence of desire' associated with passive character (*CW* xix. 410).

Having argued that active character was superior to passive character and having extended this argument from character to national character, Mill easily developed his argument further to conclude that popular government, based on active participation, was superior to despotic government, or, indeed, any form of rule where the populace were mainly the passive recipients of a top–down system of government. From this position Mill moved in numerous directions in support of institutions that reflected or advanced active character through participation in government, like the open ballot. Or, paradoxically, he restricted the operation of popular government to those societies where active character was sufficiently developed to support such a government (see *CW* xix. 413ff.). Nevertheless, Mill was not developing a typology of constitutions, but rather the first tentative steps in a science of politics. The steps were fully in accordance with his depiction of the development of a social science in the *Logic*, as a predictive science linked to an art of government. Our concern in the *Considerations* is with the extent to which the idea of active character can serve as the foundation of the whole science of politics even in the limited and tentative form developed in this text. Mill would presumably want to develop additional precepts regarding character and perhaps clarify where some aspects of character conflicted with others as between active and passive character on the one hand and self-regarding and other-regarding character on the other. In the very distinction between active and passive character Mill seemed to treat any potential conflict between self-regarding and other-regarding character as being overcome. Nevertheless, Mill made it clear that his early orientation in the *Logic* was serious and was not subsequently abandoned. This orientation also explains why the *Considerations* cannot be read as simply a textbook on government, like any other one that preceded it. Mill not only questioned a science of politics divorced from social science and advanced a social science based on character and national character, but he also seemed to abstract the idea of society from political society. The significance of this abstraction is not entirely clear. At times Mill seemed to challenge the relevance of government to human progress. In *On Liberty* the liberty of the individual is treated in society mainly apart from the traditional institutions of government and even apart from ideas of liberty that depend on these institutions. In the best form of government, active participation might well replace traditional ideas of command and obedience, as a polity based on science and art in his terms discovered new forms of decision-making and new ways of understanding the traditional processes of government.[17]

II

The Spell of Comte

5

A Dialogue Concerning Philosophy

The extensive correspondence between Mill and Comte takes us to the heart of Mill's philosophy, and forms a bridge between Mill's two great published works, *System of Logic* and *Principles of Political Economy.*[1] The correspondence also enables us to understand Comte's influence, positive and negative, on the evolution of Mill's thought. A close study of what often reads like an early Platonic dialogue (see Rosen 1968, 1973) also reveals the forms and limits of Mill's thought and personality. I have already alluded to their correspondence in various chapters and will continue to do so in this chapter and in the remainder of the book. Here, I shall examine the correspondence as an independent work. In the next chapter I shall look at it in relation to Mill's later publication, *Auguste Comte and Positivism*, where Mill presented, almost in passing, a mature statement of his views.

In the *Autobiography* Mill wrote briefly and without enthusiasm regarding his epistolary experience:

But for some years we were frequent correspondents, until our correspondence became controversial, and our zeal cooled. I was the first to slacken correspondence; he was the first to drop it. I found, and he probably found likewise, that I could do no good to his mind, and that all the good he could do to mine, he did by his books. This would never have led to discontinuance of intercourse, if the differences between us had been on matters of simple doctrine. But they were chiefly on those points of opinion which blended in both of us with our strongest feelings, and determined the entire direction of our aspirations. (CW i. 219)

As for the adequacy of the *Autobiography* in capturing Mill's feelings for and his indebtedness to Comte, one might consider Bain's remark comparing the correspondence with the *Autobiography*:

The Autobiography gives...the general effect produced upon him by the whole work [the *Cours*], which he perused with avidity as the successive volumes appeared; but does not adequately express the influence in detail, nor the warmth of esteem and affection displayed in...their correspondence.... (Bain 1882: 70–1)

Furthermore, while Mill rightly called attention in the *Autobiography* to the combination of intense feeling and philosophical debate that animated the correspondence and perhaps distinguished it from other similar correspondence between philosophers, he did not capture its significance for posterity, as he himself experienced it, particularly in the early years. For example, when Mill suggested in 1842 that Comte need not pay the postage on his letters to Mill (as the East India Company paid the postage for all letters addressed to Mill at the office) he added (as a humorous aside): 'for I see no inconvenience for the inhabitants of India to support a part of the expense of a philosophic correspondence of which, one can hope that the future of humanity, there as elsewhere, will obtain some fruit' (*CW* xiii. 540). The reader of the passage in the *Autobiography* quoted above will not find much sense of the momentousness of the occasion or that the future of humanity entered into the concerns of the correspondents. Nor will they discover the details of Mill's difficult struggle to realize his aspirations to become a philosopher and logician and be accepted by a philosopher like Comte, whom he had admired since he was a young man.

There are numerous aspects of the correspondence that deserve careful and sustained attention. Those which illuminate the correspondence as a whole enable us to see it as a literary work on its own, while other aspects bring to view generally neglected elements of Mill's life and work, or provide insights into Mill's approach to philosophy and, particularly, to writing philosophical works. Particular themes, for example, religion, or the nature of social science, though important in the Mill–Comte correspondence, will be discussed in other chapters which give fuller attention to these subjects. Our attention will be confined here to the correspondence itself.

1. *Comte's Role in Mill's Evolving Philosophy*

Let us begin by examining another passage from Bain's study of Mill, where he remarked:

His work, as a great originator, in my opinion, was done. The two books [*System of Logic* (1843), *Principles of Political Economy* (1848)] now before the world were the main constructions that his accumulated stores had prepared him for; and I do not think that there lay in him the materials of a third at all approaching to these. It is very unlikely indeed that he was even physically capable of renewing the strain of the two winters—1842–3 and 1846–7. His subsequent years were marked by diminished labours on the whole; while the direction of these labours was toward application, exposition and polemic, rather than origination; and he was more and more absorbed in the outlook for social improvements. (Bain 1882: 91)

Bain's comment points to what one might call the spine of Mill's achievement: the two great works on logic and political economy. Although Bain recognized the significance of later works like *On Liberty*, *Utilitarianism*, and *Considerations on Representative Government* (much discussed in recent decades) and treated them at length, he emphatically called attention to the two works that not only established Mill's reputation but also brought out most Mill's originality and comprehensiveness as a thinker. Though limited to a few years, the Mill–Comte correspondence mirrored that period of creativity and intense intellectual labour. It brought to life Mill's thinking about these works, the decisions that determined their form and content, and, particularly, the interaction between Mill and Comte that seemed, positively and negatively, to determine how Mill eventually conceived them.

   Mill, himself, was aware of the fact that his completion of the *Logic*, which stimulated the correspondence in the first place, meant that he was embarking on a new dimension to his career as a philosopher:

I enter into a time of my life in which I am placed for the first time to learn to what point my purely philosophic activity, through my opinions and ability, is able to provide a real influence in our country, or at least on its most advanced men. (*CW* xiii. 503)

Although one might read this passage as a philosopher's declaration of independence, appropriate to the production of a great new treatise, yet, characteristically, as Mill continued the sentence, his diffidence emerged so that his ambitions by the end of the passage declined from influence on the ideas of his country generally to an influence on some leading thinkers in his own country, many of whom he would have known since he was a youth. In line with this diffidence, Mill regarded Comte as 'one of the great intellects of our time, whom I regard with the most esteem and admiration' (*CW* xiii. 490). In this very first letter Mill wrote of 'the great intellectual debts' he owed to Comte and referred to Comte's 'great philosophic work' with obvious admiration (*CW* xiii. 488). At this point Mill had just completed the *Logic* but was unwilling to publish it until he had read the final volume of Comte's *Cours* and adopted whatever he found of value for the final book of the *Logic* on social science. He knew that Comte would not agree with the way he emphasized the logic of method apart from and over the various sciences, though he admitted that method could not be wholly independent of particular scientific doctrines. Mill reconciled these views, which lay at the heart of the *Logic*, by writing of his work that it did not possess any permanent philosophic character, only 'transitory value' which nevertheless he considered to be 'real, at least for England' (*CW* xiii. 491–2). Thus, so deferential was Mill to Comte that he was willing to regard his own major philosophical work as one of mere passing importance, except perhaps in England, where deficiencies in national character required a study like his own. As for Comte's work and his own relationship to it, Mill wrote: 'I would be very happy, if I believed myself capable of taking a truly important, though secondary part, in this great work' (*CW* xiii. 510). Mill considered deferring the publication of the whole of the *Logic* so as to revise it completely once Comte's volume was finished. Had he possessed the *Cours* in its entirety earlier, prior to his drafting the *Logic*, he might even have translated it rather than producing his own work, or, at least, he might have organized his *Logic* differently (see *CW* xiii. 530).

When Mill presented his reasons for not thoroughly revising his work or abandoning it entirely, he wrote that he was reluctant to abandon material, part of which he had completed prior to his reading the *Cours* (*CW* xiii. 530). He also offered, as we have seen, what might be considered strategic reasons for proceeding with the publication of the *Logic*. He thought that the work was particularly suited to attract the attention of the most advanced thinkers in England, as it linked his ideas on logic with 'the school of Hobbes and Locke' (*CW* xiii. 530). This school was closer to Comte and positivism than that of 'the German school which reigns today and now tramples it underfoot'. He was sufficiently confident that his

Logic would strike a blow against this ontological school in England, which might eventually be a mortal blow. This was considered by Mill as an important task in its own right, 'since this school alone is essentially theological and its doctrine is presented as the national support of the old social order, and not only in terms of Christian, but also of Anglican ideas' (*CW* xiii. 530). Thus, while the *Logic* itself was presented famously as providing a methodological 'common ground' where the 'partisans of Hartley and Reid, of Locke and of Kant, may meet and join hands' (*CW* vii. 14), Mill's account of his strategy in the correspondence with Comte reveals more of a battleground than a forum for philosophical peace.

Part of Mill's reluctance to publish the *Logic* as it was written was due to his acceptance of positivism and his ardent desire to be a disciple of Comte's philosophy.[2] It must seem strange that the greatest work of Britain's most eminent philosopher in the nineteenth century, a work that would dominate philosophical logic for several decades, was published with the author expressing serious reservations about the validity of some of the main theses presented there. Only Comte (and the readers of their correspondence) would know that the *Logic* did not necessarily represent Mill's final position.

We can thus see from the correspondence that the *Logic* appeared in the context of great uncertainty about his own work in logic and enormous deference concerning Comte's philosophy. The correspondence brings all of this to light in a highly dramatic fashion. Besides considering the *Logic* as a transitory work, part of an ongoing struggle between fundamentally opposed views of philosophy, it is also considered of relative value in relation to Comte's achievement in the *Cours* and the development of philosophy in England. When reading the *Logic*, however, we see merely parts (particularly, those concerned with social science) of Comte's *Cours* adopted with clear acknowledgement, and without any issues of discipleship and hence relative standing to Comte's work arising.

II. *Mill Turns to Political Economy*

Comte's involvement in the development of Mill's work on political economy was just as striking, though with an outcome one might not have foreseen. The first substantial reference to political economy in the correspondence came from Comte (*CG* ii. 22) who responded to Mill's location of his own early work in 'Benthamism'

(*CW* xiii. 489). Clearly, Bentham and 'Benthamism' (a term occasionally used by Mill to include Bentham and James Mill) were embraced as precursors, but also rejected as inadequate by both Mill and Comte, though possibly for different reasons. Comte made the specific link between political economy and Benthamism and believed that it had been superseded by his social science. Mill, however, referred mainly to Bentham's logic and his hostility to traditional metaphysics. At this point, with the *Logic* still unpublished and book 6 incomplete, no differences between the two philosophers were raised. Comte was happy to see that Mill was bred in Benthamism and believed that he would soon move (as Comte had done) to embrace 'sociological positivism' in which political economy had no distinct role.[3]

In the *Logic*, however, Mill both adopted Comte's sociology (and particularly the distinction between social statics and social dynamics), and at the same time left space for political economy as a distinct science. In the first edition (which Comte would have read), Mill wrote:

Mr. Comte... pronounces the attempt to treat political economy, even provisionally, as a science apart, to be a misapprehension of the scientific method proper to Sociology...; I cannot but think that he has overlooked the extensive and important practical guidance which may be derived, in any given state of society, from general propositions such as those above indicated; even though the modifying influence of the miscellaneous causes which the theory does not take into account, as well as the effect of the general social changes in progress, be provisionally overlooked. (*CW* viii. 903 and n.)

Mill regarded political economy as a science concerned with the satisfaction of the 'desire of wealth' with the applicable psychological law being that a greater gain was preferable to a smaller one (*CW* viii. 901).[4] Since Mill readily acknowledged Comte's position on the status of political economy (an acknowledgement, however, he dropped in the 1846 edition), Comte could easily take the view that if Mill's background prevented him from fully embracing positive sociology at this point, he was heading in the right direction, and would eventually adopt Comte's views on political economy.

But several developments prevented this easy transition to positivist sociology. By January 1844 the *Logic* had been published and read by Comte. Mill had been ill during the winter of 1843–4, so ill that his correspondence was briefly interrupted. Feeling an inability even to think, he was unable to make his customary first draft of his letter to Comte (see *CW* xiii. 619). With the assistance of Harriet Taylor he had already by this time mounted his critique of Comte's rigid account of social statics based on a somewhat dogmatic view of phrenology. Mill could not accept the domestic role assigned to women in the permanent institutions of society (determined by brain size in comparison with men) or the limited scope Comte gave to education. Mill thought that the development of his own science of ethology would lead to an improved social science. Comte was not enthusiastic about Mill's idea of ethology, though he was willing for Mill to pursue his research if it meant that their views would ultimately converge.

Furthermore, Mill was placed in a difficult position because, having completed the *Cours*, Comte was considering a four-volume study of sociology, but he had declared that he would not publish any of it until all the volumes were completed (see *CG* ii. 221–2). Thus, with Mill feeling diffident about his capacity to write a full treatise on ethology, saying that his thoughts were not 'ripe' and would not be so 'for some time', and Comte being unwilling even to publish his own work as each volume was completed, Mill might well have felt blocked in pursuing his study of ethology. After all, he had waited a long time for the completion of the *Cours* and felt he needed Comte's assistance to pursue the development of a positive sociology in which they both believed.

At this time political economy seemed to come to Mill's rescue. Due to the success of the *Logic* he was given the opportunity to bring together four previously published essays on political economy, written in 1830, with a longer essay on method, published in 1836, all of which were published in 1844 as *Essays on Some Unsettled Questions of Political Economy* (*CW* xiii. 626; see also *CW* xiii. 630; iv. 229–339). He then announced to Comte that he was also going to write a work on political economy, that it would be 'a work of several months', and that his object was to bring Adam Smith up to date (*CW* xiii. 626). Even at first glance, Mill's plan seems absurd, as no one, especially any one as ill as Mill had been, could create so ambitious a work, covering virtually all of political economy and seventy years of recent industrial and commercial history, in a few months. Mill also acknowledged to Comte that 'I know what you think of current political economy. I have a better opinion of it than you do' (*CW* xiii. 626).

This rapid change of plan from writing a treatise on ethology to a treatise on political economy seemed sudden, premature, and wholly against the current of Mill's attempts to reconcile his views with those of Comte. He tried in the correspondence to reassure Comte that he was not abandoning positivism. He insisted that his work would emphasize that all conclusions were wholly provisional. He would also try to distinguish between 'general laws of production', which were common to all industrial societies, and 'the principles of distribution and of the exchange of wealth', which assumed 'a particular state of society', reflecting a similar distinction in Comte's thought. 'I believe,' he continued, 'that this treatise can have, especially here, a great provisional utility, and that it will serve powerfully to make the positive spirit penetrate into political discussions' (CW xiii. 626).

Much to Mill's surprise, Comte responded by supporting Mill's project: it will make 'the positive spirit prevalent in many estimable minds who have not been penetrated by it but nevertheless are on the way' (CG ii. 249). But he qualified his remark to emphasize the tentative nature of economic analysis, which must not be separated from either static or dynamic sociological analysis. For both Comte and Mill, it seems, political economy had temporary usefulness only.

Mill was delighted with Comte's support. Besides agreeing with Comte's reservations, he added:

It also seems to me that taking for a general model the grand and beautiful work of Adam Smith, I would have important occasions to spread directly several of the principles of the new philosophy, as Adam Smith did for many of the principles of negative metaphysics with regard to its social applications, without stimulating offence by deploying any flag. (CW xiii. 631)

The flag was, in the case of Mill and Comte, for positive sociology. But it is doubtful that the members of this party, consisting in England, at least, of not many more than the two leaders, were marching in the same direction. The proposed science of ethology itself challenged Comte's close connection of phrenology (together with biology and physiology) with sociology. Mill's conceptions of character and national character, based on associationist psychology, threatened to undermine Comte's direct deductions from phrenology to sociology. Ethology might be seen as a science that could feed into a more flexible social statics and be wholly hostile to Comtean sociology. Nevertheless, to turn from ethology to political economy might well be interpreted as full-scale retreat on Mill's part, a retreat to what Comte called 'Benthamism' and which Comte regarded as already superseded by positivism (see Collini et al. 1983: 134ff.).

In March 1846, nearly two years after Mill turned to pursue his work in political economy and towards the end of their correspondence, he returned to the role of political economy in the study of society (see *CW* xiii. 698). Although Mill's language here is somewhat obscure, he is clearly saying that, contrary to Comte, sociology must depend on a theory of human nature (i.e. psychology and ethology), and sociology cannot progress without the cultivation of these sciences. Without this cultivation sociology is only capable of limited advances, and by the study of political economy, Mill believed that he was contributing to this limited progress. Mill then held out the prospect of a return to the study of ethology in one form or another. But he did not offer Comte much hope that he would follow Comte to produce a social science based on phrenology or some other physical account of the brain. If Bain was correct about Mill's intellectual exhaustion after he completed the work on political economy, Mill certainly showed the way forward by encouraging Bain's works on psychology and character and the new edition of his father's essay on psychology. He also pursued ethology in numerous contexts from the status of women to human liberty and to prospects for representative government.

In all of this writing one is aware of a continuing dialogue with Comte, positive and negative, and that Mill's two major works, on logic and political economy, bear the marks of this dialogue (see Bain 1882: 72, 88–9). Mill's young friend, Gustave d'Eichtal, who introduced Mill to Comte's writings, explained the basis of their mutual attraction to Comte and to each other: 'What brought us together was not abstract ideas but our character and our desire to be apostles' (quoted in Pickering 1993: i. 507) Whether or not Mill was an apostle has yet to be determined. What d'Eichtal usefully called attention to was that his and Mill's attraction to Comte was not based simply on Comte's ideas, in spite of Mill's statement to the contrary in the *Autobiography*.

III. *Mill's Dialogue with Comte*

To distinguish the Mill–Comte correspondence from other works of Mill, such as the *Autobiography*, one must call attention to aspects of their dialogue that animated the lengthy exchange of letters. Pickering has suggested that Comte represented 'the perfect friend that Mill had been seeking for years'. She quotes in support of this view Mill's letter to John Sterling of April 1829 concerning his yearning for a friendship 'where there would be the "feeling of being engaged in the pursuit of a common object, and of mutually cheering one another on, and helping one another in an arduous undertaking. This . . . is one of the strongest ties of individual sympathy"' (Pickering 1993: i. 533–4, quoting from *CW* xii. 30).[5] She thus sees some of the dynamic that took Mill to Comte in the relationship with Sterling. There is some truth in Pickering's approach in that Mill and Comte emphasized (as did Mill in relation to Sterling) that disagreements between them might in time disappear (see *CW* xiii. 489; *CG* ii. 36). But Mill in the 1840s was a different sort of person than he was in the 1820s, and his relationship with Comte, unlike that with Sterling, was confined to their correspondence (as Mill declined Comte's invitation to come to Paris). Additionally, Comte had to compete with Mill's devotion to Harriet Taylor. When Mill referred to the death of Sterling in a letter to Comte, he emphasized Sterling's character and capacity for sympathy (*CW* xiii. 637). Comte responded warmly but referred to Sterling's 'high value, mental as well as moral', as though feelings of friendship alone would not be sufficient to sustain a relationship (*CG* ii. 287).

Nor is it possible to see Comte as leading Mill away from Benthamism in the 1840s, as Mill believed Sterling's Coleridgean philosophy might have achieved in the 1820s. As we have seen, not only were Comte's doctrines regarded by the two philosophers in the 1840s as intended to complete Benthamism, but also Mill's decision to pursue political economy represented at least in Comte's terms a dramatic return to 'Benthamism'. To suggest, as Pickering does, that in adopting Comte's 'social vision', Mill was rejecting Benthamism and that 'positivism . . . seemed to fill the gap created by Mill's rejection of Benthamism' is superficial (with regard to Mill's ties to Bentham's philosophy) and ultimately false (Pickering 1993: i. 535).[6]

The evolving relationship between Mill and Comte that underpinned the correspondence cannot be understood either in terms of friendship, discipleship, or even brotherly love. Admittedly, Mill referred to Comte at one point as 'my older brother in philosophy' and called attention to Comte's 'fraternal manner' (*CW* xiii. 591). Comte also referred slightly earlier to Mill's proposed visit as 'fraternal' and noted that he had not had a relationship of this kind for a long time, as he had lost his own brother more than twenty years earlier (*CG* ii. 141–2).

If we, even provisionally, discount the roles of apostleship, discipleship, friendship, fraternity, and what Pickering (2009: ii. 70) calls 'their game of mutual admiration' in our attempt to understand their correspondence, it might be possible to make some progress by turning away from the ties that might have held the two correspondents together and towards the way in which the correspondence, as an ongoing and developing project, engaged their attention. Bain has provided us with some clues. Comte was frank in his remarks and 'circumstantial and minute in his accounts of his ways'. Mill was 'unusually open' and wrote about his mental and physical health in a way he had never shared with anyone (Bain 1882: 73).[7] Although it would be easy to see this frank attention to detail and openness as reflecting their relationship, it will be suggested here that the relationship, in so far as it developed beyond a brief exchange concerning Mill's *Logic* and Comte's *Cours*, depended on the underlying structure and logic of the correspondence itself. Both correspondents were engaged in a philosophical and literary activity that underpinned the correspondence, even in its highly detailed and practical dimensions.

Comte was very attentive to Mill's comments and replied to almost every point that Mill made in his letters. As a result, Comte's letters were usually longer than those of Mill, due to the fact that he combined this seemingly pedantic attentiveness to Mill's statements with the development of his own points. Comte would also often enlarge on themes and provide information and circumstantial material that Mill found of interest. Comte's engagement with Mill, however, was based on deeper foundations. Mill's unannounced appearance in his eccentric, isolated, and somewhat dreary life gave him an important point of focus. Mill was clearly, in Comte's eyes, the most promising of the very few followers that existed in either France or Britain. For Comte, the success of his philosophical system rested on his persuading Mill to move forward towards its full adoption. If Mill was eager, he encouraged him; if he was reluctant to develop key tenets (such as phrenology, for example), Comte patiently suggested texts and offered reasons for Mill to consider aspects of his approach; and if he seemed to reject Comte's philosophy (as, for example, in the case of the status of women), Comte accepted Mill's deviance as a problem that would disappear in time as he came to appreciate positivist philosophy more fully.

By November 1843 after each had written twenty letters and when Mill had already cancelled his trip to Paris, Comte was reluctantly forced to admit that there were serious issues between them. Nonetheless, Comte could still remark that, instead of the school of positivism consisting of himself alone, there were at least two members in France and possibly two (Mill and Bain) in England. While Mill finally stood up to Comte, one might be puzzled as to why he failed to challenge Comte's assumption concerning intellectual progress towards truth. Comte possessed a theory about how one developed within the philosophy of positivism that was part of an understanding of his philosophy. He noted at one point that he formed his opinions of philosophers not from their works, but on the basis of their conversations, or, in Mill's case, their correspondence (*CG* ii. 51–2). From this comment, it would appear that the *Cours* or Mill's *Logic* counted for little as opposed to the correspondence, and Comte seemed to have developed an approach that made Mill's agreement with him a badge of truth. Although Mill reluctantly disagreed with Comte, he clearly failed to turn in his badge, even though a public association with Comte for a variety of reasons was not to his advantage.

We have so far failed to understand why Mill hesitated to challenge Comte's view that agreement between them was a badge of truth. Both Comte and Mill developed strategies and a rhetoric that sought agreement between them as a major object of their correspondence. Comte, as we have seen, was obviously working from within his system, and 'agreement', even 'truth', meant, for him, Mill's acceptance of his conception of positivism. Mill had become increasingly aware of this problem but was reluctant to challenge Comte's position. The reason for his reluctance might well have been that Mill had different philosophical reasons for seeking agreement with Comte than Comte had for seeking agreement with Mill.

From the beginning of his work on logic (as we have seen), Mill felt that he was engaged in a great struggle against an enemy he referred to by a variety of names such as 'intuitive', 'metaphysical', 'German', 'ontological', and 'transcendental', to name a few.[8] In his first letter he praised Bentham for 'his systematic opposition to the explanation of phenomena by ridiculous metaphysical entities, the uselessness of which he taught me to feel from earliest youth' (*CW* xiii. 489). Comte gave Mill's experience a more political context when he referred to the potential for positivism 'to contain efficiently today the imminent irruption of metaphysical theories which threaten to subvert all sociability' (*CG* ii. 23). For Comte, the negative, critical philosophy that he associated with the

Enlightenment (or with Benthamism) had experienced decline and was unable to defeat these metaphysical theories. Only positivism could achieve that, as the negative philosophy had been 'constricted . . . before having finished its task' (*CG* ii. 23).

For Mill, however, the impetus for his hostility to 'metaphysical' theories was at the foundation of his *Logic*, and was behind the strategy of focusing on an English audience to make metaphysical ideas depend on a logical assessment of evidence.[9] But he knew that he could only succeed partially and in England alone. What Comte had held out was a doctrine to defeat metaphysical theories. At one point in their correspondence Comte asked Mill his opinion of Comte studying German philosophy. After discussing this topic Mill wrote regarding positivism: 'In future one can choose; no longer will one be forced to go towards the German camp to find a clearly formulated philosophic system. For us, positivism has now unfurled its flag' (*CW* xiii. 575). The metaphors of 'camp' and 'flag' are clearly military, but Mill's object was not wholly an aggressive one. He sought agreement with Comte, because only with such agreement could the 'flag' of positivism be unfurled, and Mill could lead the charge against German philosophy. Mill also provided in this letter a frank account of his own encounter with German philosophy:

I cannot perhaps give you a very decided opinion, having myself read neither Kant nor Hegel, nor any other chiefs of this school. I have known them only from their English and French interpreters. This philosophy, for me, has been very useful. It has corrected the exclusively analytic aspect in my thought, as nourished by Bentham and French philosophers of the eighteenth century. Add to this its critique of the negative school, and especially a real, though incomplete sense of the laws of historical development and of the development of the different conditions of man and society. A sense for this, is, I believe, most developed in Hegel. I still had need for all of this, but you do not. When I later attempted to read some German philosophic works, I found that I already possessed all that was useful for me, and the rest was tedious to the point where I could not continue the reading. (*CW* xiii. 576)

Mill's advice to Comte was not to proceed with the study of German philosophy, but to learn the German language and read Goethe. His own experience, however, was highly instructive and revealed his antipathy to any philosophy with transcendental ambitions. For Mill, what he called the 'Scottish school' (meaning mainly Hume and Smith) was far superior to the German, and Mill referred to this school as an important link in the development of positivism.

Comte also acknowledged the importance of the 'Scottish school' in his early development (see *CG* ii. 291).

We can see here and in numerous other examples that what Mill sought from Comte was a philosophical system that would enable him to defeat the German-inspired metaphysical systems or the intuitionism that underpinned much current philosophical work in Britain. Hence, agreement between the two on the character of positivism as a philosophical system was important to Mill, but it was mainly to enable him to wage war against his philosophical opponents in England. In his correspondence Mill ran up against a major obstacle, that Comte's version of positivism, based on a denial of liberty, phrenology, and an inferior role for women in society, was utterly foreign to Mill's position regarding psychology and ethology. Despite great efforts, he and Comte could not be reconciled, except perhaps by agreeing to differ. Behind the cloak of the needs and demands of national character, Mill fashioned a kind of positivism for England, a half-way house, still incomplete. English character itself perhaps required a different approach, and agreement with Comte was no longer a philosophical imperative.

6

The Mature Mill

We turn now to consider Mill's more mature views with regard to social and political ideas. Such a consideration does not require an account of a system and the foundations on which a system might be constructed. We misunderstand Mill if we see his work in terms of a system, such as utilitarianism or the 'art of life', or even as a contribution to a 'theory' (see e.g. Lyons 1994; Berger 1984). At a time when a 'theory of justice' became important, due to the work of Rawls and others, Mill scholars sought to present Mill's position in terms of a theory of justice. But, for Mill, there was no theory of justice, if only because justice might differ in different societies and at different times (see below, Chapter 11).

Mill's philosophy might better be understood in terms of a number of journeys. Even where he discussed such abstract themes as the characteristics and the classification of the sciences, he did so in terms of old and new sciences and how they impinged on each other and on new and expanding views of life and society. Mill was also one of the most autobiographical of philosophers, as may be seen in both the *Autobiography* and the correspondence with Comte. These autobiographical accounts are part of the journeys in philosophy.

Mill's social and political philosophy was concerned with development, improvement, changes in direction, and the method of reform for individuals, institutions, and societies. It was open-ended, and Mill used terms like 'improvement', 'cultivation' (including 'self-cultivation'), 'civilisation', and 'progress' to depict changes in society and the individual that he was attempting to understand and encourage. He drew on traditional philosophers, such as Aristotle, Bacon, Hobbes, and Locke, and numerous logicians, political economists, and others for his basic tools and ideas, and he faithfully recorded his debts in these respects. But Mill also developed deep and complex emotional relationships with thinkers like Comte, Harriet Mill, Bain, Bentham, his father, Grote, Sterling, and others. What was distinctive about the latter figures was his engagement with them as well as with their ideas. This group was directly part of Mill's personal journey. To put this point more strongly, one might say that they formed the motor of this journey, and Mill needed them to enable him to move through life creatively. What distinguished Mill's engagement with Aristotle or Adam Smith from his engagement with Comte was his emotional involvement with his philosophical friend. The same may be said of Mill and Harriet and Mill and his father, but the most important of these with respect to Mill's philosophy was Comte.

Mill did not necessarily agree with Comte, but whatever the chemistry of their mutual involvement (recall that they never actually met) and however much they disagreed, it was Comte who provided the materials for Mill to move forward from the Bentham camp and then to return to it with an enhanced understanding. When we examine Mill's liberalism in this chapter, we shall see how Mill first adopted Comte's perspective, then rejected it, and finally formed his own view of combining 'metaphysical' doctrines associated with the Enlightenment, dismissed by Comte, with the perspective of society which he had developed. We see this perspective emerge from Mill's philosophical struggle with Comte. Under the guidance of Comte, Mill attempted to move from the thought of the eighteenth century to that of the nineteenth century, from the metaphysical (negative) dimension to the more fully positive one. Mill then rejected the despotic implications of Comte's position and attempted to reintroduce the negative Enlightenment thought into his mature philosophy. We shall see these moves worked out in this chapter and additionally in those chapters on liberty, religion, social-ism, and the subjection of women. Even here, where we take up Comte's use of cerebral hygiene, we shall see first Mill's acceptance of the practice and then his rejection of it. But in the process of accept-ance and rejection, we note that Mill dismissed system-building by the one person with whom he tended to agree but who became addicted to systems through cerebral hygiene. Mill then replaced Comte's position with an engaged dynamic fuelled by active character, cultivation, improvement, and progress.

1. *Why* Auguste Comte and Positivism *was Written*

The Mill–Comte correspondence has been treated in this book as an important text for understanding the development of Mill's thought, particularly, in relation to his major works, *System of Logic* and *Principles of Political Economy*. It has been given the status in Mill's corpus of a distinct work and even the Millian equivalent of a Platonic dialogue.

The correspondence has provided numerous insights into Mill's life and character, and, arguably, a fuller and more accurate account of the key events and decisions surrounding the most creative period in his life than one finds in the *Autobiography*. The correspondence also reveals the complexity of the development of his moral and political philosophy. For example, in examining Mill's liberalism in this chapter, we shall see how his political ideas do not develop in a straightforward way from his inheritance of the ideas of Bentham and James Mill. Although Mill in the end retains some of these ideas, they develop through an intense struggle with the ideas of Comte which he partly accepted and partly rejected.

The correspondence by no means ended Mill's encounter with Comte. It is necessary to go further into their intellectual relationship, and to consider the correspondence in light of Mill's essay, *Auguste Comte and Positivism* (1865), published twenty years later. Most commentators use *Auguste Comte and Positivism* as a major late work to explore the development of Mill's social and political ideas on their own, with the correspondence occasionally employed to elucidate the text. However, with the correspondence given here as high a status as the text, *Auguste Comte and Positivism* will be studied in part to elucidate the themes of the correspondence. This new perspective will draw our attention back to the 1840s and will allow us to see for the first time just how far Mill moved during the correspondence from being a disciple of Comte to a major critic, and then back into what might be called the Bentham camp through the new orientation towards political economy. *Auguste Comte and Positivism* will confirm this movement, and will show, additionally, how the encounter with Comte affected the development of Mill's ideas, positively and negatively, in the spheres of liberty, morality, logic, and political economy as well as with regard to the role of philosophy in society, the separation of spiritual and temporal powers, political organization, religion, and phrenology, to name a few.

Instead of emphasizing why Mill wrote *Auguste Comte and Positivism*, Robson assists our perspective by focusing on the significance of the long delay from the first proposal to write on Comte made to him as early as 1851.[1] At that time, with both Comte and Harriet Taylor Mill still alive, and the correspondence with Comte probably fresh in his mind, he stated abruptly to John Chapman, who had taken over the *Westminster Review*, that he had no intention of writing on the *Cours* nor did he think that a translation would be 'either useful or successful' (*CW* xiv. 77; x, p. cxxx). Mill thus seemed highly reluctant to resume any contact with Comte or with his ideas. As Robson points out, once Harriet Martineau's abridged translation of the *Cours* was published (see Martineau 1853), Mill reconsidered but still declined the proposal. Both he and Harriet Mill did not wish to be associated with Martineau,[2] yet this did not seem to be the deciding factor, as Mill would have been free to write about Comte apart from the Martineau book. Mill wanted to write about Comte's atheism, but felt that the *Westminster* would not allow him to discuss the matter freely. In addition, he felt that Chapman wanted him to write more favourably about Comte than he was inclined to do. What motivated him to consider the project seriously, at least in 1854, 'was the great desire I feel to atone for the overpraise I have given Comte & to let it be generally known to those who know me what I think on the unfavourable side about him' (*CW* xiv. 134; x, p. cxxxi).

The project was reconsidered when Mill learnt in 1863 of the impending publication of Émile Littré's biography of Comte, *Auguste Comte et la philosophie positive*, which he might have thought would contain numerous references to himself (see Littré 1863: 400–65). Mill referred to Littré as 'the only thinker of established reputation' (*CW* x. 329) who was a disciple of Comte in relation to certain aspects of the *Cours* but not with regard to Comte's later writings, and who was eventually rejected by Comte. Mill did not refer specifically to himself, but his own path seemed close to that of Littré, and indeed he structured *Auguste Comte and Positivism* to concentrate on the *Cours* in the first part and to attack Comte's later absurdities in the second. In Mill's work Littré arguably became an image of Mill himself, and Mill contrasted this image with the more dedicated disciples of whom Comte showed greater approval.[3] Comte demanded 'unqualified acceptance' of his ideas and the kind of disciple he preferred was 'one whom no difficulty stops, and no absurdity startles' (*CW* x. 329). That these disciples existed reflected 'the personal ascendancy he exercised over those who approached him; an ascendancy which for a time carried away even M. Littré, as he confesses, to a length which his calmer judgment does not now approve' (*CW* x. 329).

The Littré biography, and Mill's perceived similarity to Littré, provided an incentive to clarify in a comprehensive way, his relationship with Comte.[4] After considerable debate as to the *form* an article or articles would take, and a two-year postponement to write and publish *Examination of Sir William Hamilton's Philosophy* (*CW* ix), Mill settled to his task to write *Auguste Comte and Positivism* as two essays for the *Westminster Review* and subsequently as a volume published in the same year (see Mill 1865*a*: 339–405 and 1865*b*: 1–42, reprinted in *CW* x. 261–368).

In the *Autobiography* Mill's account of *Auguste Comte and Positivism* was remarkably detached from what seemed to animate him in the correspondence. He noted that he 'had contributed more than any one else to make his [Comte's] speculations known in England' through his remarks in the *Logic*. At that time Comte was little known in France and became known to a larger group in England mainly through Mill's *Logic*. Mill then wrote that, because Comte was 'so unknown and unappreciated', Mill did not criticize his weak points but felt it a duty to 'give as much publicity as one could to the important contributions he had made to philosophic thought'. By 1865 Comte had numerous followers and was widely known in many countries to friends as well as enemies, 'as one of the conspicuous figures in the thought of the age'. Mill then concluded his comment in the *Autobiography* by suggesting that the task of sifting the good and bad aspects of Comte's thought fell upon him as 'a special obligation', presumably, because he had failed to criticize Comte publicly for his inadequacies, while praising his contributions in the *Logic* (*CW* i. 271). Mill might have added that, with both Comte and Harriet Mill now dead, he felt free to speak his mind, or that it was the correspondence rather than the *Logic* that needed redressing, as in successive editions of the *Logic* Mill had altered the text and in fact indicated his rapidly decreasing enthusiasm for aspects of Comte's thought. In addition, Mill may well have realized that sooner or later the Mill–Comte correspondence would be published, and though the correspondence was not discussed in *Auguste Comte and Positivism*, it surely hovered in the background.

II. *The Changed Role of the* Logic

With regard to his *Logic*, Mill made an abrupt change of stance from the correspondence. Instead of seeing his work as a temporary resting place (with particular reference to England) in the march of positivism, to be superseded by Comte's own work, Mill now held up the *Logic* to assess the validity of Comte's philosophy. For example, he criticized Comte for failing to recognize the importance of the Aristotelian syllogism in deduction, and with regard to induction, he wrote that 'he has no canons whatever. He does not seem to admit the possibility of any general criterion by which to decide whether a given inductive inference is correct or not.' Mill then maintained: 'He therefore needs a test of inductive proof; and in assigning none, he seems to give up as impracticable the main problem of Logic properly so called' (*CW* x. 292). In a revealing footnote regarding his own *Logic*, Mill added: 'But we cannot discover that he was indebted to it for a single idea, or that it influenced, in the smallest particular, the course of his subsequent speculations' (*CW* x. 293n.).[5] What Pickering has called 'the game of concord' in the correspondence seems to have meant not concord, but simply agreement with Comte (Pickering 1993: i. 531; 2009: ii. 70: 'their game of mutual admiration'). When one reflects on the correspondence, it becomes clear that Mill entered into it by nearly abandoning the main themes of induction and deduction that were developed in the *Logic*. At best one might say that Mill historicized the *Logic*, and the issues on which they disagreed were not ones of logic, but mainly concerned with social statics and the status of women. One might have thought that Mill, the logician, would have insisted at least that logic had a role to play in the proof of Comte's key propositions and the future of their joint programme. This insistence only appeared twenty years later in *Auguste Comte and Positivism* and not in their correspondence.[6]

We might pause here to consider Comte's practice of 'cerebral hygiene' (a practice 'not without philosophic bearings') which he adopted, according to Mill, 'for the sake of mental health' (*CW* x. 329–30). He described Comte's cerebral hygiene as an abstinence from all reading (books, learned journals, newspapers, etc.) except for some poetry in various ancient and modern languages. In his correspondence Comte added that his cerebral hygiene was also compatible with regular attendance at the Italian opera during the season. He justified the practice as follows:

I am too well adapted to such a system of cerebral hygiene to change now, especially since it facilitates my elevating and maintaining without effort the most general views as well as the most pure and impartial sentiments. But, in spite of this regimen, that I believe necessary to the full development of my philosophic life, I am far from indifferent to the effect of my work on our intellectual milieu, although nowadays I hardly have time or the means to perceive it. (*CG* ii. 20–1)

Mill was flattered when Comte set aside this practice in order to read the *Logic*, but he never questioned the practice itself. When one considers Mill's footnote in *Auguste Comte and Positivism* about Comte's reading the *Logic*, but not taking anything from Mill's text (see *CW* x. 293n.), which was fairly obvious in the correspondence, one wonders if cerebral hygiene had made it impossible by that time for Comte to learn from others beyond the extent to which others agreed with him. In *Auguste Comte and Positivism* Mill granted that cerebral hygiene could be advantageous to a mind like Comte's, allowing it to concentrate on highly difficult and abstract thought. As he already possessed 'an ample stock of materials', he might have been justified in feeling that he had learnt enough in preparation for writing his own works. But Mill was nonetheless also highly critical of the practice, and used arguments regarding truth from *On Liberty* to show its deficiencies. Comte or anyone else practising cerebral hygiene could never arrive at 'the whole truth' on any issue:

That he should effect this, even on a narrow subject, by the mere force of his own mind, building on the foundations of his predecessors, without aid or correction from his contemporaries, is simply impossible. He may do eminent service by elaborating certain sides of the truth, but he must expect to find that there are other sides which have wholly escaped his attention.
(*CW* x. 330).

In addition, Mill pointed out how cerebral hygiene could pose 'the gravest dangers' to the philosopher's mind (*CW* x. 330). These dangers included losing all sense of measure and standard that would tell him when he was departing from common sense. Mill continued:

Living only with his thoughts, he gradually forgets the aspect they present to minds of a different mould from his own; he looks at his conclusions only from the point of view which suggested them, and from which they naturally appear perfect; and every consideration which from other points of view might present itself, either as an objection or as a necessary modification, is to him as if it did not exist. (CW x. 331)

Mill added to this intellectual danger arising from cerebral hygiene, a moral one:

The natural result of the position is a gigantic self-confidence, not to say self-conceit. That of M. Comte is colossal. Except here and there in an entirely self-taught thinker,... we have met with nothing approaching to it. As his thoughts grew more extravagant, his self-confidence grew more outrageous. The height it ultimately attained must be seen in his writings, to be believed.

(CW x. 331; see also Pickering 2009: ii. 71)

In contrast to the simple acceptance of cerebral hygiene in the correspondence, here in *Auguste Comte and Positivism* it became a symbol of the denial of truth, enormous self-conceit, and even madness. Although there were many reasons for Mill not to question the practice in the correspondence (for the sake of agreement, his own diffidence, deference to a senior man, etc.), he must have thought about its implications when he wrote *On Liberty*. There is also one curious fact about this critique of cerebral hygiene. It appears at the beginning of the second part of *Auguste Comte and Positivism* where Mill set forth Comte's greatest absurdities in his writings after their correspondence had ended. But cerebral hygiene, as we have seen, also belonged to the period when Mill was a regular correspondent, and Comte was actually writing the *Cours*. Was Mill not facing the possibility that he spent six years corresponding at length with someone who was either mad or on the edge of madness? Or was he simply suggesting that Comte's absurdities did not manifest themselves until this later period? If the *Cours* belonged to this first period of Comte's life, when his philosophy was considered by Mill to be essentially sound, but Comte was nevertheless practising cerebral hygiene and also unable to learn directly from Mill's *Logic*, would not Mill have to reconsider his apparent indebtedness to Comte as expressed in the correspondence and elsewhere? Mill seemed to suggest in *Auguste Comte and Positivism* that a revised version of events would reflect better on the character of both Littré and himself (see further Wernick 2001: 23ff.; Scharff 1995: 6ff.). *Auguste Comte and Positivism* thus seemed to become a subtle way of revising the correspondence.

III. *Mill's Assessment of Comte's Philosophy*

Mill depicted the two parts of his essay initially by remarking on the truth and soundness of both periods in Comte's life. The *Cours*, discussed in the first part, was 'an essentially sound view of philosophy, with a few capital errors'. The writings of Comte's last decade were 'false and misleading', though interspersed with 'a crowd of valuable thoughts, and suggestions of thought' (*CW* x. 265). Mill was also anxious to distinguish in both parts not only what was true in Comte's thought from what was false but, additionally, what was original from that 'which belongs to the philosophy of the age, and is the common inheritance of thinkers' (*CW* x. 265). Mill pointed out that this latter task would not be a difficult one. Comte himself rarely claimed to be original when he was not, and 'was eager to connect his own most original thoughts with every germ of anything similar which he observed in previous thinkers' (*CW* x. 265).

Mill began his analysis of Comte's originality by providing a definition of Comte's conception of positive philosophy:

We have no knowledge of anything but Phænomena; and our knowledge of phænomena is relative, not absolute. We know not the essence, nor the real mode of production, of any fact, but only its relations to other facts in the way of succession or of similitude. These relations are constant; that is, always the same in the same circumstances. The constant resemblances which link phænomena together, and the constant sequences which unite them as antecedent and consequent, are termed their laws. The laws of phænomena are all we know respecting them. Their essential nature, and their ultimate causes, either efficient or final, are unknown and inscrutable to us. (*CW* x. 265–6)

Mill noted that Comte claimed no originality for this conception, but linked it to the beginning of modern science and thinkers like Bacon, Descartes, and Galileo. He partially accepted Comte's position, but believed that it was Hume who first conceived this view as a whole, though Hume went beyond Comte in his scepticism about such laws of phenomena. Following Hume, Mill referred to Thomas Brown, Bentham, James Mill, and finally, to Sir William Hamilton's doctrine of the relativity of human knowledge (*CW* x. 266–7).[7]

Mill then proceeded to provide an account of Comte's system and its originality. He brought out the historical dimension of his various tripartite divisions and paid particular attention to Comte's concern with the classification of the sciences.[8] This theme, important earlier in Diderot's preface to the *Encyclopédie*, Bentham's

Chrestomathia, and Mill's *Logic*, remained so during much of the nineteenth century. New sciences emerged and others were cast aside. We have seen how it impinged on Mill with Comte's rejection of political economy as a distinct science in favour of sociology.

But let us turn to Comte's creation of the science of sociology, where Mill might be expected to have been most indebted to Comte's work. Here we see the familiar themes that animated the correspondence reappear. Comte's treatment of political economy, women, social statics, and social dynamics receive more critical attention here than in the correspondence, with Mill not hesitating to use logic to assess the validity of some of Comte's ideas. Further-more, having now established himself as a political economist as well as a logician, Mill was not reluctant to dismiss Comte's stric-tures on political economy. Indeed, Mill rejected out of hand Comte's view that political economy was 'unscientific, unpositive, and a mere branch of metaphysics'[9] by referring to 'how extremely superficial M. Comte can sometimes be' (*CW* x. 305).

In his criticisms of Comte Mill developed his more recent emphasis on liberty, which had not featured strongly in the corres-pondence. At that time Bain discerned a difference of view between Grote and Mill on the issue of Comte's conception of liberty.[10] Due to his close ties with both Grote and Bain, Mill would have been well aware of Grote's view of Comte as the harbinger of despotism, but he did not directly address the point in the correspondence. Besides Comte's tendencies to develop a despotic system, Mill also had to confront the problem of Comte's rejection of much of the 'liberal creed' (*CW* x. 301) as belonging to 'metaphysics' and to be rejected or, at least, reconceived in terms of positive sociology.

IV. *Comte and Liberalism*

As was the case in all the sciences, Comte believed that sociology (including ethics and politics) passed or must pass through theo-logical, metaphysical, and positive dimensions. Although Mill was critical of the way Comte at times formulated these ideas in the context of physical science as well as social and political science, he seemed to have accepted this approach with some reservations. If theological politics was connected with doctrines associated with, for example, the divine right of kings, Comte seemed to link metaphysical politics with various modern movements ('the revolutionary, the radical, the democratic, the liberal, the free-thinking, the sceptical, or the negative and critical school or party in religion, politics, or philosophy') all of which shared a single characteristic. They were 'mere instruments of attack' on the old system but had no claim to possess positive truth (*CW* x. 301).

Mill then considered what he took to be major tenets of liberalism, including freedom of expression and liberty of conscience, and showed how Comte opposed any legal restraints on these freedoms. Nevertheless, he found no role for liberty of conscience in his system. Because there was no liberty of conscience in other sciences, like physics, chemistry, and biology, Comte believed that there should not be any in social and political science, a position that harmonized with his approval of phrenology and rejection of psychology. In Mill's view Comte held:

[T]he opinions of mankind should really be formed for them by an exceedingly small number of minds of the highest class, trained to the task by the most thorough and laborious mental preparation: and that the questioning of their conclusions by any one, not of an equivalent grade of intellect and instruction, should be accounted equally presumptuous, and more blamable, than the attempts occasionally made by sciolists to refute the Newtonian astronomy.

(*CW* x. 302)

At the outset Mill recognized some truth in Comte's position, but felt that this truth was liable to 'perversion' in its use or application (*CW* x. 302–3). After granting that Comte made ample provision for education in society, so that the opinions of the highest class could be challenged by an educated populace, Mill criticized him for taking his argument too far. Comte believed that that all modern metaphysical doctrines were, almost by definition, purely negative, and rejected the truth of many ideas that could also be true when reconsidered from a positivist perspective. With regard to freedom of expression, Mill believed that all Comte needed to assert was that the liberty to hold and express a creed should not be confused with the truth of the creed (see *CW* x. 303).

Mill proceeded to note a number of doctrines connected with liberalism (as part of the negative, metaphysical approach to politics) that Comte, somewhat illogically, rejected out of hand, even though they might have been restated in a positive way. The first was that a government should not engage in such activities as those promoting social progress, but should restrict its scope to keeping the peace.

Because such a view had been advanced on the grounds of preserving the abstract rights (a metaphysical doctrine) of the individual, Comte simply rejected it. Mill, however, believed that it could be maintained as a positive doctrine on other grounds and should be considered as to whether or not it was true or false as a positive doctrine. Mill agreed with Comte that 'there are no absolute truths in the political art, nor indeed in any art whatever' (CW x. 303), and considered that the doctrine of laissez-faire, without qualification, was unscientific and unpractical. Nevertheless, he believed that it was also true that those who advanced the doctrine were usually ('nineteen times out of twenty') (CW x. 303) closer to the truth than those (like Comte) who denied the doctrine. Mill also turned to the idea of equality that Comte treated as a negative notion of protest against inequalities inherited from the medieval tradition. For Comte, in a modern society where people were educated to respect the dignity of all human beings, they would organize themselves on the basis of unequal aptitudes, with some under the direction of others. Mill's view here was that Comte never considered the possibility that, granted that equality might have some merit, that merit might be facilitated better by governments or social institutions than by the social groupings of individuals in society (CW x. 304).

In a similar manner Mill considered the notion of the sovereignty of the people. Comte regarded it as part of the negative, metaphysical doctrine to overturn the divine right of kings. In this sense Mill agreed with Comte's rejection of it, but then added that there was also a positive dimension to it 'which claims the direct participation of the governed in their own government, not as a natural right, but as a means to important ends, under the conditions and with the limitations which those ends impose' (CW x. 304). If we understand Mill correctly, he was challenging Comte's position of rejecting out of hand ideas like equality, popular sovereignty, etc. that belonged to the negative and revolutionary tradition and were part of nineteenth-century liberalism. Although Mill agreed in part with Comte's critique of the negative, revolutionary schools, he nonetheless insisted that there was much of importance held by members of these schools to be considered by and incorporated into positivism. As we shall see, by making these assertions, Mill refused to embrace Comte's intellectual (and spiritual) despotism.[11]

v. *Political Economy and Social Science*

Mill then considered how Comte, when faced with the theological school on the one hand and the 'democratic and metaphysical' school on the other, 'of no value except for the destruction of the former', developed a positive social science. He pointed out that the weakness of Comte's position emerged particularly in his consideration of the value of political economy, which was, for Mill, 'the only systematic attempt yet made by any body of thinkers, to constitute a science, not indeed of social phænomena generally, but of one great class or division of them' (*CW* x. 305). For Comte, though expressing a reservation in favour of Adam Smith's 'preparatory studies for science', political economy was dismissed, as we have seen, as 'unscientific, unpositive, and a mere branch of metaphysics' (*CW* x. 305). Where Comte invoked the term 'metaphysical', Mill saw in it simply Comte's attempt to create a 'comprehensive category of condemnation' (*CW* x. 305). Mill was then scathing of Comte's approach to political economy. He maintained that Comte's single useful point, that the conditions of national wealth had to be studied in relation to the level of civilization and advancement in various societies, was already widely recognized by most political economists.[12]

Mill granted, however, that there were errors in the work of political economists. They tended to ascribe universality to aspects of human nature that were local or temporary. According to Mill, they neglected 'the wonderful pliability of the human mind' (*CW* x. 306) and failed to appreciate that human beings could be produced of a wholly different character from the way they were then. Mill next turned to consider the method of social science and again used the precepts, developed in the *Logic*, including those based on Comte's ideas, to develop a historical, relative doctrine, embracing social statics and dynamics, but with the additional emphasis (as in the *Logic*) on psychology.

vi. *Spiritual and Temporal Powers*[13]

As Mill discussed Comte's particular contributions to social science, he referred to Comte's emphasis on a wide and thorough liberal education open to all in society prior to specialist education. He then noted Comte's emphasis on 'a Spiritual Power' in society. The authority possessed by scientists in their own sciences would be extended to positive philosophers to direct education in society, but subject to the conditions that these philosophers took no part in the sphere of 'temporal government' (*CW* x. 313). This was called by Mill and Comte the separation of spiritual and temporal powers, and the separation left the positivist philosophers entirely in control of education. For Mill, such control of education as a spiritual power would lead to 'nothing less than a spiritual despotism' (*CW* x. 314). On the one hand, the involvement of 'the philosophic class' in education to take the place of the traditional role played by the clergy must be advantageous to society. On the other hand, such power in a centralized authority would soon become despotic not only in education but also in society. If Comte believed that the temporal power would be so strong that it would pay scant regard to the spiritual authority, Mill replied that this admission would mean that the ideal society, as envisaged by the positivist philosophers, would always remain an ideal and, given the separation of spiritual and temporal powers, could never come into existence. Nevertheless, Comte's idea of a spiritual power was, for Mill, hostile to liberty.

In a manner reminiscent of what I have earlier called 'the method of reform' (see Chapter 3), Mill approached this problem by invoking contrary positions:

M. Comte has got hold of half the truth, and the so-called liberal or revolutionary school possesses the other half; each sees what the other does not see, and seeing it exclusively, draws consequences from it which to the other appear mischievously absurd. (*CW* x. 313)

Mill's position with regard to social science and the institutions that constituted a good society was clearly neither that of Comte nor that of the liberal or revolutionary school. According to Mill, for example, Comte had rejected all checks on temporal power (so prominent in the Bentham school in terms of representative institutions and numerous legal and institutional checks on the abuse of power). Comte favoured only unlimited freedom of expression and criticism plus the 'counsels and remonstrances' of the spiritual power (*CW* x. 327). He failed, in Mill's view, to see what was seen by 'the Bentham school', namely, that despotism could only be prevented by institutional checks. Comte also failed to see what was missing in his conception of the institution of the spiritual power itself, that it omitted to emphasize what was necessary for preventing the abuse of this power, the cultivation of individual liberty and spontaneity in society (see *CW* x. 327).

Mill thus sought to combine the negative school that emphasized constitutional and institutional checks on temporal power, and individual freedom and spontaneity as a check on spiritual power. These positions stood in opposition to Comte's view in the *Cours* and in their correspondence, but at the time of the correspondence, Mill did not emphasize his dissent from them. Here, Mill invoked a way of taking what was useful and progressive in Comte and 'the Bentham school' (through the 'method of reform') and devised new conceptions of progressive reforming politics based on new ideas of liberty. Mill concluded that Comte had not in fact 'created' sociology, as he believed he had in the *Cours*. Yet Mill still generously gave him credit for providing a 'conception of its method' that was 'much truer and more profound than that of any one who preceded him, as to constitute an era in its cultivation' (*CW* x. 327). If he had not created the science of sociology, he had established the conditions for its creation. For Mill, Comte would have had greater influence on the development of social science, if he had not believed he had already created the science. In Mill's opinion he then proceeded wrongly to attempt 'to build upon its foundation the entire fabric of the Political Art' (*CW* x. 327).

VII. *Epicurean Morality*

In the severe critique of Comte in the second part of *Auguste Comte and Positivism*, Mill again invoked the importance of liberty against Comte's more extreme position. In dismissing Comte's approach to morality ('M. Comte is a morality-intoxicated man. Every question with him is one of morality, and no motive but that of morality is permitted': *CW* x. 336), Mill returned to the arguments of *On Liberty* and his critique of Calvinism (see Rosen 2003*a*: 203ff.; *CW* xviii. 265ff.; cf. Semmel 1998: 50). As for Comte's conception of religion, Mill wrote:

The most prejudiced must admit that this religion without theology is not chargeable with relaxation of moral restraints. On the contrary, it prodigiously exaggerates them. It makes the same ethical mistake as the theory of Calvinism, that every act in life should be done for the glory of God, and that whatever is not a duty is a sin. (*CW* x. 337)

Mill went on to see an 'intermediate space' between duty and sin—what he called 'the region of positive worthiness' (*CW* x. 337). He then gave his own account of morality which differed from that of Comte to allow for spontaneity within this sphere: 'since the notion of a happiness for all, procured by the self-sacrifice of each, if the abnegation is really felt to be a sacrifice, is a contradiction'. Mill repeated his belief that Comte's view of morality was close to that of the 'extreme' Calvinists in that 'he requires that all believers shall be saints, and damns them (after his own fashion) if they are not' (*CW* x. 338). In presenting his own view Mill sketched out this intermediate position, aspects of which allowed considerable space for egoistic pleasures and satisfactions:

We do not conceive life to be so rich in enjoyments, that it can afford to forego the cultivation of all those which address themselves to what M. Comte terms the egoistic propensities. On the contrary, we believe that a sufficient gratification of these, short of excess, but up to the measure which renders the enjoyment greatest, is almost always favourable to the benevolent affections. (*CW* x. 339)

To this Epicurean position (see Wilson 2008) Mill then added an argument that, in placing these personal enjoyments under the banner of morality, individuals should be encouraged to cultivate 'the habitual wish to share them with others, and with all others, and scorning to desire anything for oneself which is incapable of being so shared' (*CW* x. 339). He then excepted only one inclination—the love of domination or superiority—which he thought could not be shared in this manner without violating morality. Mill's position was that already developed in *On Liberty* and was given an extended social dimension in the religion of humanity:

As a rule of conduct, to be enforced by moral sanctions, we think no more should be attempted than to prevent people from doing harm to others, or omitting to do such good as they have undertaken. Demanding no more than this, society, in any tolerable circumstances, obtains much more; for the natural activity of human nature, shut out from all noxious directions, will expand itself in useful ones. This is our conception of the moral rule prescribed by the religion of Humanity. (*CW* x. 339)

Mill then turned to what he called 'an unlimited range of moral worth' up to 'the most exalted heroism' where an ascetic discipline, reminiscent of the Stoics, could rival Comte's emphasis on altruism and achieve a similar goal (*CW* x. 339).

VIII. *Liberty and Despotism*

In the second part of his essay, Mill was both highly complimentary and severely critical of Comte's later writings, though his compliments were encapsulated in sentences where criticisms at the end might seem to overwhelm compliments at the beginning (see *CW* x. 367–8). But his most severe criticisms seem to have been aimed at the denial of liberty in Comte's later positivism. Mill concluded that Comte's system placed absolute power in the hands of four people (three bankers and one pontiff) and meant that 'entire subjugation and slavery' was recommended as the highest evolution of humanity. 'It is the most warning example we know', Mill wrote, 'into what frightful aberrations a powerful and comprehensive mind may be led by the exclusive following out of a single idea' (*CW* x. 351).

Nevertheless, as we have seen, the roots of Comte's inclination towards despotism were present in different forms in the earlier *Cours* as well as in the later writings. If Mill did not dwell on liberty in the correspondence, in *Auguste Comte and Positivism* he not only emphasized liberty, but also, at times, seemed to use it to replace ethology, as the key to a progressive social science and to morality itself. Yet, Mill's conception of liberty was underpinned by a notion of active character, if not by an actual science of ethology. Where active character existed, liberty, by leaving humans free so long as they did not harm others, would enable morality and happiness to develop and flourish.

This principle of liberty, based on a conception of active character, thus formed the basis of morality, as well as the religion of humanity. If Grote, as we have seen, thought that Mill's sympathies with Comte were in danger of destroying his commitment to liberty, by *Auguste Comte and Positivism* Mill was clearly on the side of liberty. He not only readopted and re-emphasized in his writings those aspects of liberty he inherited from Bentham and his father, but he also created in *On Liberty* a new conception of social liberty to counter the Comtean tendency to use a social morality to establish 'a despotism of society over the individual' (*CW* xviii. 227). If, as Ryan (1998: 498) has suggested, *On Liberty* 'has the marks of Mill's ambivalence about Comte all over it', in *Auguste Comte and Positivism* Mill clearly and unequivocally established the liberty principle in opposition to Comte's sociology.[14] That Mill retained a conception of the religion of humanity, as we shall see in Chapter 12, did not involve his acceptance of Comte's tendency towards despotism.

III

Principles of Political Economy

7

The Circle of Liberty

1. *'Civil, or Social Liberty'*

The object of this and the following four chapters is to explore themes in the *Principles of Political Economy* (1848), such as liberty, equality, democracy, co-operation, socialism, and justice, which are important in Mill's later thought. Let us begin with the idea of liberty. As is widely known, Mill's *On Liberty* presents an analysis of what he called, somewhat oddly, 'Civil, or Social Liberty', which was defined as 'the nature and limits of the power which can be legitimately exercised by society over the individual' (*CW* xviii. 217). The oddness of the phrase, 'Civil, or Social liberty', on which few scholars comment (see e.g. Berger 1984: 227–9; see also Scarre 2007), is at least twofold. First, the account of liberty employed by Mill differed somewhat from that used throughout the eighteenth-century British tradition from Locke to Price, Bentham, and many others (see Rosen 1992: 27–39). As for civil and social liberty, the traditional idea of civil liberty offered to secure and even to enlarge liberty by the instruments of law and government. Mill's notion of 'Civil, or Social liberty', though referring to 'power', pointedly failed to mention law or government as sources or causes of this 'power'. The reason for this 'failure', so to speak, is that Mill seemed to shift his emphasis away from law and government to that of society in general. The idea of society exercising power, presumably through social or public opinion, while not wholly new, was a conception that was by no means widely used or developed (see Rosen 1983: 19–40; Odugbemi 2009).[1]

Second, the idea of social liberty may well constitute the first sustained discussion of this sort of liberty. So far as I know, the novelty of social liberty has not been noted or appreciated.[2] Mill linked the notions of society and social with Comte, and in *On Liberty*, when he used the phrase, 'the despotism of society over the individual', he referred directly to Comte (*CW* xviii. 227). But the use and development of the phrase 'social liberty' seems to belong much more to Mill himself, as Comte was less interested in liberty in his conception of society (see Chapter 6 above).

The originality of the redefinition of civil liberty and the creation of social liberty was declared by Mill himself in the second sentence of his essay. Following his definition of 'Civil, or Social liberty' in terms of 'the nature and limits of the power which can be legitimately exercised by society over the individual', he wrote:

A question seldom stated, and hardly ever discussed, in general terms, but which profoundly influences the practical controversies of the age by its latent presence, and is likely soon to make itself recognised as the vital question of the future. (*CW* xviii. 217)

This sentence seems to stress the novelty as well as the importance of Mill's conception of liberty. Not only was Mill exploring an idea of liberty 'seldom stated, and hardly ever discussed', but he was also writing for the future, where it seemed certain that it would play a greater role than at the time *On Liberty* was published. Nevertheless, in the third and final sentence in this opening paragraph, Mill seemed to move in the opposite direction in denying any novelty to his conception:

It is so far from being new, that, in a certain sense, it has divided mankind, almost from the remotest ages; but in the stage of progress into which the more civilized portions of the species have now entered, it presents itself under new conditions, and requires a different and more fundamental treatment. (*CW* xviii. 217)

What has 'divided mankind' from 'the remotest ages' was presumably 'the struggle between Liberty and Authority', which had taken different forms at different periods. Hence that aspect of liberty, though fundamental, was not new. Novelty, if it rested anywhere, was with the conception of 'Civil, or Social liberty'. It is true that Mill's novelty extended elsewhere, as Riley suggests, in the individual's 'absolute' freedom to choose among self-regarding acts (see Riley 1998*a*: 28). But his very conception of 'one very simple principle' was his main claim to novelty, though he worked out the structure of this new conception of liberty elsewhere, mainly in the earlier *Principles*. In the *Principles* (and in the *Logic* with ideas related to character and progress) Mill undertook the initial exploration and development of different conceptions of liberty. *On Liberty*, a more derivative work, attempted to provide a synthesis of these different ideas and to apply the new principle developed there.

In asserting that *On Liberty* is closely linked to the *Principles*, published eleven years earlier, and needs to be interpreted in this manner, it is clear that I am moving in a different direction from much recent and contemporary scholarship. Few commentators in recent decades have paid much attention to the *Principles* in relation to *On Liberty*. Rees (1985), Ten (1980), and Lyons (1994) seem to ignore the *Principles* entirely. Gray (1996: 62–3, 92, 95, 101) alludes to the *Principles* at several specific points for comparison and elucidation, but does not link the two works in any systematic manner. Berger (1984: 251–4, 293) and Scarre (2007: 110) refer to the *Principles* in relation to *On Liberty*, but only rarely. An exception is Hollander (1985: ii. 677) who writes that 'the general rule formalized in *On Liberty* which dictates the legitimate scope of social control...appears...in the *Principles*...with special reference to the role of government in economic affairs'. Another exception is Riley (see 1998a: 116–19) who frequently refers to the *Principles* and develops important interpretations of *On Liberty* in relation to the earlier work. Among historians of economic thought, the *Principles* is more carefully studied and is occasionally linked to *On Liberty*, if only by virtue of Mill's discussion of laissez-faire (see Schwartz 1972: 105–52; Hollander 1985: ii. 677–769). But few, if any, commentators have attempted to read the *Principles* as a foundation for the later *On Liberty*, to see if some of the perplexing aspects of *On Liberty*, for example, the material in the chapter on 'Applications', might be more clearly understood in the context of the earlier discussions in the *Principles*.

One major reason for the general indifference to the *Principles*, particularly among so-called 'revisionist' commentators, may well be the preoccupation with using *On Liberty* to raise or resolve questions concerning Mill's utilitarianism. In setting out his focus for studying *On Liberty*, Ten, for example, writes: 'The question then is whether Mill's defence of liberty is consistently utilitarian' (Ten 1980: 5). Ten answers his question and anticipates his conclusion by asserting: 'In this book I have tried to show that Mill's case for liberty is not wholly reconcilable with a consistent version of utilitarianism' (Ten 1980: 9). Ten, of course, assumes that there is some point, besides being a useful academic exercise, in seeking to reconcile liberty and utility at the level they are presented. If Mill is not a consistent utilitarian, for Ten and others, he might nonetheless be considered a consistent 'liberal', and his famous essay admired on other grounds. The fact that *On Liberty* contains no substantial discussion of utilitarianism, and *Utilitarianism* contains no serious discussion of liberty, while both themes are discussed directly or indirectly in the *Principles*, does not seem to trouble many recent commentators.

Fortunately, Mill himself has supplied the reader with a relevant and suitable context for the discussion of liberty in *On Liberty* through the discussions of liberty in the earlier *Principles*. Arguments in the *Principles* may even be regarded as supplying the foundations for important aspects of *On Liberty*. I believe that the last issue that concerned Mill was reconciling liberty and utility in the two essays on these topics. Liberty and utility were conceived in wholly different ways. Liberty was concerned with action and character (see Ball 2010: 51–2), while utility was the basis of all moral and political philosophy. Doubtless, interesting philosophical discussions have emerged from attempts to reconcile these two notions at some level of abstraction, particularly with regard to liberty and justice (see Berger 1984: 229), but in this chapter we shall be concerned with liberty alone.

I shall first examine Mill's approach to liberty in the *Principles* and see how he altered the traditional conception, particularly with regard to the role of government and law in providing security of persons and property (sections II–IV). I shall then explore the foundations he established for a new kind of liberty that he initially depicted in terms of 'a circle of liberty' that was linked to the idea of laissez-faire, elaborately developed in the final book of the *Principles*, and to the idea of active character, developed in the *Logic* and elsewhere (section V). To conclude, I shall return to *On Liberty* to see how Mill applied these ideas concerning liberty to the perplexing part of *On Liberty* (section VI) concerned with 'Applications'.[3]

II. *Security*

The traditional conception of liberty contains an element of paradox. Liberty on its own, a freedom to do as one pleases without restraint or constraint, is clear enough, but the idea that restraints and constraints can actually enlarge or enhance liberty seems intuitively wrong. Yet, civil liberty, by proposing restraints on others to prevent them from violating one's rights or interests, is precisely of this character. John Locke, for example, wrote about liberty as though this intuition did not exist. Liberty took one out of the chaos and insecurity of the state of nature and into a condition of security marked by an enlargement of liberty. Put simply, a settled rule of law enlarged the liberty of members of society by providing them with the security to act freely without interference from others.[4]

Bentham, however, found the distinction between liberty as doing what one pleases and liberty enlarged by law so paradoxical that he sought to distinguish between them by renaming the latter 'security' (Rosen 1992: 33–7). Mill followed Bentham, though, as we shall see, he radically reoriented Bentham's idea of security. Let us first sketch out Bentham's conception of security, which was a broader notion than that associated more narrowly with liberty under law. Security was associated with having enough subsistence for the present and future and was even associated with equality in so far as a more equal society was also more likely to respect the rules of property and protect individuals from harm. But security was particularly related to law and to that law that protected the individual's person and property from attack by others and by government itself. The enforcement of the law via the courts achieved the former and a system of representative democracy (based on the secret ballot, frequent elections, and numerous checks on the abuse of power) provided security against the latter.[5]

In the *Principles* Mill first introduced security in the context of a discussion of what determined productivity in a given society. After discussing natural conditions, the energy of labour, knowledge and skill among labourers, and the intelligence and level of morality and truthfulness in society (see *CW* ii. 101–11), he came to security. At first he seemed to follow Bentham, but the very place given to security in this long list of conditions affecting productivity should alert the reader to a difference in orientation. Mill wrote:

By security I mean the completeness of the protection which society affords to its members. This consists of protection *by* the government, and protection *against* the government. The latter is the more important. (*CW* ii. 112)

If one were to ask Bentham and other writers on liberty throughout the eighteenth century which protection was more important, they would probably say that protection by government was more important than protection against government (see Rosen 1999: 173–85). Unless there was a settled civil society, established to prevent chaos and disorder, and based on the rule of law, human beings could not progress beyond a savage condition. Refinements or changes in the forms of government must rest on the foundation of security. Mill partially rejected this doctrine. In the *Principles* the context was initially economical, although by the end it was also political. He focused on societies, particularly in Asia, where arbitrary taxation by despotic governments seriously limited production to the bare necessities (see Urbinati 2007: 66–97; Kurfirst 1996: 73–87). 'The only insecurity which is altogether paralysing to the active energies of producers,' he wrote, 'is that arising from the government, or from persons invested with its authority. Against all other depredators there is a hope of defending oneself' (*CW* ii. 113; see also *CW* ii. 403).

To support this view, Mill first referred to ancient Greek states and colonies as well as to Flanders and Italy during the Middle Ages. Here, he observed:

the state of society was most unsettled and turbulent; person and property were exposed to a thousand dangers. But they were free countries; they were in general neither arbitrarily oppressed, nor systematically plundered by their governments. Against other enemies the individual energy which their institutions called forth, enabled them to make successful resistance: their labour, therefore, was eminently productive, and their riches, while they remained free, were constantly on the increase. (*CW* ii. 113–14)

In contrast, the despotism of the Roman Empire relieved subjects from insecurity, but because they were left 'under the grinding yoke of its own rapacity, they became enervated and impoverished, until they were an easy prey to barbarous but free invaders' (*CW* ii. 114). Thus, in Mill's view security was dramatically separated from liberty, and liberty was much less reliant on the rule of law. Mill added a second argument to that regarding turbulent but free states, that law played a small role in establishing the security of persons and property, as compared with 'manners and opinions'. He stated that in England security of property 'is owing (except as regards open violence) to opinion, and the fear of exposure, much more than to the direct operation of the law and the courts of justice' (*CW* ii. 114).

III. *Statics and Dynamics*

When Mill returned to the theme of security in later books of the *Principles*, he had already introduced the distinction between economic statics and dynamics following his adoption of Comte's distinction between social statics and dynamics. Economic statics, for Mill, provided the laws that would govern those aspects of society and economy that were relatively stable and unchanging (*CW* iii. 705).

Bentham's account of liberty under law as security would appear to suit such an account of elements of society in a hypothetically stable condition. Members of society were considered as individuals with interests that were secured or should be secured by law and government. These interests were numerous and complex, but it was the task of law and government to secure them so that harm to persons and their property was prevented by law and the threat of punishment through the system of justice. Representative democracy was the final step in this chain, as it secured the interests of the people from oppression by government, and thus was embedded in a theory of constitutional liberty.

As we have seen, Mill undermined this theory by denying the importance of the rule of law and government in providing this kind of security. But he also sought to develop the idea of security within the context of economic dynamics. The last two books of the *Principles* are explicitly set forth in this context, which is concerned with economic factors as they affect humankind under changing conditions, but particularly in terms of 'progressive changes' by 'the more advanced portions of the race' (*CW* iii. 705). 'We have to consider', Mill wrote, 'what these changes are, what are their laws, and what their ultimate tendencies; thereby adding a theory of motion to our theory of equilibrium—the Dynamics of political economy to the Statics' (*CW* iii. 705). Mill focused on this 'progressive change' that seemed to characterize 'leading countries', which 'continues with little interruption from year to year and from generation to generation', and was linked with 'material prosperity' (*CW* iii. 705–6). After referring to a first condition, an increase in human power over nature through an understanding of science and its applications, he turned to a second change that determined progress in civilization, the 'continual increase' in security of persons and property (*CW* iii. 706). Mill depicted this security as follows:

The people of every country in Europe, the most backward as well as the most advanced, are, in each generation, better protected against the violence and rapacity of one another, both by a more efficient judicature and police for the suppression of private crime, and by the decay and destruction of those mischievous privileges which enabled certain classes of the community to prey with impunity upon the rest. They are also, in every generation, better protected, either by institutions or by manners and opinion, against arbitrary exercise of the power of government.   (CW iii: 706–7)

Mill's identification of the importance of security of persons and property might superficially be seen as very similar to that of Bentham and to the long line of advocates of liberty in the tradition of the social contract. The provision of this security is at the heart of the liberty to act in civil society without interference from others and government. Without it, one is plunged into the uncertainties and, possibly, the chaos of the state of nature and/or state of war. But Mill's account was not a similar theory of liberty. First, it did not apply to all people at all times and reflect their deeply held natural or human rights or most basic interests. Although traditional accounts of liberty distinguished between settled and civilized societies as opposed to anarchic ones, Mill's distinction was embedded in his account of social progress (based on economic dynamics) rather than a universally applicable principle of liberty. Second, though placed in an account of economic dynamics based on the history of various states, Mill's argument was defective, as there was no historical truth in the doctrine of an increasing security in each generation in all European states. For earlier writers, e.g. Hobbes, war was always very close whenever civil society broke down or a country was invaded. The proximity of war made more obvious the immense value of security. Mill, however, pushed war to a distant corner, as when he wrote (in the context of security) that 'wars, and the destruction they cause, are now usually confined, in almost every country, to those distant and outlying possessions at which it comes into contact with savages' (CW iii. 707). Mill thus wrongly accounted for war among 'civilized' societies and failed to anticipate the possibility of the terrible wars that would drive Europe to death and despair in the next 150 years. But it was part of his approach to see a dynamic in society that pointed in a different direction away from war and towards a civilized society.

Third, unlike some earlier writers and, particularly, Bentham, Mill did not link his account of security to the constitutions of government that tended to secure persons and property and, especially, to constitutional democracy in which individual rights or interests were secured by and against government. Mill's concerns with the dangers of democracy as a threat to civilization led him in another direction. When he contrasted savages or those in 'a rude state of society' with those in civilized society, he noted that in civilized society there was a far greater capacity for co-operation and united action (*CW* iii. 707–8). 'Accordingly,' he wrote, 'there is no more certain incident of the progressive change taking place in society, than the continual growth of the principle and practice of co-operation' (*CW* iii. 708).

Co-operation and related notions, like socialism, became important ideas for Mill and revealed the potential for new ways of organization which could transform the hostility behind the opposition between capital and labour. This potential for increased co-operation was the logical development of the interdependence caused by the dynamic growth of modern society and the increase in security of persons and property related to it. Nevertheless, however much Mill developed this idea, and however much it was related to security, he was clearly moving away from the idea that security was in effect liberty under law in so far as individual interests could be protected and in their protection the individual's freedom could be enlarged. We can thus see how the notion of security was changed in the context of economic dynamics.

iv. *Security and Liberty*

There is no doubt that Mill gave considerable importance to security of persons and property even in the dynamic side of economics and politics, as when he wrote:

Insecurity of person and property, is as much as to say, uncertainty of the connexion between all human exertions or sacrifice, and the attainment of the ends for the sake of which they are undergone. It means, uncertainty whether they who sow shall reap, whether they who produce shall consume, and they who spare to-day shall enjoy to-morrow. It means, not only that labour and frugality are not the road to acquisition, but that violence is. When person and property are to a certain degree insecure, all the possessions of the weak are at the mercy of the strong. No one can keep what he has produced, unless he is more capable of defending it, than others who give no part of their time and exertions to useful industry are of taking it from him. The productive classes, therefore, when the insecurity surpasses a certain point, being unequal to their own protection against the predatory population, are obliged to place themselves individually in a state of dependence on some member of the predatory class, that it may be his interest to shield them from all depredation except his own. In this manner, in the Middle Ages, allodial property generally became feudal, and numbers of the poorer freemen voluntarily made themselves and their posterity serfs of some military lord. (*CW* iii. 880)

This account of security might have been written by Bentham, except that, for Mill, there was no connection with liberty. Security and liberty were in Mill's view not only separate but potentially in opposition. For a second time in the *Principles* he pointed to a different kind of liberty as exhibited in the 'free cities of Italy, Flanders, and the Hanseatic league', which were free but lacked security. As Mill put it:

in the midst of turmoil and violence, the citizens of those towns enjoyed a certain rude freedom, under conditions of union and co-operation, which, taken together, made them a brave, energetic, and high-spirited people, and fostered a great amount of public spirit and patriotism. The prosperity of these and other free states in a lawless age, shows that a certain degree of insecurity, in some combinations of circumstances, has good as well as bad effects, by making energy and practical ability the conditions of safety. (*CW* iii. 881)

To avoid confusion, we should recall that Bentham had earlier separated security and liberty, and anticipated Mill's distinction between the two ideas. But Bentham emphasized security as another and less confusing name for liberty under law. He was less enthusiastic about liberty generally except in *Defence of Usury*, a fact Mill could acknowledge in his *Principles* (see Bentham 1952–4 (1787): i. 123–207; see *CW* iii. 923; see also Rosen 2003a: 114–30). In this important move in his argument Mill seemed to be saying that, given the requisite character or ethology, one marked by courage, energy, patriotism, public spirit, and practical ability, one does not need as much security of the kind admired by advocates of liberty under law. Indeed, Mill seemed to suggest that an energetic and practical character will establish both security on the one hand and liberty on the other.

If one possessed a degree of security sufficient to ensure that one could keep what one earned, a free people, living in a state of relative insecurity, even a degree of 'lawlessness and turbulence', would survive and prosper. Only under conditions of extreme oppression *by a government* would insecurity paralyse—where 'no energy of which mankind in general are capable, affords any tolerable means of self-protection' (*CW* iii:.881). Thus, as we have seen earlier, security *against* government was more important for Mill than security under government. Furthermore, at the foundation of Mill's conception of *both* security *and* liberty within the context of economic dynamics was the important assumption that what determined both was active and energetic character in society, as opposed to Bentham's account of the protection of interests.[6] If society possessed active and energetic character as well as intelligence and a willingness to take risks, security (liberty under law) was mainly irrelevant except where there was extreme oppression by government itself. At this point we might add that this extreme threat could come from oppressive regimes generally, as in China, or from the tyranny of the majority, under certain circumstances, as part of a democratic constitution.

v. *Mill's Circle*

If the foundation of society rested on active character, how did liberty fit into the account in the *Principles*? Mill depicted liberty as follows:

Whatever theory we adopt respecting the foundation of the social union, and under whatever political institutions we live, there is a circle around every individual human being, which no government, be it that of one, of a few, or of the many, ought to be permitted to overstep: there is a part of the life of every person who has come to years of discretion, within which the individuality of that person ought to reign uncontrolled either by any other individual or by the public collectively. That there is, or ought to be, some space in human existence thus entrenched around, and sacred from authoritative intrusion, no one who professes the smallest regard to human freedom or dignity will call in question: the point to be determined is, where the limit should be placed; how large a province of human life this reserved territory should include. (*CW* iii. 937–8; see also Scarre 2007: 110)

Mill's circle of human freedom was designed to reduce what he called 'authoritative' government intervention and clarify the extent of laissez-faire in relation to the individual. He conceived of the distinction between authoritative and non-authoritative intervention as a way of responding to two conflicting opinions regarding laissez-faire, one holding that government should be free to intervene in any circumstance in which such intervention could be shown to be useful, and the other, that the sphere of government was limited to 'the protection of person and property' from 'force and fraud' (*CW* iii. 936). Mill's distinction was intended to redirect the argument (by drawing on parts of the contraries) towards a distinction based on compulsory (authoritative) intervention in virtually any sphere and a role by government in providing advice and information (non-authoritative intervention) rather than compelling the individual to act or abstain from action. The circle of liberty surrounding the individual was meant by Mill to state the limits of any such authoritative intervention while leaving the door open for more widespread non-authoritative intervention.[7]

Mill's concern with the circle of liberty was thus in part an attempt to state the limits of authoritative intervention. He also sought to define what should be protected within the circle in language that clearly anticipated *On Liberty*:

I apprehend that it ought to include all that part which concerns only the life, whether inward or outward, of the individual, and does not affect the interests of others, or affects them only through the moral influence of example. With respect to the domain of the inward consciousness, the thoughts and feelings, and as much of external conduct as is personal only, involving no consequences, none at least of a painful or injurious kind, to other people; I hold that it is allowable in all, and in the more thoughtful and cultivated often a duty, to assert and promulgate, with all the force they are capable of, their opinion of what is good or bad, admirable or contemptible, but not to compel others to conform to that opinion; whether the force used is that of extra-legal coercion, or exerts itself by means of the law. (*CW* iii. 938)

At first glance self-cultivation and self-development within the circle of liberty seems compatible with an extensive social and political intervention in most aspects of life. Nevertheless, Mill's circle of liberty was also meant to be a reflection of and to accommodate active character, which would obviously not be content with solely an introspective life. To address this issue he wrote:

Even in those portions of conduct which do affect the interest of others, the onus of making out a case always lies on the defenders of legal prohibitions. It is not merely constructive or presumptive injury to others, which will justify the interference of law with individual freedom. To be prevented from doing what one is inclined to, or from acting according to one's own judgment of what is desirable, is not only always irksome, but always tends, *pro tanto*, to starve the development of some portion of the bodily or mental faculties, either sensitive or active; and unless the conscience of the individual goes freely with the legal restraint, it partakes, either in a great or in a small degree of the degradation of slavery. (*CW* iii. 938)

If, with every authoritative action with which we disagree, feelings of degradation associated with slavery are aroused, government intervention should be severely limited. Mill then tried to define the limits to authoritative intervention in the following passage:

Scarcely any degree of utility, short of absolute necessity, will justify a prohibitory regulation, unless it can also be made to recommend itself to the general conscience; unless persons of ordinary good intentions either believe already, or can be induced to believe, that the thing prohibited is a thing which they ought not to wish to do. (*CW* iii. 938)

The inward domain of the 'general conscience' and 'ordinary good intentions' apparently had a more important role to play than calculations of outward utility, except perhaps where 'absolute necessity' reigned. But this point of clarification did not establish where a line might be drawn to limit authoritative intervention and protect the individual, although restrictions on government seem as severe as the notion of liberty as security developed by Bentham. Furthermore, Mill's conception of the circle of liberty reveals more about what Mill sought to protect within the circle (i.e. inward consciousness, thoughts, feelings, and personal conduct) than it does about the circumference of the circle, where individuals interact with each other.

Nevertheless, authoritative intervention by government is only part of the story, for equally important is non-authoritative intervention. Mill depicted this in relation to liberty as follows:

It is otherwise with governmental interferences which do not restrain individual free agency. When a government provides means for fulfilling a certain end, leaving individuals free to avail themselves of different means if in their opinion preferable, there is no infringement of liberty, no irksome or degrading restraint. One of the principal objections to government interference is then absent. (*CW* iii: 938–9)

Mill saw the role of government in non-authoritative intervention in terms of the government not fully trusting individuals to pursue a given end, but not wishing to meddle in individual freedom. Mill's examples are wide-ranging. Government could establish a body with a similar purpose alongside one established by private individuals. It might have a church establishment while tolerating other religions or no religion among individuals in society. It might establish schools and colleges while leaving individuals free to teach without a licence from the government. There could be government factories or banks without any monopoly in their respective areas. There could be a state post office without a monopoly on sending letters or public hospitals without any restrictions on private practice (*CW* iii. 937).

Mill recognized that his distinction might not wholly avoid authoritative intervention by government, particularly in the form of compulsory taxation to establish these non-authoritative government institutions, plus penalties and additional costs for the evasion of taxes. Furthermore, the sheer size of government intervention in the economy and society might constitute interference with liberty. Nevertheless, the distinction between authoritative and non-authoritative intervention allowed Mill to envisage an expanded role for government in society in a way he thought would not seriously interfere with free agency and the free flow of active character.

VI. 'One Very Simple Principle' Applied

Towards the end of the *Principles* Mill set forth a clear statement of the foundations of political liberty:

The only security against political slavery, is the check maintained over governors, by the diffusion of intelligence, activity, and public spirit among the governed. Experience proves the extreme difficulty of permanently keeping up a sufficiently high standard of those qualities; a difficulty which increases, as the advance of civilization and security removes one after another of the hardships, embarrassments, and dangers against which individuals had formerly no resource but in their own strength, skill, and courage. It is therefore of supreme importance that all classes of the community, down to the lowest, should have much to do for themselves; that as great a demand should be made upon their intelligence and virtue as it is in any respect equal to; that the government should not only leave as far possible to their own faculties the conduct of whatever concerns themselves alone, but should suffer them, or rather encourage them, to manage as many as possible of their joint concerns by voluntary co-operation; since this discussion and management of collective interests is the great school of that public spirit, and the great source of that intelligence of public affairs, which are always regarded as the distinctive character of the public of free countries. (*CW* iii. 943–4)[8]

As we have seen at the outset of this chapter, Mill set out in *On Liberty* to examine 'Civil, or Social liberty'. It is fairly clear that he did not set out to discuss two different concepts of liberty, civil *and* social, as he made clear a few lines further on that he was concerned with 'one very simple principle', and not two. Furthermore, when he invoked civil *or* social liberty, he was probably not suggesting that he was simply using the two terms as synonyms to depict the same phenomena. That is to say, he did not seem to suggest that one can use 'social' interchangeably as a synonym for 'civil'. I have reached this conclusion by noting and reflecting on the comma that Mill placed after 'civil' in his phrase 'Civil, or Social Liberty'. In the context of *On Liberty* the comma seems to suggest that social liberty, a new form of liberty, has now incorporated civil liberty, and has advanced a new formulation and a new agenda of concerns. In the quotation with which this section began, we can see how security, part of the traditional conception of liberty, was mentioned and found wanting by Mill, as civilization in his view had progressed to a new level. Social liberty was intended to replace it. Social liberty was based on a new and more positive foundation, that of active character. The more negative civil liberty was replaced by intelligence and active character as a *foundation*, but not wholly dismissed, as basic security of persons and property remained part of social liberty or related to it.[9] Nevertheless, this shift in the foundation of liberty had important consequences for Mill's thought. Traditional positions related to civil liberty, such as opposition to the death penalty, support for the secret ballot, approval of the universal institution of representative democracy in all countries or, indeed, other forms of government, as part of constitutional liberty, diminished or disappeared following his abandonment of security of persons and property as the foundation of liberty. His indifference to the costs to society via increased taxation to pay for non-authoritative intervention seems another consequence, as does his willingness to see liberty benefit from 'turmoil and violence', perhaps implying a less fulsome appreciation of the importance of the enforcement of a settled rule of law in all circumstances.[10]

But let us examine further how Mill used and developed this new conception of liberty as 'one very simple principle' in *On Liberty*. We might see this to best effect in the final chapter of *On Liberty*, to which Mill gave the title 'Applications'.[11] The chapter as a whole seems to lack a logical structure in relation to the two 'maxims' he set out at the beginning, or, indeed, to the 'one very simple principle'.[12] Mill admitted at the outset that the time was not ripe to develop and trace all the consequences of the maxims. Instead, he proposed to consider several examples to illustrate them.

Why did Mill need to illustrate the maxims? If he were simply attempting to show how the distinction between self-regarding and other-regarding actions might be drawn or what was meant by 'harm to the interests of others', he needed only to refer the reader to the considerable literature on liberty. If A strikes B over the head with a stick, though the circumstances might be complex, the act is clearly an other-regarding act harmful to B. A might well be held accountable to society and punished for his action. To explore numerous mitigating factors and additional circumstances might be useful, but the principle is clear enough. We can see what is happening in relation to it. But Mill was concerned with social liberty as well as liberty under law and, particularly, with a social liberty that transformed liberty. He was particularly concerned with the circle of liberty. He sought to illuminate the circle that surrounded each individual in society. Even though we can see the individual, despite Mill's discussions in the *Principles* and in *On Liberty*, the circle remained somewhat obscure, even invisible. To illustrate means to make clearer, brighter, to bring from darkness into light. The 'Applications' that Mill examined should thus reveal what we cannot see, the circumference of the circle of liberty surrounding each individual that Mill sought to embed in society. I shall not comment on all of these here, but select several for examination.

The first illustration dealt with the damage caused to the interests of others through competition. Mill granted that where an individual pursued successfully a legitimate object—among his examples was a competitive examination or succeeding in an 'overcrowded profession'—others would inevitably suffer pain and loss (say, from wasted exertion or from disappointment) in the competition. A student of Mill's second maxim might conclude that the actions of the successful competitor were 'prejudicial to the interests of others'. For example, some of the other competitors might be dyslexic, suffer from anxiety, etc. and also suffer pain from participation in the system of competitive examination itself. Hence, government or other social institutions might on the grounds of liberty abandon or prohibit the use of such examinations. But even though he recognized that the practice might cause pain and harm to others, Mill did not reach this conclusion. He wrote that it is 'by common admission, better for the general interest of mankind, that persons should pursue their objects undeterred by this sort of consequences'. 'In other words,' he continued, 'society admits no right, either legal or moral, in the disappointed competitors, to immunity from this kind of suffering; and feels called on to interfere, only when means of success have been employed which it is contrary to the general interest to permit—namely, fraud or treachery, and force' (*CW* xviii. 292–3).

On what grounds did Mill reach this conclusion? At first glance it might be seen as a deduction from the utility principle that in turn overrides the liberty principle. Harm to others is caused by competition, but the greatest happiness in society is advanced by such a system. On balance, then, competitive examinations might be regarded more as advancing happiness in society than retarding it. This might well be the case, but Mill's language was not focused on pain and unhappiness. Mill invoked 'common admission' and a society that admitted no legal or moral right to immunity from competitive examinations.

Mill clearly insisted that the interests of society seemed to take precedence over the interests of the individual in competitive examinations and other related practices. The reason for this was not only based on calculations of utility, but also on an understanding of social liberty, expressed in terms of the circle of liberty surrounding the individual. In this first 'application' Mill brought to view an aspect of the circle otherwise invisible. Even though competition might lead to harm to the interests of others, it was to be encouraged, as it enabled many individuals to realize their ambitions and objects.[13]

More importantly, one can see here not only the problem of preventing harm to others, but also the invocation of the importance of active character and the kind of institutions and practices that would allow such character to flourish and a progressive society to develop. Rather than puzzling over whether or not Mill was able to distinguish clearly between the consequences of self-regarding and other-regarding actions and practices, we can see his argument as revealing an important dimension to the circle of liberty that ought to surround everyone. That he came down on the side of promoting competition should not be seen as diminishing individual liberty, but as expanding it within the circle, and hence expanding the circle.

The legitimacy of competition was an important issue for Mill. On one level it was relevant to the reform of corruption in public offices and other institutions. At another level it was also a key issue within socialist thought where competition in piecework meant greater rewards for those who worked hardest and fastest. Most socialists favoured rewarding all equally, or some variant of this approach. Mill, however, favoured competition (with unequal rewards) as an application of social liberty based on active character.[14]

Mill's second example was concerned with trade, which he accepted as a 'social act' affecting 'the interest of other persons' that came 'within the jurisdiction of society' (*CW* xviii. 293). At one time government tended to regulate prices and the actual processes of manufacture. More recently, free trade was seen as superior on the grounds of cheapness and quality of the various articles involved in trade. But, in principle, society, for Mill, could govern all aspects of trade and could choose government intervention when necessary. Some problems concerning free trade should be without question subject to regulation, e.g. prevention of fraud through adulteration, regulation of safety in dangerous occupations, sanitary precautions, etc., though Mill recognized that there were issues of liberty even here, as it was always better to leave people to look after themselves rather than to impose controls on them. Mill then mentioned three examples concerned with the freedom to purchase and consume items, like alcohol, opium, and poisons, which were at some points prohibited. Mill claimed that they clearly raised issues of individual liberty as opposed to general problems of free trade.

Mill's discussion at this point might easily have been questioned, as it is by no means clear why issues of liberty applied only to the buyers and not to the producers and sellers. A worker might want to be free to work in a hazardous occupation without the expense of acquiring elaborate health and safety equipment, because he needed the money to feed and educate his family. Such a desire for freedom belongs to the realm of liberty as much as to free trade. Unfortunately, Mill did not dwell on this question, and hastened to introduce the issue concerned with the extent to which society and government might act to prevent crime in the future. For example, liberty might dictate that a mature individual should be free to purchase and consume intoxicating drinks, but should society and government be able to take steps to prevent acts of public drunkenness or to punish those who from drunkenness failed to provide for their families?

Mill admitted that such preventive steps suggested 'obvious limitations' to the maxim that 'purely self-regarding misconduct cannot properly be meddled with in the way of prevention or punishment' (CW xviii. 295). In other words, he was admitting here that when placed under any scrutiny the realm of freedom, if derived simply from the conception of self-regarding conduct, must be small and becoming smaller, partly because few acts of self-regarding conduct are wholly self-regarding, and social and governmental regulation, for purposes of preventing crime and other socially offensive acts, may be necessary. As for the former, he upheld the freedom for individuals to act in ways concerned only with themselves which, if done publicly, might be prohibited as offences against decency. Mill continued with further examples of an increasingly diminishing liberty, as seen from the perspective of self-regarding conduct, that culminated in his example with the individual not being free 'in this and most other civilized countries' to sell oneself or allow oneself to be sold into slavery (*CW* xviii. 299). Surely, one might think, here is a self-regarding act that should escape prohibition or regulation. But Mill concluded his analysis of this example: 'The principle of freedom cannot require that he should be free not to be free. It is not freedom, to be allowed to alienate his freedom' (*CW* xviii. 300). If we look at this controversial example from the perspective of self-regarding conduct, there may be an obvious paradox in Mill's diminution of liberty for the sake of liberty. There is also nothing explicit in the example concerned with harm to others. But Mill's circle of liberty has a different and more important foundation, that of active character, and the expansion of the circle of liberty requires the continual exercise of active character, which would not usually be possible in a condition of bondage, self-imposed or imposed by others. The expansion of active character should lead to an enlargement of the circle, which should be beneficial to the individual and to society. If the circle of liberty depended on self-regarding conduct alone, it would be continually diminishing in the context of regulation and prevention in modern civilized societies. But if the circle of liberty depended on active character, one can employ what Mill called in the *Principles* non-authoritative intervention to increase liberty of the individual in the context of regulation.

The circumference of the circle of liberty is becoming more visible by these illustrations as is the dependence of the circle on active character. Consider the example of education, where, above all, Mill thought active character could and should be cultivated (see Kurer 1991: 160–70). He began with what was 'almost a self-evident axiom' that the state should 'require and compel the education, up to a certain standard, of every human being who is born its citizen' (*CW* xviii. 301). Though Mill stated his principle forcefully, he was well aware of the fact that this 'almost' self-evident axiom had not received the force of law in Britain and the father (or other responsible adult) was free to ignore such a principle. In place of freedom to educate or not, Mill proposed state requirement and compulsion. In place of the sharp diminution of freedom regarding education, Mill proposed to reinstate freedom to avoid the state actually providing the education by requiring the father to arrange it. Mill thus sought to avoid what he called 'a despotism over the mind' as well as what he called 'a moral crime' against the child and society by failing to educate him or her properly (*CW* xviii. 302). The details of Mill's arrangements for state examinations and public certificates, intended to ensure that education was organized on a satisfactory basis, need not concern us now, but they are part of the cultivation of active character and the enlargement of the circle of liberty. My circle of liberty is enlarged as I develop the character and tools through education to function in a modern society. My father's realm of self-regarding activity, based perhaps on his interest in utilizing his son's labour for his own ends rather than for the future prospects for the son, is diminished and ultimately dismissed as an obstacle to liberty.

VII. *Conclusion*

How did Mill reconcile the two kinds of liberty, civil and social, when they came into conflict, as they clearly did in the chapter on 'Applications' in *On Liberty*? On the one hand, the individual might exercise his or her freedom by agreeing to enslavement in order to safeguard life and some aspects of liberty. On the other hand, such an act might be seen as a violation of liberty that might well destroy the cultivation of individuality, the potential development of active character (see Ball 2010: 51), and taking advantage of opportunities presented in a modern, progressive society. The liberty established by the laws of property and contract (and which reflect civil liberty) seem at variance with that embodied in a society based on the expansion of the circle of liberty. Seen in this light, and from the perspective of the circle of liberty, traditional notions of civil liberty may well be found wanting.

Rees (1985: 166) interprets the example of the person who fails at a competitive examination as someone whose pains might be discounted in so far as the pains received are outweighed by benefits elsewhere. While this interpretation makes some sense, it omits Mill's own concern that social considerations *within the liberty principle* outweigh the pain suffered by the person whose freedom is violated in the competitive examination. This is achieved by virtue of the emphasis placed on the cultivation of active character within the circle of liberty, which is part of social liberty.[15] Rees seems not to appreciate that (a) the failure at competitive examinations involves harm to one's interests and is a violation of liberty; and (b) that is discounted by virtue of a far more important element in the principle of liberty.

8

The Journey to Socialism: From Liberty and Representative Democracy to Co-operation

I turn now to trace out in the next chapters how Mill used his starting points in active character and social liberty to develop a thesis that aimed at the realization of a form of socialism. It is important to appreciate that a good deal of Mill's argument was developed in the *Principles,* and was embedded in the economic ideas established there. The move to this focus on economic ideas did not diminish or restrict Mill's theory but, on the contrary, seemed to enlarge it, as these economic ideas also included import-ant reflections on society and politics.[1] Mill consciously linked his thought to the main tradition of a philosophical political economy, stemming from David Hume and Adam Smith. As we have seen in the argument with Comte, Mill regarded this tradition as suffi-ciently substantial to form the basis of his next work in social science. He was able to develop at the same time a notion of liberty that served as a foundation for *On Liberty,* itself, and a theory of industrial and political organization that culminated in socialism. That he was able to do so did not make Mill an ideological socialist as opposed to an ideological liberal, but reflected his philosophical and rhetorical skills in reconciling the two positions on a different level.

Before turning to Mill's journey to socialism, I shall briefly examine another journey he might have taken, and which was taken by numerous radicals, from liberty as security to representative democracy. This journey began, for Mill, with the legacy of the Benthamite radicals, but was interrupted by Alexis de Tocqueville's *Democracy in America*, where he discovered a number of problems in modern democracy that he shared with the French philosopher. Instead of a journey culminating in representative democracy Mill chose another journey through co-operation that culminated in a form of socialism. Put more simply, due to its defects representative democracy could not constitute Mill's vision of the highest political aspirations for humankind. To understand how Mill began to think in these terms, it is necessary to begin with his encounter with Tocqueville, which steered him into a cul-de-sac where he was more concerned with curbing the abuses of democracy than with its aspirations.

1. *The Legacy of Tocqueville*

Many commentators have discussed either at length or in passing Mill's indebtedness to Tocqueville. Kahan, for example, writes that 'Mill's view of modern society was heavily influenced by Tocqueville, and his classic *On Liberty* (1859) is largely a meditation on themes from *Democracy [in America]*' (Kahan 2010: 116). Brogan notes that Tocqueville was far too ill to read the copy of *On Liberty* Mill had sent to him, but if he had, 'he would have seen his own influence stamped deep on almost every page of Mill's masterpiece' (Brogan 2006: 627; see also Zunz 2006: 373–4). Nevertheless, there are only two brief references to Tocqueville in *On Liberty* (*CW* xviii. 219, 274). In the first Mill invoked the phrase, 'tyranny of the majority', as an evil against which society needed to be 'on its guard'. He then proceeded to distinguish between a majority tyranny enforced by public institutions and that enforced by society itself through opinion and feeling. Mill referred to the latter form of majority tyranny as being far more severe and insidious than a political tyranny, as it enslaved the soul itself (*CW* xviii. 220).

The second reference to Tocqueville was similar, though there was no explicit reference to *Democracy in America*. He cited Tocqueville for noting that recently all Frenchmen of the present decade (1850s), as opposed to earlier decades, increasingly tended to resemble one another. Mill thought that the same was true for England, and for a solution he turned to von Humboldt's emphasis on individual freedom and a 'variety of situations' (*CW* xviii. 261, 274). These two references to Tocqueville in *On Liberty* on their own suggest that this work was not necessarily intended to serve as a meditation on *Democracy in America*, nor that Tocqueville's influence was 'stamped deep' on 'almost every page' of *On Liberty*.

A number of scholars have noted a more problematic relationship between Tocqueville and Mill. In his earlier book on Mill, Tocqueville, and Burckhardt, Kahan (1992: 6) develops a less effusive view of Tocqueville's influence and acknowledges a debate among scholars (Mueller, Mayer, and Lerner on the one hand and Pappé, Lively, and Mill himself on the other). The reference to Mill is to the *Autobiography* (*CW* i. 199–201) where in the context of a discussion of the development of his political ideas, he noted that the changes in his way of thinking were 'already complete' prior to his encounter with Tocqueville (*CW* i. 199). Mill then wrote:

My new tendencies had to be confirmed in some respects, moderated in others: but the only substantial changes of opinion that were yet to come, related to politics, and consisted, on one hand, in a greater approximation, so far as regards the ultimate prospects of humanity, to a qualified Socialism, and on the other, a shifting of my political ideal from pure democracy, as commonly understood by its partisans, to the modified form of it, which is set forth in my *Considerations on Representative Government*. (*CW* i. 199)

This passage and those which follow it are not entirely clear. One can gain some clarification by noting that 'pure democracy' meant Benthamite representative democracy. Mill seemed to confirm the thesis that I have been advancing that the development of his political thought regarding 'social liberty' co-operation, and socialism, which are the subjects of this part of the book, owed little directly to Tocqueville and were developed earlier in his career, probably in relation to Comte (see Pappé 1964: 231). As Mill developed his ideas on democracy, however, he was more indebted to Tocqueville, and this was manifested in the *Considerations* and in his work on centralization. From Tocqueville, Mill learnt both 'the excellencies of Democracy' and 'the specific dangers which beset Democracy, considered as the government of the numerical majority' (*CW* i. 199, 201). He dealt specifically with the latter in the *Considerations*, leading Robbins to suggest that the *Considerations* was 'as much a plea for adequate safeguards against the abuses of democracy as an argument for proceeding for its realization' (Robbins 1952: 203). If we reflect on what Mill said, though he was highly circumspect and not entirely clear, the influence of Tocqueville, as we have just noted, seems mainly confined to the cul-de-sac where Mill wrote more on curbing the abuses of democracy and less on the nature and future of liberty and democracy. Of course, this observation still has to assess what Tocqueville's notion of the 'tyranny of the majority' meant in Mill's political thought. In the mean time we might provisionally agree with Kahan who wrote in his first book that Tocqueville did not 'drastically' alter Mill's ideas. 'His work acted to accelerate the pace of Mill's own independent intellectual development' (Kahan 1992: 6). That development, one might add, largely took place in relation to the work of Comte rather than to Tocqueville.

Pappé has made several important observations concerning this issue of Tocqueville's influence on Mill. First, he notes that Bain 'did not attribute any material importance to the influence which Alexis de Tocqueville might have exerted upon Mill' (Pappé 1964: 217). As we have seen elsewhere, due to the closeness of his relationship with Mill, Bain's observations were usually insightful and accurate. Second, Pappé calls attention to an important development within Mill's thought. Between 1835 and 1840, when Mill was writing on Tocqueville's *Democracy in America*, Tocqueville 'was consistently allocated a prominent place within a pre-existing school of thought' (Pappé 1964: 219). Thus, not only was Tocqueville often cited and quoted, but he was clearly recognized as an important writer in a distinct intellectual tradition which Mill shared. Nevertheless, if one examines Mill's two great works, the *Logic* and the *Principles*, written in the 1840s, in which he referred to numerous thinkers, Tocqueville is not mentioned at all in approximately two thousand pages. In addition, one might add that his name is not mentioned in the lengthy correspondence between Comte and Mill as a thinker or a source of Mill's ideas. But Pappé also points out that, with a few minor exceptions, Tocqueville's name does not appear for two decades after Mill's second review of *Democracy in America* in 1840, even though both reviews were highly favourable.

Pappé is also insightful in calling attention to the tendency in Mill 'to punish by silence or turn his back on those who had disappointed him' (Pappé 1964: 221). I have noted in my research a number of examples that might serve as illustrations of this tendency (see e.g. Rosen 2010: 67–83). Mill's 'silence' regarding Tocqueville followed Mill's belief, expressed in a letter of 9 August 1842, that Tocqueville had accepted a corrupting and potentially violent nationalism prevalent among the French people, and had rejected France's peaceful and civilizing role in the world (Pappé 1964: 223–4; see also Varouxakis 2002b: 141–6; Brogan 2006: 387–8). Mill could not accept this move for France and would not adopt a similar role for England. Although Mill began to cite Tocqueville again in the late 1850s, by that time his indebtedness was not clearly stated and developed. Besides the evolution of Mill's ideas during this period there is, of course, also the question of the evolution of Tocqueville's own ideas, between the publication of the two volumes of *Democracy in America*, not to speak of Tocqueville's changing views on French nationalism and on other issues.[2]

Let us turn now to examine several other issues concerning Tocqueville on which Mill commented in his own work. The evolution of Mill's critique of democracy depended in part on his response to Tocqueville's account of American democracy in 1835 and 1840 (see *CW* xviii. 47–90, 153–204). One idea he seemed to take from Tocqueville was the inevitability of democracy rapidly spreading to European states. There would be no choice of constitutions, such as between aristocracy and democracy, but, nonetheless, there would be a choice within democracy between a free society and despotism (see *CW* xviii. 56–7; see also *CW* xviii. 158).[3] Furthermore, while the security for 'a rational democracy' was accepted by Mill, Tocqueville, and other earlier writers on this subject, as consisting of the power of the people not to govern but to remove their governors (*CW* xviii. 71; see also *CW* xviii. 15–46), this alone, for Mill and Tocqueville, would not prevent a democracy from becoming tyrannical. Tocqueville emphasized great dangers arising from a new kind of tyranny, the kind exercised over opinions. According to Mill:

M. de Tocqueville's fears, however, are not so much for the security and the ordinary worldly interests of individuals, as for the moral dignity and progressiveness of the race. It is a tyranny exercised over opinions, more than over persons, which he is apprehensive of. He dreads lest all individuality of character, and independence of thought and sentiment, should be prostrated under the despotic yoke of public opinion.   (*CW* xviii. 81; see also *CW* xviii. 175)

Mill's interest in this problem existed throughout his life though his proposed solutions took different forms at different times, from the idea of a 'clerisy' and other kinds of elites to oppose ignorance and mediocrity, to the cultivation of character, including national character, generally in society. As we have seen, he also minimized somewhat the centrality of security, from its exalted position in Bentham's thought as the basis of liberty.

Just as important as these doctrines, which feature in Mill's mature writings, was Mill's recognition of the importance of Tocqueville's study of American democracy for its contribution to method. Not only did he emphasize 'the tyranny of the majority', but he showed how such a phenomenon could be studied. As Mill wrote:

> The importance of M. de Tocqueville's speculations is not to be estimated by the opinions which he has adopted, be these true or false. The value of his work is less in the conclusions, than in the mode of arriving at them. He has applied to the greatest question in the art and science of government, those principles and methods of philosophizing to which mankind are indebted for all the advances made by modern times in the other branches of the study of nature. It is not risking too much to affirm of these volumes, that they contain the first analytical enquiry into the influences of Democracy. (CW xviii. 156)

For Mill, Tocqueville's method was that of a philosopher using induction to study a democratic society and deduction to extend our knowledge of such inductions to human beings in other societies. He depicted Tocqueville's method as a mixture of the Baconian and Newtonian approaches (see CW xviii. 157). Furthermore, Tocqueville's position encouraged Mill to explore democracy, not only as an abstract political constitution, but also as an important factor in the development of the economy and society, including national character. This is not to say that Mill took his ideas of economics from Tocqueville but that he could see democracy as embedded in the economy and society as a result of his adaptation of Tocqueville's method (see Welch 2001: 68).

Tocqueville's legacy seemed to deter Mill from following in the footsteps of the radical supporters of representative democracy. He was opposed to the tyranny of the majority and for the same reasons as Tocqueville. I shall examine Mill's critique of democracy in the next section. But Mill also sought other goals following his critique of the unsatisfactory nature of modern industrial societies. This aspect of his thought owed little to Tocqueville, and tends to confirm my thesis that Mill's journey to socialism also owed little to

Tocqueville's thought (see Kahan 2010: 103–5; see also Lively 1962: 100–1, 220–1).

II. *Liberty and Representative Democracy*

The idea of representative democracy that Mill would have inherited from the Benthamite radicals was based on the foundation of liberty. Society consisted of numerous individuals (or families) each enjoying security of person and property established and enforced by the legal system and government. This security gave members of society an enhanced freedom from interference with their interests by other members of society. Nevertheless, government might be tempted to use its power not only to establish domestic security and protect the society from invasion but also to oppress the people it was intended to secure. The representative system or representative democracy would allow these individuals to enhance their security and protect their interests by electing and removing their rulers from office. This would be achieved through practices like a widespread suffrage, secret ballot, roughly equal constituencies, and freedom of speech and assembly.

Mill believed that such a representative democracy would not necessarily enhance security, because the power placed in the hands of the majority would enable it to oppress minorities. The idea that a popular government was simply the power of the nation over itself, and therefore could not be oppressive, ignored this vital fact regarding the tendency of majorities to oppress minorities. As Mill wrote in the *Principles*:

Experience, however, proves that the depositories of power who are mere delegates of the people, that is of a majority, are quite as ready (when they think they can count on popular support) as any organs of oligarchy, to assume arbitrary power, and encroach unduly on the liberty of private life. The public collectively is abundantly ready to impose, not only its generally narrow views of its interests, but its abstract opinions, and even its tastes, as laws binding upon individuals. (*CW* iii. 939)

In this passage Mill seemed to make the important point that he was not only concerned with political majorities oppressing political minorities, but also with the majority turning on its own people and oppressing at least some of them in a way that undermined what he called the 'liberty of private life'. Furthermore, he seemed to suggest that the potential for such an encroachment on the liberty of private life tended to be stronger under a democracy than under other forms of government. This potential for tyranny by the masses in a democracy was, for Mill, one of the worst features of modern life:

And the present civilization tends so strongly to make the power of persons acting in masses the only substantial power in society, that there never was more necessity for surrounding individual independence of thought, speech, and conduct, with the most powerful defences, in order to maintain that originality of mind and individuality of character, which are the only source of any real progress, and of most of the qualities which make the human race much superior to any herd of animals. (CW iii. 939–40)

For Bentham, of course, what made human beings superior to a herd of animals was the security that enabled humans to make plans for the future, and to deny themselves immediate satisfactions in order to achieve greater (and more civilized) satisfactions in the future. Democracy was part of the process that would guarantee these future pleasures through the enhanced security achieved by the power to remove corrupt or tyrannical rulers from office. Yet, as we have seen, Mill rejected this approach in favour of a different notion of freedom based on active character. And in rejecting Bentham's view, he also rejected in part his defence of representative democracy.

It is tempting to argue that Mill's critique of democracy was mainly a response to changing conditions, or to new ideas. Perhaps, following Tocqueville's account of American democracy, he could see dangers in democracy that an earlier generation could not have seen. In part, this must be true, though it is equally true to say that Mill's opposition to democracy was founded on a different account of liberty based on active character in a progressive society. Mill might be seen as the champion of an 'originality of mind' and an 'individuality of character' that, contrary to Bentham, was 'the only source of real progress' and the qualities that separated humans from a herd of animals. Bentham was more willing to accept people as they were, as largely, though not wholly, self-regarding beings and whose complex bundles of interests were to be protected by civil society. He believed that the rule of law and bills of rights could be translated into institutions that did not deny liberty. For Mill, this approach would not necessarily secure a progressive society or the progressive elements in any society, or provide the freedom that individuality of character required. Thus, Mill may well have not seen anything different in democracy than Bentham saw, but given his idea of liberty, he

rejected it as a solution to the problem of securing individual freedom within the state. Mill's idea of freedom stressed the encouragement of active character within the state, based on laissez-faire,
rather than traditional ideas of civil liberty directed at securing
interests.

Mill's critique saw representative democracy as much a part of the
problem of oppression in society as part of any solution to it. In a
memorable passage he wrote:

A democratic constitution, not supported by democratic institutions in detail,
but confined to the central government, not only is not political freedom, but
often creates a spirit precisely the reverse, carrying down to the lowest grade in
society the desire and ambition of political domination. In some countries the
desire of the people is for not being tyrannized over, but in others it is merely for
an equal chance to everybody of tyrannizing. Unhappily this last state of the
desires is fully as natural to mankind as the former, and in many of the conditions
even of civilized humanity, is far more largely exemplified. In proportion as the
people are accustomed to manage their affairs by their own active intervention,
instead of leaving them to the government, their desires will turn to repelling
tyranny, rather than to tyrannizing: while in proportion as all real initiative and
direction resides in the government, and individuals habitually feel and act as
under its perpetual tutelage, popular institutions develope in them not the desire
of freedom, but an increased appetite for place and power; diverting the intelligence and activity of the country from its principal business, to a wretched
competition for the selfish prizes and petty vanities of office. (*CW* iii. 944)

What will direct individuals away from bullying, tyrannizing, and 'a
wretched competition for the selfish prizes and petty vanities of office'
is not representative democracy or civil liberty, but active character,
which somehow can be translated into a different sort of society. At
the heart of this society was the 'growth of the principle and practice of
co-operation' (*CW* iii. 708). One commentator has written: 'Far from
abandoning the principle of democracy, viewed in terms of his conception of political theory, John Stuart Mill, I argue, deserves—along
with Tocqueville—to be recognized as the theorist of democratic
society.' He then proceeds to link socialism (viewed as an economic
concept by Mill) with democracy so that 'socialism is the *economic*
form of democracy' (Ashcraft 1998: 175, 176). But Mill did not simply
follow Tocqueville. His position followed his encounter with Comte
and the development of social liberty. Mill remained a critic of representative democracy, and his attitude towards socialism had a different foundation (see also Ashcraft 1989: 105–26). Co-operation and, to a
certain extent, socialism was thus the political manifestation of social

liberty in the same sense as representative democracy was, for the Benthamites, the political manifestation of civil liberty. To see how one might arrive at co-operation and co-operative institutions from a starting point in liberty, we shall return to Mill's conception of active character which is the foundation of his theory.

III. *Active Character*

At one point in the *Principles* where Mill was discussing laissez-faire, he considered objections to this doctrine on the grounds that government intervention in numerous spheres of life was necessary for progress. He then distinguished between 'book and school' instruction (to which we shall return) and what he called 'the business of life':

The business of life is an essential part of the practical education of a people; without which, book and school instruction, though most necessary and salutary, does not suffice to qualify them for conduct, and for the adaptation of means to ends. Instruction is only one of the desiderata of mental improvement; another, almost as indispensable, is a vigorous exercise of the active energies; labour, contrivance, judgment, self-control: and the natural stimulus to these is the difficulties of life.   (*CW* iii. 943; see also Hansen 2005)

Mill was anxious to point out that he was not saying that the difficulties of life constituted some sort of good in itself. But he was arguing that the inevitable difficulties of life could bring forth the exercise of energy and active character towards a variety of ends. Where a people habitually looked to their government to solve problems of joint concern rather than solve them for themselves, the faculties of ordinary people became only half developed. Furthermore, if knowledge and practical skill were retained within a ruling class and were not diffused throughout society, the system approached a despotism.

We come now to Mill's conception of 'the only security against political slavery' (*CW* iii. 943–4). He did not look to representative democracy or any other constitution as a remedy, but to the condition of ordinary people. In an important passage he wrote:

Experience proves the extreme difficulty of permanently keeping up a sufficiently high standard of those qualities [intelligence, activity, and public spirit]; a difficulty which increases, as the advance of civilization and security removes one after another of the hardships, embarrassments, and dangers against which individuals had formerly no resource but in their own strength, skill, and courage. It is therefore of supreme importance that all classes of the community, down to the lowest, should have much to do for themselves....

The role of government in this grand enterprise was:

not only [to] leave as far as possible to their own faculties the conduct of whatever concerns themselves alone, but should suffer them, or rather encourage them, to manage as many as possible of their joint concerns by voluntary co-operation; since this discussion and management of collective interests is the great school of that public spirit, and the great source of that intelligence of public affairs, which are always regarded as the distinctive character of the public of free countries. (*CW* iii. 944)

It is tempting to think of Mill's remedy for political slavery as an exercise of a Rousseauian conception of the general will. But Mill was not advancing either this or, more generally, a conception of civic virtue. His fundamental belief was in the cultivation of active character outside the state, even against the state. Its foundations were in laissez-faire and not any kind of democracy or popular government, unless, as in ancient Periclean Athens, the public realm served to stimulate active character in private life (see Rosen 2004: 181–94).

Mill's emphasis on laissez-faire, i.e. 'restricting to the narrowest compass the intervention of a public authority in the business of the community', led him to assert as a guiding principle that laissez-faire 'should be the general practice: every departure from it, unless required by some great good, is a certain evil' (*CW* iii. 944–5). But, as we have seen in Chapter 7, laissez-faire was not the same as the minimal state, as a good deal of government intervention was allowable as *voluntary* intervention under the principle of laissez-faire.

As a general rule Mill believed that those people who actually worked on various projects were better judges of them than government and its officials. Hence, not only did laissez-faire generally support the development of active character, but it also recognized the superior competence of those who actually worked on and developed these projects. Nevertheless, Mill did not believe that consumers of goods and services possessed a similar competence to judge the quality of the goods and services they received. Where such judgements were important, the decisions could not be left to the market alone and might well require government intervention. Furthermore, how can those matters that concern the improvement of human character be judged by those whose judgement was to be improved? 'The uncultivated', Mill wrote, 'cannot be competent judges of cultivation. Those who most need to be made wiser and better, usually desire it least, and if they desired it, would be incapable of finding the way to it by their own lights' (CW iii. 947).

Unlike some believers in laissez-faire (Mill cited Charles Dunoyer as an example of one holding the opposite view: see CW iii. 948n.), Mill believed that education might in principle be provided by government for the people. As we have seen in Chapter 7, education could be based in part on a voluntary principle and be placed in the camp of laissez-faire, in so far as pupils, for example, might not be compelled to attend any particular school. Furthermore, in a curious addition Mill believed that state provision could well extend to the provision of additional education for the few gifted children on the principle of the importance of 'keeping up the perpetual succession of superior minds, by whom knowledge is advanced, and the community urged forward in civilization' (CW iii. 948n.).

We have seen how Mill stressed 'the business of life' apart from formal education as an important resource for the development of active character. Mill also extended this emphasis on the cultivation of active character to education itself. Instruction could enlarge the faculties that underpinned active character, and act favourably on the 'spirit of independence' (CW iii. 949). The state provision of education provided 'help towards doing without help' (CW iii. 949). In this spirit Mill developed a number of arguments, such as questioning the capacity of private charity to provide education, particularly at the elementary level, and recommending that government did so, either at no expense to the children or for a tiny payment. Nevertheless, government should not practise authoritative intervention in any institution of education. Mill called such intervention 'despotic' (CW iii. 950). He attempted to depict the non-authoritative role of government in education as follows:

Though a government, therefore, may, and in many cases ought to, establish schools and colleges, it must neither compel nor bribe any person to come to them; nor ought the power of individuals to set up rival establishments, to depend in any degree upon its authorization. It would be justified in requiring from all the people that they shall possess instruction in certain things, but not in prescribing to them how or from whom they shall obtain it.   (CW iii. 950; see also xviii. 301–4)

The kinds of arguments Mill developed with regard to education as an exception to the strict application of laissez-faire were then extended to the treatment of lunatics, idiots, infants, or lower animals, that is to say, where they were unable to take an intelligent view of their own interests (*CW* iii. 951). Mill reminded his readers, however, that because women, unlike children, could be judges of their own interests, they should be free from government control (for example, from government control over hours of labour). Furthermore, as in *On Liberty* (see *CW* xviii. 299–300), Mill also rejected any legal enforcement of a contract in perpetuity, holding that freedom of contract should apply in these cases (*CW* iii. 953).

Without following Mill's arguments concerning the limits of laissez-faire in detail, and his further uses of the distinction between voluntary and involuntary intervention, it is clear that, despite his belief in laissez-faire, Mill could envisage on the one hand a wide range of intervention by government:

In the particular circumstances of a given age or nation, there is scarcely anything really important to the general interest, which it may not be desirable, or even necessary, that the government should take upon itself, not because private individuals cannot effectually perform it, but because they will not. At some times and places, there will be no roads, docks, harbours, canals, works of irrigation, hospitals, schools, colleges, printing-presses, unless the government establishes them; the public being either too poor to command the necessary resources, or too little advanced in intelligence to appreciate the ends, or not sufficiently practised in joint action to be capable of the means. This is true, more or less, of all countries inured to despotism, and particularly of those in which there is a very wide distance in civilization between the people and the government: as in those which have been conquered and are retained in subjection by a more energetic and more cultivated people. (*CW* iii. 970)

Nevertheless, even in the context of what might be considered a necessary despotic rule, where few aspects of life were the province of active character, Mill added a note of caution concerning the limits of government intervention:

A good government will give all its aid in such a shape, as to encourage and nurture any rudiments it may find of a spirit of individual exertion. It will be assiduous in removing obstacles and discouragements to voluntary enterprise, and in giving whatever facilities and whatever direction and guidance may be necessary. (*CW* iii. 970–1)

Where there was no private enterprise, aid might be given in a way to serve as 'a course of education for the people in the art of accomplishing great objects by individual energy and voluntary co-operation' (*CW* iii. 971).

For Mill, there were numerous ways in which active character could be enhanced or diminished by government and, particularly, by the legal system. In writing on this theme, here as well as else-where, he was aware of the close connections between law, society, economy, and morality. For example, at one point in the *Principles* he stressed the importance of 'probity and fidelity' with regard to promises and contracts on which the economy and society depended not only for material prosperity but also for the encouragement of 'integrity and trustworthiness' in society as moral virtues with a bearing on character (*CW* iii. 886). Unfortunately, and particularly in England, the law was widely used to resist such probity and fidelity either by the employment of unjust litigation or by the use of one's wealth within the legal system to resist just claims. Mill's concern with morality in this context was also a concern for the develop-ment of character in a progressive society. As he continued:

> If again, the law, by a misplaced indulgence, protects idleness or prodigality against their natural consequences, or dismisses crime with inadequate pen-alties, the effect, both on the prudential and on the social virtues, is unfavour-able. When the law, by its own dispensations and injunctions, establishes injustice between individual and individual; as all laws do which recognise any form of slavery, as the laws of all countries do, though not all in the same degree, in respect to the family relations; and as the laws of many countries do, though in still more unequal degrees, as between rich and poor; the effect on the moral sentiments of the people is still more disastrous.
> (*CW* iii. 886)

When Mill referred here to 'the moral sentiments of the people', he was not only invoking earlier philosophers, like Adam Smith, but he was also referring to the character of the people and how that char-acter might be improved in society by changes in the law. In another example he examined recent changes in insolvency laws which, in his view, had a strong and direct influence on the development of character in society (*CW* iii. 910).

Of greatest importance to Mill's conception of the development of character was the condition of the working classes. In this area Mill invoked laissez-faire and opposed restrictions on voluntary combin-ations of workers and on strikes, so long as compulsion was not used to force workers to join a union or to take part in a strike. While Mill deplored the tendency in unions not to allow distinctions between 'the energetic and the idle, the skilful and the incompetent', he nonetheless strongly opposed the use of law and punishment to prohibit trade unions (*CW* iii. 934). At stake at this time was the prospect of 'the elevation of the character and condition of the entire body' of the working class, which had 'at last become a thing not beyond the reach of rational effort' (*CW* iii. 931). Thus, in focusing on the working classes in society, Mill was expressing a belief that with freedom (laissez-faire), the character of these classes could be transformed, and society as a whole could see advantageous developments of character.

iv. *Co-operation*

If from liberty (as laissez-faire), Mill saw the development of active character, then from active character he saw the development of co-operation.[4] What did Mill mean by co-operation? When asked by George Jacob Holyoake, the historian of the co-operative movement, to suggest a definition, Mill was quoted as saying:

'It is not co-operation,' he said, 'where a few persons join for the purpose of making a profit by which only a portion of them benefit. Co-operation is where the whole of the produce is divided. What is wanted is that the whole working class should partake of the *profits of labour.* (Holyoake 1906: i. 306)[5]

Why, one might ask, did he hold co-operation in such high esteem? First, liberty, for Mill, meant primarily social liberty, and the social dimension to liberty was voluntary co-operation in social projects. Second, he did not believe that individuality and co-operation need be at odds under the umbrella of liberty. Third, he felt that the time was ripe in advanced civilizations for the rapid and rational improvement of all members of society and this might only be achieved by the implementation of the co-operative principle. Finally, the growth of co-operation, both with regard to its principles and its increased practice in society, in turn reflected the progressive changes taking place in society.

These reasons might suggest the importance of co-operation in Mill's thought, but would not capture either the urgent need to solve problems facing growing industrial societies or the remedies he proposed for the problems. Mill's belief in co-operation was not meant to be 'utopian' but practical, and he saw in legal restrictions an important barrier to progress. As for urgency, he wrote:

I must repeat my conviction, that the industrial economy which divides society absolutely into two portions, the payers of wages and the receivers of them, the first counted by thousands and the last by millions, is neither fit for, nor capable of indefinite duration: and the possibility of changing this system for one of combination without dependence, and unity of interest instead of organized hostility, depends altogether upon the future developments of the Partnership principle. (*CW* iii. 896)

As for practicality, Mill sought to bring combination among work-men under the umbrella of laissez-faire. Such combinations would be seen as private contracts best left to develop without government interference, just as other private companies were mainly left to develop without state interference. This invocation of liberty as laissez-faire would address the need to develop active character in the working classes in much the same way as Mill envisaged the 'business of life' working to develop such character. In a lengthy though important passage, Mill wrote:

It is, above all, with reference to the improvement and elevation of the working classes that complete freedom of the conditions of partnership is indispens-able. Combinations such as the associations of workpeople... are the most powerful means of effecting the social emancipation of the labourers through their own moral qualities. Nor is the liberty of association important solely for its examples of success, but fully as much so for the sake of attempts which would not succeed; but by their failure would give instruction more impressive than can be afforded by anything short of actual experience. Every theory of social improvement, the worth of which is capable of being brought to an experimental test, should be permitted, and even encouraged, to submit itself to that test. From such experiments the active portion of the working classes would derive lessons, which they would be slow to learn from the teaching of persons supposed to have interests and prejudices adverse to their good; would obtain the means of correcting, at no cost to society, whatever is now erroneous in their notions of the means of establishing their independence; and of dis-covering the conditions, moral, intellectual, and industrial, which are indis-pensably necessary for effecting without injustice, or for effecting at all, the social regeneration they aspire to. (*CW* iii. 903–4)

For co-operatively based working-class societies, Mill referred to such institutions as friendly societies and the co-operative move-ment, in particular, to the Rochdale Pioneers (*CW* iii. 904n.; see also Holyoake 1893). But he was also willing to accept trade unions and even the apparently destructive character of strikes (see *CW* iii. 932–3; see also Fawcett 1860). He regarded these as essential elem-ents in free markets. I shall examine these ideas further in later chapters, focused more directly on the working classes and social-ism, but at this point it is important to recognize that Mill knitted together his own view of social liberty with active character and co-operation, especially in relation to the working classes.

A final area where Mill invoked laissez-faire against government interference was in the sphere of freedom of opinion and publication. I mention it here partly because of the role it played later in *On Liberty*, and partly to show its connection with Mill's idea of social liberty. Laissez-faire enabled Mill to insist that without freedom of opinion and publication, unrestrained by law or public opinion, active character could not develop. A regime that insisted on giving approval to all opinions in politics, morals, law, and religion would be fatal to economic prosperity and create in society a 'general torpidity and imbecility' which would prevent progress even in the 'common affairs of life' and lead to a loss of previous gains (*CW* iii. 935). As examples he referred to conditions in Spain and Portugal for two hundred years after the Reformation. He also referred to conditions in England with regard to violations (including imprisonment) of the freedom of expressing unorthodox views on religion and the possibility of such penalties being inflicted on those who were considered to be advocates of 'Chartism or Communism'. But he granted that most restraints on 'mental freedom' came less from law or government and more from what he called 'the intolerant temper of the national mind', based not on bigotry or fanaticism but on habits of thought and action that in turn followed from a rigid adherence to custom, and enforced by social penalties (*CW* iii. 935). Laissez-faire, it seems, would be the starting point for developing freedom of opinion, and then active character would challenge the habits and customs that had developed to oppose it.

9

From Co-operation to Socialism

---

1. *The Journey to Socialism*

In the *Principles* Mill made the following point regarding co-operative societies:

Eventually, and in perhaps a less remote future than may be supposed, we may, through the co-operative principle, see our way to a change in society, which would combine the freedom and independence of the individual, with the moral, intellectual, and economical advantages of aggregate production; and which, without violence or spoliation, or even any sudden disturbance of existing habits and expectations, would realize, at least in the industrial department, the best aspirations of the democratic spirit, by putting an end to the division of society into the industrious and idle, and effacing all social distinctions but those fairly earned by personal services and exertions.

(*CW* iii. 793)

Later, in the *Autobiography* he wrote:

The notion that it was possible to go further than this in removing the injustice— for injustice it is whether admitting of a complete remedy or not—involved in the fact that some are born to riches and the vast majority to poverty, I then reckoned chimerical; and only hoped that by universal education, leading to voluntary restraint on population, the portion of the poor might be made more tolerable. In short, I was a democrat, but not the least of a Socialist. We were now much less democrats than I had been, because so long as education continues to be so wretchedly imperfect, we dreaded the ignorance and especially the selfishness and brutality of the mass: but our ideal of ultimate improvement went far beyond Democracy, and would class us decidedly under the general designation of Socialists. (*CW* i. 239).[1]

In these two passages we can see Mill attempting to declare and support a major change in political and economic orientation. In the first he raised the banner of co-operation as the way forward to a new kind of democracy based on overcoming class and other social divisions.[2] In the second he maintained that he had abandoned the traditional view of representative democracy and, together with Harriet Mill, looked to socialism as a way of remedying the problems of class conflict and its relationship to private property. The link between co-operation and socialism was crucial to the development of his thought, and my object in this and the next chapter is to explore this link. In this chapter I shall concentrate on Mill's essays in the *Principles*, 'Of the Stationary State' (*CW* iii. 752–7) and 'Of the Probable Futurity of the Labouring Classes' (*CW* iii. 758–96) to establish the context for his discussions of socialism. We shall then examine in the next chapter the accounts of the varieties of socialism both in the *Principles* and in the 'Chapters on Socialism'.

II. *The Stationary State*

Mill considered the 'stationary state' in the context of his earlier distinction between economic statics and dynamics.[3] The stationary state belonged to the realm of dynamics, where Mill was led to challenge the views of earlier economists who saw the end of economic development in terms of 'the extinction of prosperity' and a 'pinched and stinted' condition for the masses (*CW* iii. 752–3). Mill used the metaphor of the stationary state to refer not to an end but, paradoxically, to a beginning. It could in fact represent a starting point for major improvement in existing conditions. He was not attracted to the 'ideal of life' which held that 'the normal state of human beings' was one of 'trampling, crushing, elbowing, and treading on each other's heels' (*CW* iii. 754). Although he could appreciate that competition for power might be necessary in 'the progress of civilization', he thought that 'the best state for human nature' was one in which 'while no one is poor, no one desires to be richer, nor has any reason to fear being thrust back, by the efforts of others to push themselves forward' (*CW* iii. 754).

Mill would leave 'backward countries' to concentrate on increasing production, while in advanced countries a better distribution, assisted by restraints on population growth and limitations on inheritance, was necessary. He looked forward to a condition of society with a well-paid and fairly prosperous labouring class, no enormous fortunes in society beyond what might be 'earned and accumulated' in a single lifetime, and a larger group of people free of 'coarser toils', and able 'to cultivate freely the graces of life' (CW iii. 755). This larger (and expanding group) would provide examples of this cultivation for those who were not, or not yet, in similar circumstances.

The stationary state of capital in the economy should thus not imply a stationary condition of human improvement. On the contrary, there would be greater scope 'for all kinds of mental culture and moral and social progress; as much room for improving the Art of Living, and much more likelihood of its being improved, when minds ceased to be engrossed by the art of getting on' (CW iii. 756). Mill asked if most mechanical inventions had actually lightened anyone's daily toil. The population had been able to increase, though most of this increase had been forced to spend their lives in what Mill called 'drudgery and imprisonment'. Manufacturers and others had become rich and the middle classes could lead more comfortable lives. But there had been little change in the state of the labouring classes for whom the stationary state would allow them 'to effect those great changes in human destiny' (CW iii. 756–7).

Mill's conception of the stationary state was conceived as an economic concept involving a stable amount of capital in an advanced society.[4] It represented a shift in emphasis from the production of goods and the accumulation of wealth to its distribution in society, where it could be used to free men and women from toil and drudgery. In one sense it followed directly from his earlier treatment of economic dynamics where he emphasized the increasing power over nature acquired by mankind, increases in the efficiency of human exertion, and a diminution of the costs of production. All of this was related to the development of free trade, where commodities could be produced throughout the world using cheaper labour. 'As civilization spreads,' he wrote, 'and security of person and property becomes established, in parts of the world which have not hitherto had that advantage, the productive capabilities of those places are called into fuller activity, for the benefit of their own inhabitants and of foreigners' (CW iii. 711).

Mill used the idea of the stationary state to take economic dynamics to a new level. He wrote at one point that his object in the chapter was 'to deprecate a false ideal of human society' (*CW* iii. 758). Once a certain level of economic development had been achieved, he thought that we need not concentrate exclusively on a highly competitive and ever-growing economy. For Mill, not only were other economists wrong in seeing no alternatives to such a society committed only to economic development, but they were also wrong in seeing the end of such a society, if and when it came, as a sorry state of affairs. On the contrary it presented numerous opportunities for individual human development, but, just as important, opportunities for the improvement of society as a whole. In this latter respect the development of a socialism based on co-operative principles became particularly important.

If one were looking at the stationary state as some sort of utopian blueprint to be realized in the future, it would be easy to criticize Mill's vision. He failed to take into account the possibility of major wars in the future between and within civilized countries, and the military establishments and the massive defence industries necessary to support them. He also failed to appreciate ongoing and intensifying religious conflicts and other forms of social and ethnic division. He seemed at times unaware of the negative side of free trade and globalization. He continually lamented the inadequacy of education to transform lives, while, at the same time, clinging to it as the most important force for social change. But the stationary state was not a blueprint for action. It simply raised the possibility that we need not continue to live in the manner in which we were currently living, and, particularly, new developments might emerge from the working classes themselves to bring about this or a similar transformation. The discussion of the stationary state thus led directly into his longer essay bearing the unusual title, 'Of the Probable Futurity of the Labouring Classes'.

III. *Two Theories Regarding the Working Classes*

As in many of his essays, Mill began his discussion with two contrary theories from which he seemed to extract a third one.[5] In this case, the theories were concerned with the future state of the manual labourer in Britain. The first was depicted as the theory of dependence and security in which the rich were to look after, educate, and give morality and religion to the poor. He depicted this relationship as follows:

The rich should be *in loco parentis* to the poor, guiding and restraining them like children. Of spontaneous action on their part there should be no need. They should be called on for nothing but to do their day's work and to be moral and religious. Their morality and religion should be provided for them by their superiors, who should see them properly taught it, and should do all that is necessary to ensure their being, in return for labour and attachment, properly fed, clothed, housed, spiritually edified, and innocently amused.   (*CW* iii. 759)

Mill realized that the rich had never in the past played this role nor were they likely to do so in the future. Nevertheless, he regarded this theory as an 'ideal of the future' held by those 'whose dissatisfaction with the present assumes the form of affection and regret towards the past' (*CW* iii. 759). The belief itself exercised an 'unconscious influence on the opinions and sentiments of numbers who never consciously guide themselves by any ideal' (*CW* iii. 759–60). In this sense, this first theory exercised and would continue to exercise a considerable influence over members of society. As a practical proposal, however, Mill thought it useless. By the time the superior classes were improved sufficiently to govern the inferior classes, the latter would be too improved to accept being governed by them.

Despite the inadequacy of the theory in relation to current society and, indeed, to past practice, Mill attempted to account for its 'seductive' influence. In a curious passage he wrote:

Though the facts of it have no prototype in the past, the feelings have. In them lies all that there is of reality in the conception. As the idea is essentially repulsive of a society only held together by the relations and feelings arising out of pecuniary interests, so there is something naturally attractive in a form of society abounding in strong personal attachments and disinterested self-devotion. Of such feelings it must be admitted that the relation of protector and protected has hitherto been the richest source.   (*CW* iii. 760; see also a similar discussion in Chapter 13 below)

Mill then continued to elaborate his thesis by showing that the feelings surrounding the relationship between protectors and protected were among the most fundamental in society:

Hence, in an age of lawless violence and insecurity, and general hardness and roughness of manners, in which life is beset with dangers and sufferings at every step, to those who have neither a commanding position of their own, nor a claim on the protection of some one who has—a generous giving of protection, and a grateful receiving of it, are the strongest ties which connect human beings; the feelings arising from that relation are their warmest feelings; all the enthusiasm and tenderness of the most sensitive natures gather round it; loyalty on the one part and chivalry on the other are principles exalted into passions. (*CW* iii. 760)

Mill then argued that the feelings just enumerated had a 'beautiful and endearing character', and he would not want to deprecate or diminish them (*CW* iii. 761). The theory, however, belonged to a bygone age, and was no longer relevant to contemporary life. One might have thought that Mill would turn to other ideals or models of care and protection, for example, that of mother and child, parents and children, or even the good shepherd. It is arguable that these were still relevant to contemporary society and could motivate and inspire those who were in suitable positions to care for and improve those who were weaker or less fortunate than themselves. The age of chivalry might have passed but there were abiding concerns, for example, of parents caring for and protecting children that were based on feelings that were widely felt in society.

Mill emphatically rejected this approach. In civilized societies he felt that people no longer required this protection and hence need not feel gratitude and affection for it. The law provided the protection that a system of chivalry and loyalty might perhaps have provided in an earlier age. But he also had a more important point to make. In contemporary society under the rule of law, the individual did not need protection from others, but only protection from his or her protectors. In a dramatic passage, he wrote:

The so-called protectors are now the only persons against whom, in any ordinary circumstances, protection is needed. The brutality and tyranny, with which every police report is filled, are those of husbands to wives, of parents to children. That the law does not prevent these atrocities, that it is only now making a first timid attempt to repress and punish them, is no matter of necessity, but the deep disgrace of those by whom the laws are made and administered. No man or woman, who either possesses or is able to earn an independent livelihood, requires any other protection than that which the law could and ought to give. (*CW* iii. 761; see also Chapter 13 below)

Not only did Mill reject the theory as belonging to a past age, but he also tried to show in this dramatic fashion that, as for the working classes, the search for protectors and educators was the wrong way forward. If so, let us consider the second contrary which was based not on the search for protectors but on the working classes taking matters into their own hands and showing that their interests were often opposed to those of their employers. The process that began with the Reformation, with ordinary people obtaining the skills of reading and writing (see also *CW* xviii. 50), had ensured that the working classes would not accept the prescription of religion and morality from others. As Mill put it:

The poor have come out of leading-strings, and cannot any longer be governed or treated like children. To their own qualities must now be commended the care of their destiny. Modern nations will have to learn the lesson, that the well-being of a people must exist by means of the justice and self-government, the *dikaiosúne* and *sophrosúne*, of the individual citizens.

Mill then continued by observing:

Whatever advice, exhortation, or guidance is held out to the labouring classes, must henceforth be tendered to them as equals, and accepted by them with their eyes open. The prospect of the future depends on the degree in which they can be made rational beings. (*CW* iii. 763)

As Mill developed these ideas, he seemed to align himself clearly with the theory of self-dependence. He called attention to a pattern of self-education (as opposed to school education) that had been spreading among the labouring classes, where many could read newspapers and other publications. For example, he praised the Lancashire spinners and weavers, who with intelligent insight, based on their reading newspapers and obtaining other sources of information, did not blame employers or the government during a recent crisis in cotton manufacturing. 'The institutions for lectures and discussion,' he wrote, 'the collective deliberations on questions of common interest, the trades unions, the political agitation, all serve to awaken public spirit, to diffuse variety of ideas among the mass, and to excite thought and reflection in the more intelligent' (*CW* iii. 763–4). This pattern of self-education, based on self-dependence, could and would be reflected in other aspects of economic, political, and social life. Ultimately, the theory of self-dependence raised the important issue of the forms of economic association appropriate for such a theory. One form, that of the dependence of workers on masters, with opposite interests and little motivation to remedy their mutual distrust and antagonism, was clearly rejected as not being part of the way forward, particularly, as it had a bad effect on both the employers and workers.

If Mill clearly rejected the theory of dependence in its current form, what was the point of making such a theory one of the two contrary theories at the outset? Usually, when Mill posed such contrary theories, he found merit in aspects of both contraries (though usually greater merit in the more progressive one) and formed a synthesis of the two in his resolution of the issue. At first glance, Mill had wholly rejected the theory of dependence as belonging to a bygone age and irrelevant to the present time. Nevertheless, it would be a mistake to reach this conclusion. If he rejected dependence, he did not reject deference, as in the following passage:

It is quite consistent with this, that they should feel respect for superiority of intellect and knowledge, and defer much to the opinions, on any subject, of those whom they think well acquainted with it. Such deference is deeply grounded in human nature; but they will judge for themselves of the persons who are and are not entitled to it. (CW iii. 764–5)

Furthermore, Mill thought that self-dependence would not preclude the use of the legislature and other institutions of the state to accede to their demands and enforce them through legislation. Self-dependence was not intended to be a theory of anarchism. Thus, in both deference to knowledge and superior skill and in the use of hierarchies associated with law and government, Mill seemed to retain elements of the theory of dependence.

There was a further use of the theory. Mill was attracted to the assumption, implicit in the chivalrous ideas of protecting and being protected, that relations between rich and poor or capitalists and workers need not necessarily turn on self-interest and pecuniary benefit alone. The theory of self-dependence meant initially a shift in power to the working classes and liberation from dependence on capitalists and other wealthy members of society. But in order for the theory to succeed, it was necessary to move beyond power and self-interest and introduce other values into the theory. These values (concerned with association and co-operation) need not be the same as those associated with chivalry, but the theory of dependence showed that one could realistically envisage an ideal economy where values beyond narrow economic ones could flourish in daily life, even though (as with chivalry) they had not existed in recent history.

This point takes us to the most important element Mill took from the first contrary, i.e. the theory of dependence. If one considers the title of the chapter, 'On the Probable Futurity of the Labouring Classes', undoubtedly carefully chosen, one's attention is drawn to the phrase 'probable futurity'. Whatever this phrase was intended to mean, it should be clear that Mill's 'futurity' was not intended to be 'utopian', that is to say, located 'nowhere', except to serve as a critique of existing society. Mill's theory of association was intended to be realized in the future. Furthermore, it was not meant to be one of several theories that might be realized in the future, but was considered by Mill to be *probable*. There was a scientific basis in this attempt to predict the future, even though, like the theory of chivalry, the movement away from the mutually destructive and exploitive relationship between rich and poor in an entire modern society had never taken place in the past. When Mill, for example, wrote that 'it will sooner or later become insupportable to the employing classes to live in close and hourly contact with persons whose interests and feelings are in hostility to them' (*CW* iii. 767), he was not making a vague reference to the future. He was making a definite prediction that was qualified only by the fact that he was unable to be definite concerning the time span involved. The theory of dependence allowed him to believe that people in fact would act on the basis of such a theory. In Mill's day, there were numerous people who believed deeply and acted on the theory that one of their main tasks in life was to look after the poor and provide food, clothing, shelter, and moral and religious support for them. As we have seen, it was in Mill's view an 'ideal of the future' in which people retained the feelings that in turn worked unconsciously to direct action. It is fair to say that Mill sought a similar basis for his theory of association, though clearly one with a very different content.

IV. *Co-operative Associations*

Until the present age Mill noted that the worker had but two alternatives: either he worked for a master or he worked for himself. Now, however, it was no longer necessary to choose between these two alternatives. Large-scale production and successful experiments with workers' associations meant that workers and capitalists need not occupy two hostile camps with the former to earn their living with as little effort as possible and the latter simply supplying funds and taking profits. Mill, however, looked to the 'probable futurity' in which new possibilities had opened up, as when he wrote:

The form of association, however, which if mankind continue to improve, must be expected in the end to predominate, is not that which can exist between a capitalist as chief, and workpeople without a voice in the management, but the association of the labourers themselves on terms of equality, collectively owning the capital with which they carry on their operations, and working under managers elected and removable by themselves. (*CW* iii. 775)

Here we see the theory of self-dependence in action. Mill explicitly drew on the evolution of the idea of workers' associations in the theories of Owen and Blanc and the practice following the revolution of 1848 in France, where such associations were established. But Mill was concerned with far more than the mechanics of the workers' associations themselves. He could see in them the ideas that could govern social and political life in the future. Mill suggested that the associations, which would embody active character, could also inculcate virtue and improve character. They might contribute to enhanced feelings of personal worth and dignity, and the rules of the associations would change to reflect lessons learnt and new ways of organization. For example, instead of rules governing discipline being more lax, they were stricter in the associations, but were not felt to be so, due to the fact that the rules were self-imposed and more carefully followed. Furthermore, the associations at first opposed reward based on effort (including piecework) and rewarded all workers equally. Subsequently, they abandoned this system of reward and adopted one that first gave to all a fixed amount for subsistence and then divided the remainder according to work done. These changes reflected actual experience within the associations. Mill was fairly optimistic about the development of the co-operative associations:

It is hardly possible to take any but a hopeful view of the prospects of mankind, when in two leading countries in the world, the obscure depths of society contain simple working men whose integrity, good sense, self-command, and honourable confidence in one another, have enabled them to carry these noble experiments to the triumphant issue which the facts recorded in the preceding pages attest. (*CW* iii. 791)

Mill's optimism and enthusiasm was not diminished by the fact that many associations, as they became successful, transformed themselves into joint stock companies. He noted with special regret that this had happened to the Manufacturing Society of Rochdale. He realized that this sort of change would mean that individual capitalists would gain a considerable advantage over the associations, as the latter would give up the gains to be achieved by association in terms of productivity as well as the development of character (*CW* iii. 792). Individual capitalists were also more likely to take risks and adopt innovations. Nonetheless, Mill remained hopeful regarding the future of co-operative associations, seeing in them 'the best aspirations of the democratic spirit' (CW iii. 793).

The reference to 'the best aspirations of the democratic spirit' is an important one, as it suggests that Mill's idea of co-operative association or socialism was meant to be the fullest ethical and social realization of democracy. Although he qualified himself by confining this development to what he called 'the industrial department', his account of the associations clearly and pointedly transcended economics. The success of the associations depended on their being the source of education in 'moral and active qualities'. They were also inclusive societies and capitalists were free to join them. They would give rights to women, which he referred to as 'a transformation' (assuming that women were given equal rights) that 'would be the nearest approach to social justice, and the most beneficial ordering of industrial affairs for the universal good, which it is possible at present to foresee' (CW iii. 793–4).

Mill had thus looked to a foreseeable future—a futurity—and aligned himself with co-operative associations and considered this form of socialism as the embodiment of social justice. As though to remind us that a 'probable futurity' was meant to be a dynamic concept, he also stated some reservations concerning the current form of co-operative associations. Although he developed these reservations more completely in the 'Chapters on Socialism', he emphasized here the fact that many socialists opposed competition in the associations and wrote against competition, regarding it as a source of economic evil. Mill defended the importance of competition as a means of raising wages and also lowering the costs of labour. There could be competition between associations, if not between individuals (though Mill also defended in the 'Chapters on Socialism' piecework and hence individual competition). If there was no competition, there would be monopoly which he called 'the taxation of the industrious for the support of indolence, if not plunder' (CW iii. 794). With competition between associations, at least, consumers would benefit. But socialists saw competition as a source of low wages and capitalist exploitation. In Mill's view, however, they commited a 'common error' in neglecting 'the natural indolence of mankind; their tendency to be passive, to be the slaves of habit, to persist indefinitely in a course once chosen' (CW iii. 795).[6] He feared that stagnation would replace improvement. Even though competition was not an ideal condition, he asserted that 'no one can foresee the time when it will not be indispensable to progress' (*CW* iii. 795) and will not underpin innovation. Without innovation the various associations would be left behind.

The emphasis by Mill on the importance of competition reminds us of the emphasis he placed on improvement, progress, and innovation. Such a vision need not conflict with the idea of the stationary state, which also had individual liberty and opportunity at its core. Nor need it conflict with his vision of socialism which did not aspire to absolute equality in distribution but to another conception of justice that gave rewards according to exertion. His conception of socialism did conflict with the existing system of capitalism which he thought had replaced competition with exploitation. The future health of the working classes depended on their gradually replacing this system of exploitation with one of co-operation that embodied individual liberty and competition, as well as social improvement. Mill foresaw this condition in the future.[7] But we do not yet have any sense of a timescale, or even a sense of urgency beyond the acknowledgement of the danger of continuing with a system, even one incorporating representative democracy, that was so patently destructive of the highest aspirations of mankind. These topics were tackled in the 'Chapters on Socialism'.

10

Justice and Private Property in the *Principles* and 'Chapters on Socialism'

According to Helen Taylor's 'Introductory Notice', the 'Chapters on Socialism' (1879), an incomplete and unfinished work, was written in a rough format in 1869 (*CW* v. 705). The date of composition is significant. Mill explicitly linked the work with the new Reform Act of 1867 (30 & 31 Victoria, c. 102). We shall first examine this link, which might be seen as the immediate context of the work. Mill began the essay by referring briefly to a wider context, the existence of manhood suffrage in the United States of America, its extension in France since 1848, and in some states within the German Confederation (*CW* v. 705–6). He then turned to the Reform Act of 1867 in the following terms:

> but the last Reform Act admitted within what is called the pale of the Constitution so large a body of those who live on weekly wages, that as soon and as often as these shall choose to act together as a class, and exert for any common object the whole of the electoral power which our present institutions give them, they will exercise, though not a complete ascendancy, a very great influence on legislation.   (*CW* v. 706)[1]

This new power in the constitution, Mill continued, consisted for the first time in Britain of people without an obvious interest in upholding inequalities of property. In other words, the defence of private property could not be based simply on the personal interest of those who controlled the government. The laws of property needed a further justification that took into account the general welfare. This new justification, however, had to take into consideration British national character. We learn in this introductory material that the British character tended to be sceptical, and hence mass political movements, especially those demanding sudden changes, were unlikely to occur. Nevertheless, as Mill noted, the shift of electoral power to a considerable body of the people was permanent, and the fact that little use of this power had been attempted thus far only represented a temporary delay. He seemed to sense that here was an opportunity, perhaps a unique opportunity, to consider the consequences in Britain of the passage of electoral power to the working classes, but this opportunity required a new way of approaching the subject (see Ryan 1974: 197; Robson 1968: 258–9). He dismissed out of hand the traditional approach (perhaps associated with Bentham and James Mill) of focusing on constitutions. Alternatively, he might have been tempted to write another treatise on government to supplement the *Considerations on Representative Government*. But throughout the 'Chapters on Socialism' there is no reference, directly or indirectly, to the *Considerations*. Mill seemed to be looking in a different direction. As he wrote:

The political aims will themselves be determined by definite political doctrines; for politics are now scientifically studied from the point of view of the working classes, and opinions conceived in the special interest of those classes are organized into systems and creeds which lay claim to a place on the platform of political philosophy, by the same right as the systems elaborated by previous thinkers.   (*CW* v. 707)

'Chapters on Socialism' was clearly meant to be a contribution to a scientific study of politics from the point of view of the working classes. It is surely presented from the perspective of recent writing concerning the working classes and an appreciation of different strands of socialist thought. It might be regarded as 'scientific' in Mill's terms, in so far as it takes into consideration psychology and British national character. Like Mill's *Considerations*, which was occasioned by the failure of the reform movement in parliament to pass an Act to advance parliamentary reform, 'Chapters on Socialism' was also written for a particular time and occasioned by a particular event, in this case, the passage of the Reform Act of 1867. The time factor is important. Mill could see that the British people had only a generation to avoid conflict between 'opposite prejudices'—those in favour of 'ignorant change' and those in 'ignorant opposition to change'. Looking between the old (opposition to change) and the new ('ignorant change'), Mill sought a position in which 'the best parts of both may be combined in a renovated social fabric' (*CW* v. 708).

How did Mill suggest that social science could determine the terms of that reconciliation? First, he wrote that one needed 'to go down to the very first principles of existing society' (*CW* v. 708). Second, note that he referred to the first principles of a society that actually existed and not an ideal society. Mill was not constructing a utopian view of society, nor even looking deeply into its 'futurity'. Third, he turned to a concrete issue that had to be considered afresh, that concerning the status of the institution of private property in the particular historical context of Britain at that time. As Mill wrote:

Until the present age, the institution of property in the shape in which it has been handed down from the past, had not, except by a few speculative writers, been brought seriously into question, because the conflicts of the past have always been conflicts between classes, both of which had a stake in the existing constitution of property. It will not be possible to go on longer in this manner. (*CW* v. 708)

The issue of private property requires us to examine the earlier discussion in the *Principles*, where it was first raised in a systematic manner.

1. *Property in the* Principles

Mill's discussion of property in the earlier *Principles*, particularly the well-known writings on justice and socialism (see *CW* ii. 199–214), written to take account of the challenges posed by communist and socialist doctrines, sets the scene for this later discussion. His argument was somewhat paradoxical. The traditional arguments that were employed to discuss property had been fairly settled both in philosophy and economics. Security of property, as I have noted on numerous occasions, was an important element in the establishment of traditional civil liberty, and, for Mill, a foundation for human progress. It was rarely challenged, even though the ownership of property was wholly accidental and unrelated to virtually all known principles of justice and utility. What recommended existing property arrangements (with some exceptions) was that the status quo was preferable to the chaos that would follow a major alteration in property rights. At the time when Mill wrote, the institution of private property

> necessarily carried with it as a consequence, that the produce of labour should be apportioned as we now see it, almost in an inverse ratio to labour—the largest portions to those who have never worked at all, the next largest to those whose work is almost nominal, and so on in a descending scale, the remuneration dwindling as the work grows harder and more disagreeable, until the most fatiguing and exhausting bodily labour cannot count with certainty on being able to earn even the necessaries of life... (*CW* ii. 207)

On this account Mill granted that communism (based on equality of property and reward based on equality) should be considered a superior system to the one Mill had described. But such a comparison would not make sense. What Mill called 'the régime of individual property', as it might be 'made', had never had a fair trial in Britain or, for that matter, in any other country. Existing property laws were based on force and conquest, and despite modifications over the centuries, such foundations remained incompatible with the principles that were used to justify private property (*CW* ii. 207–8). Instead of seeing the object of private property to guarantee to individuals 'the fruits of their own labour and abstinence' (*CW* ii. 208) and establish a principle of fairness between remuneration and exertion, one found just the opposite nearly everywhere.

The paradox for Mill would seem to be that while communist and socialist writers had raised the banner of distributive justice against the existing system of private property, they might be focusing on the wrong target. The real issues might be not only different and more complex, but also the flag of social justice might better be replaced by the banner of liberty.

Private property, Mill argued, should mean in practice 'the guarantee to individuals of the fruits of their own labour and abstinence', and not the fruits of the labour and abstinence of others. There should be, in Mill's terms, an observance of 'that equitable principle'—'of proportion between remuneration and exertion' (*CW* ii. 208). This is the foundation on which private property should rest. In addition, Mill stated two conditions that should be met generally if one were to be able to choose between a system of private property and that of socialism in the best senses. The first was that of universal education and the second birth control or other forms of limits on population. If these conditions were met, poverty could be overcome, even under the existing system of property. Nevertheless, the choice between socialism and private property would not be a simple matter of promising relief from current evils, but, as Mill put it, 'a mere question of comparative advantages' (*CW* ii. 208). To this he added: 'We are too ignorant either of what individual agency in its best form, or Socialism in its best form, can accomplish, to be qualified to decide which of the two will be the ultimate form of human society' (*CW* ii. 208). Thus, Mill would appear to have no answer to the question of which form, private property on the one hand or socialism or communism on the other, would be ultimately superior, though he seemed to suggest that on many questions an ideal form of private property and a similarly ideal form of socialism (with universal education and population control) might have little to decide between them.

Mill could have left his alternatives for decision in the future. But he proceeded to advance a 'conjecture' that one major consideration would be which of the systems were consistent with human liberty—securing 'to all persons complete independence and freedom of action, subject to no restrictions but that of not doing injury to others' (*CW* ii. 208–9). As Mill briefly developed the theme of the role of liberty ('one of the most elevated characteristics of human nature': *CW* ii. 209), he returned to his problem that socialism, as an ideal system, was being contrasted with an existing system of society that Mill acknowledged was seriously flawed. As he put it, 'the restraints of Communism would be freedom in comparison with the present condition of the majority of the human race' (*CW* ii. 209). But another problem needed to be explored. The issue for Mill was 'whether there would be any asylum left for individuality of character; whether public opinion would not be a tyrannical yoke; whether the absolute dependence of each on all, and surveillance of each by all, would not grind all into a tame uniformity of thoughts, feelings, and actions'. Mill continued in the same vein, raising issues of 'the multiform development of human nature', 'diversity of tastes and talents', and freedom of expression, all of which were part of 'the mainspring of mental and moral progression' (*CW* ii. 209).

Mill then turned to examine more closely the varieties of communist and socialist doctrines and their ability to satisfy the various and competing ideas of distributive justice and other human aspirations. At the outset he first distinguished between what he took to be communism as opposed to other forms of socialism.[2] Communism was said to form 'the extreme limit of socialism' (*CW* ii. 210), and was defined as a system in which the instruments of production, land and capital belonged to the whole community. The produce was divided equally and the labour was apportioned equally. Mill acknowledged that most other varieties of socialist doctrine, for example, that of Louis Blanc, had abandoned this somewhat strict conception of communism and in France, where socialism had been introduced to a limited extent, equal distribution had been replaced by a system of piecework.

Nevertheless, Mill gave credit to communism for appealing to what he called 'a higher standard of justice' and noted that it reflected 'a much higher moral condition of human nature' (*CW* ii. 210). By comparison, remuneration on the basis of work done (the leading feature of many socialist doctrines) was unjust, because it mainly gave to those already 'most favoured by nature' (*CW* ii. 210). Those who had, tended to receive more. But Mill was willing to see this 'injustice' accepted by socialist systems, as a compromise between the higher morality of communism and the current standard of morality in existing societies. He wrote:

Considered, however, as a compromise with the selfish type of character formed by the present standard of morality, and fostered by the existing social institutions, it is highly expedient; and until education shall have been entirely regenerated, is far more likely to prove immediately successful, than an attempt at a higher ideal. (*CW* ii. 210)

Given this compromise with the high standards of communism, Mill then turned to examine St-Simonism and Fourierism, the two most important forms of non-communist socialism. He clearly admired their writings and referred to their 'intellectual power', 'their large and philosophic treatment of some of the fundamental problems of society and morality', and their position as 'among the most remarkable productions of the past and present age' (*CW* ii. 210).

According to Mill the St-Simonian scheme envisaged an unequal division of the produce of the society, with each member holding posts according to their 'vocation or capacity' (*CW* ii. 210). They were assigned different functions by the ruling authority with remuneration related to function and to the merit of the worker. A variety of schemes were proposed for choosing the ruling authority, from popular suffrage to a voluntary submission by the people based on their recognition of the mental capacity and superior virtue of the rulers.

Mill compared this proposal to that famous example of eighteenth-century writers, the rule of the Jesuits in Paraguay. Here, educated and virtuous rulers (united by a community of property) established a system in which 'a race of savages' were taught for a brief time to work for the good of the community and learn the arts of civilized life. In effect, these rulers (the Jesuits) dispensed in Mill's terms 'distributive justice to every member of the community', a process which, Mill believed, could only exist under the most extraordinary conditions (*CW* ii. 211). In an insightful passage, he wrote:

> A fixed rule, like that of equality, might be acquiesced in, and so might chance, or an external necessity; but that a handful of human beings should weigh everybody in the balance, and give more to one and less to another at their sole pleasure and judgment would not be borne, unless from persons believed to be more than men and backed by supernatural terrors. (*CW* ii. 211)

As we have seen, equality of distribution in communism, though meeting a high standard of justice, did not reflect human nature in its current state. Hence, Mill seemed to have been drawn to a form of St-Simonism, which he linked with Fourierism. Fourierism held on to the principle of private property (and even to that of inheritance). In small communities consisting of approximately two thousand members, distribution was based on a minimum remuneration to ensure subsistence to all, with the rest divided unequally according to the claims of labour, capital, and talent. Talent would be reflected in the various ranks established in the institution. Those who managed the operations would be chosen by the members. There would be no community of property, although members would live together in the same village and use centralized purchasing and selling facilities to achieve major economies by cutting out various middlemen (see *CW* ii. 212).

Fourierism would thus be opposed to the equality associated with communism and would provide for rewards for increased skill and energy. Like Owenism it also addressed the problem of providing incentives for a few people to do unpleasant and arduous work. Despite some difficulties with Fourierism, Mill seemed attracted to it, largely because its account of equality was more related to a diversity of 'tastes and talents' existing in the community (*CW* ii. 213). He called this kind of equality 'real' and contrasted it with that equality that came from 'compression' as opposed to 'the largest possible development, of the various natural superiorities residing in each individual' (*CW* ii. 213). He also believed that Fourierism could be adapted to the existing imperfect state of mental and moral development, and could be tried experimentally in any current society without risk to persons and existing systems of property. Nevertheless, Mill ended his discussion of Fourierism and other forms of 'community of property' on a sceptical note. The political economists, he suggested, 'for a considerable time to come' will mainly concentrate on private property and individual competition, with the object being the improvement and not the subversion of the system of individual property. Such an improvement, he believed, would nonetheless include 'the full participation' of all members of the community in the benefits of this system (CW ii. 214).

II. *Property and British National Character*

Let us return to the 'Chapters on Socialism'. Mill began his discussion of property[3] by contrasting one view, which was widespread in France, Germany, and Switzerland, with another view prevailing in Britain. The first view consisted of an opposition to all forms of income not based on labour, and a general hostility to private property and its privileges. These ideas had not yet been widely adopted in Britain, though 'the soil is well-prepared to receive the seeds of this description' (CW v. 709). British national character, however, tended to accept that permanent change could not be achieved suddenly. There was a general resistance to extreme theories and a hostility towards those who sought immediate revolutionary action (as some did 'even in sober Switzerland': CW v. 709) to abolish private property as well as government without any clear view of what should be done afterwards.

The extension of the franchise did not bring to an end the issue of private property but, on the contrary, raised it in an important and urgent way. One had to raise the question, was it a 'necessary evil' that, although the working classes had been liberated from slavery by law (by the Reform Act), they were still enslaved by poverty. For Mill, they were

still chained to a place, to an occupation, and to conformity with the will of an employer, and debarred by the accident of birth both from the enjoyments, from the mental and moral advantages, which others inherit without exertion and independently of desert. (CW v. 710)

Thus, the issue of private property, more prominent and urgent due to the passage of the Reform Act of 1867, raised other related issues, such as the status of inherited wealth, desert with regard to income, and the whole issue of justice. Mill proposed nothing less than a fresh examination of all social institutions and took the view that such an examination of private property should not be aimed at those who already had an interest in upholding the institution and were convinced of its value, but to those whose only interest was in 'abstract justice and the general good of the community' (*CW* v. 711). Mill's somewhat Benthamite legislator should

ascertain what institutions of property would be established by an unpreju-diced legislator, absolutely impartial between the possessors of property and the non-possessors; and to defend and justify them by the reasons which would really influence such a legislator, and not by such as have the appear-ance of being got up to make out a case for what already exists ... An impartial hearing ought, moreover, to be given to all objections against property itself.

(*CW* v. 711)

Mill had thus shifted the argument from a critique of the institution of private property or, on the contrary, its wholesale justification, to another perspective, i.e. the impartial consideration of private prop-erty from the point of view of the working class, which now had the power in Britain for the first time to make major changes to it.

III. *The Critique of Existing Society*

Mill began his impartial investigation by first listing some of the evils of existing society. The first of these, poverty, was treated with all the fury of the continental socialists whom Mill had read and admired. 'Suffice it to say,' he wrote, 'that the condition of numbers in civilised Europe, and even in England and France, is more wretched than that of most tribes of savages who are known to us' (*CW* v. 713). Mill not only recognized the state of poverty in existing so-called 'civilized' societies but he also dismissed arguments often put forward to justify continued poverty in the midst of affluence. For example, he dismissed the view that somehow poverty was 'natural' or that it represented the state of affairs where some were sacrificed for the good of the whole, that is to say, a doctrine justify-ing poverty as the outcome of a struggle of the fittest. For Mill, it was clear that poverty involved a failure of distributive justice to be observed or promoted in current society. 'The very idea of distribu-tive justice,' he wrote, 'or of any proportionality between success and merit, or between success and exertion, is in the present state of society so manifestly chimerical as to be relegated to the regions of romance' (*CW* v. 714).

A second evil concerned morality and virtue. The current state of society seemed to Mill to encourage the worst vices as well as some virtues. As he wrote:

If persons are helped in their worldly career by their virtues, so are they, and perhaps quite as often, by their vices: by servility and sycophancy, by hard-hearted and close-fisted selfishness, by the permitted lies and tricks of the trade, by gambling speculations, not seldom by downright knavery. Energies and talents are of much more avail for success in life than virtues . . . (*CW* v. 714)

Human misconduct, i.e. crime, vice, and folly, was partly due to poverty, idleness, and poor education, or no education at all.

Mill's two criticisms of the system of private property, based on poverty and on morality, were regarded as commonplace not only among socialists but also among 'levellers' generally. Socialists, how-ever, tended to add a further criticism that focused on excessive individualism, with each person competing for security and advan-tage for oneself and against the rest in a Hobbesian state of war. They were critical of what they saw as widespread under capitalism that one could only gain if others lose. Economic competition would lead to low wages, bankruptcy among producers, and the establishment of a new and complex capitalist feudalism (*CW* v. 715). Mill inserted at this point long quotations from Louis Blanc, Robert Owen, Fourier-ists, and others to substantiate and develop this view (*CW* v. 716–27).

IV. *Socialist Objections Examined*

Having apparently allied himself with the 'levelling' and socialist critique of the system of private property and the current form of capitalism, Mill then began an examination of this critique.[4] While he could acknowledge that 'the wages of ordinary labour, in all the countries of Europe, are wretchedly insufficient to supply the phys-ical and moral necessities of the population in any tolerable meas-ure' (*CW* v. 727), he disputed Blanc's view that there was a continual decline in wages, as part of the capitalist system.

As for the wages of labour, Mill developed three arguments to substantiate his view that in all countries in the civilized world ordin-ary wages of labour, measured by money or articles of consumption, were not declining, and in those countries where they were increasing, this increase was not slowing, but increasing more rapidly (see *CW* v. 727–8). The first argument was concerned with overpopulation. Mill first praised Blanc, Owen, and Fourier for appreciating the problem of overpopulation, but argued that they had wrongly adopted the view of Malthus that population would increase more quickly than subsistence and consequently force wages down. Mill rejected this view, and while he saw the pressures of population as one source of low wages, he believed that this source was diminishing. To support his position he first pointed to one consequence of increasing civilization which had led to the development of new ways of employing and maintaining labour. Second, there were new opportunities for labour to go abroad and, particularly, to 'unoccupied lands' where their wages would not necessarily decline. Third, Mill could point to improvement in 'the intelligence and prudence of the population', by which he meant generally the use of birth control to limit population (*CW* v. 729). Although Mill conceded that socialist institutions might be better placed to deal with the pressures of population, he insisted that it was not true that under the current system wages would necessarily fall.

Mill then turned to the socialist view ('very imperfect and one-sided') of the role of competition in society, which socialists generally condemned not only as a way of forcing wages down but also as a source of other evils. On the whole Mill was a strong supporter of competition in the economy. Competition for workers could lead to an increase in wages as much as to a decrease. Competition in the production of commodities could lead to a decrease in prices that was advantageous to ordinary workers. Competition did not necessarily lead, as some socialists claimed, to monopolies, as the most successful drove out one's rivals and wages then could be decreased and prices increased. Mill believed that it was very difficult for a capitalist to defeat all rivals and control wages and prices, and even where it happened, government regulation could intervene.

After a full reply to the socialist position on competition Mill qualified his position by arguing that, while competition provided the best security for the cheapness of goods, it did not necessarily provide the best security for the quality of goods. Here, he called attention to fraud, adulteration, short measure, etc. 'Thus the frauds, begun by a few,' he wrote, 'become customs of the trade, and the morality of the trading classes is more and more deteriorated' (*CW* v. 732). Nevertheless, the remedy was not the abolition of capitalism, but the regulation of trading standards, the development and use of co-operative stores, and the revision of bankruptcy and insolvency laws that seemed then to ignore the moral dimension to bankruptcy, for example, in an exclusive concentration on obtaining the most from a bankrupt to recompense creditors.

A final theme considered by Mill was the false view held by some socialists concerning the sharing of the produce of investments between the capitalists and labourers. If someone invested, for example, £20,000 for an annual return of £2,000, many socialists would regard the investor as having both the £20,000 and the £2,000, while the workers possessed only their wages. Mill disagreed. The £20,000 was invested in machinery, buildings, and various other instruments of production. The investor in effect had only the profits (the £2,000 per year) at his disposal, and the £20,000 was used mainly to satisfy the needs of the workers (CW v. 734). Although Mill acknowledged that the issue was more complex than this part of his example suggested, he insisted that it was a serious exaggeration by some socialists to insist that the worker was left under capitalism with only his wages, based on his labour.

In examining Mill's argument thus far, it is difficult not to pay tribute to his care, impartiality, and honesty in investigating the current state of society, the strengths and weaknesses of the socialist critique of capitalist society, the critique of socialist analysis and aspirations, and the time frame available to remedy the problems of capitalism. As we have seen, he rejected the view that capitalism was rapidly taking the British towards a system of indigence and poverty and thought that there was neither a crisis of that sort nor one that required the suspension of rational thought or immediate revolutionary action. Nevertheless, his remarks and approach, arguing that the Reform Act of 1867 gave political power to the working classes for the first time and that there was an urgent need of reform, were accompanied with the precise suggestion of a time frame of approximately a generation to engage with the conditions that socialism was meant to remedy and to consider which forms of socialism would lead to lasting reform. One might see Mill's progress thus far in terms of the identification of contrary positions and an attempt to reconcile these contraries. The public debate focused on irreconcilable opposites, between those who upheld 'ignorant opposition to change' and those who favoured 'ignorant change', that is to say, between those who upheld traditional rights to the unequal ownership of property, however obtained, as a 'natural right', and those who advocated immediate revolution and the public ownership of the means of production. Mill shifted the focus to the acceptance of the near-inevitability of some sort of socialism in Britain within a generation and posed a different question regarding the alternatives before him:

What is incumbent on us is a calm comparison between two different systems of society, with a view of determining which of them affords the greatest resources for overcoming the inevitable difficulties of life. And if we find the answer to this question more difficult, and more dependent upon intellectual and moral conditions, than is usually thought, it is satisfactory to reflect that there is time before us for the question to work itself out on an experimental scale, by actual trial. I believe we shall find that no other test is possible of the practicability or beneficial operation of Socialist arrangements; but that the intellectual and moral grounds of Socialism deserve the most attentive study, as affording in many cases the guiding principles of the improvements necessary to give the present economic system of society its best chance.   (CW v. 736)

Mill's new 'contraries' are the existing capitalist society on the one hand and the doctrine of socialism on the other. They might be reconciled by focusing on the alternative doctrines within socialism itself and concentrating on moral and intellectual issues that various forms of socialism aspired to resolve. These, in turn, were to be seen in a practical light as serious alternatives to capitalism, as it then existed.

v. *Revolutionary versus Experimental Socialism*

Those who are familiar with Marx's distinction between utopian and scientific socialism, with the former absorbed by and replaced by the latter (see Marx and Engels 1968: 59–62), might be surprised to encounter Mill's important distinction between revolutionary and experimental socialism. If Marx elevated revolutionary socialism to the status of a science, Mill dismissed it precisely because it was not capable of experimental trials. Additionally, it was advocated by continental socialists and not by those in touch with British national character. Marx's 'utopian socialism' was not seen as utopian at all, as these forms were capable of experimental trials in small societies or in portions of large societies. Although this distinction, which led Mill to oppose the revolutionary form of socialism, was important, it also enabled him to focus more on intellectual and moral issues rather than, for example, on theories of historical or revolutionary change.[5]

Mill characterized socialism in terms of 'the joint ownership by all the members of the community of the instruments and means of production' (*CW* v. 738). He then added the proviso that socialism did not necessarily prohibit private articles of consumption or the right to enjoy, give, or exchange such articles, when they were received. What made socialism distinctive, for Mill, was that only the instruments of production were held in common ownership. On a small scale, as advocated by Owen and Fourier, such a form of socialism seemed practical. On the scale of a nation, the management of the whole means of production was another matter. Mill granted that revolutionary socialism had a kind of popular appeal. '[W]hat it professes to do,' he wrote, 'it promises to do quickly, and holds out hope to the enthusiastic of seeing the whole of their aspirations realised in their own time and at a blow' (*CW* v. 737–8). Mill did not share in this enthusiasm, or in the optimism surrounding revolutionary politics. As he wrote:

It must be acknowledged that those who would play this game on the strength of their own private opinion, unconfirmed as yet by any experimental verification—who would forcibly deprive all who have now a comfortable physical existence of their only present means of preserving it, and would brave the frightful bloodshed and misery that would ensue if the attempt was resisted—must have a serene confidence in their own wisdom on the one hand and a recklessness of other people's sufferings on the other, which Robespierre and St. Just, hitherto the typical instances of those united attributes, scarcely came up to. (*CW* v. 737)

Mill's hostility towards revolutionary socialism was partly based on its impracticality, as it could not be tried experimentally, but was also rejected for other reasons. These other reasons were initially approached via different conceptions of distribution in a socialist society. These might include 'simple communism'—equal distribution among those who shared in the society, or Blanc's 'higher standard of justice' with distribution according to need, or Fourier's scheme of variations in remuneration. But Mill did not dwell on these distinctions and turned instead to examine the psychology of motivation that would operate in both socialist and capitalist societies. Mill's turning to psychology at this point might possibly reflect his work on the second edition of his father's *Analysis of the Phenomena of the Human Mind* (1869), published at the same time as the 'Chapters' was being written, but more probably Mill was returning to his conception of social science, as elaborated in book 6 of the *Logic*, and which established the foundations of social analysis in psychology and ethology (i.e. character and national character). To discriminate between different conceptions of distributive justice he needed a platform on which to stand. We have seen how Mill used his estimation of national character to establish an underlying disposition among the British against revolutionary change, which in turn led him to reject those forms of socialism that depended on it.

Mill now turned to examine the various versions of distributive justice from the perspective of motivation. His starting point was what he called 'the ever-present influence of indolence and love of ease' (CW v. 740) and considered this fundamental (though not unchanging fact) about human nature from the point of view of workers performing repetitive and boring tasks. The main motivation for such work, according to Mill, was that there would be economic rewards that improved the life of the workers and their families. 'To suppose the contrary,' Mill argued, 'would be to imply that with men as they now are, duty and honour are more powerful principles of action than personal interest, not solely as to special acts and forbearances...but in the regulation of their whole lives; which no one, I suppose, will affirm' (CW v. 740). Nevertheless, a socialist or communist system would have to rely on a different sort of motivation than personal interest. Mill believed that a different morality might be inculcated, but this would take time, with one generation of those who subscribed to this morality educating another generation. Furthermore, to rely even on this lengthy form of education falsely assumed that the personal limitations of the teachers, perhaps based on the circumstances of the old regime, would not be passed on to the next generation. Mill then acknowledged that, in the absence of other motivation, the managers of the socialist or communist system would have to rely on the motivation of rulers in Plato's Republic [416ff.] (1963: i.308ff.) that rulers do so in order to prevent worse rulers from gaining power (see CW v. 741).

When Mill turned to ordinary workers, he thought that, as workers under a capitalist regime, there was little incentive to perform repetitive work with energy and efficiency. While the mere presence of fellow-workers might be more effective under socialism, it might have the opposite effect, as when trade unions advocated doing less work in order to safeguard jobs and avoid putting themselves out of work.

One remedy Mill considered as a motivating factor under socialism would be the introduction of piecework, as this rewarded the energetic and efficient. But socialist doctrine had tended to oppose piecework as under this regimen workers were forced to work harder; without piecework they could earn the same amount with less exertion. Furthermore, competition, as we have seen, was generally opposed by the same thinkers. Then Mill turned to another possible source of motivation, that of 'industrial partnership', i.e. with the whole body of labourers admitted to participate in the profits (*CW* v. 743). But this way of organizing firms with workers sharing in the profits (which Mill seemed to favour) would work equally well under capitalism as under socialism. Mill was then led to the conclusion: 'It thus appears that as far as concerns the motives to exertion in the general body, Communism has no advantage which may not be reached under private property, while as respects managing heads it is at a considerable disadvantage' (*CW* v. 743).

Related to Mill's psychological insights regarding motivation was his analysis of the difficulties of justice under a communist system which distributed an equal payment to all workers. Because work varied in hardness and unpleasantness, it was difficult to apportion it equally. If it could not be apportioned equally, the principle of equality of reward would, in Mill's view, constitute an imperfect justice. If workers were to perform *all* work in turn, as a way of overcoming the imperfection in the system, the firm or the economy would have to sacrifice the benefits in production and wealth achieved by the division of labour. The view among communists that quarrelling and ill-will would disappear under their regime and would be replaced by 'harmony and unanimity' was, according to Mill, simply false. In fact, he thought that the opposite would be the case. As normal squabbles over pecuniary interest and ambition were repressed, the struggles for pre-eminence and influence in the larger collective body would intensify, as they would constitute the only channels for personal gratification. Thus, from his conception of distributive justice under communism, Mill's psychological analysis led him to conclude:

For these various reasons it is probable that a Communist association would frequently fail to exhibit the attractive picture of mutual love and unity of will and feeling which we are often told by Communists to expect, but would often be torn by dissension and not unfrequently broken up by it. (*CW* v. 745)

Mill continued by noting that under communism the individual would lack the resources and hence the opportunity to opt for private education. If the education of the society was run by the society as a whole, the individual might not only have few resources, but also little influence in society as a whole. Mill then invoked the importance of liberty in opposition to a communist regime:

The obstacles to human progression are always great, and require a concurrence of favourable circumstances to overcome them; but an indispensable condition of their being overcome is, that human nature should have freedom to expand spontaneously in various directions, both in thought and practice; that people should both think for themselves and try experiments for themselves, and should not resign into the hands of rulers, whether acting in the name of a few or of the majority, the business of thinking for them, and of prescribing how they shall act. But in Communist associations private life would be brought in a most unexampled degree within the dominion of public authority, and there would be less scope for the development of individual character and individual preferences than has hitherto existed among the full citizens of any state belonging to the progressive branches of the human family. Already in all societies the compression of individuality is a great and growing evil; it would probably be much greater under Communism, except so far as it might be in the power of individuals to set bounds to it by selecting to belong to a community of persons like-minded with themselves. (CW v. 745–6)

Mill did not altogether reject a communist system of production, as he was willing to grant that at some future period it might be found to be suited to human wants and needs. This suitability would have to be discovered by experimental trials within the system of private property, though he qualified himself by noting that current society, due to its 'demoralizing' effects on character, would not be able to provide this moral education. Hence, the trials of communism would first have to establish from one generation to another that such moral education was possible.

If Mill was sceptical of full-blown communism, he was willing to consider other forms of socialism that attempted to overcome the limitations of communism. The main form was Fourierism. Mill seemed full of praise for Fourierism: its capacity to deal with objections to communism and its possession of a more workable principle of distributive justice. Fourier even grappled with the issue of how to make labour attractive. Mill's description of a Fourierist village (see CW v. 747–8) was highly sympathetic, and he thought that the scheme should have a fair trial to assess its practicability. In spite of this strong support, Mill managed to qualify his remarks somewhat, or, at least, he insisted that his praise was directed at Fourier's industrial system alone. Fourier's 'unmistakable proofs of genius' were mixed with 'the wildest and most unscientific fancies respecting the physical world'. His conceptions of humanity's past and future were 'rash' and he held 'peculiar opinions' on social issues and, particularly, on the institution of marriage (*CW* v. 748n.).

As Mill brought this material to a conclusion, he stressed first that socialism could work then only among an elite of mankind, and it would be necessary to train people at large to accept it. Second, as for revolutionary socialism there was no way of dealing with the injustice done to those who had capital and property. Third, Mill closed on a sober note with a quotation from the account of the state of nature in Hobbes's *Leviathan*, where life was 'solitary, poor, nasty, brutish, and short' (*CW* v. 749; Hobbes 1966 (1651): 100). As Mill wrote:

> If the poorest and most wretched members of a so-called civilized society are in as bad a condition as every one would be in that worst form of barbarism produced by the dissolution of civilised life, it does not follow that the way to raise them would be to reduce all others to the same miserable state. On the contrary, it is by the aid of the first who have risen that so many others have escaped from the general lot, and it is only by better organization of the same process that it may be hoped in time to succeed in raising the remainder. (*CW* v. 749)

VI. *The Future of Private Property*

As Mill concluded his essay on socialism, he restated his view that the mere abolition of private property and competition by an act of parliament or by revolution would not necessarily lead to the establishment of a new and successful foundation for society. If socialism was to be established, it would require numerous trials and much education. Furthermore, Mill believed that private property would survive for a considerable period of time. Even where a revolutionary movement abolished it, it would return in one form or another, because there was no other foundation on which people could rely on for subsistence and security. In addition, those who benefited from the abolition of private property would be eager to safeguard that portion of public property which they managed to acquire and would be reluctant to return it to earlier possessors (see Robson 1968: 246).

Nevertheless, private property and, indeed, capitalism were not fixed systems incapable of change and improvement. As Robson points out, private property is, for Mill, always subject to utility (Robson 1968: 246; cf. Ryan 1974: 197). With the passage of the Reform Act of 1867, which gave great potential power to the working classes, there were obvious reasons for the educated minority to advance aspects of socialist doctrine as well as to oppose the premature attempts to move suddenly towards socialism. As Mill argued, proposals for reform in human institutions and practices should not depend for their support on their acceptability to existing ideas of property, but existing ideas of property should be adapted to the 'growth and improvement of human affairs' (CW v. 753). 'Under this condition,' Mill concluded, ' . . . society is fully entitled to abrogate or alter any particular right of property which on sufficient consideration it judges to stand in the way of the public good' (CW v. 753).

What is the significance of these remarks regarding property? It is difficult to say clearly and definitely that Mill either was or was not a socialist. He seemed to uphold the security and subsistence provided by a system of private property. Nevertheless, as we have seen here and elsewhere, Mill was well aware of the moral injustice and economic folly of such a system. But if a socialist system of common ownership were to replace private property, the goal to make that replacement successful would require preparation that would take time and postpone the achievement of the goal. Mill's intelligent elite, though perhaps favouring socialism, or at least recognizing its inevitability, would paradoxically seem to spend most of its time holding back its premature arrival, as such an arrival would probably mean failure.

The clue to this paradox of opposing socialism in order to succeed in introducing it may be found in Mill's *System of Logic*. He draws on the two sciences of psychology and ethology and brings his insights to bear on the theme of socialism. Psychology teaches that the vast majority of workers, particularly those engaged in boring and repetitive tasks, preferred indolence and ease to hard work. There was no motivation apart from a rarely found love of labour that could lead ordinary workers to discard self-interest and love of wealth to work only for the public good. Camaraderie and revolutionary enthusiasm might last for a short time but could not survive when Mill wrote, and the same is probably true nowadays.

As for ethology, Mill insisted that British national character was such that, unlike France, Germany, and even Switzerland, there was little taste for violent revolution or even rapid change. The character of the British emphasized caution and experiment rather than risking all on utopian dreams. Mill used the two sciences, in so far as he worked them out, to establish a unique and different kind of political art. This art was based on the prospects for the British people following the passage of the Reform Act of 1867, which placed ultimate political power for the first time in the hands of the working classes. It no longer mattered if Mill approved or disapproved of socialism. He realized that socialism in one form or another would inevitably be attempted, and those who understood these matters needed to discuss the nature of this new form of government and economic organization prior to its arrival. In assessing British national character, he realized that philosophers had only one generation to work out the meaning of this new form of society and educate the people to respond to it.

11

Distributive Justice in *Utilitarianism*

In the last chapter we have on several occasions encountered the theme of distributive justice, taken by Mill primarily from communist and socialist writers. The banner of distributive justice was also raised in criticism of the existing system of private property and was intended to serve as a guide to the systems that might replace it. In addition, different versions of distributive justice were dissected by Mill to see which ones reflected both the high ideals of justice and, particularly, their practical applications in modern industrial societies.

As we have seen, Mill recognized the importance of claims to justice by those who opposed the existing system of private property, but he insisted that such claims were directed at the wrong target. Although the existing system was a source of exploitation and misery, it might be replaced by another system of private property that was based on an 'equitable principle' that established a proportion between remuneration and exertion. This principle did not exist in the present system of private property, where remuneration was not related to exertion, and those who received the greatest rewards usually did the least work. But if remuneration was currently unrelated to exertion, it need not continue to be so and could form the basis of a future system of private property. An ideal system of private property and an ideal system of socialism might in fact have little to choose between them. Furthermore, to make the choice, if one was possible or necessary, a major issue would be which of the systems best protected and nurtured individual liberty.[1]

Mill generally gave credit to those he tended to call 'communists' for adopting a high standard of distributive justice, where the instruments of production, land and capital, belonged equally to the whole community. Labour was also equally apportioned and rewarded. Nevertheless, this system reflected a higher standard of human nature and morality than existed at that time, and, in addition, was potentially subject to a paternalism and possibly to abuses of liberty in attempts to apply it (as in the case of the Jesuits in Paraguay: see also *CW* xix. 396). Those whom Mill tended to call 'socialists' adopted a less absolute notion of equality, as when they sought to reward work actually done. Hence, those already favoured by strength, agility, and intelligence tended to receive more. In the current state of humanity this compromise with absolute equality was considered in practice to be more acceptable. It would also require less of a violation of individual liberty to establish and maintain.

I. *Distributive Justice in* Utilitarianism

Utilitarianism contains several important allusions to these problems and debates, particularly with regard to equality and justice.[2] I have argued elsewhere that Mill adopted Bentham's conception of liberty as 'security' and developed it as a principle of justice in *Utilitarianism*.[3] Given his discussions of communism and socialism, and his anxiety that their adoption might easily threaten liberty by the introduction of compulsion regarding work and regimentation regarding reward and the conditions of work, as well as in society generally, Mill cleverly inserted a familiar account of liberty into the heart of justice.[4] Security of persons, property, and expectations, as principles of justice, also led to Mill's conception of rights.

If we translate Mill's treatment of communism and socialism in the *Principles* and the 'Chapters' into the language of security, as in *Utilitarianism*, we shall find that the ideal system of private property and individual liberty was already established as a principle of justice, and, additionally, as a part of justice that was distinguished from ordinary utility. At one level Mill was asserting that liberty as security was an important part of justice itself, both as the essence of a version of liberty and as the foundation of an account of rights. At another level he was suggesting that liberty trumped justice when the two conflicted, and they would mainly conflict when liberty opposed justice based on equality.

The actual discussion of communism and socialism occurred in relation to equality.[5] Mill introduced equality as an idea of justice, which was 'nearly allied' to impartiality (one of the five 'common attributes' of justice) (*CW* x. 243). The exact status of equality in relation to justice was unclear, though in introducing it, Mill recognized that it entered into both the conception and practice of justice, and, 'in the eyes of many persons, constitutes its essence' (*CW* x. 243). Mill, however, found equality particularly problematic in its applications to morality and politics. For example, the same people who regarded equality as the essence of justice often upheld great inequalities. In one example Mill noted that the justice of upholding the equal rights of all could easily be applied to a slave society, where the rights of slaves, such as they were, were as rigorously upheld, under a principle of equality, as those of the masters. Thus, justice as equality appeared to accommodate the most striking inequalities.

In another example, he asserted that those who regarded government as necessary and expedient did not see any injustice in granting unequal amounts of power to government officials on the one hand and the people on the other. In these examples, therefore, even though one might take the view that equality was the essence of justice, the application of the principle could lead to confusion with regard both to justice and to equality.

Mill then offered a final example:

Some Communists consider it unjust that the produce of the labour of the community should be shared on any other principle than that of exact equality; others think it just that those should receive most whose needs are greatest; while others hold that those who work harder, or who produce more, or whose services are more valuable to the community, may justly claim a larger quota in the division of the produce. (*CW* x. 244)

The differences among communists and socialists were set out in a clear and definite manner. Both presented different applications of equality and hence different (and incompatible) notions of distributive justice. In the *Principles* and the later 'Chapters', Mill posed and developed this problem, and, as we have seen earlier, these various versions of distributive justice were at the heart of the problem of the futurity of the working classes and the kinds of institutions they might adopt.

By this stage in his argument, Mill had made several important points. First, he seemed to insist that both communists and socialists validly appealed to distributive justice, but difficulties arose in the application of the principles to practice (see also Robson 1968: 248). Second, the problem of distributive justice might have to be considered apart from an analysis of justice in relation to morality and expedience. As we shall see, Mill returned to this problem at the end of *Utilitarianism*. Third, largely due to the problems encountered in the various conceptions of justice, Mill admitted to some 'embarrassment' in grasping the 'mental link' that held these different conceptions of justice (not in themselves ambiguous) together, and he restarted his study of justice in *Utilitarianism* with an examination of the etymology of the term.

By the time he returned to the specific issue of equality, Mill had already established the meaning and status of justice. For the most part justice was derived more from the Aristotelian conception of corrective rather than from the Aristotelian idea of distributive justice (see Rosen 1975: 228–40). Justice was also marked off from ordinary expediency by seeing it as a special part of morality which in turn was a special part of expediency.

Mill conceived of justice as follows:

the idea of justice supposes two things; a rule of conduct, and a sentiment which sanctions the rule. The first must be supposed common to all mankind, and intended for their good. The other (the sentiment) is a desire that punishment may be suffered by those that infringe the rule. (*CW* x. 249–50)

In addition, he emphasized the importance for justice of there being a definite person whose rights were violated and a sentiment of justice that began with an 'animal desire' to repel an injury to oneself or to one with whom one sympathized, with that sympathy potentially enlarged to include all persons (*CW* x. 250). Mill then turned to emphasize the importance of rights to security and adopted Bentham's idea of liberty as security in this new context.

II. *Equality*

None of this discussion of justice emphasized equality. When Mill finally returned to equality, he initially saw its derivation from 'the first of judicial virtues, impartiality' (*CW* x. 257). Then, he turned to two other sources of 'the exalted rank' given to equality and impartiality. The first was related to desert. If there was a duty to treat everyone according to desert, it followed that 'we should treat all equally well (when no higher duty forbids) who have deserved equally well of us, and that society should treat all equally well who have deserved equally well of it, that is, who have deserved equally well absolutely' (*CW* x. 257). Although this sentence is somewhat cumbersome, it adds to the judicial principle of impartiality a notion of reward and punishment according to desert. Following this exposition, Mill wrote dramatically that 'this is the highest abstract standard of social and distributive justice; towards which all institutions, and the efforts of all virtuous citizens, should be made in the utmost possible degree to converge' (*CW* x. 257).

Mill then turned to the second source of the 'exalted rank' given to equality and impartiality, which was located in the greatest happiness principle itself. The greatest happiness principle was 'a mere form of words without rational signification, unless one person's happiness, supposed equal in degree (with the proper allowance made for kind), is counted for exactly as much as another's' (*CW* x. 257). He continued with the well-known line that 'Bentham's dictum "everybody to count for one, nobody for more than one", might be written under the principle of utility as an explanatory commentary' (*CW* x. 257). This important exposition of the status of equality in both Bentham and Mill was then explained further in a brief footnote in which Mill criticized Spencer for arguing that the utility principle presupposed another principle, that of equality, when the utility principle actually embodied equality (*CW* x. 257n.–258n.; see Rosen 2003*a*: 230–1).

In both the footnote regarding Spencer and his discussion of 'maxims of justice' (*CW* x. 258), Mill seemed to recognize the importance of justice (including distributive justice) as operating on two levels: first, as part of the utility principle, and deducible from the greatest happiness principle itself, and second, as a more problematic part of the ongoing struggle for social improvement in most societies. Both here and elsewhere Mill was aware of how a social practice or institution could be in one age thought necessary for social existence itself (and hence clearly related to security, moral rights, and justice) while later it was seen as the epitome of injustice. As he wrote:

The entire history of social improvement has been a series of transitions, by which one custom or institution after another, from being a supposed primary necessity of social existence, has passed into the rank of an universally stigmatized injustice and tyranny. So it has been with the distinctions of slaves and freemen, nobles and serfs, patricians and plebeians; and so it will be, and in part already is, with the autocracies of colour, race, and sex. (*CW* x. 259)

What prevented steady progress towards social improvement was that many people seemed to mistake injustice for justice because they believed that social distinctions upholding inequality were necessary for social stability, and even social existence. Prior to the passage just quoted, he wrote:

And hence all social inequalities which have ceased to be considered expedient, assume the character not of simple inexpediency, but of injustice, and appear so tyrannical that people are apt to wonder how they ever could have been tolerated; forgetful that they themselves perhaps tolerate other inequalities under an equally mistaken notion of expediency, the correction of which would make that which they approve seem quite as monstrous as what they have at last learnt to condemn. (*CW* x. 258–9)

III. *A 'Theory' of Justice?*

Mill's account of justice and injustice here was intentionally paradoxical, as it was based not only on his view of justice as a historically relative and changing value in its applications, particularly in relation to equality, but also on a fairly unchanging system of morality, where justice itself seemed to rest formally on principles of security, equality, desert, etc. These principles would only change if fairly fundamental qualities of human character in its broadest senses changed. However, the use of these fairly fixed stars of justice, liberty, and happiness in the heavens of morality tended to be problematic, and Mill insisted on giving considerable attention to the problem of what he called 'applications'. How then did he resolve the issues he posed regarding the application of justice to the institutions of private property, co-operation, communism, and socialism? First, the existing system of private property was manifestly unjust in its exploitation of some by others, its emphasis on inequality of property, and on remuneration not in proportion to exertion. However, the existing system, almost by default, possessed numerous virtues. Considerable injustice and violence would be required for its destruction and replacement with other property arrangements. To retain this unjust system and gradually reform it might thus actually reduce injustice. The liberty in security of persons and their property was an important part of justice and should not be compromised (see Riley

1989: 148). Where such property arrangements were destroyed, another system of private property (perhaps, even more unjust) might eventually replace it. Hence, the abolition of private property would be more problematic in relation to justice than might be fully grasped even by those who sought its abolition.

Second, the existing system of private property might be replaced by an ideal form under which reward was more closely related to exertion and security of private property retained. This system might be introduced gradually and constitute a serious competitor to socialism in relation to justice. Third, a system of co-operation in industrial production and other aspects of society might better reflect the aspirations of the working classes to equality and justice. With the abolition of dog-eat-dog competition, co-operatives could enable some of the virtues of the stationary state to be realized. Co-operatives could also be established within the existing system of private property, where they might assist the transition to an improved system.

Fourth, the aspirations of the working classes with their new-found political power might include the complete abolition of existing capitalism and the introduction of communism or socialism. Communism, though pursuing the value of equality of condition, would be least likely to be adopted as a principle of justice, given a widespread hostility to the regimented equality implicit in its applications. Socialism, with reward according to exertion, might be more acceptable to working men who would be more likely to adopt principles of competition that would avoid economic stagnation.

Can these notions of distributive justice be reconciled and various arrangements assessed in relation to some universally applicable rules of justice? According to West (2004: 161), Mill believed that conflicting principles of justice (as in the realm of distributive justice) could be assessed and any conflict resolved by an appeal to consequences. A potential resolution of the various issues, therefore, might depend on how one conceived of consequences. Although 'consequentialism' was devised in the twentieth century, and is a philosophical category that Mill did not use in any technical sense (see West 2004: 34n.; Hooker 2010: 444–55), it might be possible to insert Mill's own method into a consequentialist theory. Nevertheless, from the perspective of Mill's own thought, that is to say, making sense of what Mill actually wrote, there might not be much point in looking to a consequentialist theory. Mill, himself, as we have seen in earlier chapters, emphasized in the *Logic* psychology and ethology, and this might be a better way forward in assessing the utility of various conceptions of distributive justice, or, for that matter, other issues or categories in human affairs. Given Mill's scepticism regarding the motivation of working men in advanced industrial societies to sustain morally the egalitarianism required by the system of justice advocated by communist writers and his commitment to individual liberty that potential regimentation in society threatened, his understanding of psychology clearly led him to discount one kind of socialism that emphasized a strict equality.

Furthermore, when one realizes the status Mill accorded to equality (as part of the utility principle itself), his critique of egalitarian forms of communism and socialism as assuming too high a moral standard for the current age and threatening to destroy individuality in the pursuit of equality might seem puzzling, if not contradictory. Although one might see these as negative consequences of such a socialist system, the arguments resonate more clearly as deductions from psychology used to understand social ideas and policies. After all, except for the Jesuits in Paraguay (hardly egalitarian in a political sense and not lasting a very long time), no strictly egalitarian system had ever been attempted and certainly not in the context of an advanced industrial society. Thus, it would be difficult to calculate the consequences of these conditions that had never existed. Nevertheless, one might still use established psychological ideas to assess them.[6] There were crucial psychological problems of maintaining motivation to work in the face of regimentation and aspiring to meet standards of equality that were too high for the workers involved. But to see these problems as imagined practical consequences of a theory of justice might seem difficult to grasp. The psychological truths possess a strength and reality that can clearly challenge and direct the principle of utility.

Ethology (or character) was the other science that underpinned Mill's method. As we saw in Chapter 10, Mill invoked a feature of British national character, which was generally opposed to sudden, violent change in politics and society, and stood in favour of gradual change, even though existing conditions might be more unjust than those that could be achieved by sudden change. This empirical observation concerning British national character seemed to set a clear obstacle to any socialist and communist doctrines aimed at equality but based on revolutionary principles. Furthermore, sudden change might be regarded as an unintended and possibly minor consequence of a revolutionary theory of justice. But by identifying British national character (admittedly, not the most precise idea), the practical problem of quickly establishing a communist regime through the expropriation of private property and nationalization of the means of production would be seen as virtually impossible (in the sense that it would require force to achieve and would not last without force) unless a major change in British national character, a gradual process in itself, first took place. Mill thus had the tools to analyse and assess different claims to distributive justice in systems of private property, socialism, and communism and point out their strengths and weaknesses.

If we reject the view that for Mill conflicting claims to distributive justice could be assessed simply by calculating consequences and that they might be reconciled by reference to equality, how did Mill conceive of the status of justice within his philosophy? Many moral philosophers take a fairly simple approach. There is such a thing as moral theory, and justice (including distributive justice) is part of it (see Lyons 1994: 3, 109). To understand Mill's theory, presumably one should read *Utilitarianism*. Lyons assumes that an understanding of justice in the fifth chapter of *Utilitarianism*, albeit a critical understanding of the theory, would deliver the truth about distributive justice. But as we have seen in the *Principles* and the 'Chapters', the theory of distributive justice might contain within it conflicting ideas and these ideas might conceivably change from day to day, year to year, generation to generation, and country to country. What is accepted as just at one time is often seen as tyrannical at another. Nevertheless, Mill's relativism and the fact that he rejected transcendent and permanent categories need not affect the status of his theory, so long as not too much is claimed for it as a 'theory'. In his analysis of 'rules of justice' in Mill, Riley writes that 'utilitarian rules of justice distribute equal rights to absolute self-regarding liberty for all mature individuals in any civil society' (Riley 2008: 68). If we set aside Riley's concern to reconcile *On Liberty* and *Utilitarianism*, with which we are not concerned here, we are left with a theory applicable to 'all mature individuals in any civil society'. Perhaps Riley should have said 'ought to distribute' because there is no suggestion that such rules actually exist in any society. But he is correct to say 'any' rather than 'every', as the latter is even further removed from the realm of possible application. One can accept this as part of Riley's account, because it offers a glimpse into the future of the potential adoption of 'rules of justice' and roughly what sort of rules they might be. Riley explains himself further when he writes that 'Mill is working with a non-standard version of utilitarianism that assigns great weight to rules of justice and its calculations of the general welfare' (Riley 2008: 69n.). He is able to incorporate into his argument the relativism as well as the importance Mill gave to justice, without claiming to determine justice pure and simple for everyone through a calculation of consequences.

One problem with Riley's way of exploring 'rules of justice' arises when we consider Mill's treatment of the claims for distributive justice. Mill can envisage, as we have seen, a society where the standards of justice are so high (strict equality of reward and treatment) that injustice is created in the compulsion and regimentation necessary to achieve this standard. This idea of a standard of justice creating injustice in its application is not problematic for Mill, as it is part of the relativism concerning justice that the human condition encounters and Mill understands through psychology and ethology. It becomes more problematic for commentators who seek a 'theory of justice' universally applicable and useful as a criterion for pronouncing clearly on various claims to justice. Those who claim, for example, that communism is just because it supports equality or that liberalism is just, because justice must be compatible with liberty, misunderstand or perhaps underestimate Mill's position. The truth is in the two sciences of psychology and ethology, which can be tested by the canons of logic and scientific method.

Some aspiration towards justice provides a sufficient foundation on which an analysis can proceed. When one overloads Mill by first calling it a 'theory of justice' and second by filling in the theory with a substantive moral doctrine applicable everywhere, the obvious points raised by Mill in examining distributive justice cannot be accommodated. For example, when Berger brings his 'theory' of justice to examine socialism, there is no place for the problems raised here in the theory. He simply summarizes Mill's views 'in a single paragraph' in that very long book (Berger 1984: 147). For it is by no means clear that Mill 'adhered' to 'basic principles of economic justice' (see Berger 1984: 166ff.). To assume that 'principles of economic justice' exist and that they are part of moral theory leaves one in a position that one cannot assess the meaning and potential application of Mill's views. To put my position more strongly, I suggest that Berger, for example, does not provide the criteria to assess the claims to distributive justice of any rule, act, or institution. This assessment requires the two sciences, psychology and ethology, and the assessment deals with how the claims to absolute or relative equality, for example, might be adopted by members of a particular society, at a particular time, given their character, the state of their education, and their psychological dispositions. Once these assessments are made, the 'theory of justice' might clarify the assessment by reference to equality, desert, impartiality, etc., but the relative merits of the claims to justice have already been determined by the applications of psychology and ethology. The role of the 'theory' is thus fairly minimal, while the insights derived from psychology and ethology enable the claims to be assessed and determined. The 'theory of justice' seems to have little to do with this determination.

IV. *Was Mill a Socialist?*

Was Mill himself ideologically a socialist? Hollander (1985: ii. 773) begins his discussion with the famous passage in the *Autobiography* (*CW* i. 239), quoted above at the beginning of Chapter 10, where Mill stated that he and Harriet Mill classed themselves under the general heading of socialists. But as he carefully analyses Mill's position, from the relationship with Harriet Mill (Hollander 1985: ii. 774) to the different positions adopted in the various editions of the *Principles* (Hollander 1985: ii. 786ff.), Hollander finds it difficult to provide a straightforward answer to the question. He insists that 'it is most important to avoid concluding that Mill can be (almost) all things to all men by failing to commit himself', and points to Mill's clear adoption of the goal of introducing co-operation to bring to an end the dependency created by class relations in capitalism (Hollander 1985: ii. 820–1; see also Claeys 1987: 145). But some have found that Mill's commitment to socialism as an economic and/or political system is highly qualified and virtually impossible to pin down (see e.g. Ten 1998: 384–95; see also Miller 2003: 213–38; 2010b).

Others take a more robust view. According to Ryan, Mill's brief remarks on socialism in the *Autobiography* give 'a perfectly credible account of his position'. For Ryan, Mill gave socialism after 1852 'a qualified welcome rather than a qualified cold shoulder' (Ryan 1974: 184). Robson refers to a change in Mill's thought:

The change is simply this: Mill became more convinced of the practicability of certain socialist plans and, as he felt the balance between socialism and free enterprise to be roughly level, he shifted from being an opponent of socialism to being a qualified supporter. (Robson 1968: 248)

Even with Robson, Mill ends up as only a 'qualified supporter', and that does not seem like firm commitment (see also van Holthoon 1971: 109). To avoid Hollander's fear that Mill might seem to be all things to all people, we might adopt a different approach. The philosopher, Henry Sidgwick, commented on Mill's approach to socialism as follows:

> But though Mill had concealed from us the extent of his Socialism, we were all, I think, conscious of having received from him a certain impulse in the Socialistic direction: we had at any rate ceased to regard the science of Political Economy as opposing a hard and fast barrier against the Socialistic conception of the ideal goal of economic progress.[7]

Sidgwick was not simply praising Mill for placing socialism on the agenda of political economy, nor was he, as Winch suggests, revealing the extent of his inspiration from Mill's 'mounting reputation as a public moralist' (Winch 2009: 204). He was providing a unique reading of Mill, seeing that Mill could not answer the question as to his commitment to socialism, because his philosophical method did not allow him to do so. But there is an answer to the question, as Sidgwick suggests, if one follows the complex arguments of his philosophy and his economics (see Riley: 1996: 68; Miller 2003: 237).

The denial that Mill had a simple answer to the question of whether or not he was a socialist is related to the fact that he was not primarily a public moralist and his avoidance of final and categorical moral positions would not permit him to become one. Among recent commentators on Mill Pappé has some insight as to how Mill regarded socialism:

> He was not instrumental in bringing about socialism. He was one of those who sensed it coming. He taught people to keep their heads in the new social and economic situation, not to be swayed by the new nor to stem the tide, but to exercise their sovereign judgment subject to analysis and to experiential insight. (Pappé 1960: 45–6; see also van Holthoon 1971: 79)

As in the passage from Sidgwick, we can see here a different view of Mill's approach to socialism. The question is less one of adhering to or opposing a view and more one of considering all sides of various issues, but without losing one's head or failing to exercise one's judgement. If Mill was not a public moralist, but primarily a philosopher and logician, an acknowledgement of that position would allow us to provide the best answer to the question as to whether or not he was a socialist.

12

God and the Religion
of Humanity

Mill's opinions regarding God and religion are fairly straightforward, yet have stimulated considerable debate. The straightforward element concerns his personal belief. 'Amen', quipped Bentham at the end of a satisfactory exchange of letters in 1827, persuading the young and reluctant Mill that his name, as editor, should be added to the title page of Bentham's *Rationale of Judicial Evidence*. To this he added: 'If you know not what that means, send to the Booksellers for a Hebrew Dictionary' (Bentham 2006: 349). Mill, himself, recognized his uniqueness, even in relation to Bentham, his father, and the long tradition of scepticism and Epicureanism in Britain, when he wrote that he had 'the destiny, very rare in my country, never to have believed in God, even in my childhood' (*CW* xiii. 560).[1] Mill's uniqueness should not be underestimated, as it gave him a detachment from religious controversy throughout his life (see also Cowling 1990: 79). He could never have written a work like Bentham's *Not Paul, But Jesus* (1823), as he lacked both the background of being raised in a faith and the passion which rebellion against such a faith might engender. Even when he considered seriously various substitutes for religion or theology (e.g. the religion of humanity), his position was measured, and he considered characteristically all sides of these issues, thus avoiding simple hostility to religion or one-sided arguments.[2]

I. *Mill's Self-Censorship*

Let us begin this chapter by considering how one who had no belief in God could still write about religion in the context of nineteenth-century England. In his first letter to Comte, Mill distinguished religion in England from the rest of Europe by referring to its greater 'roots' in England, despite the loss of its traditional civilizing role. 'It is regrettable, I believe, for us, that the revolutionary philosophy, which was very active a dozen years ago today has fallen into decrepitude before finishing its work' (*CW* xiii. 489–90). By 'revolutionary philosophy' Mill meant the Enlightenment philosophers who sought to undermine, if not overthrow, existing religion and theology via their writings. This theme of religion regaining ground in the nineteenth century in Britain recurred in a number of his letters to Comte.[3]

In his second letter Mill spelt out the attitude towards religion that had guided him in the composition of *A System of Logic*:

> You should not ignore the fact that for us, as writers, if we avow openly antireligious or even antichristian opinions, it would compromise not only one's social position, . . . but also, and more seriously, one's chance of being read. I take risks already, when I set aside the religious point of view and abstain from rhetorical eulogies of providential wisdom, generally made by philosophers, including unbelievers, in my country. I allude rarely to this order of ideas and do not attempt to awaken any religious antipathy in the vulgar reader. I believe that I have written in a manner that no reader, either Christian or unbeliever, cannot understand the true character of my opinions, though I rely on the worldly prudence which generally prevents religious writers from noting, without necessity, the irreligion of a mind of some scientific value.
>
> (*CW* xiii. 491–2)

These remarks were made by Mill after he had written the *Logic* but prior to its publication, where his care in its organization and composition in fact led to a wide acceptance among both believers and unbelievers. He continued in the same letter by pointing out his intentional use of some terminology—'certain expressions of metaphysical origin'—which would be particularly acceptable to believers, but Mill gave these terms definitions which stressed a positive sense and eliminated any meaning that could not be referred to either observable phenomena or abstract names for phenomena (*CW* xiii. 492).

There is, however, another side to Mill's position as a unique unbeliever. In the same letter that he declared his uniqueness to

Comte, he could refer to a grand vision of positive philosophy (as embodied in Comte's *Cours*), that it was capable 'of taking possession of the high social role that only religions have imperfectly filled' (*CW* xiii. 560). Here, for Mill, was a social philosophy that could serve as the basis of 'a general regeneration of human morality', and an 'idea of Humanity', and was the only idea that was capable of 'replacing that of God' (*CW* xiii. 560). Mill's enthusiasm for Comte's system as a way of replacing God with humanity and his later advocacy of a religion of humanity were never meant to elevate humanity to divine status or even to transform it into a transcendental category, but to see in a wholly secular philosophy the possibility of living without the idea of God.

It is important to appreciate Mill's caution, as well as his enthusiasm. When he was sent by Comte in April 1844 a copy of his *Discours sur l'esprit positif*, a summary of his position in the *Cours* (see Comte 1845: 1–108), Mill reacted negatively to the essay. He opposed any translation into English of either the essay or the *Cours*. For both, Mill wrote, repeating his sentiments expressed with regard to the *Logic* more than two years earlier:

The time has not come when, without compromising our cause, we can in England direct open attacks against theology, including Christian theology. We can only avoid the problem by eliminating it from all philosophical and social discussion and by passing over all questions which relate to it. Consequently, it seems to me that the propaganda your works will not fail to cause in England will occur by their being read in the original. Those who have a certain scientific culture and religious emancipation, or even semi-emancipation, are nearly always capable of reading your book in French and translation would not be of any utility. (*CW* xiii. 625–6)

Nearly a year later in January 1845 Comte proposed the establishment of a new journal, a '*Positive Review*' (*CG* ii. 320). For a variety of reasons, Mill reacted with horror to this proposal and one of the reasons concerned religion. Mill cited Grote's view that at that time in England 'the philosopher bows low with affectation before the priest' and expressed his own belief that a journal, unlike a book, might well provoke a religious reaction (*CW* xiii. 657). Seven months later, when Comte had proposed yet another publication, Mill again responded negatively: 'To place positivism in open contradiction to all religion is, perhaps, in my view, a very inopportune use of it in England today' (*CW* xiii. 671). The public, he believed, associated atheism with the 'school of Diderot and d'Holbach'.

While he granted that there might be some advantage in allowing Comte's atheism, so very different from this earlier school, to be discussed in public, his position was clear:

Today, I think it is necessary, in writing for England, to remain absolutely silent on the question of religion, except to strike indirectly at religious beliefs as one can. This reserve is especially necessary for a writer already known for having professed openly antireligious opinions, because the directors of reviews will examine such matters more closely than in any other case. (*CW* xiii. 671)

In dealing with the reviews or other publications Mill proposed that one should treat a subject 'as if religion did not exist' (*CW* xiii. 671). In other words scientists were then beginning to undermine religious belief in a number of subjects from geology to physiology without ever referring to religion. The same development could take place within philosophy, as Mill had successfully attempted to achieve in the *Logic*, where he set religious or theological controversy apart from theories of scientific proof and logical analysis. Furthermore, he warned Comte of the consequences of publicly attacking religious belief:

But today the publication, in English, of a pamphlet in your name, where all religious belief is openly dismissed, will probably close to you all journals of this country. Anti-religious *words* are feared and dismissed here more than opposition to religion itself. (*CW* xiii. 671)

As we can see in these passages, Mill was particularly sensitive to English national character. His decision to publish the *Logic* was based in part on its being appropriate for the state of philosophy in England rather than for possessing a 'permanent philosophic character' (*CW* xiii. 491). At numerous points Mill invoked national character, often to oppose a view of Comte, who (as a self-proclaimed citizen of Western Europe) was not willing to give much credence to Mill's position. But Mill was never a nationalist (see Varouxakis 1998, 2002a, 2007). 'I have stood for a long time,' he wrote to Comte, 'in a type of open opposition against English national character, which in many respects is antipathetic to me, and to which I prefer the French, German, or Italian character.' Yet, at the same time he could write that he had 'since he was a youth, . . . occupied himself with the study of the English character' (*CW* xiii. 696–7). His remarks about the discussion of religion in England should not be seen as reflecting his own views, which strongly supported freedom of religion and freedom of expression. But Mill felt that France was far in advance of England with regard to the public discussion of religion. The freedom Comte enjoyed in France was not present in England, and if this fact was not taken to heart, the future philosophical, political, and literary publications not only of Comte but also of Mill, who publicly supported him, would be in danger of a rapid decline in public acceptance.

II. *Separation of Spiritual and Temporal Powers*

Mill's personal attitude towards God and religious orthodoxy is relatively clear, despite his acceptance in the composition of his works of numerous concessions to the power of religion in England. But there are aspects of his thought that are more difficult to understand, partly because they emerge from his relationship with Comte and partly because they are connected with important ethical and political ideas. One idea is the doctrine of the separation of spiritual and temporal powers. As we have seen in Chapter 6, Comte had established the principle that the philosopher should avoid participation in political life. At first Mill was reluctant to accept it, but eventually he embraced it with considerable enthusiasm, though also with some reservations.

Mill's reluctance was based on a number of factors. He felt that in England (as opposed to France) no member of the elite would pay much attention to anyone who did not engage in public life. He also felt that 'sociological speculations' could not make much progress in England as long as England had not experienced its '1789' (*CW* xiii. 493), and that required an active involvement in political life. Comte, it seems, was intent on protecting philosophy from a dilution either by mediocre minds, which would drift towards practical politics, or waste time and energy on pointless political projects. Philosophy, left to its own devices, would lead the way to regeneration in Europe. Just how this was to be effected was by no means clear, though he rejected Mill's view that England had not experienced its '1789'. As far as Comte was concerned, the French Revolution was for all of Europe (including England).

While Mill was rereading the fifth volume of the *Cours* in February 1842, prior to his completion of the *Logic* and prior to Comte's completion of the sixth and final volume, he wrote:

I can at least indicate, that for me the most positive and certain result of the study of the fifth volume is a complete conviction of the great principle that alone among contemporary philosophers you have enunciated, that of the definitive separation of the two powers, temporal and spiritual. (*CW* xiii. 501)

Mill continued by asserting that this 'definitive separation' meant that each of these powers must develop 'in a totally distinct manner'. But in his way of ending a sentence by qualifying (even opposing) his main thesis, he added that his view 'does not for me imply the impossibility that the same individual can participate to a certain point in the work of both' (*CW* xiii. 501–2). In explaining himself, he wrote:

I think on the contrary that a partially active education is necessary for the perfection of the speculative education, as all philosophers accept that a specu-lative education is necessary for active life. (*CW* xiii. 502)

If Mill's new position seemed to adopt Comte's idea of the separation of spiritual and temporal powers, he so qualified his acceptance as to make the reader feel that he had not accepted it at all, particularly if 'a partially active education' is necessary 'for the perfection of the speculative education'. However, Mill did proceed to clarify his position in an important way:

I am, nonetheless, radically cured, and this by your work, of any tendency towards the utopian doctrines, which look to place the government of society in the hands of philosophers, or even to make it depend on high intellectual capacity more generally. (*CW* xiii. 502)

Mill admitted that he had been tempted by the doctrine of the rule of philosophers, which he had found in Saint-Simon and which he believed might favour intellectual progress. Yet, as in China, rule by an intellectual elite would in the end corrupt the intellectual class, stifle progress, and produce a form of rule which Mill called a 'pedantocracy' (see *CW* xiii. 502). What developed in China was rule by a majority of mediocre scientists and scholars who lacked any originality or deep insight. Mill noted that he had anticipated his new position, adapted from Comte, to an extent by his own concep-tion of the actual historical conditions for progress in societies. He found that in these societies there were two progressive forces and the ruling party was never able to incorporate both of them or to repress one or the other. If they had tried and failed, the society might well disintegrate (like Athens) or if they succeeded, they would eventually produce a static state (like China). Mill believed

217

that he had found in this theory of historical progress a reply to 'any political system, democratic or Benthamist' (*CW* xiii. 502). And he employed part of this approach in the *Logic*. But he also recognized that he had not yet worked out how to apply his own insight to modern politics. This dimension he found in Comte's doctrine of the separation of spiritual and temporal powers.

Nevertheless, when Mill returned to his personal role in relation to politics in 1842, he repeated his view, contrary to that of Comte, that in England, 'I still find the parliamentary tribune the best chair of public education for a well-placed philosophic sociologist'. This philosophic sociologist 'might seek to make ministers or to direct them according to his ideas, but abstain from involvement except probably at those critical moments, such as those I do not believe are far distant' (*CW* xiii. 503). Perhaps Comte might be satisfied with this limited separation of powers. For Mill, however, he could refer a month later to the continued antagonism between temporal and spiritual powers as a condition for human progress, as a new area of common agreement between them.

In spite of this lingering disagreement between Mill and Comte over the philosopher's engagement in politics, Mill held to the doctrine of the separation of the two powers, and, most importantly, to the belief that regeneration in society would depend on the development of a spiritual force. As he wrote:

I appreciate the wise reserve that you have used in your opinion that immediate discussion of political institutions, properly called, are premature, at least of the temporal order. You have brought out very well the feeling that social regeneration depends now on spiritual development, which is more and more evident to enlightened spirits due to the failure for almost a century of all theoretical and practical attempts to renew the state of humanity by institutions alone. (*CW* xiii. 553)

So far, we can see Mill aligning himself with Comte's position. The temporal power in Comte's view was to be left to its own devices, and mainly placed in the hands of captains of industry. The spiritual power would reside in a highly organized group of philosophers who would control education, live simply on a state stipend from the temporal power, and proceed to effect an intellectual and moral regeneration of society. Nevertheless, Mill seemed slightly uneasy with this simple arrangement. He pointed in addition to the 'highly regarded' leaders of 'the proletarian political movement' who put forth both political projects and ideas of 'morality and intellectual culture for the popular masses' (*CW* xiii. 553). Even though these ideas were based on the much criticized (by Comte and Mill) 'metaphysical and negative philosophy', and supported democratic institutions, Mill seemed sympathetic to their position and sought to take up some issues of temporal reform (organization of industry, representative institutions, etc.). Comte dismissed these issues as irrelevant to the current state of European society:

the political efficacy appropriate to the metaphysical and negative philosophy, still dominant, is henceforth essentially finished, and the great revolution of the West can only make a crucial step forward under the general ascendency of a new and fully positive philosophy, which will spontaneously assimilate into itself all that remains of the purely critical spirit... (*CG* ii. 107)

Comte's vision of the role of a positive philosophy was at this stage a defence of philosophy and philosophers and had little to do with religion, except for the fact that the philosophers would take over the educative role in society traditionally reserved to the clergy. Indeed, he seemed to rely on this vision of the role of the philosopher even in his struggles with his French detractors and his English financial supporters (see e.g. *CG* iii. 47).

When Mill later wrote *Auguste Comte and Positivism*, he could not avoid the theme of the separation of spiritual and temporal powers, but his response was considerably different. In part I, where he discussed the material known to him at the time of their correspondence two decades earlier, he seemed to adopt some aspects of Comte's conception of a spiritual power. Both were concerned with the consequences of narrow, specialized education and favoured 'a large and liberal general education' (*CW* x. 312). But, as we have seen in Chapter 6 where Mill's application of the new liberty principle in this work was discussed, Comte's 'spiritual authority' was now seen as 'spiritual despotism' (*CW* x. 314). Furthermore, instead of criticizing the negative, metaphysical school for a hundred years of failure to provide the ideas that would reform positively the temporal institutions of society, Mill invoked his notion of contraries with Comte and the negative, revolutionary schools each holding half of the truth. Mill now believed that Comte's conception of spiritual power, embedded in a centralized bureaucratic institution, would not only be despotic, but would also destroy the very principle of the separation of the two powers and be 'repugnant to mankind' (*CW* x. 314).

As Mill considered Comte's later writings in the second part of *Auguste Comte and Positivism*, he also criticized Comte's idea of spiritual power. Comte seemed to have replaced the quest for scientific truth about society with a system created out of his own imagination. Yet, at its foundation remained the separation of spiritual and temporal power, with the former the only 'counterpoise' to the absolute power of civil rulers (*CW* x. 344). As Mill explored the details of these aspects of Comte's idea of spiritual power, the more he rejected them, and he became increasingly content to invoke intellectual liberty in place of spiritual power or look to Benthamite institutional reforms to ensure progress in the civil sphere. It is thus fairly clear that the idea of spiritual power and the separation of spiritual and temporal power, however much embraced by Mill, remained a means of achieving mainly political ends, and to the extent that Comte sought to provide a religious dimension (using the language of Roman Catholicism to do so), Mill retreated from the doctrine.

III. *The Religion of Humanity*

As we have seen, Mill was attracted to the idea of a religion of humanity. He shared this attraction, if not the precise doctrine, with Comte, for neither of them, if they adopted a religion, believed in a God.[4] Mill wrote of Comte's ideas in *Auguste Comte and Positivism*:

He made no change in the purely negative attitude which he maintained towards theology: his religion is without a God. In saying this, we have done enough to induce nine-tenths of all readers, at least in our own country, to avert their faces and close their ears. To have no religion, though scandalous enough, is an idea they are partly used to: but to have no God, and to talk of religion, is to their feelings at once an absurdity and an impiety. Of the remaining tenth, a great proportion, perhaps, will turn away from anything which calls itself by the name of religion at all. Between the two, it is difficult to find an audience who can be induced to listen to M. Comte without an insurmountable prejudice. (*CW* x. 332)

Mill's attempt at humour and the curious way he addressed his readers while at the same time describing Comte's position, prepared the way for an important declaration about both Comte and himself:

Though conscious of being in an extremely small minority, we venture to think that a religion may exist without a belief in a God, and that a religion without a God may be, even to Christians, an instructive and profitable object of contemplation. (*CW* x. 332)

Mill then proceeded to depict the logical conditions for such a religion without God and some of the characteristics of Comte's religion. He first stated several necessary conditions for the constitution of a religion. The first was a 'creed' or conviction—'claiming authority over the whole of human life'. The second was a 'belief...respecting human destiny and duty, to which the believer inwardly acknowledges that all his actions ought to be subordinate'. This 'deliberately adopted' belief should be accompanied by a third condition, a 'sentiment'—'sufficiently powerful' to give the creed 'the authority over human conduct to which it lays claim in theory' (CW x. 332).

Mill then proceeded to argue that what Comte had developed constituted a religion. He cited Carlyle's remark in *Sartor Resartus* (1837: 170) that a belief in the 'Infinite nature of Duty' was religious, and remarked:

M. Comte believes in what is meant by the infinite nature of duty, but he refers the obligations of duty, as well as all sentiments of devotion, to a concrete object, at once ideal and real; the Human Race, conceived as a continuous whole, including the past, the present, and the future. (CW x. 333)

Mill's evocation of Comte's 'Grand Etre'—the human race—was developed with considerable skill. Not only could it constitute a religion, but it solved a number of difficulties associated with religion. Mill also noted that it need not be anthropocentric and could be extended to cover the duty of humankind towards inferior animals, as well as duties towards humanity, past, present, and future (see CW x. 334). He concluded this depiction of Comte's religion of humanity with strong support. It is clear that Mill had adopted the idea of a religion of humanity, but his subscription did not mean that here was a church with a membership of two or, possibly, a few more members. He added, to his acceptance of the legitimate development of Comte's philosophy into a religion, an important remark that 'all other religions are made better in proportion as, in their practical result, they are brought to coincide with that which he aimed at constructing' (CW x. 335). In other words, this outward-looking religion would seek to have other religions conform to its precepts, but not necessarily to adopt the details of Comte's version of it.

At the very point where Mill was most fully extolling Comte's creation, he asserted that Comte had made a fundamental error. This error, as we have seen in Chapter 6, consisted in making the good of humanity the standard of right and wrong, and then insisting on altruism (a term coined by Comte) as the only motive for conduct (see *CW* x. 335). In discussing Comte's religion, he also compared it with 'extreme' Calvinism in so far as whatever was not a moral duty was a sin (see *CW* x. 337).[5] Mill then proceeded to criticize Comte's conception of religion as a denial of individual liberty. '[T]he notion of a happiness for all, procured by the self-sacrifice of each, if the obligation is really felt to be a sacrifice, is a contradiction' (*CW* x. 338). Mill invoked a number of themes from *On Liberty* and focused these on the question of moral duty.[6] This position was repeated by Mill in his *Autobiography*, where he wrote:

for Comte's work recognizes no religion except that of Humanity, yet it leaves an irresistible conviction that any moral beliefs, concurred in by the community generally, may be brought to bear upon the whole conduct and lives of its individual members with an energy and potency truly alarming to think of. The book stands a monumental warning to thinkers on society and politics, of what happens when once men lose sight, in their speculations, of the value of Liberty and of Individuality. (*CW* i. 221)

In the *Autobiography* Mill also dismissed Comte's later work, *Système de Politique Positive* as 'the completest system of spiritual and temporal despotism, which ever yet emanated from a human brain, unless possibly that of Ignatius Loyola' (*CW* i. 221). In *On Liberty*, itself, Mill developed this critique, linked to Carlyle, and when he came to Comte, he again referred to the *Système* as 'establishing (though by moral more than by legal appliances) a despotism of society over the individual, surpassing anything contemplated in the political ideal of the most rigid disciplinarian among the ancient philosophers' (*CW* xviii. 227).

As we have seen, Mill retained the view that Comte's idea of a religion of humanity was flawed from the outset by its establishment of a spiritual despotism. We have also noted Mill's attempt to apply the principles of *On Liberty* to Comte's conception of moral duty. The point to be noted here is that in *On Liberty* and the *Autobiography* Mill did not reveal his sympathies for a religion of humanity (but see *Utilitarianism*: *CW* x. 232), while in *Auguste Comte and Positivism*, as we have seen, he did so, but rejected Comte's version of it. In the *Autobiography*, especially, Mill seemed to leave the reader with the impression that a religion of humanity was inherently despotic. In *Utilitarianism* Mill did not invoke a religion of humanity, Comtean or otherwise. But he did assert that utilitarianism was compatible with religion in numerous respects.

'If it be a true belief,' he wrote, 'that God desires, above all things, the happiness of his creatures and that was his purpose in their creation, utility is not only not a godless doctrine, but more profoundly religious than any other' (CW x. 222). 'If it be meant that utilitarianism does not recognize the revealed will of God, as the supreme law of morals,' he continued, 'I answer, that an utilitarian who believes in the perfect goodness and wisdom of God, necessarily believes that whatever God has thought fit to reveal on the subject of morals, must fulfil the requirements of utility in a supreme degree' (CW x. 222). Nevertheless, this clear compatibility between utilitarianism and a belief in God is not the same thing as a religion of humanity without any God. At least in *Utilitarianism* Mill did not proclaim utilitarianism as the basis of a religion of humanity, even though it might easily have been conceived by Mill as supplying the ethical foundation for one.

In both 'Utility of Religion' (CW x. 403–28) and 'Theism' (CW x. 429–89), two of the three posthumously published essays on religion (the third was 'Nature': CW x. 373–402), Mill briefly returned to the idea of a religion of humanity, though in these instances without any reference to Comte or, for that matter, to utilitarianism. According to Helen Taylor's 'Introductory Notice', 'Utility of Religion' was written in the 1850s. She also noted that Mill completed 'Theism' in 1873 (the year of his death; see CW x, pp. cxxiii, 371–2).[7]

Mill's discussions of a religion of humanity were reserved for the very end of both 'Utility of Religion' and 'Theism'. In 'Utility of Religion' Mill approached the religion of humanity as part of an answer to the question of why cultivated minds persisted in their need for religious belief. He advanced one simple reason, that human knowledge was severely limited, but the desire to know was boundless. With elegance and insight Mill developed this theme into the urge by cultivated people to explore through religion and, additionally, by poetry a 'region' where 'imagination is free to fill up the vacancy with the imagery most congenial to itself; sublime and elevating if it be a lofty imagination, low and mean if it be a grovelling one' (CW x. 419). Mill had no doubt that religion was considered of value by many individuals. It was 'a source of satisfaction and of elevated feelings' (CW x. 420), and Mill would not deny the reality and importance of such feelings by associating them with delusion or false consciousness imposed by churchmen, moralists, and rulers. He posed this question:

whether in order to obtain this good, it is necessary to travel beyond the boundaries of the world which we inhabit; or whether the idealization of our earthly life, the cultivation of a high conception of what *it* may be made, is not capable of supplying a poetry, and, in the best sense of the word, a religion, equally fitted to exalt the feelings, and (with the same aid from education) still better calculated to ennoble the conduct, than any belief respecting the unseen powers.   (*CW* x. 420)

In a curious argument Mill first accepted that many people would think that such a religion, based on 'the smallness and insignificance of life', would lead to the adoption of the so-called Epicurean maxim of 'let us eat and drink, for to-morrow we die' (see *CW* x. 420; see also 1 Corinthians 15: 32). Mill was content to adopt a part of this maxim:

To make the most of the present for all good purposes, those of enjoyment among the rest; to keep under control those mental dispositions which lead to undue sacrifice of present good for a future which may never arrive; to cultivate the habit of deriving pleasure from things within our reach, rather than from the too eager pursuit of objects at a distance; to think all time wasted which is not spent either in personal pleasure or in doing things useful to oneself or others; these are wise maxims, and the 'carpe diem' doctrine, carried thus far, is a rational and legitimate corollary from the shortness of life.   (*CW* x. 420)

Mill's invocation of Epicureanism clearly distinguished his version of a religion of humanity from that of Comte. But this element by no means exhausted his approach to the problem of the shortness of life. He continued:

Let it be remembered that if individual life is short, the life of the human species is not short; its indefinite duration is practically equivalent to endlessness; and being combined with indefinite capability of improvement, it offers to the imagination and sympathies a large enough object to satisfy any reasonable demand for grandeur of aspiration. If such an object appears small to a mind accustomed to dream of infinite and eternal beatitudes, it will expand into far other dimensions when those baseless fancies shall have receded into the past.   (*CW* x. 420)

Mill's last line regarding 'infinite and eternal beatitudes' as 'baseless fancies' would not endear him to churchmen, but his main object was not to detract from supernatural religion so that the religion of humanity would satisfy human aspirations. He sought instead to show how various secular ideas—he used the example of Rome—could take on characteristics of a religion, as the devotion to Rome by Romans and even by a philosopher, like Cicero, did. This devotion took on the strength and characteristics of a morality, but equally other aspects of morality could take on characteristics of a religion. The knowledge that great figures from the past—Mill mentioned Socrates, Howard, Washington, Antoninus, or Christ—would have been sympathetic to one's actions, or that one was attempting to act in the same spirit that motivated them, 'has operated on the very best minds, as a strong incentive to act up to their highest feelings and convictions' (CW x. 422).

Mill then brought his thoughts together in an important passage regarding the religion of humanity:

To call these sentiments by the name morality, exclusively of any other title, is claiming too little for them. They are a real religion; of which, as of other religions, outward good works (the utmost meaning usually suggested by the word morality) are only a part, and are indeed rather the fruits of the religion than the religion itself. The essence of religion is the strong and earnest direction of the emotions and desires towards an ideal object, recognized as of the highest excellence, and as rightfully paramount over all selfish objects of desire. This condition is fulfilled by the Religion of Humanity in as eminent a degree, and in as high a sense, as by the supernatural religions even in their best manifestations, and far more so than in any of their others. (CW x. 422)

Mill clearly had placed the religion of humanity on a collision course with traditional religions and, particularly, with Christianity. He argued that in a number of respects the religion of humanity was superior to Christianity and other supernatural religions. First, he noted that it was 'disinterested': 'It carries the thoughts and feelings out of self, and fixes them on an unselfish object, loved and pursued as an end for its own sake' (CW x. 422). In contrast, supernatural religions cultivated the selfish feelings in the way they used threats and promises with respect to a future life. Mill granted that some believers in supernatural religions had been highly unselfish, directing their minds not towards threats and promises, but emphasizing 'the idea of a Being to whom they looked up with a confiding love, and in whose hands they willingly left all that related especially to themselves' (CW x. 422). Yet, for most ordinary minds religion appealed to selfish feelings by its promises of salvation and threats of damnation, and Mill believed the religion of humanity was superior due to the absence of this dimension.

Second, Mill pointed to the confusions and sophistry involved in reconciling different aspects of Christianity. The God of nature ruled over a 'clumsily made and capriciously governed' creation, and yet one must somehow conceive this God as embodying 'absolute perfection', in spite of the 'blind partiality, atrocious cruelty, and reckless injustice' one finds in the created world (*CW* x. 423). Mill conceded that the God of revelation, as in the Sermon on the Mount, was a more benign and loving figure, but in Christianity this figure had to be reconciled with the God of creation. What particularly troubled Mill was the effect on the mind of all the sophistry and confusion involved in attempting such reconciliations and its effects on individual development. Those who survived this intellectual confusion seemed to do so only by assuming that the ways of God and Providence were mysterious and that divine morality was some-how different from ours. But, if this was the case, the worship of moral perfection in God became pointless (*CW* x. 424).

Third, Mill turned to what he called 'the moral difficulties and perversions' involved in revelation and which were distinct from the otherwise highly moral sayings of Christ. Mill's main example was the contradiction he thought was involved in the creation of a hell and, additionally, in the creation of 'countless generations of human beings with the certain foreknowledge that he was creating them for this fate' (*CW* x. 424). Mill asserted that numerous doctrines, like 'atonement and redemption, original sin and vicarious punishment', as well as belief in Christ's divine mission as a condition for salva-tion, were actually foreign to the words of Christ, and hence not necessarily ascribable to Christianity (*CW* x. 424). Nevertheless, he thought that every form of Christianity contained one moral contra-diction, namely that the religion was not given to all, but to a 'favoured minority'. Millions of people had lived and died without this divine remedy for sin and suffering. Additionally, the 'divine message' was not presented in a way that cultivated minds could easily accept, thus creating a gulf between scientific knowledge and Christianity (*CW* x. 424).

Mill mentioned the possibility of selective belief in Christian doctrines so as to preserve one's devotion without 'any perversion of the moral sentiments' (*CW* x. 425), by setting aside any doctrine that conflicted with the beauty and beneficence of the Gospels or in nature. Mill referred to Plato, to Manicheanism, and, curiously, to a similar creed 'devoutly held by at least one cultivated and conscien-tious person of our day', which held: 'that all the mass of evil which exists was undesigned by, and exists not by the appointment of, but in spite of the Being whom we are called upon to worship' (*CW* x. 425). Mill argued that this doctrine could incorporate a morality without contradiction, but he held that it was no substitute for a religion of humanity.

Mill's final argument for the religion of humanity arose from his consideration that supernatural religions apparently had the advantage of extending to individuals the possibility of life after death. He dismissed those who were so utterly selfish as to seek another selfish life after death, but with respect to the unselfish, he wrote that, as they became happier in their lives, they would feel less of a need to prolong them and to seek other lives after death. Those who had never been happy were most inclined either to prolong their lives or to seek another one. He then contrasted those believers in the religion of humanity who would be happy to survive longer than the current span of life, but at some point 'would have had enough of existence, and would gladly lie down and take their eternal rest' (*CW* x. 427).

The religion of humanity was thus meant to be a real religion, and its superiority over supernatural religions was based on moral clarity and logical consistency. It could incorporate the life and sayings of Jesus, not as the son of God, but as one who, as he wrote in 'Theism', his final work on religion, was 'in the very first rank of men of sublime genius of whom our species can boast' (*CW* x. 487–8). Mill continued:

When this pre-eminent genius is combined with the qualities of probably the greatest moral reformer, and martyr to that mission, who ever existed upon earth, religion cannot be said to have made a bad choice in pitching on this man as the ideal representative and guide of humanity; nor, even now, would it be easy, even for an unbeliever, to find a better translation of the rule of virtue from the abstract into the concrete, than to endeavour so to live that Christ would approve our life. (*CW* x. 488)

In addition, Mill looked to Christianity, once purged by 'rational scepticism', to give assistance to the religion of humanity, which would be, as Mill put it, 'the religion of the Future' of which 'I cannot entertain a doubt' (*CW* x. 489).

iv. *Mill and Religion*

Mill's writing on the religion of humanity in 'Utility of Religion' and 'Theism' completed his development from the 1820s, where he first began to take seriously the social importance of religion in society and Coleridgean ideas, such as the clerisy (see Knights 1978: 1, 37, 146–7). Yet, this chapter, for the most part, confirms Bain's view concerning Mill and religion, and, particularly Christianity:

It has been said by his opponents, with some show of plausibility, that Mill was at bottom a religious man...[W]e may call his aspirations and hopes for a bright future to the race, a religion of humanity....[T]he fact remains, that in everything characteristic of the creed of Christendom, he was a thorough-going negationist. He admitted neither its truth nor its utility. (Bain 1882: 139–40)

The starting point for this chapter was an appreciation of Mill's uniqueness in matters of religion, the fact that he was raised without a belief in God and never possessed one. Whatever the foundations and the aspirations of his version of a religion of humanity, it was confined to humanity alone—past, present, and future. While it could include the welfare of animals, it did not include God. Mill wrote eloquently of the importance of the morality of Jesus, but so could a sceptic like Bentham in *Not Paul, But Jesus* (see Bentham 1823: 394). Nevertheless, there was an important difference between Bentham and Mill. Bentham was critical of Christianity, tried to undermine its teachings, and had nothing with which to replace it. At times it seemed as if Mill shared this view. Mill, however, gave a new twist to this assault on religion and followed Comte in attempting to replace Christianity with a religion of humanity, though one that Comte would have rejected because of its embodiment of individual liberty.

Mill's development of a religion of humanity, his sympathy with the arguments for design in 'Nature' (see *CW* x. 448), his appreciation that religion served profound human needs, and his interest in writers from Plato to Coleridge who explored inner human qualities that would respond positively to religion—all of this supports the view (contrary to that of Bain) that Mill was 'at bottom a religious man'. In recent years more has been made of this position, with Mill's attitude towards religion used to develop new and more attractive forms of liberalism that are more sympathetic to religion than were Mill's predecessors, Bentham and James Mill (see Eisenach 2002: 189–216; Devigne 1998: 231–56; Megill 1998: 301–16; Capaldi 2004: 339–50). Those more critical of Mill on religion have seen in his attitude and his sympathy with Comte a disquieting illiberalism. One feature common to those who applaud Mill's liberalism on account of his views on religion as well as to those who criticize Mill because of the way he turned the philosophy he inherited into a 'proselytizing liberalism' and a 'narrow and intolerant creed' (see Knights 1978: 141, quoting from Cowling 1963) is a failure to deal with the consequences of Mill's engagement with Comte.

Those who have approached Mill on religion from the perspective of Comte seem to have a different understanding of their relationship. But even here there are difficulties. According to Wright, 'the first and most famous of Comte's British followers was John Stuart Mill, who emerged from initial enthusiasm through subsequent disillusion to become a firm believer in the need for a reformed religion of humanity, divested of its founder's authoritarian politics and personal idiosyncrasies' (Wright 1986: 40). As Wright points out, by 1848 Mill grasped the importance of Comte's work in transforming humanity (the *culte de l'humanité*) from a substitute for religion to the status of a religion (Wright 1986: 44; *CW* xiii. 738–9). After tracing the effects of Comte's ideas through transformations in *Utilitarianism*, *On Liberty*, and elsewhere, he concludes that Mill 'was the great reformer of Positivism, modifying many of Comte's ideas but also giving them a much wider publicity than they might otherwise have achieved' (Wright 1986: 50).

Pickering's study of Comte also contains important remarks on Mill's use of Comte's ideas on religion, though she notably depicts Mill, like Comte, as 'an early unbeliever', when, in fact, he never believed at all (Pickering 1993: i. 507). Furthermore, she is also unaware of the complex relationship between Bentham and James Mill on the one hand and J. S. Mill on the other with regard to social and political issues, as, for example, their views on education (see Pickering 1993: i. 513). Nevertheless, she is one of a few scholars to have paid close attention to the details of the interaction between Mill and Comte in their correspondence (see also Pickering 2009: ii. 70–113). She also provides the fullest discussion so far of Comte's views on the separation of spiritual and temporal powers. Of special interest are her critical remarks regarding Comte's vision of society:

He had, for example, vastly overestimated the decline of religion and the military spirit. And when he claimed that the government had completely abandoned the intellectual and moral realm, he overlooked the censorship to which he himself was subject as well as the governmental regulations about the educational system that had prevented him from becoming part of the University. Much of Comte's theory derived from wishful thinking. (Pickering 1993: i. 669)

Besides 'wishful thinking', as the basis of parts of his theory, Pickering has seen, for example, in Comte's doctrine of the separation of spiritual and temporal powers, not necessarily the remedy for 'conservatism, authoritarianism, and intellectual megalomania' that Comte sought to establish, but in fact a new conservatism, authoritarianism, and intellectual megalomania (Pickering 1993: i. 672). As Mill gradually became aware of these aspects of Comte's thought and then the way Comte's madness emerged in his later writings, he retreated to the position of the *Logic*, which, though adopting a considerable number of Comte's ideas, used the doctrine he once thought of abandoning in favour of Comte's evolving position as a continuing foundation for his own social science. Instead of Wright's conception of Mill as a reformer of Comtean positivism, it is perhaps more accurate to say that Mill's own view was more of a retreat from positivism to the negative philosophy of Bentham and James Mill. Mill left just enough of the religion of humanity to establish a vision of humanity itself as part of the moral aspirations of mankind.[8]

13

Conclusion: Liberty and Despotism in *The Subjection of Women*

In this concluding chapter my main object will be to use Mill's late essay, *The Subjection of Women* (1869) (*CW* xxi. 259–340), to draw together a number of the themes developed in the earlier chapters of the book.[1] Berger has written that the *Subjection* 'was one of his most important works': not only 'his most radical and far-reaching social tract', but also 'a place where the most central themes in his moral philosophy are brought to bear on an issue of vital practical concern' (Berger 1984: 195–6).[2] My study of the *Subjection* will build on, but also differ from that of Berger. He treats the essay as an important work of Mill's philosophy, looking back to and inspired by the *Logic* and the *Principles*. He also appreciates Mill's development of the concept of character and his evocation of equality and justice. In addition to the these themes, I shall also examine others that have run through Mill's thought, as developed in this book, such as religion, the future, civilization, utility, and progress. At the outset, however, Mill's rhetorical method will be considered to establish a continuing preoccupation with the use of contrary themes to provide the starting points and parameters for Mill's arguments. This part of the chapter will show how Mill's careful attention to rhetoric and to what I have called his 'method of reform' influenced the presentation of his philosophy, and has led wrongly to accusations of inconsistency and contradiction from scholars who have failed to take these aspects of his thought into consideration.

In this chapter we shall also see that Mill developed in the *Subjection* a striking thesis concerned with despotism, which might be regarded as a foundation of his political thought.[3] Through an understanding of its main characteristics in the context of the oppression of women, Mill attempted to state the conditions for bringing to an end this despotic condition and despotism in society more generally. Without such movement in society he believed that the liberty and justice he sought to develop could never be realized.

1. *Mill's Method*

According to Hamburger, Mill's rhetoric, at least in *On Liberty*, but also most probably in the *Subjection*, is intended to disguise, conceal, equivocate, and mislead. 'He wrote less as one seeking to present the truth,' he continued, 'than as a practitioner of rhetoric seeking to shape beliefs' (Hamburger 1999: 203; see also Carlisle 1991: 211). Hamburger also juxtaposes Mill and Socrates in writing that 'in spite of his admiration for Socrates, Mill avoided following the Socratic example of forthrightly stating doubts and opinions about the most sensitive issues and sacred matters. Mill instead was cautious and reticent' (Hamburger 1999: 203).

Let us turn to Mill's rhetorical method in the *Subjection*. Contrary to Hamburger, I suggest that Mill's approach might be considered 'Socratic', as his method of identifying contrary views and then attempting to resolve or reconcile them places one directly in the midst of a dialectical argument concerning the subject to be addressed.[4] Mill was not a public moralist in the sense that he held to a philosophical or political position which he simply advanced and defended in a series of propositions. He could easily have argued in a straightforward manner that human happiness or utility generally required that women should be freed from various legal and societal restraints and constraints, as part of the gradual and steady improvement of humanity. But such an argument, however compelling, would not address the complexities of the relationships between men and women in his day and in the future. In place of a straightforward argument, supposedly based on utility, Mill's starting point was the identification of a series of contrary views that enabled him to identify directly what in the informal logic of ordinary men and women would enable them to advance towards freedom in society and in the family.[5] In order to address this question, he sought to avoid, as he did in the *Logic*, any intractable stalemate between those who adhered to the principles of utility and those who upheld divine or natural law as the foundation of morality and politics. The latter would be tempted to ignore or simply reject such arguments as Mill might set forth and hence undermine his attempts to deal with subjection generally and particularly with the subjection of women. There was no need to deal with ultimate principles. Let us first identify the contrary views he sought to identify and reconcile. The first contrary was set forth in terms of an opinion he had held 'from the very earliest period', the 'principle of perfect equality' between men and women. The opposing principle was 'the legal subordination of one sex to the other', which Mill declared to be 'wrong in itself, and now one of the chief hindrances to human improvement'. Mill saw in his opposition to this latter part of the contrary an 'arduous' task, but its arduousness was not due to any theoretical difficulties. It was arduous because he needed to overcome 'a mass of feelings' that supported the arguments (such as they were) for the legal subordination of women. 'So long as an opinion is strongly rooted in the feelings,' he wrote, 'it gains rather than loses in stability by having a preponderating weight of argument against it' (*CW* xxi. 261). Those who adhered to this opinion tended to hold on to it, because it was rooted in feelings. Instead of adopting a better argument, they set forth further arguments in opposition to the ones that defeated them. Furthermore, their feelings gained in power by being almost universally accepted and highly popular. Mill felt that in these circumstances intellectual arguments had little power except among elites in advanced modern societies.

Mill thus revealed a second pair of contraries, related to the first, that of reason on the one hand and feeling on the other. As for reason, he was content to apply ordinary logical arguments. There were two doctrines he sought to undermine: first, men had a right to command and women were under an obligation to obey; and, second, men were fit for government and women were unfit. He could undermine these with examples and counterarguments. As for feeling, a different approach was required. He explained this approach by returning to a theme developed, as we have seen in Chapter 3, in the essays on 'Bentham' and 'Coleridge', that of the reaction of the nineteenth century against the eighteenth (see e.g. *CW* x. 125). If, for Mill, the eighteenth century ascribed infallibility to reason, the nineteenth did the same for instinct. The primacy of instinct was not to be overlooked:

For the apotheosis of Reason we have substituted that of Instinct; and we call everything instinct which we find in ourselves and for which we cannot trace any rational foundation. This idolatry, infinitely more degrading than the other, and the most pernicious of the false worships of the present day, of all of which it is now the main support, will probably hold its ground until it gives way before a sound psychology, laying bare the real root of much that is bowed down to as the intention of Nature and the ordinance of God. (*CW* xxi. 263)

Mill's reference to false worship and idolatry (see Rosen 2006: 129) that would eventually succumb to a 'sound psychology' invoked several themes from the *Logic*, as did his opposition to the use of ideas like 'Nature' and 'God', in support of various arguments. But how would Mill defeat those, obviously the majority even in advanced societies, who relied on instinct or feeling rather than argument? By identifying their position in terms of a false move in logic that had taken place in the nineteenth century, he sought to return those who acted, or believed they had acted, on instinct or feeling to the standards of rationality enshrined in the eighteenth century, and, particularly, in Bentham and James Mill. One element that Mill retained in this context, however, from the nineteenth-century reaction was Coleridge's reliance on history. Mill again turned to history, at this time to undermine the feelings supporting the legal subordination of women, and stated that he too would accept this position 'unless... custom and feeling from age to age can be shown to have owed their existence to other causes than their soundness, and to have derived their power from the worse rather than the better parts of human nature' (*CW* xxi. 263). This challenge was advanced in a fairly light-hearted way by Mill who was confident of a successful outcome.[6] He began by insisting that the social system that incorporated the subordination of women to men was based paradoxically only on theory, as no other system had ever been practically tried. He then argued that this system 'arose simply from the fact that from the very earliest twilight of human society, every woman (owing to the value attached to her by men, combined with her inferiority in muscular strength) was found in a state of bondage to some man' (*CW* xxi. 264).

By insisting that the subjection of women could be historically shown to be simply an example of slavery and nothing else, Mill sought to undermine those doctrines justifying this condition. Was it probable from the perspective of the nineteenth century that God or Nature had ordained the legal bondage of women? With so many institutions connected with slavery, and particularly African slavery in the new world, being abolished (the American civil war ended just four years prior to the publication of the *Subjection*), Mill argued that the time had come to re-examine the institution of slavery that underpinned the subjection of women. By turning to slavery, he was able to see its institutions as existing in history and already mainly abolished except in the case of women. The legal subordination of women was thus a mere historical convention that could be changed and need not exist in the future. The foundation in feeling, instinct, divine or natural law became an illusion. But why should we look to what Mill called 'perfect equality', as that too could be changed, abolished, or reinterpreted perhaps as 'equal slavery'? The answer is that 'perfect equality' is a manifestation of the higher parts of our psychology and our character.

Let us return, however, to what Mill called the 'law of the strongest' on which the bondage of women and other forms of slavery was based. He recognized that his identification of this previously all-pervasive principle contained an element of paradox in that modern morality and civilization had rejected it. In these countries, Mill wrote, 'nobody professes it, and, as regards most of the relations between human beings, nobody is permitted to practise it' (*CW* xxi. 265). He regarded this state of affairs as somewhat paradoxical, as the right of the strongest was still being enforced in relations between men and women in these same advanced nations.

Mill had already used the phrase, 'law of the strongest', in 1850 (and doubtless elsewhere and at other times) to criticize Carlyle's attack on the 'rights of Negroes' (see *CW* xxi. 87–95; Goldberg 2005: 125–35; see also Jones 2005: 184; Varouxakis 2005: 137–53). Here, Mill referred to the 'old law of the strongest' in terms of 'a law against which the great teachers of mankind have in all ages pro-tested' (*CW* xxi. 87). Mill may well have been alluding to the argu-ment between Socrates and Thrasymachus at the beginning of Plato's *Republic* where the notion that justice could be defined as what is in the interest of the stronger was famously rejected (see Plato [338Cff.] (1963: i.47ff.). But he was clear about the modern significance of the law of the strongest. 'The history of human improvement,' he wrote, 'is the record of a struggle by which inch after inch of ground has been wrung from these maleficent powers, and more and more of human life rescued from the iniquitous dominion of the law of might' (*CW* xxi. 87). Mill continued by showing how persistent were moral principles based on power, and how reluctant most people were to abandon them. But why would the subjection of women be among the last to disappear? In an insightful passage he wrote:

It was inevitable that this one case of a social relation grounded on force, would survive through generations of institutions grounded on equal justice, an almost solitary exception to the general character of their laws and customs; but which, so long as it does not proclaim its own origin, and as discussion has not brought out its true character, is not felt to jar with modern civilization, any more than domestic slavery among the Greeks jarred with their notion of themselves as a free people. (*CW* xxi. 265)

There are two points in this passage worth emphasizing. First, the compatibility of domestic slavery among the ancient Greeks with their view of themselves as a free people is a fairly exact analogy of the legal bondage of women in otherwise free modern societies. Second, the way to wean these societies away from this situation was to identify the condition of servitude and discuss it in these very terms. In place of Victorian sentimentality and religiosity, Mill advanced a very different image of so-called domestic bliss.[7]

He explored the law of the strongest in some detail, as he attempted to show how pervasive it was throughout history from the earliest times to its continued existence in advanced societies (see *CW* xxi. 265-7). He also emphasized how pervasive throughout these societies was the exercise of power by men over women:

The clodhopper exercises, or is to exercise, his share of the power equally with the highest nobleman. And the case is that in which the desire of power is the strongest: for every one who desires power, desires it most over those who are nearest to him, with whom his life is passed, with whom he has most concerns in common, and in whom any independence of his authority is oftenest likely to interfere with his individual preferences. (*CW* xxi. 268)

After discussing a range of arguments, from Aristotle to representatives of the southern states of America, that proclaimed the 'naturalness' of subjection, and, in the case of women, that such subjection was voluntary, Mill proceeded to reveal how deeply engaged both men and women were in this subjection. Men eagerly sought more than could be achieved with the direct exercise of power. As Mill wrote:

Men do not want solely the obedience of women, they want their sentiments. All men, except the most brutish, desire to have, in the woman most nearly connected with them, not a forced slave but a willing one, not a slave merely, but a favourite. They have therefore put everything in practice to enslave their minds. (*CW* xxi. 271)

In this respect as well as in others, Mill emphasized the importance of psychological factors leading to the formation of character, but in this case leading to a false position of subjection, where many women did not personally feel their condition as one of subjection or, indeed, slavery. Mill argued with considerable passion:

When we put together three things—first, the natural attraction between opposite sexes; secondly, the wife's entire dependence on the husband, every privilege or pleasure she has being either in his gift, or depending on his will; and lastly, that the principal object of human pursuit, consideration, and all objects of social ambition, can in general be sought or obtained by her only through him, it would be a miracle if the object of being attractive to men had not become the polar star of feminine education and formation of character. (*CW* xxi. 272)

From this condition, men imposed a character on most women, as a means of enslaving them. They were to be meek, submissive, and would resign their wills into the hands of men as part of their sense of being sexually attractive. Nevertheless, such meek submission ran in opposition to the main tendency of modern society towards liberty and, particularly, freedom of choice.

II. *Despotism*

As Mill delved deeply into the kind of subjection that marked modern societies, he brought to light not only the true condition of women and the current structure of the institution of marriage, but also the nature of despotism itself.[8] In the first chapter of the *Subjection* Mill sought to uncover despotism in the status of women. In the second chapter, while he set out to examine the marriage contract, he soon changed course to examine the analogy between despotism in marriage and political despotism. Mill later wrote in the *Subjection* (though dealing with a slightly different theme): 'Not a word can be said for despotism in the family which cannot be said for political despotism' (*CW* xxi. 286). As we look more closely, it appears that he was arguing that it was the family rather than the polity that exhibited more clearly and strikingly the evils of despotism. Furthermore, there could be no remedy for political despotism without a reform of the social institution of the family. Where law and government were involved, it was law and government as directed at the family and not simply at the overall constitution of the polity. Law could as easily enhance despotism in the family as relieve it. Indeed, the exploration of the analogy between despotism in the polity and despotism in the family was not Mill's major concern. The problem to be solved was despotism in the family, and the analogy with despotism more generally merely served to make it more visible. For many, probably the majority of Mill's readers, the image of the family was one of domestic peace and contentment in the context of hearth and home. However, the analogy enabled Mill to see oppression and evil where others saw domestic bliss. But the important point was Mill's revelation of a social despotism that functioned in and through the institution of marriage and prevented the development and improvement of the character of men and women in numerous aspects of social life.

Mill's exploration of despotism continued as he focused on the family and relationships between husbands and wives and parents and children. In examining relationships between superiors and dependents Mill uncovered what he called 'the nursery of these vices of character' (CW xxi. 288). The following passage is a good example of his analysis and his rhetoric:

A man who is morose or violent to his equals, is sure to be one who has lived among inferiors, whom he could frighten or worry into submission. If the family in its best forms is, as it is often said to be, a school of sympathy, tenderness, and loving forgetfulness of self, it is still oftener, as respects its chief, a school of wilfulness, overbearingness, unbounded self-indulgence, and a double-dyed and idealized selfishness, of which sacrifice itself is only a particular form: the care for the wife and children being only care for them as part of man's own interests and belongings, and their individual happiness being immolated in every shape to his smallest preferences. What better is to be looked for under the existing form of the institution? (CW xxi. 288–9)

Though women, in Mill's view, had little power to resist, they could retaliate by making the lives of their husbands uncomfortable. This exercise of power he called 'the power of the scold' or 'the shrewish sanction' (CW xxi. 289). Nevertheless, he admitted that this power was not very successful in ending despotism and tended only to establish a counter-tyranny and to make victims of husbands who least sought to establish a tyranny. The power a woman might gain was, in effect, self-defeating, as it moved her further away from liberty and the power to assert her own rights (see CW xxi. 289–90). Mill used the example of the favourite slave of the sultan who had the power to tyrannize over other slaves and to obtain the enjoyment such tyranny might provide. But she should never have been a slave or have had power over other slaves. The same was true for the typical wife: 'She neither knows nor cares which is the right side in politics, but she knows what will bring in money or invitations, give her husband a title, her son a place, or her daughter a good marriage' (*CW* xxi. 290).

To the question, who should be the ultimate authority in the family, Mill replied that there need not be a single ruler. He looked instead to the model of a business partnership where there were no rulers. For a marriage to become a partnership of equals, it should be established by mutual consent. Otherwise, the analogy with a business partnership, where either partner was free to leave, could not be sustained.[9]

The establishment of equality of rights thus became a first step towards the change in character and behaviour mainly by women but also by men. Mill wrote: 'I believe that equality of rights would abate the exaggerated self-abnegation which is the present artificial ideal of feminine character, and that a good woman would not be more self-sacrificing than the best man' (*CW* xxi. 293).

Let us examine Mill's argument in greater detail. The existing state of marriage had produced a despotism of men over women. Feminine character had become self-sacrificing, sycophantic, and, perhaps, where possible, even shrewish. The development of this character, what we might call a feminine personality, was not based on any permanent characteristics of the female sex. These had developed from the age-old state of despotism that existed in marriage and society. Introduce equal rights and a modicum of liberty within the institution of marriage and the personalities of both women and men would change. Not only would the despotic regime of marriage be reformed, but the character of the people involved would also change for the better.

The possibility of fairly simple alterations to character by changes in circumstances ran counter to the emphasis on nature and permanence emphasized by those who supported the status quo. But Mill had in the *Subjection* moved the argument away from the false consciousness associated with the subordination of women, and revealed first a despotism lurking within family life, and, second, a historical, alterable foundation that could lead to equality. From a focus on marriage and the family he also took the argument concerning despotism to social life more generally. He sought to allow women to compete with men for jobs, rewards, honours, etc. in various occupations from which they had been excluded. In doing so, he invoked notions like 'justice' and 'equal moral right', and repeated his view of the importance of competition which would enable women (and men) to progress in society (see *CW* xxi. 300). He rejected the view of phrenologists who believed that a difference in the size of male and female brains could be used to justify, in effect, the subjection of women (see *CW* xxi. 310–12). In place of these phrenological speculations, he asserted the importance of differences in character.

In this material Mill returned to the arguments and positions adopted earlier in the *Logic*. But here in the *Subjection* he used this material and this approach to focus on the issue of despotism. He even used the failure to tackle the study of psychology and character in a major way to discredit the doctrines that had been advanced to justify the subjection of women as a 'natural' condition. How could such a theory be accepted, he asked, when the alternative had not yet been fully examined? Nor could such a theory be accepted once people recognized the despotic character of this particularly odious form of modern slavery. In a striking passage he wrote:

The law of servitude in marriage is a monstrous contradiction to all the principles of the modern world, and to all the experience through which those principles have been slowly and painfully worked out. It is the sole case, now that negro slavery has been abolished, in which a human being in the plenitude of every faculty is delivered up to the tender mercies of another human being, in the hope forsooth that this other will use the power solely for the good of the person subjected to it. Marriage is the only actual bondage known to our law. There remain no legal slaves, except the mistress of every house. (*CW* xxi. 323)

We might ask precisely which principles Mill thought belonged to the modern world and which belonged to outmoded institutions that supported despotism. The principles of the modern world would include not only liberty, equality, justice, and utility, but also what one might call intellectual and emotional virtues that could provide the insights and guide the despots to reject the benefits of such subjection. There are two points worth making here. First, Mill not only emphasized individual liberty as the key principle involved to end despotism in the family (see *CW* xxi. 323), but he also emphasized principles like equality and justice. At stake was not simply the liberation of the individual, but the transformation of society that would eventually allow the cultivation of individuality to take place. This transformation would in turn require numerous families to experiment with different arrangements and be guided by those who understood how to proceed. Second, as the transformation of the family was only part of the change necessary, and as the end of subjection would require important changes in the law to allow women to compete with men in society, there was a question of power that needed to be addressed. Education and cultivation would not on their own solve the legal restrictions that supported the subjection of women.

Mill was not entirely clear as to how the end of subjection was to be achieved. In part, he could not be clear, because he had no means to predict the future. Nevertheless, from the point of view of the philosopher he could explore psychology, character, institutions, and history to examine future trends and possibilities. We have seen how he had dramatically revealed the widely esteemed institution of marriage to be a despotic system linked with laws in urgent need of reform.[10] We have also seen how the key to progress lay with changes to moral understanding and practice within the family. We shall explore further in due course the importance of introducing equality into the family as a prelude to further change. But let us look first at Mill's understanding of the role of religion, mainly Christianity, in the transformation of society in the future.

III. *Religion*

In light of the discussions of Mill's views on religion in general and Christianity in particular in earlier chapters, one might expect his account of the role of Christianity in marriage to be somewhat ambivalent. Mill noted that women were traditionally forced into marriage either directly or sold by their fathers. The Christian church might have required formal consent by a woman, but in the end only by taking monastic vows might she be saved from being placed under the husband's power of life and death (see *CW* xxi. 283). In spite of the widespread belief that the development of civilization and the influence of Christianity had 'restored to the woman her just rights', Mill believed that the current position of women was, as we have seen, worse than that formerly occupied by African slaves (*CW* xxi. 284).

In the *Subjection* Mill alluded at several points to links between Christianity and values associated with the end of subjection. At one point he referred to the equality of human beings as part of Christian teaching, if not of Christian practice (see *CW* xxi. 293). At another point he referred to the Christian love of freedom that was superior to an ancient ideal of liberty, which he depicted in terms of disdain for a yoke on oneself, but accepting the imposition of subjection on others for one's self-glorification (*CW* xxi. 295). At still another point, he identified justice with Christianity (see *CW* xxi. 326). Finally, he referred to the importance of women in persuading 'northern conquerors' to soften their military passions and adopt Christianity (*CW* xxi. 327).

As for the issue of a duty of obedience required by Christianity, Mill admitted that Christianity might require such obedience in its 'formularies' regarding marriage, and St Paul did say: 'Wives, obey your husbands' (Colossians 3:18: *CW* xxi. 296). But Mill insisted that the injunction to obedience in the marriage ceremony was not an essential part of Christianity, and that St Paul was more concerned to avoid rebellion against existing laws at that time than to prevent change and improvement in the future. In an important passage he wrote:

To pretend that Christianity was intended to stereotype existing forms of government and society, and protect them against change, is to reduce it to the level of Islamism or of Brahmanism. It is precisely because Christianity has not done this, that it has been the religion of the progressive portion of mankind, and Islamism, Brahmanism, &c., have been those of the stationary portions....

To this he added:

There have been abundance of people, in all ages of Christianity, who tried to make it something of the same kind; to convert us into a sort of Christian Musselmans, with the Bible for a Koran, prohibiting all improvement: and great has been their power, and many have had to sacrifice their lives in resisting them. But they have been resisted, and the resistance has made us what we are, and will yet make us what we are to be. (*CW* xxi. 296)

In this material Mill saw Christianity as involved in an important struggle within itself to be on the side of an advancing civilization that would end the subjection of women. The contrast between Christianity (or some part of it) and Islam highlights the wider struggle for the end to this subjection.

For Mill to enlist Christianity in this struggle against subjection and slavery will not seem odd to those who have read Mill's remarks on the religion of humanity, as he was not opposed to religion except when it became a force opposed to a progressive civilization. He could see in Christianity a source of those feelings that in one of his initial contraries could oppose the feelings underpinning opposition to change in the status of women. Furthermore, Christianity embodied a regard for equality, justice, and freedom that could be mobilized, just as it had been for the abolition of slavery.

Mill also suggested that among the higher classes in England 'a great majority' of married couples had already adopted and lived with the ideal of equality (CW xxi. 295). Moral sentiments, such as these, were thus in advance of existing legislation and could lead the struggle to abolish these unjust laws. Mill believed that this comparatively small elite was 'the very foundation of my hopes' (CW xxi. 295), but did it in fact exist? And if it did, would its members advocate such changes for the rest of society? One can see here how important the progressive element in Christianity could be (see August 1976: 213; see also Jones 2007). But from Mill's other writings it is clear that Christianity itself lacked the dynamism and the truth to lead the revolution.

iv. *The Future*

Mill turned to look elsewhere for those who might possess the authority and power to lead women out of subjection.[11] At one point he wrote:

To see the futurity of the species has always been the privilege of the intellectual élite, or those who have learnt from them; to have the feelings of that futurity has been the distinction, and usually the martyrdom, of a still rarer élite. Institutions, books, education, society, all go on training human beings for the old, long after the new has come; much more when it is only coming. (CW xxi. 294)

Who are the 'intellectual elite', and what did Mill mean by the 'rarer elite'? The first part of the question might be answered fairly simply. The intellectual elite would consist of progressive philosophers of a sort who had read and understood a work like Mill's *Logic* or the *Principles*. They could provide an intellectual leadership that might show the way, but they were by no means sufficient to complete the task. They could see that 'the true virtue of human beings is fitness to live together as equals' and this, of course, included women as well as men (CW xxi. 294). This insight into the future was, however, only an intellectual insight. The passage on the 'still rarer elite', which possessed the feelings of the future, and possibly the 'martyrdom', contained an allusion (though not explicitly) to

Christianity or some other form of belief. But the point of the 'still rarer elite' was to show that Mill was looking to a few who could lead a country to end the subjection of women by virtue of strong feelings about equality and liberty, say, a Martin Luther King in recent times or the Abolitionists at the time of slavery.

But these elites, on their own, would not have been sufficient. Mill earlier referred to the whole movement of modern history that supported this vision of equality between men and women in the future:

the course of history, and the tendencies of progressive human society, afford not only no presumption in favour of this system of inequality of rights, but a strong one against it; and that, so far as the whole course of human improvement up to this time, the whole stream of modern tendencies, warrants any inference on the subject, it is, that this relic of the past is discordant with the future, and must necessarily disappear. (CW xxi. 272)

As we shall see, it was not necessarily history that taught Mill that on the subject of equality the past was 'discordant with the future' and the inequalities of the present must 'necessarily' disappear.[12] History, while better understood in Mill's day than in earlier periods, enabled students to see the importance of external factors in the development of character and its variableness. But the study of history on its own would not lead to the insights concerning equality as well as improvement and progress more generally. What they needed to bring to its study were the sciences of psychology and ethology (including national character), as well as an understanding of the role of necessity in human nature and affairs.

Among those who have discussed Mill's attitude towards the future, Nicholson has written:

In other words, Mill always intended to address an audience in the future.... To that extent the verdict of his contemporaries was irrelevant: it was superficial, short-sightedly ignoring the deeper social tendencies hostile to human freedom. Mill was content to be judged by the future. (Nicholson 1998: 470)

That Mill wrote for and was content to be judged by the future must surely be true. Nicholson is at this point referring to On Liberty, though his comments would also apply to the Subjection and other works. He cites and quotes (see Nicholson 1998: 469) from the Autobiography (CW i. 259–60) in which Mill attempted to provide a brief account of his method. Here, he distinguished between those who looked at 'present facts' rather than at 'tendencies'. These underlying tendencies would appear to make one sceptical of the facts before one's eyes, and in periods of transition would enable one to see the future or some aspects of the future and, possibly, what should be done to face it. In the context of *On Liberty* Mill wrote of this transitory period and its aftermath as follows:

At such times people of any mental activity, having given up many of their old beliefs, and not feeling quite sure that those they still retain can stand unmodified, listen eagerly to new opinions. But this state of things is necessarily transitory: some particular body of doctrine in time rallies the majority round it, organizes social institutions and modes of action conformably to itself, education impresses this new creed upon the new generations without the mental processes that have led to it, and by degrees it acquires the very same power of compression, so long exercised by the creeds of which it has taken the place. (*CW* i. 259–60)

On Liberty, for Mill, had a special use particularly to prevent such inevitable compression from stifling opinions that would limit progress and destroy individuality (see *CW* i. 260). Similarly, the *Subjection* might stimulate the reform of the law with regard to rights to property and other rights both in marriage and in the modern world (such as with respect to universal suffrage). Nevertheless, was Mill writing for the future? It is important to emphasize that Mill was not a utopian in the sense that he pictured a future state or a return to an idealized past state. He saw tendencies, and these tendencies were based on ideas and principles, like equality, justice, and liberty. His method was to seek out contrary opinions both in favour and opposed to his position. Out of both contraries he looked for elements that might combine to advance a possible state of affairs he could envisage in the future, e.g. marriage based on equality. He could see the sources of the opinions and emotions that would take one there. I have called his method the method of reform, as it envisaged gradual reform, generation after generation, as new ideas and feelings helped to move the human race towards an improved condition.

v. *Equality, Justice, Liberty, Utility*

In the opening paragraph of the *Subjection*, as we have seen, Mill expressed the grounds of his opinion regarding the relationship between men and women in terms of 'a principle of perfect equality' (*CW* xxi. 261).[13] Throughout the work, he referred to such a principle and its manifestations, though he employed a variety of terms to do so, e.g. 'equal justice' (*CW* xxi. 265, 336); 'equality of rights' (*CW* xxi.

293); 'equal right' (*CW* xxi. 326); 'equal moral right' (*CW* xxi. 300); 'just equality' (*CW* xxi. 299); 'equality' (*CW* xxi. 293, 294–5, 336); 'justice' (*CW* xxi. 293, 294, 301, 324–5); and 'equal freedom' (*CW* xxi. 281). He seemed almost casual in his use of this terminology, and made no attempt to define and distinguish his terms. He did not attempt to delineate clearly the sphere of liberty from that of equality or distinguish between utility and equality or justice.

Even though Mill announced at the outset that the guiding principle was 'perfect equality', there is reason to believe that a major theme of the *Subjection* was that of liberty (see Berger 1984: 196; August 1976: 212). After all, it takes no great imagination to think that the remedy for subjection, slavery, and despotism is liberty of some sort. Yet Mill only embraced liberty with considerable qualification, and often linked it to equality or justice. He was aware of several difficulties in the use of the idea of liberty in the contexts of the family and society. He noted, as we have seen, that liberty in the context of the family, if applied to the man, might only enhance the subjection of the woman. If, for example, liberty in society leads to the legalization of divorce, subsequent remarriage could lead to the reimposition of despotism. Society would have to be radically reorganized to end subjection, and that reorganization would have to be based on equality as well as liberty.[14]

Nevertheless, Mill did not neglect liberty. If equal justice should govern social life and relationships within marriage, there remained the private individual for whom liberty would be a great benefit. As Mill wrote somewhat dramatically:

But it would be a grievous understatement of the case to omit the most direct benefit of all, the unspeakable gain in private happiness to the liberated half of the species; the difference to them between a life of subjection to the will of others, and a life of rational freedom. (*CW* xxi. 336)

Mill strongly asserted the importance of freedom: 'After the primary necessities of food and raiment, freedom is the first and strongest want of human nature' (*CW* xxi. 336). He distinguished between a freedom that was appropriate to a lawless society and a later more rational freedom for those who understood and valued reason and duty. Under this form of freedom individuals accepted the restraint of reason, but were not willing to accept the will of others in the use of this restraining force. He wrote:

the communities in which the reason has been most cultivated, and in which the idea of social duty has been most powerful, are those which have most strongly asserted the freedom of action of the individual—the liberty of each to govern his conduct by his own feelings of duty, and by such laws and social restraints as his own conscience can subscribe to. (*CW* xxi. 336)

Mill not only valued this freedom but he also argued that even in an imperfect form it was superior to any form of rule by a 'good and skilful administration' (*CW* xxi. 337). If the manifestation of such freedom was rude and imperfect, it was, even in this form, superior in that it enhanced 'consciousness of working out their own destiny under their own moral responsibility' (*CW* xxi. 337), and this kind of liberty was applicable to women as well as men.

Mill followed this praise of liberty for men and women by noting that, if women were denied or forced to suppress this liberty, they turned instead to the exercise of power over others. As he wrote, 'an active and energetic mind, if denied liberty, will seek for power: refused the command of itself, it will assert its personality by attempting to control others' (*CW* xxi. 338). Some might argue that liberty and power go together, and, as Locke argued, liberty is a power to perform certain acts (see Cranston 1953: 23). But, for Mill:

The love of power and the love of liberty are in eternal antagonism. Where there is least liberty, the passion for power is the most ardent and unscrupulous. The desire of power over others can only cease to be a depraving agency among mankind, when each of them individually is able to do without it: which can only be where respect for liberty in the personal concerns of each is an established principle. (*CW* xxi. 338)

As we examine this 'established principle', we can see that it is simply a restatement of the heart of Mill's philosophy. Active character is at the foundation of human personality. Without its cultivation, as we have already seen, various vices, like envy and, as here, love of power, develop. The vices are deeply held in individuals and in the case of women, Mill wrote of 'women's passion for personal beauty, and dress and display; and all the evils that flow from it, in the way of mischievous luxury and social immorality' (*CW* xxi. 338). Without providing the freedom that allowed for the development of active character, women were placed in this corrupting position, and men suffered as well from the inability of civilization to flourish.[15]

We can now see that above the foundation of active character, liberty, in the form Mill conceived it, vied with power to allow such character to flourish. Furthermore, liberty seemed also to require equality and a form of justice in order to achieve the distribution of liberty. Without equality and justice, we are left with a society that would eventually rest wholly or in part on power and despotism. Liberty, equality, and justice were thus necessary to end the subjection of women.

But what is the role of utility? Shanley has noted that 'there is much dispute over whether the controlling principle of Mill's critique in the *Subjection* is equality or utility' (Shanley 1998: 419n.). One might also note that there seems to be a large number of controlling principles from active character to liberty, from equality to justice, and from progress to improvement and civilization. The role of utility and the language of utilitarianism are not emphasized in the *Subjection* but are present nonetheless. The invocation of happiness is somewhat muted, as compared with justice and equality, though at the end of the essay he could confidently assert that 'an enjoyable life' and 'the happiness of human beings' required an end to inequality between the sexes (*CW* xxi. 339–40). But even where utility was not explicitly invoked and discussed, its role was important. At the beginning of the final chapter Mill wrote:

There remains a question, not of less importance than those already discussed, and which will be asked the most importunately by those opponents whose conviction is somewhat shaken on the main point. What good are we to expect from the changes proposed in our customs and institutions? Would mankind be at all better off if women were free? If not, why disturb their minds, and attempt to make a social revolution in the name of abstract right? (*CW* xxi. 323)

These questions were posed in a utilitarian fashion, looking for their answers to an assessment of benefits and burdens, pleasures and pains, and consequences in the future. But did Mill intend to use equality, justice, and liberty in opposition to or in conflict with utility?

If we look carefully at the way Mill employed these ideas, we can see that they were not regarded as ideal criteria by which to judge existing arrangements. It is arguable that behind these ideas lurked the utility principle which played an important role in Mill's discussion. First, equal justice and perfect equality on their own would not provide such criteria to evaluate law or custom, and Mill never defined and clarified the ideas sufficiently for them to do so. Although utility would not provide such criteria, it could orient their use towards the future. Justice and equality in the concrete senses suggested by Mill (e.g. equal rights within marriage, equal suffrage, equal opportunities for employment, etc. in progressive societies that valued improvement and civilization) might be adopted. Here utility directed reform towards future realization. As we have seen, the orientation towards the future was crucial to Mill in the *Subjection* as well as elsewhere, and clearly the utility principle (embodying happiness as pleasure, and the absence of pain) stood as a magnet drawing the present into the future by giving meaning and direction to various moral concepts. If equal liberty had little meaning on its own, under the guidance of utility, it could advance, for example, equal rights to education to be realized by future legislation.

Second, the utility principle also provided a unifying theme for these ideas. Mill was able to move from equality to justice to liberty in part because utility provided the context in which it made sense to invoke them. On its own 'perfect equality' between men and women was a formal idea without much content. In the context of specific issues in the law governing marriage, where a despotism of men over women currently reigned, it made sense intellectually and emotionally.

Third, as we have seen throughout this chapter (and elsewhere in the book) utility functioned mainly within a dynamic context. We do not know precisely what institutions and customs will exist in the future, but we can see where we are going. Many might oppose moving in the direction of equality between the sexes, and look to 'nature' and 'religion' for sources of stability to oppose such moves. But the underlying trends in society (even at the time Mill wrote) favoured such progress in economically advanced, largely Christian societies, because once despotism in the family and society was fully revealed, its abolition became an issue as important as the abolition of slavery.

If we look briefly at Mill's essay, *Utilitarianism*, we do not find any arguments that conflict with the treatment of utility here. In the first chapter of *Utilitarianism* Mill attempted to use the paradigms of science and art to show the limitations of the principles of morality attaining the kind of certainty and absoluteness that many claimed for them. He referred in the first paragraph to what might be called another 'Socratic moment' (see Chapter 2 above) in which Socrates in Plato's *Protagoras* is said to have founded 'the theory of utilitarianism against the popular morality of the so-called sophist'.[16] This reference to Socrates (rather than to the more familiar figures in the Epicurean tradition: see Rosen 2003*a*: 15–28, 172–4; Bentham 1983*c*: 299ff.) seems very precise, though it is used by Mill to show that more than 2,000 years of debate concerning the criterion of right and wrong and the question of the *summum bonum* have led to the creation of many 'sects and schools' but no clear resolution of the issues raised. Thus, the precise identification of the founder and the time of the discovery of the theory has not helped to establish it in the minds of thinkers. Similarly, as Mill looked at the sciences, he pointed out that the first principles of even the most precise sciences, like mathematics, and particularly algebra, were obscure. Though the elements of these sciences, as they were taught to students, were clear and coherent, the first principles were 'as full of fictions as English law and of mysteries as theology' (CW x. 205). The elementary notions of the sciences were not like the foundations of a building, but more like the roots of a tree which performed well, even though they were not well-understood and never examined with any care.

Mill's point might be interpreted as a sceptical assessment of the ultimate principles of knowledge, but he did not assert here such a theory of knowledge. His object in this analysis was to show that the practical arts (including morality) could not exhibit more certainty with regard to foundations and first principles than the most exact sciences. To establish this thesis further he turned to the arts, where one might expect that the first principles would be more certain and definite. He pointed to those thinkers who held that there was a moral faculty, sense, or instinct that declared what was right and wrong, and he criticized those who held such a view no matter on what basis they held it. He was particularly critical of Kant's principle ('so act, that the rule on which thou actest would admit of being adopted as a law by all rational beings') as allowing 'the most outrageously immoral rules of conduct' (CW x. 207). For Mill, it seemed that the more certain the claim for the foundations of morality, the more probable was the confusion and error that would follow from it. Other thinkers seemed to believe that there was a science of morals, but had seldom made any progress in setting out the principles or even a single principle of such a science. Mill took the view that those who sought to develop a science or art of morality mainly looked to the development of a single principle or several principles (that might be ranked in precedence) to form the foundation of morality, from which practical precepts could be deduced. But proof of first principles in the sciences appeared to be virtually impossible for Mill, and equally so with regard to the arts and particularly to the art of morality or ethics. For Mill, the medical art was good in so far as it conduced to health, but it was not possible to prove that health was good. Similarly, claimed Mill, the art of music was good, in that it produced pleasure, but it was not possible to prove that pleasure was good (see CW x. 208).

Mill then set out to show what kinds of proof were relevant to utilitarianism and the critical literature is full of studies and inter-pretations of these studies.[17] What is less noticed is what Mill had already established, namely, that the importance of proof of ultimate principles in science and art had been diminished at the outset of *Utilitarianism* to become amenable to the principles of logic, as developed by Mill in the *Logic*. For example, if one argued that the basis of morality was a divine spark located in each individual and perceived by intuition, Mill could easily argue that there was no way to prove that such a spark existed. Hence, there could be numerous claims concerning the validity of ultimate principles that could not be established. When Mill wrote that the greatest happiness principle held that actions were right as they tended to produce pleasure and wrong as they tended to produce the reverse of pleasure, such a thesis became important not only for what it claimed for pleasure and pain as the basis of morality but also for what it rejected as relevant to the moral art. It rejected any use of an ultimate principle to provide the basis of deductions of valid principles of morality, applicable to all people at all times. Whatever Mill said subsequently about proof in *Utilitarianism* did not contradict the initial remarks in the first chapter, as this set limits to the later discussions. Mill wrote at the beginning of chapter 4 of *Utilitarian-ism* regarding proof: 'It has already been remarked, that questions of ultimate ends do not admit of proof, in the ordinary acceptation of the term. To be incapable of proof by reasoning is common to all first principles; to the first premises of our knowledge, as well to those of our conduct' (*CW* x. 234).[18]

Although Mill was referring to his discussion of proof with regard to the sciences and arts, he changed his language here to principles of 'knowledge' and 'conduct'. He did not explicitly deny in chapter 1 of *Utilitarianism* that the first principles were not amenable to proof, but he shifted the metaphor in chapter 1 from 'foundations' to 'roots' of trees that were often invisible. When he wrote in chapter 4 that first premises of knowledge 'may be the subject of a direct appeal to the faculties which judge of fact', he omitted to repeat his earlier point that these first principles seldom presented themselves clearly as matters of fact to 'our senses, and our internal consciousness' (*CW* x. 234). But Mill did not seek to reconcile his two positions, as his point was not concerned with matters of fact and first principles of the sciences, but with 'practical ends' (*CW* x. 234). Nevertheless, one can suspect Mill of 'stretching' his position somewhat to make 'proof' a greater possibility, first, for the sciences, and, second, for aspects of the arts concerned with conduct. Without Mill's initial acceptance, however, that full proof was not possible in the sciences and arts, one might be tempted to reject Mill's argument in this later chapter. But even here, where he turned from knowledge of fact to knowledge of practical ends, Mill carried with him his scepticism regarding the sciences and arts. He limited his 'proof' regarding happiness as an end to the empirical fact that people desire happiness. And he took another contentious step in his argument that happiness was the ultimate end and other ends, such as virtue, are means to the ultimate end. Nevertheless, the view expressed here concerning utility standing in the foreground and playing a unique role of encouraging the practical arts to use ideas like liberty, equality, and justice to advance coherently towards the future is not subject to any possible criticism from what Mill wrote in *Utilitarianism*. Indeed, *Utilitarianism* allows the student of the *Subjection* to understand the underlying structure of its arguments.

VI. *Character*

Ryan (1974: 156) has noted perceptively that character or ethology was 'the great intellectual weapon which *The Subjection of Women* relies on' (see also Okin 1980: 222; Goldstein 1980: 324–5; Ball 2010: 46–8). He made this remark in the context of his discussion of Mill's denial that social arrangements were 'natural'. Ethology was also employed by Mill in numerous other contexts, all of which relied on the assumption that character, social institutions, and the ideals that seemed to govern them were mainly the product of changeable external factors. But Mill admitted that he was in some difficulty with this fundamental principle.[19] He was unable to establish a science of ethology, even though he believed strongly that the ingredients for such a science were present. As we have seen, the increased study of history was of considerable assistance as, like ethology, it showed 'the extraordinary susceptibility of human nature to external influences' (*CW* xxi. 277). But the study of history could not replace ethology, because 'in history, as in travelling, men usually see only what they already had in their own minds; and few learn much from history, who do not bring much with them to its study' (*CW* xxi. 277). Although Mill praised the great improvements in the study of history in the nineteenth century, and saw its relevance to the study of ethology, the analogy with travelling seems almost to defeat his view of its importance. If we only see what is already in our minds, history would almost seem to be irrelevant, except perhaps to suggest that what is in our minds can change. But with regard to a subject like the natural differences between men and women (a subject on which phrenology claimed it could provide a full account), Mill first acknowledged widespread ignorance of the subject and then suggested that the answer might be found in 'an analytic study of the most important department of psychology, the laws of the influence of circumstances on character' (*CW* xxi. 277). Mill seemed to turn from history to psychology. But this somewhat cumbersome reference to psychology in terms of an analytic study of its most important department is really meant to be a reference to logic. In an important (though lengthy) passage, Mill spelt out just how logic would help to determine the essential differences between the sexes:

For, however great and apparently ineradicable the moral and intellectual differences between men and women might be, the evidence of their being natural differences could only be negative. Those only could be inferred to be natural which could not possibly be artificial—the residuum, after deducting every characteristic of either sex which can admit of being explained from education or external circumstances. The profoundest knowledge of the laws of the formation of character is indispensable to entitle any one to affirm even that there is any difference, much more what the difference is, between the two sexes considered as moral and rational beings; and since no one, as yet, has that knowledge, (for there is hardly any subject which, in proportion to its import-ance, has been so little studied), no one is thus far entitled to any positive opinion on the subject. Conjectures are all that can at present be made; conjectures more or less probable, according as more or less authorized by such knowledge as we yet have of the laws of psychology, as applied to the formation of character. (*CW* xxi. 277–8)

Mill's depiction of the way forward was thus derived from the heart of his logic.[20] In this respect his views were unchanged from this earlier period. The science of psychology was not sufficiently positive in its findings about the differences between the sexes, but drawing on logic, it could use negative evidence while remaining sceptical regarding other kinds of evidence. For example, the fact that numerous female monarchs were excellent rulers provided some negative evidence to undermine the widespread view that women were by nature unfit to rule, without establishing the opposite view that they were equally qualified as men to do so (*CW* xxi. 302).

This use of logic might not seem to take Mill's position very far forward. But once it was realized that the common view of the character of women was that they were by nature the opposite to men, such negative evidence, as provided in the *Subjection*, could undermine this commonplace view. A few exceptions to the opinion of the natural opposition of men and women would undermine any evidence in favour of a natural subordination. Thus, very simple conjectures and discussions might bring down the foundations of the whole edifice of enslavement and false consciousness on the part of both women and men.

Mill thus had a way forward from the status quo. As for the relationship between men and women within marriage, he felt that most men knew 'absolutely nothing' of the nature of women (*CW* xxi. 280). Furthermore, much of what women wrote about marriage was based on 'mere sycophancy to men' (*CW* xxi. 279). This situation could be remedied in modern societies by providing women with liberty, and, specifically, 'equal liberty', so that the 'free play' of their faculties would provide an answer in the future. It was important, however, that women were not pushed into a position where they had to choose between not wanting to marry at all (men's fear) and despotism in marriage. The achievement of equal freedom should be accompanied by reform of the marriage contract (*CW* xxi. 280–2).

We can conclude this brief, though important, examination of Mill's use of character and the science of ethology in the *Subjection* by referring to two aspects of character that have also appeared in this and in earlier chapters. The first is Mill's emphasis on 'active' character, which seems to be an aspect of a healthy human being. In the *Subjection* Mill assumed that this was the case, and he highlighted the way a passive and sycophantic character, often found in women, was less their nature and more a perversion of it. Active character required a progressive outlet or it became perverted. Thus, it was closely allied with Mill's arguments in favour of liberty and against despotism. Where liberty was not allied to active character, Mill emphasized in the *Subjection*, as we have seen, not only the evils of passivity but also the replacement of a love of liberty with a love of power. To an extent women had an outlet for their active character in raising families and running households. But Mill emphasized that this ceased to be the case for older women who seemed to be left with religion and modest charitable work as outlets for their considerable skills. Such outlets could and did become causes of boredom and despair in later life. As for the opposition between liberty and power, Mill, as we have seen, was highly suggestive, and showed how the use of power in place of liberty could function at the psychological, social, and political levels. It became an important dimension to Mill's overall account of liberty as a *social* concept. Without liberty in society at all levels, but particularly in the family, despotism would soon establish itself even though it was never called by its true name.

The second aspect of character discussed in the *Subjection* was that of 'national' character. Mill used national character to show in part that as people behaved differently in different societies, one could use this evidence to show how circumstances affected character and how changes in circumstances could lead to the modification of character. In addition, in the *Subjection* Mill used the example of differences in national character as an analogy to establish that, depending on circumstances, women's excellence varied and could not be regarded as static and 'natural'. 'Like the French compared with the English, the Irish with the Swiss, the Greeks or Italians with the German races,' he wrote, 'so women compared with men may be found, on the average, to do the same things with some variety in the particular kind of excellence' (*CW* xxi. 309). To this he added: 'But, that they would do them fully as well on the whole, if their education and cultivation were adapted to correcting instead of aggravating the infirmities incident to their temperament, I see not the smallest reason to doubt' (*CW* xxi. 309–10).

VII. *Civilization, Improvement, and Progress*

In his early essay on 'Civilization' (1836) (*CW* xviii. 119–47), Mill began with the view that the term had a double meaning.[21] On the one hand, it referred to improvements that made individuals and societies 'farther advanced in the road to perfection; happier, nobler, wiser' (*CW* xviii. 119). On the other hand, it was used to distinguish a wealthy and powerful nation from that of savages or barbarians without any reference, for example, to happiness or wisdom. Once he had developed the clear, if somewhat artificial, distinction between 'improvement' and 'progress', as we have seen in Chapter 2, he could link civilization with both progress (e.g. from barbarism to a modern society) and improvement (e.g. through reform in society). Both uses were relevant to ending the subjection of women. At the very outset of the *Subjection* in the formulation of one of the first contraries, Mill proclaimed that the principle of the legal subordination of women was 'wrong in itself' and 'one of the chief hindrances to human improvement' (CW xxi. 261). Shortly afterwards, he linked 'the progress of civilization' with 'the improvement of the moral sentiments of mankind' (CW xxi: 264).

Mill's use of this language is not without paradox in another respect. When he criticized the 'law of the strongest', he argued that the most advanced societies had abandoned the idea and the institutions supporting it. However, these same civilized societies still adhered to the 'law of the strongest' in one important sphere—that concerned with the relationships between men and women. We can see that, for Mill, civilization did not progress uniformly throughout the world or even within societies. His conception of character and national character attempted to show, in theory at least, why such variations occurred. It was also possible to show theoretically that some portions of a civilized society were more advanced than others. There were elites in most of these societies that had marriages based on equality rather than on the law of the strongest. But the very fact that the worst sort of despotism, as we have seen, was practised in the most civilized countries, and marriage was widely celebrated as a highly civilized and civilizing legal and moral institution, threatened to undermine Mill's ideas of progress and civilization.

Mill not only employed his rhetoric and arguments to bring to light the despotism in modern societies in the legal and social relationships between men and women, but he also attempted to argue logically, using such concepts as civilization, progress, and improvement, to show that this last vestige of despotism was out of step with modernity and must necessarily disappear. History and progress formed a kind of rough standard that could be used to measure the good and evil of various institutions and societies. Despotic relationships were not always evil; for many centuries the law of the strongest was all that existed to govern relationships in societies. As societies progressed and such notions as equality, justice, and especially liberty spread throughout society, those institutions still based on despotism were bound to be challenged and found wanting. They failed to measure up to a set of standards (justice, equality, and liberty) that were part of modernity. These standards could be used to assess the good or evil generated by particular institutions. They also provided guidance for those who sought to employ the method of reform.

Given the facts of two world wars, two economic depressions, and mass murder and economic chaos on an unprecedented scale, Mill's assumptions concerning modernity and progress might seem fanciful, if not false. The facts of modern history, even in his day, should have made him more cautious in placing such emphasis on his way of viewing the future and assessing the present. Nevertheless, Mill's approach continues to have some relevance today. Consider, for example, the widely advocated doctrine of multiculturalism, which calls for the toleration of many customs and practices of different cultures in advanced, modern societies.[22] Not only should there be toleration, say its advocates, but law and public opinion should be allowed to stamp out liberty, even where the practices (such as the treatment of women within Islam) were patently opposed, as Mill himself noted, to modernity. For Mill, the liberty of modern societies required opposition to such laws and practices that led to major inequality and injustice in society. The sort of toleration called for by some contemporary multiculturalists would have been considered by Mill to be false, because no woman in a modern Western society should be required to submit to the despotism of a forced marriage, live in fear of an 'honour' killing, or be required to live generally as an inferior to a man. Mill was not an absolutist, but he used his ideas of civilization and improvement to make clear his judgements on the justice and utility of law and social institutions.

At the heart of Mill's idea of an advancing civilization was the principle of civil, or social liberty. In the *Subjection* he wrote of modern ideas and institutions:

It is, that human beings are no longer born to their place in life, and chained down by an inexorable bond to the place they are born to, but are free to employ their faculties, and such favourable chances as offer, to achieve the lot which may appear to them the most desirable. Human society of old was constituted on a very different principle. (*CW* xxi. 272–3)

Mill's liberty principle here was focused on freedom of choice (*CW* xxi. 273). It was not necessary to have a rule or law declaring that only strong-armed men could become blacksmiths, when freedom and choice determined that those who became blacksmiths were strong-armed men. Those who were weaker usually chose other occupations where they would have a better opportunity to prosper and for which they were better fit. Mill then proceeded to declare, through reasoning that should be familiar by this point, that 'the surest test and most correct measure of the civilization of a people or an age' consisted in the improvement in the status of women (*CW* xxi. 276).

As we have seen, Mill treated Christianity somewhat ambivalently in his account of progress in the improvement of women in society. On the one hand, he was highly critical of the commonplace expressions, e.g. that civilization and Christianity had already given women their just rights (*CW* xxi. 284); on the other hand, of all existing religions he believed that Christianity (as opposed to Islam and 'Brahmanism') belonged to the progressive part of humanity (*CW* xxi. 296). Christianity was also linked with justice (*CW* xxi. 326).

Nevertheless, modernity and civilization did not include only abstract ideas or progressive forces in religion. In examining chivalry, for example, Mill could see that its reforming side applied only to a few high-minded men. Modernity was achieved through 'the combined operation of numbers', and the main occupation had changed from fighting to business, that is to say, 'from military to industrial life' (*CW* xxi. 328). Modernity also depended more on law and its threat of penal sanctions than on the morality and moral sanctions associated with chivalry. Modern society could enhance the status of women throughout society by the application of law (*CW* xxi. 329). It could protect the weak and vulnerable, and still allow for what he called 'the beauties and graces of the chivalrous character' (*CW* xxi. 329). Mill also believed that women had a considerable moral and softening effect on men within the marriage bond, but that they were seldom encouraged or even allowed to develop their faculties on a larger scale beyond the family.

VIII. *Conclusion*

This chapter has been written both as a study of the *Subjection* and a conclusion to this book on Mill. Many of the themes considered in the book were developed and applied by Mill with great skill in the *Subjection*. Furthermore, we have been reminded that Mill remains a 'living' thinker who still plays an important role in numerous academic disciplines from logic to moral and political philosophy, from economics to social science, and in the debates that are part of contemporary social and political life.

In many chapters I have challenged both traditional and 'revisionist' readings of Mill's thought, drawn on both of them, and set forth new interpretations from new perspectives. Some of these are historical and biographical. New insights into Mill's thought have been established, for example, by a reconsideration of his relationship with Comte, a reinterpretation of his lifelong engagement with Bentham, and a new understanding of the 'Socratic' character of his arguments.

It is hoped that this study will stimulate others to reconsider seriously their own readings of Mill and, additionally, use him more as a profound 'contemporary' thinker than as an obscure Victorian moralist. To do so, however, we should engage with Mill at the same level as he wrote. His intellectual roots extend deeply into ancient thought from Socrates, Plato, and Aristotle to Epicurus and Epicureanism. His grasp of modern utilitarianism was not only informed by Bentham and James Mill, but also by Hume, Smith, Helvétius, and others. When he wrote on logic, he was familiar with the ancient and medieval thinkers, as well as modern logicians, including his immediate contemporaries, such as Whately, De Morgan, Boole, Hamilton, and Jevons (see Rosen 2010). When he wrote on political economy, he knew the extensive literature from Smith to contemporary writers.

Even though Mill is more accessible than ever, due to the new edition of the *Collected Works*, the new edition also makes one realize how many other important works exist that are relevant to an understanding of his thought. Nevertheless, I hope that I have presented an interpretation of the core of Mill's social and political thought (as in the *Logic*, the correspondence with Comte, and the *Principles*) and have shown the relevance of this core to works like the essays, 'Bentham' and 'Coleridge', *Utilitarianism*, *On Liberty*, *Considerations on Representative Government*, and the *Subjection of Women*. As a result, new understandings of Mill on liberty, justice, and utility have been presented.

If Mill 'lives' today, is it as a profound influence, an object of criticism, or perhaps both? As for the first, let us conclude that anyone who seeks to understand philosophy in the Anglo-American tradition will find in Mill a deep and sensitive thinker who clearly demonstrates that this tradition is concerned with a range of issues that transcends the caricature of it as concerned only with narrow, technical problems. Even where he is open to criticism, Mill provides an excellent guide to logic and methodology, though his conclusions or their applications to numerous topics seem in retrospect to be mistaken. I have suggested that this is so with regard to his predictions concerning the future of the working classes or his pronouncements on war. This chapter on Mill and the *Subjection* on its own can provide the basis of much further study. Its central theme is despotism, and its remedy is in forms of liberty and equality, particularly, in the family. Mill thus provides the starting point for the study of liberty and despotism by dismissing other starting points and by showing how this one connects with other problems in politics, ethics, and economics that are also at the heart of the modern world.

Notes

Chapter 1

1 No book on Mill can fail to refer to the splendid edn. of the *Collected Works of John Stuart Mill* (1963–91), and, particularly, to the brilliant editorial work of John M. Robson and his team. One should also mention the new edition (in progress) of *The Collected Works of Jeremy Bentham*, ed. J.H. Burns, J.R. Dinwiddy, F. Rosen, and P. Schofield (1968–) and the world-wide revival of interest in Mill, Bentham, and the development of utilitarianism.

2 Besides his mental crisis of 1826, explored in detail in the *Autobiography* (*CW* i. 137ff.), Mill suffered a further series of mental crises in 1836 (following the death of his father), in 1843 (at the time of his completion of the *Logic*), and in 1847 (prior to the publication of the *Principles*. These illnesses (by no means the last) left him unable to undertake major creative work after the *Logic* and *Principles*. The *Autobiography* is misleading in suggesting that Mill suffered a single mental crisis in 1826. On numerous occasions this book attempts to revise and correct Mill's *Autobiography*. See also Rosen 2010: 67–83, for an account of how Mill underplayed in the *Autobiography* the role of George Bentham in the development of his early interest in philosophy.

3 The correspondence, written in French, was first published as a whole in Comte and Mill 1899. For the circumstances surrounding the publication, See Vogeler 1976: 17–22. Most of Mill's letters appear in *CW* xiii, but Comte's letters are not included. The edn. of Comte's letters (Comte 1973–90) includes those of Mill, but they are consigned to notes (see vols. ii–iv), thus making the work difficult to follow as a whole. The more recent English translation (Comte and Mill 1995) provides a helpful text. See also Ch.5 n. 1 below. The translations from the original French of Comte and Mill are my own.

4 On Harriet Mill's writings see H. T. Mill 1998; A. Robson and J. Robson 1994. For accounts of the influence of Harriet on John Mill's thought, See Hayek 1951 and Pappé 1960. The idea that Mill's 'socialism' developed in the *Principles* under the influence of Harriet Mill has become almost commonplace. See e.g. Berlin 1969: 183n.

5 For a useful brief introduction and bibliographical note on James Mill, See Ball 1992: pp. xi–xxviii, xxxi–xxxiv. See also Fenn 1987 for an excellent guide to Mill's writings. In addition, one might note J. Mill 1969 with an introduction by W. H. Burston; and J. Mill 1966 with an introduction by D. Winch. The recent online publication of James Mill's Commonplace Books by the Centre for Intellectual History at Sussex University is a very welcome addition to the James Mill corpus. See James Mill, Common

Place Books, ed. Robert A. Fenn (online edn.): http://www.intellectual-history.net/Mill. I am indebted to Kristopher Grint for supplying me with this information.

6 For a recent attempt to restate one 'revisionist' position, See Brown 2010: 5ff., 36–7 (n. 2). That revisionist interpretations continue, See also Miller 2010*a*: 47–66; Riley 2010: 67–116.

Chapter 2

1 There are echoes of Mill's approach in this passage from Frege 1999: 85: 'The word "true" indicates the aim of logic as does "beautiful" that of aesthetics or "good" that of ethics. All sciences have truth as their goal; but logic is also concerned with it in quite a different way from this. It has much the same relation to truth as physics has to weight or heat. To discover truths is the task of all sciences; it falls to logic to discern the laws of truth.' There have been a number of excellent modern studies of various aspects of Mill's logic. See e.g. Jackson 1941; Kubitz 1932; Ryan 1987; Scarre 1989; Skorupski 1989.

2 Texts like Aldrich 1691 and Sanderson 1618 were still in use in this period.

3 '[W]e shall be more than satisfied if he should derive one hundredth part of the instruction from our criticism, which we have received from his work' (*CW* xi. 4).

4 Vlastos 1994: 13, 18–20, is one of a few scholars who have appreciated the significance of the Socratic elenchus and the work of George Grote, Mill's close friend, in reasserting this perspective.

5 Mill wrote translations and brief comments on nine Platonic dialogues in the 1830s, some of which were published in the *Monthly Repository* in 1834–5. See *CW* xi. 37–238. On the quotation from Mill on the *Gorgias* and *Republic*, see further Demetriou 2009: 56n.–57n.

6 In an important recent essay Demetriou 2009: 35–61 argues that Grote took as much from Mill's *Logic* and *On Liberty* for his own interpretations of Plato, as Mill took from Grote.

7 Not all classical scholars share this view of liberty in Thucydides' account of Pericles' funeral oration. See e.g. Hornblower 1991: 297–9, 301.

8 For the originality of Mill's term see the *Oxford English Dictionary* and Bain 1882: 73. For a good account of Mill's use of the term with Auguste Comte, See Pickering 1993: i. 527–8, 671.

9 Comte was much taken with the term 'pedantocracy' and used it to attack those opposed to positivism, to him personally in the École Polytechnique, and elsewhere. See *CG* 1973–90: ii. 37, 43, 47, 51, 266; Pickering 1993: i. 527–8, 531, 671–2.

10 Skorupski 2006: 6 answers his question, *Why Read Mill Today?*, by seeing Mill in terms of liberalism, and he particularly emphasizes the foundation of liberty of thought within his liberalism.

11 See e.g. Eisenach 1998: 3–7 and references to 'liberal' and 'liberalism' in the index to Urbinati and Zakaras 2007: 384.

Chapter 3

1 Ryan 1974: 190 is among very few commentators even to refer to 'Mill's long-drawn-out attempt to make something of both Bentham and Coleridge, to reconcile Liberals and Conservatives'. He does not, however, go on to discuss method in the *Considerations*, based on these earlier essays. Nor does he consider Mill's method in his earlier discussion of 'Bentham' and 'Coleridge' (See Ryan 1974: 53–8).

2 For a fuller discussion of the evolution of Mill's philosophic radicalism from Bentham's radical philosophy, see Rosen 2011: 257–94.

3 On the difficulties of assessing Mill's indebtedness to Coleridge, see Turk 1988: 44ff. See also p. 232, where he writes: 'Coleridge's influence was probably effective, not only in single ideas, but in the formulation of a whole method of truth.' However, Turk fails to consider how Mill utilized Coleridge not only with regard to truth and its expression, but also as a method in practical politics.

4 Hence, other scholars have been attracted to Mill's essay on Coleridge, e.g. seeing it serve a wide range of objects. For one, 'Coleridge' is 'the best introduction to Coleridge's writings' (Barrell 1972: p. xxvi), or, as Leavis thought, an important work providing insights into Victorian intellectual history (Leavis 1980: 12–13). One might note Morrow's belief that Mill's essay led to the liberal political philosophy accompanying the rise of English Idealism in writers like T. H. Green and J. H. Muirhead (Morrow 1990: 164), or Williams's Marxist interpretation of Mill's essays on Bentham and Coleridge as forming a prologue to much subsequent 'English thinking about society and culture' (Williams 1958: 49).

5 For a discussion of Mill's institutional proposals in relation to earlier radicalism, See Rosen 1983: 183–99.

Chapter 4

1 The novelty of Mill's approach may be seen in the fact that those who earlier classified the arts and sciences tended to regard politics as a distinct subject for study. See Diderot's 'Systême Figuré des Connoissances Humaines', which was prefixed to the French *Encyclopédie*, where 'politique' was a branch of philosophy related to morality and jurisprudence and shared this position with economics. In Bentham's *Chrestomathia* the subject appeared under ethics which was divided

NOTES TO CHAPTER 4

into private ethics and state-regarding ethics. Under the latter he included internal government and international politics, with the former divided into legislation and administration. Further divisions followed. Neither Diderot nor Bentham adopted a category called social science. For both tables See Bentham 1983a (1817): 158, 178 (following pages). Bentham mistakenly ascribed the authorship of the first table to D'Alembert rather than to Diderot, a mistake that has tended to be repeated in Bentham scholarship. See the correction in Bentham 1998: 58n. I am grateful to Professor David Adams and Dr John Hope Mason for advice and assistance on this and related issues. For a starting point with regard to the question of a science of politics, See Hume 1985 (1748): 14–31. As we shall see, Mill uses some elements of Hume's approach (emphasis on liberty, moderation, and character), but Mill's thought develops differently in its emphasis on social science rather than political science, and in its critical attention in the *Logic* to the nature of the sciences.

2 Mill wrote: 'It thus appeared, that both Macaulay and my father were wrong; the one in assimilating the method of philosophizing in politics to the purely experimental method of chemistry; while the other, though right in adopting a deductive method, had made a wrong selection of one, having taken as the type of deduction, not the appropriate process, that of the deductive branches of natural philosophy, but the inappropriate one of pure geometry, which not being a science of causation at all, does not require or admit of any summing-up of effects. A foundation was thus laid in my thoughts for the principal chapters of what I afterwards published on the Logic of the Moral Sciences...' (*CW* i. 167–9).

3 In the *Autobiography* Mill wrote: 'If I am asked what system of political philosophy I substituted for that which, as a philosophy, I had abandoned, I answer, no system: only a conviction, that the true system was something much more complex and many sided than I had previously had any idea of, and that its office was to supply, not a set of model institutions, but principles from which the institutions suitable to any given circumstances might be deduced' (*CW* i. 169).

4 See also Robson 1968: 141. The evidence for Mill's abandonment of ethology comes mainly from Bain. See Bain 1882: 78–9, 84; 1904: 159, 164. Many commentators have adopted this view. See e.g. Feuer 1976: 86–110; Capaldi 1973: 409–20; 2004: 177–8; Semmel 1984: 64n.–65n.; Burns 1976: 8; Reeves 2007: 170–1; 236. This view of the abandonment of ethology has been challenged by Ball 2000: 25–48; 2010: 35–56 (at 2010: 35 Ball provides a list of those who have accepted the abandonment thesis). Ball's position is discussed further below. For a recent attempt to develop Mill's idea of character, See Card 2010: 481–93.

5 In Bentham 1983a (1817): 61, Bentham e.g. wrote: 'As between *art* and *science*, in so far as they are distinguishable, *art* is that one of the two that seems entitled to first mention, as being first and most independent—in *value*, and thence in *dignity*, in so far as dignity consists in *use*: for, of

science, the value consists in its subserviency to *art*; of *speculation*, the value consists in its subserviency to *practice*. Of the two, *art*, when it is not itself the *end*, stands nearest to the end: with reference to this end, whatsoever of *science* stands connected with it, is but as a *means*.'

6 See Spencer 1864. See also Ch.6 n. 8 below.

7 In an earlier work (Collini *et al.* 1983: 130), Collini seems to agree in part with the position taken here: 'His views on the philosophic method appropriate to the study of politics are deserving, therefore, of fuller consideration than we would, in other cases, feel at all tempted to bestow on such matters. And, in fact, methodological and substantive issues are, as so often, closely intertwined, with the question of the formation of "character", both individual and national, providing the main common motif.' Nevertheless, Mill was not an 'intellectual' in the sense that Jones (2007: 256ff., drawing on Collini 2006: 46–8) ascribes to Mill's contemporary, Mark Pattison. Using Collini's definition of a 'subjective sense of intellectual' that denotes 'a particular commitment to truth-seeking, rumination, analysis, argument, often pursued as ends in themselves', which took the form, for Pattison, of 'the high conception of learning (*Wissenschaft*) and the academic vocation that emerged from Germany' (Jones 2007: 260), it is possible to see in Mill an opposing figure—a Socratic philosopher (who knows nothing) and an Epicurean—with foundations in pleasure and pain—rather than an intellectual *per se*.

8 Bentham 1983*a* (1817): 22. In the 1st edn. Bentham quoted from an article in the *Monthly Magazine* (1 Apr. 1814), but Southwood Smith, the editor of the version of *Chrestomathia* that appeared in Bentham 1838–43, chose the longer and more graphic account from the *Gentleman's Magazine* (Feb. 1814). See Bentham 1983*a* (1817): pp. xxiv, 425.

9 Bentham, of course, was not the first to discover ennui. He probably developed his ideas from the writings of Helvétius, but he gave the topic a new context. See Rosen 2003*a*: 82–96, esp. 93ff.

10 Like Mill, Bentham belonged to the modern Epicurean tradition which generally recognized that intellectual pleasures were superior to sensual ones. See Rosen 2003*a*: 15–28, 166–84. In developing the doctrine of higher pleasures Mill, contrary to some commentators, did not subsequently disagree with Bentham, and his utilitarianism accepted both the notion of qualities of pleasure and the importance of higher or intellectual pleasures. Where Mill disagreed with Bentham was in his introduction of Stoicism into his Epicureanism (See Rosen 2003*a*: 180–4) in order to use his version to oppose that of Carlyle. Mill did not write in *Utilitarianism* that it was better to be Socrates satisfied than a fool satisfied, but that it was better to be Socrates *dissatisfied* than a pig satisfied (see *CW* x. 212).

11 In a little-known passage Bentham wrote: 'Thus it is, that weeds of all sorts, even the most poisonous, are the natural produce of the vacant

mind. For the exclusion of these weeds, no species of husbandry is so effectual, as the filling the soil with flowers, such as the particular nature of the soil is best adapted to produce. What those flowers are can only be known from experiment; and the greater the variety that can be introduced, the greater the chance that the experiment will be attended with success' (Bentham 1983*a* (1817): 24–5). Thus education in a wide sense could fill the vacant mind and replace these poisonous weeds with flowers.

12 In Aug. 1843 Mill wrote to Comte that 'we have made for our common philosophy a conquest of the first order: it is that of young Bain'. 'He is a true thinker', Mill continued, after acknowledging his help with the *Logic* (*CW* xiii. 594–5). A year later in Oct. 1844, Mill was even stronger in his admiration of Bain and his appreciation of his importance to the joint positivist legacy Mill and Comte hoped to leave. 'I see only Bain', he wrote to Comte, 'in whom, if I would die tomorrow, I would be certain to leave a successor' (*CW* XIII. 638). As for the accuracy of his prediction regarding Bain flying the flag of positivism, See Bain 1904: 54, 145–6, 153–4, 156–9, 194, 202. Bain's attempts to delay the publication in French of the Mill–Comte correspondence is recorded in Vogeler 1976: 20. More generally, See Cashdollar 1989: 21, which begins with the relationships between Bain, Mill, and Comte. Mill also regarded highly Spencer's *Principles of Psychology* (Spencer 1855), but did not treat it with the same enthusiasm that he devoted to Bain's work (see *CW* xi. 342n.; see also viii. 853n.).

13 As Mill wrote (*CW* viii. 905): '[I]t must appear that the laws of national (or collective) character are by far the most important class of sociological laws. In the first place, the character which is formed by any state of social circumstances is in itself the most interesting phenomenon which that state of society can possibly present. Secondly, it is also a fact which enters largely into the production of all the other phenomena. And above all, the character, that is, the opinions, feelings, and habits, of the people, though greatly the results of the state of society which precedes them, are also greatly the causes of the state of society which follows them; and are the power by which all those of the circumstances of society which are artificial, laws and customs for instance, are altogether moulded: customs evidently, laws no less really, either by the direct influence of public sentiment upon the ruling powers, or by the effect which the state of national opinion and feeling has in determining the form of government, and shaping the character of the governors.' Of course, Hume is an important predecessor in writing on national character (Hume 1985 (1748): 197–215). See Varouxakis 1998: 375–91; 2002*a*: 54ff. Varouxakis is one of the few recent commentators on Mill to appreciate the significance of national character in his social science. See also Romani 2002; Mantena 2007: 308.

14 Bain was a careful student of Mill and wrote on this point: 'Political freedom is not exactly the same thing as Self-government, but is not complete without that addition' (Bain 1870: ii. 290).

15 For different interpretations of the distinction between active and passive character, See Holmes 2007: 327; Ball 2010: 35–56.

16 As Mill wrote (*CW* xix. 407): 'The self-benefiting qualities are all on the side of the active and energetic character: and the habits and conduct which promote the advantage of each individual member of the community, must be at least a part of those which conduce most in the end to the advancement of the community as a whole.'

17 Cf. J. Mill 1937, where Mill retained the emphasis on traditional forms of government, based on interests, and did not rely on any conception of character for his theory of government. Nevertheless, arguably, Mill's theory was based on interests in society and these social interests determined the most appropriate form of government, in this case, representative government. Perhaps, J. S. Mill's starting point was not too distant from his father's position. See also the way J. Mill 1813: 97 *contrasted* law and character by suggesting that 'laws are but so many imperfect substitutes for the defects of character'. In addition, see the critique of J. S. Mill's attempt to abstract society from the institutions of political society in Cornewall Lewis 1852: i. 51–2. If nothing more, Mill began a debate about the character of the 'political' that continues to the present time (see Philp 2007).

Chapter 5

1 This remarkable exchange of letters began on 8 Nov. 1841 and the last of the eighty-nine letters was sent on 17 May 1847. The letters were originally written in French, as Mill, who initiated the correspondence, was fluent in French from his visit to Samuel Bentham's family in the early 1820s (See Rosen 2010: 67–83). Although both writers claimed that their letters were not written with an eye on eventual publication (and, with minor exceptions, neither kept copies of their own letters: see *CW* xiii. 619), the full set survived, with the originals in the hands of the two who received them (See Vogeler 1976: 17–22). The delay in their publication as a single work until 1899 for Lévy-Bruhl's French edn., and 1995 for the English tr. by Haac might suggest that the significance of the correspondence as a whole was slow to be appreciated. The publication of Mill's letters without those of Comte in the Toronto edn. of Mill's *Collected Works* did not help to bring the correspondence as a coherent text to scholarly attention, and Mill scholars generally, though familiar with the outline of the relationship with Comte, have not focused on the correspondence as a whole (see Mill 1963–91, *CW* xiii where the letters may be found). In Comte's *Correspondance générale et confessions* (1973–90: ii–iv) both Comte's and Mill's letters are included, though Mill's

letters are placed in the notes, thus making it difficult, even here, to read the correspondence as a single work.

2 By 'positivism' both Comte and Mill referred to what they saw as a new doctrine for a new period in history. In confining its scope to positive facts and observable phenomena, and using these as the basis of knowledge of the arts and sciences, positivism rejected both the theological philosophies of the medieval period as well as their transcendental successors, and the 'negative', sceptical philosophies associated with the Enlightenment. The negative character of Enlightenment philosophy could not provide foundations for a science of society, and without such a science there could be little progress in understanding human beings as individuals and members of society. Mill sought to develop these foundations in the sciences of psychology and ethology, while Comte emphasized phrenology and physiology more generally. But Comte had initially formulated the three stages of human development from the theological to the critical (also called 'metaphysical' but related to the Enlightenment) to the positive (scientific and reconstructive).

3 See Weinberg 1982: 165–72, which provides an account of Comte's early enthusiasm for political economy, particularly his admiration of Adam Smith. This early acceptance of political economy was abandoned by the time he wrote 'Early Essays' (Comte 1911) and the *Cours* (Comte 1830–42). Political economy became, for Comte, 'purely metaphysical' and its usefulness belonged to the past, where it was used to discredit earlier industrial policies. See Weinberg 1982: 173. Regarding the term, 'metaphysical', see Ch.6 n. 9 below.

4 As I have noted in Ch.4, Mill excluded political science as a separate science and stated that a discussion of forms of government must be part of political ethology and hence part of social science. Political economy differed from this categorization due to its distinct psychological law that could form the basis of this unique science also concerned with society.

5 Sterling and F. D. Maurice were the 'Coleridgeans' in the London Debating Society and were considered by Mill as representing a radical force in politics, but one opposed to Benthamite radicalism. When Sterling attacked Bentham in a debate, Mill made a sharp defence of Bentham, and as a result Sterling resigned from the Society. The letter to Sterling was a successful appeal to resume their friendship which lasted until Sterling's death in 1844. The letter also contains one of the very few references (outside the *Autobiography*) to Mill's first mental crisis. See also Ch.3 above.

6 In Pickering's 'Final Analysis of their Relationship' (Pickering 2009: ii. 97–113), she repeats her thesis that Mill rebelled against a Benthamite 'philosophy based on selfishness and a narrow view of happiness' (Pickering 2009: ii. 98), and omits to consider Mill's return to Benthamism. Concerning Bentham and selfishness, Mill simply wrote: 'There is

no selfishness in Bentham's doctrines' (*CW* xiv. 78). Like Bentham, his view of happiness was based on pleasure and pain. Nevertheless, Comte played an important role not only in Mill's 'rebellion' but also in his return to Benthamism. That Mill 'returned' to some of Bentham's doctrines by the time he wrote *Utilitarianism* has been a matter of some discussion by scholars in recent decades (see e.g. Hollander 1985: ii. 602–3, 605; Schwartz 1972: 58; Robson 1968: 35; Scarre 1996: 91). Hollander acknowledges an important earlier debt to Jacob Viner who wrote in 1949: 'The intellectual history of Mill is in large part a history of faithful discipleship, then of rebellion from, and finally of substantial return to the Benthamite set of doctrines' (Viner 1991: 154). Viner was not mainly concerned with the formulation of the principle of utility but with Halévy's thesis ascribing a doctrine of 'natural or spontaneous harmony of interests' to Bentham (Viner 1991: 162; see e.g. Halévy 1928: 108). Viner argued that Bentham never accepted this doctrine, and that Mill's approach to laissez-faire in the *Principles* followed that of Bentham (reflecting a partial return to Benthamite principles). Like Bentham, Mill, as we shall see in Ch.7, was fully prepared to envisage considerable government intervention in the economy. Hollander takes the idea of a rebellion and return from Viner but applies it differently. He criticizes the work of Schumpeter who took as his understanding of Bentham, the view of Bentham that Mill expressed in the essays of the 1830s. For Schumpeter, this view of Mill never changed. For Hollander, Schumpeter missed entirely the evolution of Mill's thought, not only because he did not read Mill properly, but also because he misread Bentham. Bentham did not hold the doctrine ascribed to him by Schumpeter. Hollander accepts Mill's own view in the *Autobiography* that 'I had now completely turned back from what there had been of excess in my reaction against Benthamism' (*CW* i. 237; see also *CW* i. 227). In the preface to *Dissertations and Discussions* (1859) Mill wrote briefly of his regret concerning his overly strong sympathy 'with the reaction of the nineteenth century against the eighteenth' (*CW* x. 494). Hollander admits that the conception of a 'return' is not entirely clear in Mill and refers to 'some difficulty in getting a grip on Mill's centre of gravity' (Hollander 1985: ii. 638). At this point in Mill's life, he was closely linked with Harriet Taylor, and tended to play down the extent of his 'return' to Benthamite ideas. Mill stressed his progress, hand in hand with Harriet, particularly towards socialism, which is hardly a Benthamite position (See Hollander 1985: ii. 638–9). Nonetheless, Hollander finds considerable evidence of Mill's 'return' which is difficult to dispute. Where his argument is somewhat flawed is in his failure to appreciate the link between Mill and Comte. Hollander is fully aware of the importance of Mill's reading in 1829 Comte's brief essay, 'Système de politique positive' (1824). In his first letter to Comte in 1841 he referred to this essay as giving his ideas 'a strong bump', and he continued by saying that 'with other causes but more than they, determined my exit from the Benthamite section of the revolutionary school in which I was a pupil' (CW xiii. 489). If Comte's role in Mill's rebellion against Benthamite ideas is clear, his role in the 'return' is more difficult to determine. Hollander goes astray somewhat by ignoring the significance of Mill turning to political economy in their correspondence and assuming that Auguste Comte and Positivism 'provides us with a convenient summary of Mill's considered opinion' (Hollander 1985: i. 171). In my view the starting point for understanding Auguste Comte and Positivism, a complex work, is in the correspondence. When Mill finished the Logic, he was still thinking of writing a treatise on ethology and contributing with Comte to a new positivist social science. The possibility of contributing further to political economy after his successful publication of Essays on Some Unsettled Questions of Political Economy (1844) (CW iv. 229–339) was surely in his mind, but so was the increasing difficulty of working with Comte on any project. Of course, Mill brought with him into the Principles a number of ideas he took from Comte (see CW xiii. 626). First, he would adopt the view that all laws or conclusions were merely provisional. Second, he would distinguish between the laws of production and those of distribution, reflecting Comte's distinction between social statics and social dynamics. Third, he would not regard various states of economic society as unchanging. Fourth, although Mill regarded his proposed treatise as being of only passing usefulness, he also considered it highly relevant to the support of positivism in its current intellectual and political struggles (See Weinberg 1982: 177). However, one must not be tempted to conclude that Mill's work on political economy was as a faithful disciple of Comte. Weinberg draws attention to the unique feature of Mill's Principles in his bringing together two distinct sciences and methods: 'the retention of economics as a deductive discipline and the adoption of sociology as a historical science' (Weinberg 1982: 390). Although this move might appear to present the Comtean Mill as providing a synthesis of the two sciences, it also marks off a path (that of political economy) which Comte had rejected and would not accept (See Weinberg 1982: 173). The principle of laissez-faire to which Mill (following Bentham) gave prominence in the Principles was also rejected by Comte as introducing disorder and even anarchy into his fairly rigid system of social statics based on the determinism embedded in phrenology. In so far as political economy incorporated the idea of 'spontaneous development', and incorporated laissez-faire, it would seem that Mill's move to write on political economy was in fact a return to Bentham and Benthamism. In what did Mill's return to Bentham and Benthamism consist? I have already argued that Mill's hedonism, despite apparent evidence to the contrary, represented a continuation of Bentham's position (with an added dose of Stoicism), as both were clearly working within the Epicurean tradition (See Rosen 2003a: 15–28, 166–84). There is no return to Bentham, based on a distinct break, but perhaps a stronger appreciation in Utilitarianism and earlier in the essay on Whewell (CW x. 165–201) that he and Bentham were closer on this crucial question than has been commonly thought. Similarly, Mill's insistence (against Comte) on the importance of ethology represented a continuation of his Benthamite roots that emphasized the importance of education in the formation of character. Mill's adoption of laissez-faire in the *Principles* and *On Liberty* also represent a continuation of Bentham's views from the early *Defence of Usury* (Bentham 1952–4 (1787): i. 123–207), which in turn was given a prominent role in the *Principles*. There are numerous other spheres where Mill continued the Benthamite tradition, such as in giving justice (as security) a prominent role under the principle of utility or in his emphasis (with his father) on associationist psychology. None of this refers to an explicit 'return' to Benthamism, as he never left it. My thesis is that the so-called 'return' was less a return and more a departure from Comte at the time when Mill made the decisive move in 1844 to write the *Principles*. It represented a change of focus from Comtean sociology to economics and a return to Benthamism, a move that Comte was quick to spot. Where the move touched on fundamentals, it is to be found in Mill's insistence on the primacy of the idea of liberty. Liberty becomes a major theme not only in *On Liberty* but also in the *Principles*, in his socialism, and in the *Subjection*, to name a few. Mill's account of liberty represented a crucial 'return' from the rigidity and despotism associated with Comtean positivism and the 19th cent. to the ideas of the Enlightenment adopted by Bentham and embedded in the utilitarian tradition. This element in Mill's thought is fully evident in the correspondence and in *Auguste Comte and Positivism*.

7 Bain 1882: 73 wrote: 'In 1842 and 1843, the letters on both sides were overflowing with mutual regard. It was Comte's nature to be very frank, and he was circumstantial and minute in his accounts of himself and his ways. Mill was unusually open; and revealed, what he seldom told to anybody, all the fluctuations in his bodily and mental condition.'

8 For some further insight into Mill's hostility towards 'German' philosophy, see the account of his relationship with Theodor Gomperz in Weinberg 1963: 9ff. On the ambiguity associated with the use of 'metaphysics' and 'metaphysical', see below Ch.6 n. 9.

9 The full title of Mill's *Logic* is: *A System of Logic Ratiocinative and Inductive, Being a connected View of the Principles of Evidence and the Methods of Scientific Investigation*. The title reflects Mill's concern with evidence as well as his experience of editing Bentham's *Rationale of Judicial Evidence* (Bentham 1827).

Chapter 6

1 See *CW* x, pp. cxxix ff. Pickering 2009: ii.109n. wrongly suggests 1854 and thus misses the more purely philosophical dimension in Mill's reluctance, as opposed to any hostility to Martineau.

2 Packe 1954: 321 has written: 'it is clear that [Mill] already thought her a cantankerous and opinionated creature, the hard and narrow core of the sectarian radicalism he was trying to puncture. He never liked her: she was not his friend. And from the first she disapproved of Harriet for being frivolous.'

3 See Pickering 2009: iii. 33–52, where she provides a full account of Littré's defection from the positivist camp with many issues similar to those found to be troubling Mill, such as the status of political economy and the proposed treatment of women. Nevertheless, she clearly distinguishes between the positions of Littré and Mill with regard to Comte (see Pickering 2009: iii. 50). See also Littré 1866.

4 According to Pickering 2009: iii. 3, in *Auguste Comte and Positivism* Mill 'helped spread this view of the discontinuity in his [Comte's] development'. Pickering, herself, disputes the opinion that there was an 'abrupt break' between Comte's 'first' and 'second' careers (Pickering 2009: iii. 4), and states that one object of the final 2 vols. of her biography is to 'highlight the continuity in his trajectory'. She also notes that, contrary to Mill, Littré 'spoke openly about his devotion to positivism' 'even at the end of his life' (Pickering 2009: iii. 50). My chapters on Mill and Comte here have been written mainly from the perspective of Mill, and I have noted several examples of Mill showing his appreciation of aspects of Comte's later as well as his earlier writings and, in addition, criticizing Comte for positions and convictions held in both periods. Thus, from Mill's point of view, there was continuity, but he certainly wanted to dissociate himself from what he considered to be Comte's later absurdities. That Mill played down Comte's earlier absurdities (such as cerebral hygiene—see below) was perhaps meant to protect his reputation and moderate his overly sympathetic view of Comte's achievements in the *Logic*, correspondence, and elsewhere. See also Scharff 1995.

5 For Pickering (2009: ii. 72), Comte's interest in Mill's *Logic* was mainly due to its praise of Comte. 'Comte knew very well that Mill was giving him the respectability he needed and making him famous. He intended to take full advantage of his good fortune.'

6 It is tempting to suggest that Mill's self-doubt and deference to Comte in the correspondence is reflected in the *Logic* itself by Mill's apparent restriction of Comte's influence to book 6 concerned with social science. This view might then enable the critic of my argument concerning the importance of Comte to minimize the importance of the correspondence on Mill's thought as a whole and also minimize the importance of Comte in the development of Mill's thought. The view developed here, based on the correspondence, grants that while Comte did not directly affect Mill's book 3 on induction, he had a profound influence not only on book 6 but also on the whole of the *Logic*. First, Comte's views on the relationship between science and art and the classification of the sciences relates to the whole of the *Logic*. Second, Comte's position on the historical nature

of ideas is also important with regard to Mill's conception of truth throughout the *Logic*. Third, Comte on the character of religion has a direct effect on Mill's conceptions of the purpose of logic and the importance of empirical truth. The very notion of the importance of positive science forming the basis of truth also runs through the whole of the *Logic*.

7 For an account of Comte's indebtedness to Hume, See Pickering 1993: i. 311–13.

8 Mill wrote: 'It is not at first obvious how a mere classification of the sciences can be not merely a help to their study, but itself an important part of a body of doctrine; the classification, however, is a very important part of M. Comte's philosophy' (*CW* x. 279). See also Spencer 1864. For the importance of the classification of the sciences in Mill's thought, see above, Ch.4 n. 1.

9 There may be some confusion regarding the use of 'metaphysics' or

'metaphysical' by the two philosophers. Comte used it, as here, to refer to the negative, critical thought that was associated with the Enlightenment and which had to be rejected and replaced by positivism. Metaphysical thought had also replaced earlier theological thought in the Enlightenment. But Mill also used the term 'metaphysical' to refer to transcendental, 'German' philosophy that was part of the 19th-cent. reaction to the Enlightenment and was opposed by Mill's *Logic*. Hence, the second use might be seen as in conflict with the first. As this chapter demonstrates, Mill incorporated a good deal of what Comte called metaphysics into his 'return' to the Bentham school, while at the same time criticizing the tendency of Comte, as well as German philosophy and Anglican Christianity, to exhibit metaphysical tendencies associated with transcendental ideas. In the context of Comte's criticisms of political economy, Mill wrote that Comte used the category of metaphysics as a 'comprehensive category of condemnation in which he places all attempts at positive science which are not in his opinion directed by a right scientific method' (*CW* x. 305). This passage reflects Mill's critique of Comte for not appreciating the more lasting truths of Enlightenment thought.

10 According to Bain: 'The delicate part of the situation was that Grote, who began admiring Comte, as Mill did, although never to the same degree, was yet strongly adverse to his sociological theories, especially as regarded their tendency to introduce a new despotism over the individual. Indeed, his admiration of Comte scarcely extended at all to the sociological volumes. He saw in them frequent mistakes and perversions of historical facts, and did not put the same stress as Mill did upon the Social analysis—the distinction of Statics and Dynamics, and the Historical Method; in fact, he had considerable misgivings throughout as to all the grand theories of the French school on the Philosophy of History. But the repression of liberty by a new machinery touched his acutest

susceptibility; he often recurred in conversation to this part of Comte's system, and would not take any comfort from the suggestion I often made to him, that there was little danger of any such system ever being in force' (Bain 1882: 75).

11 For a brief study of contemporary liberalism that shows the importance of Mill's thought (though not the debate with Comte) to its evolution, See Kelly 2005.

12 Mill wrote: 'None of them pretend that the laws of wages, profits, values, prices, and the like, set down in their treatises, would be strictly true, or many of them true at all, in the savage state (for example), or in a community composed of masters and slaves. But they do think, with good reason, that whoever understands the political economy of a country with the complicated and manifold civilization of the nations of Europe, can deduce without difficulty the political economy of any other state of society, with the particular circumstances of which he is equally well-acquainted' (CW x. 305–6).

13 A further discussion of this theme in the context of Mill's religious views appears in Ch.9 below.

14 For different accounts, which stress Mill's agreement with Comte, See Wright 1986: 45ff. and Pickering 1993: i. 518–19.

Chapter 7

1 Later in the chapter when Mill asserted 'one very simple principle', he referred to 'compulsion and control' by means of 'physical force in the form of legal penalties, or the moral coercion of public opinion' (CW xviii. 223). But in elucidating the principle, the power of law and government was minimized in favour of what seemed to be a moral principle belonging to a 'civilized community' (CW xviii. 223).

2 See the edns. of the Oxford English Dictionary, where the phrase has not been included either under 'social' or 'liberty'. Rousseau is an important precursor in the use of 'social', as in 'social contract', but Mill probably simply took the 'social' directly from Comte, and attached it to liberty.

3 See also the earlier treatment of freedom of thought and expression in Ch.2 above.

4 'The End of Law', Locke wrote, 'is not to abolish or restrain, but to preserve and enlarge Freedom', for 'where there is no Law, there is no Freedom' (Locke 1988 (1698): 306 (ii. 57)). See also Locke 1988 (1698): 283–4 (ii. 22). (The additional references are to the Second Treatise and paragraph numbers.)

5 For Bentham on security, see further Long 1977: 74–83; Rosen 1983: 67–75; 1987: 121–38; Kelly 1990: 71–103.

6 This statement represents a change of view concerning Mill's conceptions of liberty and security, based on the work of Rees 1985, Gray 1996, Ten 1980, and others, presented in Rosen 1987: 121–38. At that time I was concerned to state the extent to which Mill took his ideas of liberty and justice from Bentham, and I had not yet explored the *Principles* in any depth. As a result, I could not state clearly the additional foundations of Mill's thought, particularly, the continuing significance of his idea of active character.

7 See Gray 1996: 62–3 for an assessment of the link between Mill's distinction and the principle of liberty in *On Liberty*.

8 The final sentences of *On Liberty* restate in a different context the sentiments expressed here. See *CW* xviii. 310.

9 See Skinner 1998: pp. ix–x, 82–4, where he contrasts 'neo-roman' views of liberty and those associated with 'classical liberalism'. Mill's ideas of liberty would not fit into either of Skinner's categories. Skinner's distinction would disqualify Mill as a liberal, even though Mill identified himself with liberalism, as numerous subsequent commentators have pointed out (see e.g. Levin 2003: 68). Furthermore, according to Skinner (1998: 84), 'the key assumption of classical liberalism' is 'that force or the coercive threat of it constitute the only forms of constraint that interfere with individual liberty'. Mill's rejection of civil liberty as the *foundation* or 'key assumption' in liberalism in favour of social liberty involves, as we have seen, the acceptance of active character, turmoil, and even violence in its development, as well as widespread interference by government in individual lives. Furthermore, the concept of social liberty does not fit well into Skinner's more political 'neo-roman' or republican category of liberty. Mill's social liberty intentionally lacks this political dimension by focusing on the people in society. See also Rosen 2004: 190–1.

10 See also Williams 1989: 102–11, who presents numerous examples of Mill's support for political violence.

11 As Riley 1998a: 146 points out: 'Much of the literature relating to application of the liberty doctrine is unhelpful. Some commentators are so hostile and/or confused that they claim Mill perversely abandons his "one very simple principle" in this fifth chapter, leading them roundly to dismiss his whole approach.' For an example of this confusion See Himmelfarb 1974: 109–39. Few, if any, commentators have suggested that the key to understanding the 'Applications' chapter might be found in the *Principles*.

12 'The maxims are, first, that the individual is not accountable to society for his actions, in so far as these concern the interests of no person but himself. Advice, instruction, persuasion, and avoidance by other people if thought necessary by them for their own good, are the only measures by which society can justifiably express its dislike or disapprobation of his conduct. Secondly, that for such actions as are prejudicial to the

interests of others, the individual is accountable, and may be subjected either to social or to legal punishment, if society is of opinion that the one or the other is requisite for its protection' (*CW* xviii. 292).

13 See Jacobson 2000: 276–309, who presents a different argument to challenge the conventional view that the harm principle is the foundation of the doctrine of liberty.

14 See Hollander 1985: ii. 775–6, for an appreciation of the importance of competition in Mill's thought. Rees 1985: 153 seems to think that the issue of competition is one supported by all who engaged in the practice. While it was a practice Mill supported, it was not universally favoured in theories of distribution within socialist thought, where a greater emphasis was placed on equality.

15 This emphasis on the importance of social liberty in Mill does not extend to any acknowledgement that the essay *On Social Freedom* (See Fosdick 1941) was written by Mill himself. Rees 1985: 175–85, 201–3, has examined the text in detail, and for numerous biographical as well as textual reasons, correctly concludes that it was not written by Mill. The editors of Mill's later correspondence (*CW* xv. 792n.) as well as Rees 1985: 203 suggest that the author might have been E. R. Edger who had sent an essay to Mill in the early 1860s for Mill to advise him concerning his abilities to pursue a career in philosophy. The question has been raised, but not answered, as to how or why the essay remained in Mill's papers, which led to it being published in 1907 and republished in 1941 as a work of Mill himself. A tentative hypothesis might be that Mill kept it and might have referred to it, if he had decided to write more on the subject of social liberty. The interpretation of liberty in the *Principles* and in *On Liberty* with the emphasis on social liberty suggests that he might have had this in mind. I am grateful to Peter Nicholson for bringing this volume to my attention.

Chapter 8

1 For an excellent study of the 18th-cent. link between economics and political theory, as a way of seeing the context of Mill's journey to socialism, See Hont 2005.

2 For differences in Tocqueville's view of the 'Tyranny of the Majority' in the 2 vols. of *Democracy in America*, See Drescher 2006: 34–5 and Richter 2006: 269. For a more elaborate comparison between the two thinkers, See Hamburger 1976: 111–25.

3 See also Manent 2006: 111: 'For Tocqueville, in fact, the same social "base"—"democracy"—can correspond to two antithetical political regimes, one democratic in the ordinary sense of the word, the other "despotic", but involving a novel form of despotism.'

4 For the importance of co-operation in Mill, see the discussion by Claeys 1987: 145.

5 Holyoake 1906: i. 306 added his own definition: 'Co-operation is an industrial scheme for delivering the public from the conspiracy of capitalists, traders, or manufacturers, who would make the labourer work for the least and the consumer pay the utmost, for whatever he needs of money, machines, or merchandise. Co-operation effects this deliverance by taking the workman and the customer into partnership in every form of business it devises.' See also Holyoake 1906: i. 3–6; 1873a: 1–29. For another brief account of the idea of co-operation, See Holyoake 1873b: 1–16.

Chapter 9

1 As Stafford 1988: 123 has written, the reference to socialism here was never retracted and, particularly, not in the 'Chapters on Socialism'. Claeys 1987: 142 draws attention to Bain's remark (1882: 90) that the 'Chapters on Socialism' 'shows the wide gulf that still separated him and them' (i.e. Mill and the Socialists), and notes that many writers have followed Bain's position in seeing the 'Chapters' as a step backward from socialism. However, recent writers (Claeys refers to Gray 1979: 273–4) have argued that there was little change in Mill's view between the *Principles* and the 'Chapters'. It will be argued in the next chapter that, if there are differences, they may be accounted for by differences in context and strategy rather than by changes in any ideological sense for or against socialism.

2 In Ch.8 I stressed that there was no direct link between representative democracy and socialism. For Mill to refer to 'the best aspirations of the democratic spirit' would not establish such a link, but would take one back to the ideas of active character and co-operation, which serve as foundations for socialism.

3 On the distinction between economic statics and dynamics and Mill's indebtedness to Comte, see further Weinberg 1982: 391.

4 For a brief discussion of the stationary state in relation to Ricardian economics, See Riley 1998b: 310–15; See also Urbinati 2011: 242–5.

5 I have discussed Mill's method on numerous occasions in approaching similar moral and political issues in terms of a 'method of reform' (see Ch.3 above). This is not to deny, as Ryan (1974: 184–5) has suggested, that Mill also possessed 'propagandist intentions', which also dictated his approach in various works, and, particularly, his writings on socialism.

6 On other aspects of Mill's honesty with regard to the working classes, see *CW* i. 274–5. See also Kinzer *et al.* 1992: 64–5.

7 See Pappé 1960: 45–6 for a view of what Mill's foresight consisted.

Chapter 10

1 See also Kinzer 2007: 175; Kinzer *et al.* 1992: 90ff.; Winch 2009: 82.

2 Mill's distinction between communism and socialism was not always a clear one, perhaps, reflecting usage at this point in the 19th cent. Nevertheless, Mill seems to have a fairly clear distinction in mind when he uses these terms. Furthermore, in discussing his views on various socialist writers, I have focused on his reading of their ideas. It would be useful to sort out how well Mill read these writers, but no attempt has been made to do so here. But See Claeys 2011: 521–55.

3 On the different discussions of property in the *Principles* and the 'Chapters', See Ryan 1974: 185. See also Schwartz 1972: 181; Hollander 1985: ii. 785.

4 Claeys 1987: 143 observes that the differences between the 'Chapters' and Mill's earlier writings emerge at this point in the critique of socialist objections to the current system. However, he adds (rightly in my view) that 'the actual drawbacks of the workings of any socialist system which the "Chapters" pointed to are in fact little different from those he had alluded to previously'.

5 A good deal more might be written to compare and contrast Mill and Marx. Robson 1968: 275–6 has noted that Mill knew little of Marx (but see *CW* xxxii. 220) and that Marx was little known in England in the period up to Mill's death in 1873. See Feuer 1949: 297–303. Contrasting Mill and Marx, Robson added that Mill was opposed to violent revolution, but he was in favour of a moral and intellectual revolution. Mill found such ideas as a dictatorship of the proletariat 'puerile' and rejected any emphasis on class war. Mill also opposed too much emphasis on central control and felt that communists and socialists had presented an inadequate account of the institutions of the state. At a deeper level, Mill's understanding of history emphasized 'intellect, idea and individual', and while not ignoring economic factors, rejected a hard determinism like that of Marx. Finally, Marx (like Comte, but unlike Mill) ignored logical problems, such as proof, generalizations from data, etc. See further Ryan 1974: 183, 161–3, 165, 174, 240. For a more elaborate study and comparison of Marx and Mill, See Duncan 1973.

Chapter 11

1 C. L. Ten (1998: 372) writes: 'In the end it was his overriding concern for the fate of individual freedom and development which guided all his social and political proposals.' Nevertheless, Ten seems to ignore the issue of justice, particularly, distributive justice, as an important issue in the context of socialism. See also Ten 1980.

2 Most moral and political philosophers who write on utilitarianism do not consider the issue of distributive justice in Mill's *Utilitarianism* in any detail. See e.g. Crisp 1997: 155–71, esp. 157; Crisp 1998: 136–50; Raphael

2001: 126–38; Donner 1998: 282–91. An exception is West 2004: 161ff. See also Berger 1984: 153, 157–204; Riley 1989: 143.

3 See e.g. Rosen 1987: 121–38; 1992: 25–39; 2003*a*: 185–206, 245–55.

4 Mill's conception of justice as security of persons and property might well form a basis of his opposition to sudden and violent change in the system of property ownership.

5 I have discussed this material in earlier publications in relation to Bentham's and Mill's ideas of distribution mainly to reject the view that classical utilitarianism required or allowed for the punishment of some to achieve the greater happiness of others. See Rosen 2003*a*: 228–31, esp. 230–1. Part of this discussion was concerned with the status of equality, and I contrasted H. L. A. Hart's view of equality in Bentham (as a weighting principle) and in Mill (as confused) with my own conception of equality as being a distributive principle. Nevertheless, there was more to Mill's discussion of equality than this debate, however important, suggests, and in Mill's consideration of communism and socialism, further insights have been obtained.

6 See further Miller 1998: 68–81, for an appreciation of the importance of Mill's psychology in *Utilitarianism*. But See also Miller 2010*b*: 217. In addition, See Vogler 2001; Wilson 1990, for a more general account of Mill's psychology.

7 Sidgwick 1904: 242. This passage came to my attention in Winch 2009: 203.

Chapter 12

1 In the *Autobiography* (*CW* i. 45) Mill wrote: 'I am thus one of the very few examples in this country, of one who has, not thrown off religious belief, but never had it: I grew up in a negative state with regard to it.' In contrast with the correspondence between Mill and Comte, Mill did not in the passage from the *Autobiography* make the clear distinction between God and religion. It may be another example of his greater frankness in the correspondence than in his published works.

2 Sell 2004 is one of a very few writers to have recently attempted to explore Mill's religious thought in its own terms without a preoccupation with other issues, such as liberty and liberalism (see e.g. Cowling 1990: pp. xii–xiii; Hamburger 1999: 108–48; Eisenach 2002: 189–216). Although there is much to praise in the book, particularly, its thorough reading of Mill's texts as well as the literature on Mill by Mill's own contemporaries (See also Sell 1997), his work suffers from several confusions. Among the most important is his failure to distinguish between God on the one hand and religion on the other. Sell 2004: 1 knows that Mill was raised by his father, not as a dogmatic atheist, but in an environment that excluded God. Yet he suggests in a chaptertitled 'The Omnipresence of God' that 'whether

we read Mill's published works or his letters, God, or at least religion, is not far away' (Sell 2004: 27). I would argue that, although Mill discussed religion in numerous contexts, he did so without the presence of a transcendent God. Sell 2004: 76 e.g. quotes the passage regarding God from the letter to Comte, in the text above, but fails to see the importance of Mill's distinction and his emphasis on being raised without God and never having believed in God. This being without God tends to make Mill's religious views seem somewhat odd, leading Sell to refer 'to a certain tiresomeness in his subsequent writings which is characteristic of many fashionable pundits, then as now, who debunk Christianity' (Sell 2004: 6). This sort of commentary mistakenly links Mill with 'fashionable pundits' who debunk Christianity, when, in fact, he was often sympathetic to Christianity (as opposed to other religions) and was a unique figure in 19th-cent. England. Sell 2004: 6 also asks 'whether Mill succeeded, or even seriously attempted to succeed, in the first duty of the honourable critic, namely, that of seeking to "get under the skin" of the quarry by the expenditure of effort and the employment of imaginative sympathy'. How Mill might have been expected to get 'under the skin' is not clear, and one suspects that any failure of 'imaginative sympathy' was due less to his being a 'fashionable pundit' and more to his unique position. A second confusion may be found in Sell's tendency to use the *Autobiography* as a faithful record of Mill's life. As we have seen in Mill's account in the *Autobiography* of his visit to France in 1820–1 (See Rosen 2010: 69–72) or in his account of his relationship with Comte (see Chs. 5 and 6 above), the *Autobiography* should not be regarded as simply an attempt to state accurately the main events and influences of his life, but as a work that is part of his philosophical corpus and might contribute (though not conclusively) to an account of the evolution of some of his philosophical views. Sell uses the *Autobiography*, wrongly in my view, to see defects in Mill's character that profoundly affected his views on religion or at least brought confusions to these views. Sell writes of Mill's 'mode of thought' that 'it oscillates between theoretical positions, with the result that he can land himself in contradiction' (Sell 2004: 18). My position is that Mill's views on God and religion are fairly clear (and certainly not contradictory) once one separates God from religion. There are difficulties and these arise (as we shall see) from Mill's encounter with Comte, which may be more fully understood from his correspondence with Comte than from the *Autobiography*. Sell 2004: 104 is right to see that Mill derived his idea of a religion of humanity from Comte, and works out his own conception in relation to Comte. But the significance of such a religion (as we shall see) reflects Mill's overall commitments in logic and, particularly, in social and political philosophy. For example, the religion of humanity arguably enabled Mill to develop a more universal moral doctrine than his character-based historically relative morality seems to suggest is possible. Sell grasps some of this when he criticizes philosophers for ignoring

Mill's work on religion in their own accounts of Mill's thought (See Sell 2004: 69; see also 1, 20–1). But his criticism of Mill on religion over some alleged contradiction as well as superficiality assumes a view of theistic religion which was utterly foreign to Mill, despite Sell calling him 'a God haunted man' (Sell 2004: 178). For a brief account of the place of religion in Mill's thought, See Winch 2010: 63–5.

3 Eisenach 2002: 189–216 virtually ignores Comte and the Mill–Comte correspondence in his important essay on Mill and religion. See also Britton 1976: 21–34.

4 For a helpful study of Mill and the religion of humanity, See Vernon 1989: 167–82.

5 Mill wrote: 'The most prejudiced must admit that this religion without theology is not chargeable with relaxation of moral restraints. On the contrary, it prodigiously exaggerates them. It makes the same ethical mistake as the theory of Calvinism, that every act in life should be done for the glory of God, and that whatever is not a duty is a sin' (*CW* x. 337).

6 For a wide-ranging recent study of Mill's 'moral theory', focusing on 'revisionist' interpretations roughly since Gray, See Brown 2010: 5–45. Brown, however, does not consider the moral implications surrounding Mill's conception of the religion of humanity.

7 With regard to 'Utility of Religion', the material on the religion of humanity could have been added to the text at the same time as he was writing 'Theism' and not composed in the 1850s. Compare *CW* x. 422–8 and 488–9. Although there is no evidence to suggest that this was necessarily the case, except for the location of the discussions at the end of the respective texts, it would also make sense, as *Auguste Comte and Positivism* (published in 1865) seems to have been the first public discussion of this topic.

8 Compare Sell 2004: 95, who suggests that Mill's religion of humanity involves him in 'playing God'. Sell 2004: 102 also quotes from Hamburger 1991: 166: 'When one considers the accumulated effects of education, public opinion, and the trained conscience that internalizes the morality of the Religion of Humanity, one is left with an individual that was indoctrinated, socially pressured, and internally restrained'. The view presented in this chapter rejects both of these assertions.

Chapter 13

1 There is no intention here to assess Mill's *Subjection* from the perspective of modern feminism or from a comparison of the writings of Harriet and John Mill on the status and prospects of women. Commentators have been concerned mainly with an assessment of Harriet Mill's abilities as a thinker and writer, an estimation of her influence on Mill over a wide

range of issues, and his recognition of the importance of that influence. See e.g. Packe 1954: 347, 370ff.; Hayek 1951: 14ff. Pappé 1960: 24–9 is less enthusiastic about Harriet Mill's influence. According to J. S. Mill, with regard to their 'joint productions' (as he referred to those works published in the 2-vol. collection of essays, *Dissertations and Discussions*: See Mill 1859; *CW* xxi. 393 and n.), he claimed only to be Harriet's 'editor and amenuensis'. For these 'joint productions', he proposed in a letter of August 1853 that her name should be on the title-pages, since she was 'the originating mind, the Bentham' and he was merely 'the Dumont' (*CW* xiv. 112). As for Harriet Mill's essay, 'The Enfranchisement of Women' (1851), Himmelfarb 1974: 183–6 has argued that the work was mainly that of Harriet rather than that of John Mill. This view has largely been adopted by Collini and Robson in *CW* xxi, where they reassess the evidence. See *CW* xxi, pp. xxxii and lxxiv–lxxvii. A. and J. Robson 1994: p. vii also take the view that 'there is no question now that Mill would have been less effective in the cause without the companionship of Harriet and Helen Taylor'.

2 Berger's view of the *Subjection*, published in 1984, by no means reflected that of traditional Mill scholarship which largely neglected the work. See Tulloch 1989: 3. Even where it was highly praised, as by Bertrand Russell, who regarded it and *On Liberty* as superior to the *Logic* and the *Principles*, it tended to be dismissed. In Russell's opinion e.g. the importance of the *Subjection* had been diminished, because he thought that its work had already been accomplished, an opinion widely challenged by the feminist movement since the 1970s (See Russell 1968: 10–11). Berger, however, seems to have absorbed the feminist appreciation as well as the critique of Mill's *Subjection*. See also Okin 1980: 202–3. For an appreciation of the *Subjection* by a contemporary of Mill, see Morley 1970 (1874): 153. Not all estimations at that time were full of praise. See e.g. Stephen 1873: 203ff., 237–8.

3 Mill's view of the subjection of women and its connection with slavery was formed early in his life. See *CW* xviii. 55n. On the connection between slavery and dependence, see Skinner 1998: pp. ix, 40ff.

4 See Rosen 1968: 105–16; 1973: 307–16, for attempts to explore the Socratic method from the perspective of all of the interlocutors and not just Socrates in two Socratic dialogues of Plato. While this approach is not that of Mill, it attempts to capture Plato's approach to reconciling opposing views. It is also important to note that the use of the Socratic method is not confined to Plato's early or middle dialogues. Aristotle is an important figure in the development and extension of the Socratic approach in logic and ethics. For Mill's discussion of Aristotle, see *CW* xi. 475–510. See also Grote 1872.

5 See Tulloch 1989: 6–8, who identifies Mill's use of contraries, but does not see how they drive the arguments forward.

6 '... for to prove this, is by far the easiest portion of my task' (*CW* xxi. 263).

7 According to Tulloch 1989: p. xiv, Freud called attention to Mill's use of the analogy with slavery and rejected it on the grounds that women were simply different from men with different natures that emphasized 'beauty, charm, and sweetness'. See Jones 1953: i. 192–3.

8 See Shanley 1991: 165–72 for an appreciation of the theme of slavery in Mill's essay. See also Hirschmann 2003: 62. August 1976: 212 compares *On Liberty* with the *Subjection*, saying that *Liberty* 'lays siege to the general evil of oppression' and the *Subjection* 'assaults the peculiar evil of society's most prevalent form of oppression'. Early modern feminism (*c.*1970) tended to overlook this dimension in Mill's essay. In emphasizing the distinction between the liberal pursuit of legal rights for women on the one hand and their social position in the family on the other, Rossi 1970: 7, e.g. omits to consider Mill's concern with despotism. It is worth noting that, while Morley 1970 (1874): 153–4 felt that Mill went to the heart of the subjection of women, he also did not see the essay as a study of despotism. Nor have numerous recent feminist writers who have emphasized 'patriarchalism' rather than despotism. According to Zerilli 1994: 96, 'in light of his critique of the domestic ideal as a vehicle of male power, commentators have puzzled over the shortcomings of Mill's most sustained indictment of patriarchy, *The Subjection of Women*'. Tulloch 1989: 5 defines patriarchy as 'a particular form of gender relations involving hierarchical relationships, and legal and social domination of women by men. Sex thus acts to confer both privilege and disability in a way Mill deplored.' Tulloch clearly states in this passage that Mill deplored patriarchy. Other feminist writers have taken a different view and have argued that, despite Mill's apparent rejection of patriarchalism, he nonetheless embraced it. See Zerilli 2005: 185n.–186n.; Okin 1980: 230. It is important to note that the terms 'patriarchal' and 'patriarchalism' were not frequently used by Mill and not obviously in the *Subjection*. The dictionary definition of 'patriarchal' refers mainly to rule by a father or father-figure, and only in this limited sense does it refer to 'gender relations'. Mill would not have been inclined to use the term 'patriarchal', as the *Subjection* was concerned with despotism (linked with enslavement and tyranny), while 'patriarchy' and 'patriarchalism' (linked more with monarchy) could refer to a more benevolent form of rule. Mill referred more commonly to 'paternal' and 'paternalism' (and usually critically), but this was not a theme in the *Subjection*.

9 As Kamm 1977: 197ff. and numerous other feminists have pointed out, Mill's reluctance to support the legal possibility of divorce at the time raised difficult problems. As Mill knew, the indissolubility of marriage in a society, where women had few independent legal rights to a separate existence, might actually protect women. Furthermore, where divorce was legally permitted, remarriage under such a regime could involve

individuals voluntarily abandoning their liberty, a position he condemned in *On Liberty* and elsewhere. Mill also believed in 'perfect equality' and would know that his position was difficult to reconcile with such a goal. Mill himself was privately very clear about his position. In a letter to John Nichol (18 Aug. 1869), he wrote: 'I thought it best not to discuss the questions about marriage & divorce along with that of the equality of women; not only from the obvious inexperience of establishing a connexion in people's minds between equality, & any particular opinions on the divorce question, but also because I do not think that the conditions of the dissolubility of marriage can be properly determined until women have an equal voice in determining them, nor until there has been experience of the marriage relation as it would exist between equals. Until then I should not like to commit myself to more than the general principle of relief from the contract in extreme cases' (*CW* xvii. 1634, cited in Okin 1980: 203, 330n.). This passage seems to me to be fully compatible with my position on Mill's rhetoric. He did not want to compromise his fundamental commitment to equality. Furthermore, to understand more fully the application of equality to marriage and divorce required not only the idea of equality but also a sufficient equality in society so that women themselves had an equal opportunity to determine the rules respecting marriage and divorce. Not to take this position would be like establishing ideal conditions for marriage and divorce for female African slaves before they were emancipated. One must be suspicious of a number of recent feminist positions on this issue. Okin, who has examined the same passage in Mill's letter, tends to read it in terms of Mill playing down or omitting his 'radical ideas', in order to maintain the respectability of the women's rights movement (Okin 1980: 203). If there is any merit in my argument, Mill's passage has nothing to do with radicalism versus liberalism and nothing to do with respectability. It has a lot to do with rhetoric and strategy. Goldstein 1980: 320 has criticized Mill for stopping 'dead short at the brink of radical alteration of the traditional marriage institution'. On the contrary, Mill embraced 'radical alteration', because he embraced 'perfect equality' for women to determine in the future what those arrangements should be. See also Morales 1996: 21ff.

10 '... one of John Stuart Mill's great insights in *The Subjection of Women* was his observation that the decision to marry for the vast majority of women could scarcely be called "free"' (Minow and Shanley 1997: 90).

11 For a different and more critical account of Mill's attempts to assess and determine the future, See Ring 1991: 50–1, 72. See also the earlier remarks of Annas 1977: 179–94.

12 August 1976: 212 suggests that Mill writes here 'with almost Marxian inexorableness'.

13 For a brief account of the significance of equality in Mill's *Subjection* in the context of Victorian and modern feminism, See Shanley 1989: 63–7. See also Berger1984: 196–7; Okin 1980: 202–3; Morales 1996.

14 See these ideas worked out without direct reference to Mill, but in the context of 'battered women' in Hirschmann 1997: 194ff.

15 Mill alluded to the example, prominent in Bentham's *Chrestomathia* (Bentham 1983a (1817): 21–2; see also Ch.4 above) of a man who retired from active employment and whose lack of activity led to 'ennui, melancholy, and premature death' (*CW* xxi. 338). Without mentioning Bentham (or any other writer) by name, Mill pointed out that a similar condition in women was almost never considered. After a lifetime of raising a family and running a home, a woman was left with no outlet for her abilities and character. Mill's remark and subsequent discussion (*CW* xxi. 338–40) might or might not have contained an intentional allusion to Bentham, but one cannot help noting that Bentham, now highly regarded as an early feminist (See Boralevi 1987: 165–6), failed to refer specifically to the condition of women in terms of despotism or potential liberty in society, even though he saw no reason for denying women the right to vote or for opposing their liberty in any other respect (See Sokol 2011). But he did not seem to imagine that the case for the cultivation of intellectual pleasures might require a specific focus on the condition of women.

16 See Crisp 1998: 111–12, for an assessment of Mill's remark.

17 For a useful and brief account, See Crisp 1997: 67ff.

18 Hall has correctly written: 'Chapter iv is, I wish to urge, simply an explication of a certain sort of consideration that an empiricist can use to gain acceptance for an ethical first principle, the first principle in this instance (though it is not used as a mere illustration, for Mill does wish to get his readers to accept it) being, of course, that of utility' (Hall 1969: 159–60).

19 Mill wrote: 'Of all difficulties which impede the progress of thought, and the formation of well-grounded opinions on life and social arrangements, the greatest is now the unspeakable ignorance and inattention of mankind in respect to the influences which form human character' (*CW* xxi. 277).

20 As Morley 1970 (1874): 153 wrote: 'The little book on the Subjection of Women, though not a capital performance like the Logic, was the capital illustration of the modes of reasoning about human character...'

21 'It sometimes stands for human improvement in general, and sometimes for certain kinds of improvement in particular' (*CW* xviii. 119).

22 See Parekh 2000; Barry 2001. See also Parekh 2002: 133–50; Barry 2002: 204–38.

Bibliography

Primary Sources

Aldrich, H., *Artis Logicae Compendium* (Oxford: Oxford University Press, 1691).

Bain, A., [Review of Mill's *System of Logic*] *Westminster Review*, 39 (1843), 412–56.

——*The Senses and the Intellect* (London: John W. Parker & Son, 1855).

——*The Emotions and the Will* (London: John W. Parker & Son, 1859).

——*On the Study of Character including An Estimate of Phrenology* (London: Parker, Son, and Bourn, 1861).

——*Mental and Moral Science. A Compendium of Psychology and Ethics* (London: Longmans, Green, and Co., 1868).

——*Logic*, 2 vols. (London: Longmans, Green, Reader, and Dyer, 1870).

——*Mind and Body: The Theories of their Relation* (London: Henry S. King and Co., 1873).

——*John Stuart Mill, A Criticism: with Personal Recollections* (London: Longmans, Green and Co., 1882).

——*Autobiography* (London: Longmans, Green, and Co., 1904).

Bentham, J., [Gamaliel Smith], *Not Paul, But Jesus* (London: John Hunt, 1823).

——*Rationale of Judicial Evidence, specially applied to English Practice*, ed. J. S. Mill, 5 vols. (London: Hunt and Clarke, 1827).

——*The Works of Jeremy Bentham*, ed. J. Bowring, 11 vols. (Edinburgh: W. Tait; and London: Simpkin Marshall, 1838–43).

——'Defence of Usury', in *Jeremy Bentham's Economic Writings*, ed. W. Stark, 3 vols. (London: George Allen & Unwin, 1952–4 [1787]), i. 123–207.

——*The Collected Works of Jeremy Bentham*, ed. J. H. Burns, J. R. Dinwiddy, F. Rosen, and P. Schofield (London: Athlone Press; and Oxford: Clarendon Press, 1968–).

——*Chrestomathia*, ed. M. J. Smith and W. H. Burston (*The Collected Works of Jeremy Bentham*) (Oxford: Clarendon Press, 1983a [1817]).

——*Constitutional Code, Volume I*, ed. F. Rosen and J. H. Burns (*The Collected Works of Jeremy Bentham*; Oxford: Clarendon Press, 1983b [1830]).

——*Deontology, together with A Table of the Springs of Action and Article on Utilitarianism*, ed. A. Goldworth (*The Collected Works of Jeremy Bentham*) (Oxford: Clarendon Press, 1983c).

——*An Introduction to the Principles of Morals and Legislation*, ed. J. H. Burns and H. L. A. Hart, with a New Introduction by F. Rosen (*The Collected Works of Jeremy Bentham*) (Oxford: Clarendon Press, 1996 [1789]).

——'Legislator of the World': Writings on Codification, Law, and Education, ed. P. Schofield and J. Harris (The Collected Works of Jeremy Bentham) (Oxford: Clarendon Press, 1998).

——The Correspondence of Jeremy Bentham, xii. July 1824 to June 1828, ed. L. O'Sullivan and C. Fuller (The Collected Works of Jeremy Bentham) (Oxford: Clarendon Press, 2006).

Bulwer, E., England and the English, 2 vols. (London: Bentley, 1833).

Carlyle, T., Sartor Resartus, 2nd edn. (Boston: Munroe, 1837).

Coleridge, S. T., On the Constitution of Church and State, According to the Idea of Each, ed. J. Barrell (London: J. M. Dent & Sons Ltd., 1972 [1830]).

Comte, A., Cours de philosophie positive, 6 vols. (Paris: Bachelier, 1830–42).

——'Discours Préliminaire, sur l'esprit positif', in Traité Philosophique D'Astronomie Populaire (Paris: Carilian-Goeury and Victor Dalmont, 1845), 1–108.

——Système de politique positive, 4 vols. (Paris: L. Mathias, 1851–4).

——Early Essays in Social Philosophy, tr. H. Dix Hutton and ed. F. Harrison, (London: George Routledge and Sons, 1911).

——Correspondence générale et confessions, 8 vols., ed. P. E. de Berrêdo Carneiro, P. Arnaud, P. Arbousse-Bastide, and Angèle Kremer Marietti (Paris: École des Hautes Études en Sciences Sociales and Vrin, 1973–90).

——Early Political Writings, ed. H. S. Jones (Cambridge: Cambridge University Press, 1998).

——and Mill, J. S., Lettres Inédites de John Stuart Mill à Auguste Comte Publiées Avec Les Réponses De Comte et une Introduction par L. Lévy-Bruhl, ed. L. Lévy-Bruhl (Paris: Félix Alcan, 1899).

——The Correspondence of John Stuart Mill and Auguste Comte, tr. and ed. O. Haac (New Brunswick, NJ, and London: Transaction Publishers, 1995).

Encyclopædia Metropolitana; or, Universal Dictionary of Knowledge, On an Original Plan, ed. Henry J. Rose, Hugh J. Rose, and E. Smedley, 29 vols. (London: B. Fellowes et al., 1845).

Fawcett, H., 'Strikes, their Tendencies and Remedies', Westminster Review, NS 18 (1860), 1–23.

Fosdick, D. (ed.), On Social Freedom by John Stuart Mill (New York: Columbia University Press, 1941).

Grote, G., Aristotle, ed. A. Bain and G. Robertson, 2 vols. (London: Murray, 1872).

——A History of Greece, 12 vols. (London: J. M. Dent & Sons, 1940 [1846–56]).

Hobbes, T., Leviathan, ed. M. Oakeshott (New York: Collier Books, 1966 [1651]).

Holyoake, G. J., John Stuart Mill As Some of the Working Classes Knew Him (London: Trübner & Co., 1873a).

——The Logic of Co-operation, (London: Trübner & Co., and Manchester: Co-operative Printing Society, 1873b).

——*The History of the Rochdale Pioneers*, (London: George Allen & Unwin Ltd., 1893).

——*The History of Co-operation*, Revised and Completed, 2 vols. (London: T. Fisher Unwin, 1906).

Hume, D., 'That Politics May Be Reduced to a Science' and 'Of National Characters', in *Essays, Moral, Political, and Literary*, ed. E. Miller (Indianapolis: Liberty Fund, 1985 [1748]), 14–31, 197–215.

Lévy-Bruhl, L., *La Philosophie d'Auguste Comte* (Paris: Félix Alcan, 1900).

Lewis, G. Cornewall, *A Treatise on the Methods of Observation and Reasoning in Politics*, 2 vols. (London: J. W. Parker and Son, 1852).

Littré, É., *Auguste Comte et la philosophie positive* (Paris: Hachette, 1863).

——*Auguste Comte et Stuart Mill* (Paris: Germer Baillière, 1866).

Locke, J., *An Essay Concerning Human Understanding*, ed. P. Nidditch (Oxford: Oxford University Press, 1975 [1690]).

——*Two Treatises of Government*, ed. P. Laslett (Cambridge: Cambridge University Press, 1988 [1698]).

Martineau, H., *The Positive Philosophy of Auguste Comte, Freely Translated and Condensed*, 2 vols. (London: John Chapman, 1853).

Marx, K., and Engels, F., *Selected Writings in One Volume* (London: Lawrence & Wishart, 1968).

Mill, H. T., *The Complete Works of Harriet Taylor Mill*, ed. J. Jacobs and P. Payne (Bloomington and Indianapolis: Indiana University Press, 1998).

Mill, James, [Review of] 'A New View of Society: or Essays on the Principle of the Formation of Human Character, and the Application of the Principle to Practice. By one of His Majesty's Justices of the Peace for the County of Lanark. Essays First and Second', *The Philanthropist*, 3 (1813), 93–119.

——*Analysis of the Phenomena of the Human Mind*, 2nd edn., ed. A. Bain, A. Findlater, G. Grote, and J. S. Mill, 2 vols. (London: Longmans, Green, Reader, and Dyer, 1869).

——*An Essay on Government*, ed. E. Barker (Cambridge: Cambridge University Press, 1937 [1824]).

——*Selected Economic Writings*, ed. D. Winch (Edinburgh and London: Oliver & Boyd, 1966).

——*James Mill on Education*, ed. W. H. Burston (Cambridge: Cambridge University Press, 1969).

——'Education' in *Political Writings*, ed. T. Ball, (Cambridge: Cambridge University Press, 1992 [1824]), 139–94.

——Common Place Books, ed. R. Fenn (online edn.), 2011: http://www.intellectualhistory.net/Mill.

Mill, J. S., *Dissertations and Discussions*, 2 vols. (London: Parker, 1859).

——'The Positive Philosophy of Auguste Comte', *Westminster Review*, 83 (1865a), 339–405.

——'Later Speculations of Auguste Comte', *Westminster Review*, 84 (1865b), 1–42.

——*Collected Works of John Stuart Mill*, ed. J. M. Robson, 33 vols. (Toronto: University of Toronto Press, and London: Routledge & Kegan Paul, 1963–91).

Morley, J., 'Mr. Mill's *Autobiography*', in P. Stansky (ed.), *Nineteenth-Century Essays* (Chicago and London: University of Chicago Press, 1970 [1874]), 139–63.

Plato, *The Republic*, tr. P. Shorey, 2 vols. (London: William Heinemann; and Cambridge, Mass.: Harvard University Press, 1963).

Sanderson, R., *Logicae Artis Compendium*, 2nd edn. (Oxford: A. Lichfield, 1618).

Sidgwick, H., 'The Economic Lessons of Socialism', in *Miscellaneous Essays and Addresses* (London: Macmillan and Co., 1904), 235–48.

Spencer, H., *The Principles of Psychology* (London: Longman, Brown, Green, and Longmans, 1855).

——*The Classification of the Sciences: to which are added Reasons for Dissenting from the Philosophy of M. Comte* (London: Williams and Norgate, 1864).

Stephen, J. F., *Liberty, Equality, Fraternity* (London: Smith Elder, 1873).

Whately, R., *Elements of Logic* [based on 2nd edn, of 1827], ed. R. McKerrow (Delmar, NY: Scholars' Facsimiles and Reprints, 1975).

Secondary Sources

Annas, J., 'Mill and the Subjection of Women', *Philosophy*, 52 (1977), 179–94.

Ashcraft, R., 'Class Conflict and Constitutionalism in J. S. Mill's Thought', in N. Rosenblum (ed.), *Liberalism and the Moral Life* (Cambridge, Mass.: Harvard University Press, 1989), 105–26.

——'John Stuart Mill and the Theoretical Foundations of Democratic Socialism', in E. Eisenach (ed.), *Mill and the Moral Character of Liberalism* (University Park, Pa.: Pennsylvania State University Press, 1998), 169–89.

August, E., *John Stuart Mill, A Mind at Large* (London: Vision Press, 1976).

Ball, T., 'Introduction', in James Mill, *Political Writings*, ed. T. Ball (Cambridge: Cambridge University Press, 1992).

——'The Formation of Character: Mill's "Ethology" Reconsidered', *Polity*, 33 (2000), 25–48.

——'Competing Theories of Character Formation, James vs. John Stuart Mill', in G. Varouxakis and P. Kelly (eds.), *John Stuart Mill—Thought and Influence. The Saint of Rationalism* (London and New York: Routledge, 2010), 35–56.

Barrell, J., 'Introduction', in S. T. Coleridge, *On the Constitution of Church and State*, ed. J. Barrell (London: J. M. Dent & Sons, 1972).

Barry, B., *Culture and Equality: An Egalitarian Critique of Multiculturalism* (Cambridge: Polity Press, 2001).

——'Second Thoughts—and Some First Thoughts Revived', in P. Kelly (ed.), *Multiculturalism Reconsidered: Culture and Equality and its Critics* (Cambridge: Polity Press, 2002), 204–38.

Berger, F., *Happiness, Justice, and Freedom: The Moral and Political Philosophy of John Stuart Mill* (Berkeley, Los Angeles, and London: University of California Press, 1984).

Berlin, I., *Four Essays on Liberty* (London, Oxford, and New York: Oxford University Press, 1969).

Boralevi, L., 'Utilitarianism and Feminism', in E. Kennedy and S. Mendus (eds.), *Women in Western Political Philosophy* (Brighton: Wheatsheaf Books, 1987), 159–78.

Britton, K. W., 'John Stuart Mill on Christianity', in *James and John Stuart Mill: Papers of the Centenary Conference*, ed. J. M. Robson and M. Laine (Toronto and Buffalo, NY: University of Toronto Press, 1976), 21–34.

Brogan, H., *Alexis de Tocqueville, A Biography* (London: Profile Books, 2006).

Brown, D. G., 'Mill's Moral Theory: Ongoing Revisionism', *Politics, Philosophy & Economics*, 9 (2010), 5–45.

Burns, J. H., 'J. S. Mill and Democracy, 1829–61', in J. B. Schneewind (ed.), *Mill, A Collection of Critical Essays* (London: Macmillan, 1969), 280–328.

——'The Light of Reason: Philosophical History in the Two Mills', in J. M. Robson and M. Laine (eds.), *James and John Stuart Mill: Papers of the Centenary Conference* (Toronto and Buffalo, NY: University of Toronto Press, 1976), 3–20.

Capaldi, N., 'Mill's Forgotten Science of Ethology', *Social Theory and Practice*, 2 (1973), 409–20.

——*John Stuart Mill: A Biography* (Cambridge: Cambridge University Press, 2004).

Card, R. 'Situationist Social Psychology and J. S. Mill's Conception of Character', *Utilitas*, 22 (2010), 481–93.

Carlisle, J., *John Stuart Mill and the Writing of Character* (Athens, Ga., and London: University of Georgia Press, 1991).

——'Mr. J. Stuart Mill, M. P., and the Character of the Working Classes', in E. Eisenach (ed.), *Mill and the Moral Character of Liberalism* (University Park, Pa.: Pennsylvania State University Press, 1998), 143–67.

Cashdollar, C. D., *The Transformation of Theology, 1830–1980, Positivism and Protestant Thought in Britain and America* (Princeton: Princeton University Press, 1989).

Claeys, G., 'Justice, Independence, and Industrial Democracy: The Development of John Stuart Mill's Views on Socialism', *Journal of Politics*, 49 (1987), 122–47.

——'Non-Marxian Socialism 1815–1914', in G. Stedman Jones and G. Claeys (eds.), *The Cambridge History of Nineteenth-Century Political Thought* (Cambridge: Cambridge University Press, 2011), 521–55.

Collini, S., 'Introduction', in *The Collected Works of John Stuart Mill*, xxi (Toronto: University of Toronto Press; and London: Routledge & Kegan Paul, 1984), pp. vii–lvi.

——'Introduction' in J. S. Mill, *On Liberty, with The Subjection of Women and Chapters on Socialism*, ed. S. Collini (Cambridge: Cambridge University Press, 1989), pp. vii–xxvi.

——*Public Moralists, Political Thought and Intellectual Life in Britain 1850–1930* (Oxford: Clarendon Press, 1991).

——*Absent Minds: Intellectuals in Britain* (Oxford: Oxford University Press, 2006).

——Winch, D., and Burrow, J., *That Noble Science of Politics, A Study in Nineteenth-Century Intellectual History* (Cambridge: Cambridge University Press, 1983).

Colmer, J., 'Editor's Introduction', in *On the Constitution of the Church and State*, ed. J. Colmer (The Collected Works of Samuel Taylor Coleridge, 10) (Princeton and London: Princeton University Press, 1976), pp. xxxiii–lxviii.

Cowling, M., *Mill and Liberalism*, 2nd edn., 1990 (Cambridge: Cambridge University Press, 1963).

Cranston, M., *Freedom, A New Analysis* (London: Longmans, Green, and Co., 1953).

——'Introduction', in Rousseau, *The Social Contract* (Harmondsworth: Penguin Books, 1968), 9–43.

Crisp, R., *Mill on Utilitarianism* (London: Routledge, 1997).

——'Introductory Materials' and 'Notes' in *J. S. Mill, Utilitarianism* (Oxford and New York: Oxford University Press, 1998), 3–43, 111–53.

Demetriou, K., 'Grote on Socrates: An Unpublished Essay of the 1820s in its Context', *Dialogos*, 3 (1996), 36–50.

——*George Grote on Plato and Athenian Democracy: A Study in Classical Reception* (Frankfurt: Peter Lang, 1999).

——'Socratic Dialectic and the Exaltation of Individuality: J. S. Mill's Influence on G. Grote's Platonic Interpretation', *Quaderni di Storia*, 69 (2009), 35–61.

——*Studies on the Reception of Plato and Greek Political Thought in Victorian Britain* (Farnham, Surrey, and Burlington, Vt.: Ashgate Publishing, 2011).

Devigne, R., 'Mill on Liberty and Religion: An Unfinished Dialectic', in E. Eisenach (ed.), *Mill and the Moral Character of Liberalism* (University Park, Pa.: Pennsylvania State University Press, 1998), 231–56.

Donner, W., *The Liberal Self, John Stuart Mill's Moral and Political Philosophy* (Ithaca, NY, and London: Cornell University Press, 1991).

——'Mill's Utilitarianism', in J. Skorupski (ed.), *The Cambridge Companion to Mill* (Cambridge: Cambridge University Press, 1998), 255–92.

——'Morality, Virtue, and Aesthetics in Mill's Art of Life', in B. Eggleston, D. Miller, and D. Weinstein (eds.), *John Stuart Mill and the Art of Life* (Oxford and New York: Oxford University Press, 2011), 146–65.

Drescher, S., 'Tocqueville's Comparative Perspectives', in C. Welch (ed.), *The Cambridge Companion to Tocqueville* (Cambridge: Cambridge University Press, 2006), 21–48.

Duncan, G., *Marx and Mill, Two Views of Social Conflict and Social Harmony* (Cambridge: Cambridge University Press, 1973).

Eggleston, B., Miller, D., and Weinstein, D., 'Introduction', in *John Stuart Mill and the Art of Life* (Oxford and New York: Oxford University Press, 2011), 3–18.

Eisenach, E., 'Introduction', in E. Eisenach (ed.), *Mill and the Moral Character of Liberalism* (University Park, Pa.: Pennsylvania State University Press, 1998), 1–12.

——'Mill and Liberal Christianity', in *Narrative Power and Liberal Truth, Hobbes, Locke, Bentham, and Mill* (Lanham, Md.: Rowman & Littlefield, 2002), 189–216.

Fenn, R., *James Mill's Political Thought* (New York and London: Garland, 1987).

Feuer, L., 'John Stuart Mill and Marxian Socialism', *Journal of the History of Ideas*, 10 (1949), 297–303.

——'John Stuart Mill as a Sociologist: The Unwritten Ethology', in J. M. Robson and M. Laine (eds.), *James and John Stuart Mill: Papers of the Centenary Conference* (Toronto and Buffalo, NY: University of Toronto Press, 1976), 86–110.

Fisch, M., 'Alexander Bain and the Genealogy of Pragmatism', *Journal of the History of Ideas*, 15 (1954), 413–44.

Frege, G., 'The Thought: A Logical Inquiry', in S. Blackburn and K. Simmons (eds.), *Truth* (Oxford: Oxford University Press, 1999), 85–105.

Goldberg, T., 'Liberalism's Limits, Carlyle and Mill on "The Negro Question"', in B. Schultz and G. Varouxakis (eds.), *Utilitarianism and Empire* (Lanham, Md.: Lexington Books, 2005), 125–35.

Goldstein, L., 'Mill, Marx, and Women's Liberation', *Journal of the History of Philosophy*, 18 (1980), 319–34.

Gray, J., 'John Stuart Mill on the Theory of Property', in A. Parel and T. Flanagan (eds.), *Theories of Property: Aristotle to the Present* (Waterloo, Ontario: Wilfred Laurier University Press, 1979), 257–80.

——*Mill on Liberty: A Defence* (London and New York: Routledge, 1996).

Guillin, V., 'Auguste Comte and John Stuart Mill on Sexual Equality: Historical, Methodological, and Philosophical Issues', PhD thesis (London School of Economics, 2005).

Halévy, E., *The Growth of Philosophic Radicalism*, tr. M. Morris (London: Faber & Faber, 1928).

Hall, E., 'The "Proof" of Utility in Bentham and Mill', in J. B. Schneewind (ed.), *Mill, A Collection of Critical Essays* (London: Macmillan, 1969), 145–78.

Hamburger, J., 'Mill and Tocqueville on Liberty', in J. M. Robson and M. Laine (eds.), *James and John Stuart Mill, Papers of the Centenary Conference* (Toronto and Buffalo, NY: University of Toronto Press, 1976), 111–25.

——'Religion and *On Liberty*', in *A Cultivated Mind: Essays on J. S. Mill Presented to John M. Robson* (Toronto: Toronto University Press, 1991), 139–81.

——*John Stuart Mill on Liberty and Control* (Princeton and Oxford: Princeton University Press, 1999).

Hansen, H., 'Mill on Inference and Fallacies', in D. Walton and A. Brinton (eds.), *Historical Foundations of Informal Logic* (Aldershot: Ashgate, 1997).

——'"The Great Business of Life": Mill and Argumentation', paper presented at the International Society for Utilitarian Studies Conference, Dartmouth College, USA, Aug. 2005.

Hayek, F., *John Stuart Mill and Harriet Taylor, Their Correspondence and Subsequent Marriage* (London: Routledge & Kegan Paul, 1951).

Himmelfarb, G., *On Liberty and Liberalism, The Case of John Stuart Mill* (New York: Alfred A. Knopf, 1974).

Hirschmann, N., 'The Theory and Practice of Freedom: The Case of Battered Women', in M. Shanley and U. Narayan (eds.), *Reconstructing Political Theory, Feminist Perspectives* (Cambridge: Polity Press, 1997), 194–210.

——*The Subject of Liberty, Toward a Feminist Theory of Freedom* (Princeton and Oxford: Princeton University Press, 2003).

Hollander, S., *The Economics of John Stuart Mill*, 2 vols. (Oxford: Basil Blackwell, 1985).

Holmes, S., 'Making Sense of Liberal Imperialism', in N. Urbinati and A. Zakaras (eds.), *J. S. Mill's Political Thought, A Bicentennial Reassessment* (Cambridge: Cambridge University Press, 2007), 319–46.

Hont, I., *Jealousy of Trade, International Competition and the Nation-State in Historical Perspective* (Cambridge, Mass., and London: Harvard University Press, 2005).

Hooker, B., 'Consequentialism', in J. Skorupski (ed.),*The Routledge Companion to Ethics* (London and New York: Routledge, 2010), 444–55.

Hornblower, S., *A Commentary on Thucydides*, i (Oxford: Oxford University Press, 1991).

Jackson, R., *An Examination of the Deductive Logic of John Stuart Mill* (London: Oxford University Press, 1941).

Jacobson, D., 'Mill on Liberty, Speech, and the Free Society', *Philosophy & Public Affairs*, 29 (2000), 276–309.

Jones, E., *Sigmund Freud, Life and Work*, 3 vols. (London: Hogarth Press, 1953).

Jones, H. S., 'John Stuart Mill as Moralist', *Journal of the History of Ideas*, 53 (1992), 287–308.

——'The Early Utilitarians, Race, and Empire: The State of the Argument', in B. Schultz and G. Varouxakis (eds.), *Utilitarianism and Empire* (Lanham, Md.: Lexington Books, 2005), 179–87.

——*Intellect and Character in Victorian England, Mark Pattison and the Invention of the Don* (Cambridge: Cambridge University Press, 2007).

Kahan, A., *Aristocratic Liberalism, The Social and Political Thought of Jacob Burkhardt, John Stuart Mill, and Alexis de Tocqueville* (New York and Oxford: Oxford University Press, 1992).

——*Alexis de Tocqueville* (New York and London: Continuum, 2010).Kamm, J., *John Stuart Mill in Love* (London: Gordon and Cremonesi, 1977).

Kelly, P., *Utilitarianism and Distributive Justice: Jeremy Bentham and the Civil Law* (Oxford: Clarendon Press, 1990).

——*Liberalism* (Cambridge: Polity Press, 2005).

Kinzer, B., *J. S. Mill Revisited, Biographical and Political Explorations* (New York and Basingstoke: Palgrave Macmillan, 2007).

——Robson, A., and Robson, J., *A Moralist In and Out of Parliament: John Stuart Mill at Westminster 1865-8* (Toronto, Buffalo, NY, and London: University of Toronto Press, 1992).

Knights, B., *The Idea of the Clerisy in the Nineteenth Century* (Cambridge: Cambridge University Press, 1978).

Kubitz, O., 'Development of John Stuart Mill's *System of Logic*', *Illinois Studies in the Social Sciences*, 18/1-2 (Urbana, Ill.: University of Illinois Graduate School, 1932).

Kurer, O., *John Stuart Mill, The Politics of Progress* (New York and London: Garland Publishing, 1991).

Kurfirst, R., 'J. S. Mill on Oriental Despotism, including its British Variant', *Utilitas*, 8 (1996), 73–87.

Leavis, F. R., 'Introduction', in *Mill on Bentham and Coleridge*, ed. F. R. Leavis (Cambridge: Cambridge University Press, 1980), 1–38.

Levin, M., 'John Stuart Mill Looks at Utopian Socialism in the Years of Revolution 1848-9', *Utopian Studies*, 14 (2003), 68–82.

Lewisohn, D., 'Mill and Comte on the Methods of Social Science', *Journal of the History of Ideas*, 33 (1972), 315–24.

Lively, J., *The Social and Political Thought of Alexis de Tocqueville* (Oxford: Clarendon Press, 1962).

——and Rees, J. (eds.), *Utilitarian Logic and Politics* (Oxford: Clarendon Press, 1978).

Long, D., *Bentham on Liberty: Jeremy Bentham's Idea of Liberty in Relation to his Utilitarianism* (Toronto: University of Toronto Press, 1977).

Lyons, D., *Rights, Welfare, and Mill's Moral Theory* (New York and Oxford: Oxford University Press, 1994).

Manent, P., 'Tocqueville, Political Philosopher', in C. Welch (ed.), *The Cambridge Companion to Tocqueville* (Cambridge: Cambridge University Press, 2006), 108–20.

Mantena, K., 'Mill on the Imperial Predicament', in N. Urbinati and A. Zakaras (eds.), *J. S. Mill's Political Thought, A Bicentennial Reassessment* (Cambridge: Cambridge University Press, 2007), 298–318.

Megill, A., 'J. S. Mill's Religion of Humanity and the Second Justification for the Writing of *On Liberty*', in E. Eisenach (ed.), *Mill and the Moral Character of Liberalism* (University Park, Pa.: Pennsylvania State University Press, 1998), 301–16.

Miller, D., 'Internal Sanctions in Mill's Moral Psychology', *Utilitas*, 10 (1998), 68–81.

——'Mill's "Socialism"', *Politics, Philosophy & Economics*, 2 (2003), 213–38.

——'Brown on Mill's Moral Theory: A Critical Response', *Politics, Philosophy & Economics*, 9 (2010*a*), 47–66.

——*J. S. Mill, Moral, Social and Political Thought* (Cambridge and Malden Mass.: Polity Press, 2010*b*).

Minow, M., and Shanley, M., 'Revisioning the Family: Relational Rights and Responsibilities', in M. Shanley and U. Narayan (eds.), *Reconstructing Political Theory, Feminist Perspectives* (Cambridge: Polity Press, 1997).

Morales, M., *Perfect Equality, John Stuart Mill on Well-Constituted Communities* (Lanhan Mass.: Rowman & Littlefield, 1996).

Morrow, J., *Coleridge's Political Thought, Property, Morality, and the Limits of Traditional Discourse* (Basingstoke: Macmillan, 1990).

Mueller, I., *John Stuart Mill and French Thought* (Urbana, Ill.: University of Illinois Press, 1956).

Nicholson, P., 'The Reception and Early Reputation of Mill's Political Thought', in J. Skorupski (ed.), *The Cambridge Companion to Mill* (Cambridge: Cambridge University Press, 1998), 464–96.

Odugbemi, A. M., 'Public Opinion and Direct Accountability between Elections: A Study of the Constitutional Theories of Jeremy Bentham and A. V. Dicey', PhD thesis (University College London, 2009).

Okin, S., *Women in Western Political Thought* (London: Virago, 1980).

O'Rourke, K., *John Stuart Mill and Freedom of Expression, The Genesis of a Theory* (London and New York: Routledge, 2001).

Packe, M. St. John, *The Life of John Stuart Mill* (London: Secker & Warburg, 1954).

Pappé, H., *John Stuart Mill and the Harriet Taylor Myth* (Victoria: Melbourne University Press, 1960).

——'Mill and Tocqueville', *Journal of the History of Ideas*, 25 (1964), 217–34.

Parekh, B., *Rethinking Multiculturalism, Cultural Diversity and Political Theory* (Basingstoke and London: Macmillan Press, 2000).

——'Barry and the Dangers of Liberalism', in P. Kelly (ed.), *Multiculturalism Reconsidered, Culture and Equality and its Critics* (Cambridge: Polity Press, 2002), 133–50.

Philp, M., *Political Conduct* (Cambridge, Mass., and London: Harvard University Press, 2007).

Pickering, M., *Auguste Comte, An Intellectual Biography*, 3 vols. (Cambridge: Cambridge University Press, 1993, 2009).

Raphael, D. D., *Concepts of Justice* (Oxford: Clarendon Press, 2001).

Rees, J., *John Stuart Mill's On Liberty*, ed. G. Williams (Oxford: Clarendon Press, 1985).

Reeves, R., *John Stuart Mill, Victorian Firebrand* (London: Atlantic Books, 2007).

Richter, M., 'Tocqueville on Threats to Liberty in Democracies', in C. Welch (ed.), *The Cambridge Companion to Tocqueville* (Cambridge: Cambridge University Press, 2006), 245–75.

Riley, J., 'Justice Under Capitalism', in J. Chapman and J. R. Pennock (eds.), *Markets and Justice*, NOMOS XXXI (New York and London: New York University Press, 1989), 122–62.

——'J. S. Mill's Liberal Utilitarian Assessment of Capitalism Versus Socialism', *Utilitas*, 8 (1996), 39–71.

——*Mill on Liberty* (London and New York: Routledge, 1998a).

——'Mill's Political Economy: Ricardian Science and Liberal Utilitarian Art', in J. Skorupski (ed.), *The Cambridge Companion to Mill* (Cambridge: Cambridge University Press, 1998b), 293–337.

——'Mill's Neo-Athenian Model of Liberal Democracy', in N. Urbinati and A. Zakaras (eds.), *J. S. Mill's Political Thought, A Bicentennial Reassessment* (Cambridge: Cambridge University Press, 2007), 221–49.

——'Racism, Blasphemy, and Free Speech', in C. L. Ten (ed.), *Mill's On Liberty, A Critical Guide* (Cambridge: Cambridge University Press, 2008), 62–82.

——'Mill's Extraordinary Utilitarian Moral Theory', *Politics, Philosophy, & Economics*, 9 (2010), 67–116.

Ring, J., *Modern Political Theory and Contemporary Feminism: A Dialectical Analysis* (Albany, NY: State University of New York Press, 1991).

Robbins, L., *The Theory of Economic Policy in English Classical Political Economy* (London: Macmillan & Co., 1952).

Robson, A., and Robson, J. M., 'Introduction', in *Sexual Equality, Writings by John Stuart Mill, Harriet Taylor Mill, and Helen Taylor*, ed. A. Robson and J. M. Robson (Toronto: University of Toronto Press, 1994).

Robson, J. M., *The Improvement of Mankind, The Social and Political Thought of John Stuart Mill* (Toronto: University of Toronto Press, 1968).

——'Civilization and Culture as Moral Concepts', in J. Skorupski (ed.), *The Cambridge Companion to Mill* (Cambridge: Cambridge University Press, 1998), 338–71.

Romani, R., *National Character and Public Spirit in Britain and France* (Cambridge: Cambridge University Press, 2002).

Rosen, F., 'Piety and Justice: Plato's *Euthyphro*', *Philosophy*, 43 (1968), 105–16.

——'Obligation and Friendship in Plato's *Crito*', *Political Theory*, 1 (1973), 307–16.

——'The Political Context of Aristotle's Theory of Justice', *Phronesis*, 20 (1975), 228–40.

——*Jeremy Bentham and Representative Democracy, A Study of the Constitutional Code* (Oxford: Clarendon Press, 1983).

——'Bentham and Mill on Liberty and Justice', in G. Feaver and F. Rosen (eds.), *Lives, Liberties and the Public Good, New Essays in Political Theory for Maurice Cranston* (London: Macmillan Press, 1987), 121–38.

——*Bentham, Byron and Greece: Constitutionalism, Nationalism, and Early Liberal Political Thought* (Oxford: Clarendon Press, 1992).

——'Individual Sacrifice and the Greatest Happiness: Bentham on Utility and Rights', *Utilitas*, 10 (1998), 129–43.

——'Crime, Punishment and Liberty', *History of Political Thought*, 20 (1999), 173–85.

——*Classical Utilitarianism from Hume to Mill* (London: Routledge, 2003a).

——'Mill on Coleridge', *Telos*, 12 (2003b), 7–21.

——'J. S. Mill on Socrates, Pericles, and the Fragility of Truth', *Journal of Legal History*, 25 (2004), 181–94.

——'The Philosophy of Error and Liberty of Thought: J. S. Mill on Logical Fallacies', *Informal Logic*, 26 (2006), 121–47.

——'Parallel Lives in Logic: The Benthams and the Mills', in G. Varouxakis and P. Kelly (eds.), *John Stuart Mill–Thought and Influence. The Saint of Rationalism* (London and New York: Routledge, 2010), 67–83.

——'From Jeremy Bentham's Radical Philosophy to J. S. Mill's Philosophic Radicalism', in G. Stedman Jones and G. Claeys (eds.), *The Cambridge History of Nineteenth-Century Political Thought* (Cambridge: Cambridge University Press, 2011), 257–94.

Rossi, A. (ed.), *Essays on Sexual Equality, John Stuart Mill and Harriet Taylor Mill* (Chicago: University of Chicago Press, 1970).

Russell, B., 'John Stuart Mill', in J. B. Schneewind (ed.), *Mill: A Collection of Critical Essays* (London: Macmillan, 1968), 1–21.

Ryan, A., *J. S. Mill* (London and Boston: Routledge & Kegan Paul, 1974).

——*The Philosophy of John Stuart Mill*, 2nd edn. (Basingstoke: Macmillan, 1987).

——'Mill in a Liberal Landscape', in J. Skorupski (ed.), *The Cambridge Companion to Mill* (Cambridge: Cambridge University Press, 1998), 497–540.

Scarre, G., *Logic and Reality in the Philosophy of John Stuart Mill* (Dordrecht: Kluwer Academic Publishers, 1989).

——*Utilitarianism* (London and New York: Routledge, 1996).

——*Mill's On Liberty, A Reader's Guide* (London and New York: Continuum, 2007).

Scharff, R., *Comte After Positivism* (Cambridge: Cambridge University Press, 1995).

Schwartz, P., *The New Political Economy of J. S. Mill* (London: Weidenfeld and Nicolson, 1972).

Sell, A., (ed.), *Mill and Religion. Contemporary Responses to Three Essays on Religion* (Bristol: Thoemmes Press, 1997).

——*Mill on God, The Pervasiveness and Elusiveness of Mill's Religious Thought* (Aldershot and Burlington, Vt.: Ashgate, 2004).

Semmel, B., *John Stuart Mill and the Pursuit of Virtue* (New Haven and London: Yale University Press, 1984).

——'John Stuart Mill's Coleridgean Neoradicalism', in E. Eisenach (ed.), *Mill and the Moral Character of Liberalism* (University Park, Pa.: Pennsylvania State University Press, 1998), 49–76.

Shanley, M., *Feminism, Marriage, and the Law in Victorian England, 1850–1895* (London: I. B. Tauris, 1989).

——'Marital Slavery and Friendship: John Stuart Mill's *The Subjection of Women*', in M. Shanley and C. Pateman (eds.), *Feminist Interpretations and Political Theory* (Cambridge: Polity Press, 1991), 164–80.

——'The Subjection of Women', in J. Skorupski (ed.), *The Cambridge Companion to Mill* (Cambridge: Cambridge University Press, 1998), 396–422.

Simon, W. M., *European Positivism in the Nineteenth Century: An Essay in Intellectual History* (Port Washington, NY, and London: Kennikat Press, 1972).

Skinner, Q., *Liberty Before Liberalism* (Cambridge: Cambridge University Press, 1998).

Skorupski, J. *John Stuart Mill* (London and New York: Routledge, 1989).

——(ed.), *The Cambridge Companion to Mill* (Cambridge: Cambridge University Press, 1998).

——*Why Read Mill Today?* (London and New York: Routledge, 2006).

Snyder, A. D., *Coleridge on Logic and Learning with Selections from the Unpublished Manuscripts* (New Haven: Yale University Press, 1929).

Sokol, M., *Bentham, Law and Marriage, A Utilitarian Code of Law in Historical Contexts* (London and New York: Continuum Books, 2011).

Stafford, W., *John Stuart Mill* (Basingstoke: Macmillan Press; and New York, St Martin's Press, 1988).

Ten, C. L., *Mill on Liberty* (Oxford: Clarendon Press, 1980).

——'Democracy, Socialism, and the Working Classes', in J. Skorupski (ed.), *The Cambridge Companion to Mill* (Cambridge: Cambridge University Press, 1998), 372–95.

Thomas, W., *The Philosophic Radicals: Nine Studies in Theory and Practice, 1817–41* (Oxford: Clarendon Press, 1979).

Thompson, D., *John Stuart Mill and Representative Government* (Princeton: Princeton University Press, 1976).

Tulloch, G., *Mill and Sexual Equality* (Hemel Hempstead: Harvester Wheatsheaf, 1989).

Turk, C., *Coleridge and Mill, A Study of Influence* (Aldershot: Gower, 1998).

Urbinati, N., *Mill on Democracy: From the Athenian Polis to Representative Government* (Chicago and London: University of Chicago Press, 2002).

——'The Many Heads of the Hydra: J. S. Mill on Despotism', in N. Urbinati and A. Zakaras (eds.), *J. S. Mill's Political Thought, A Bicentennial Reassessment* (Cambridge: Cambridge University Press, 2007), 66–97.

——'An Alternative Modernity: Mill on Capitalism and the Quality of Life', in B. Eggleston, D. Miller, and D. Weinstein (eds.), *John Stuart Mill and the Art of Life* (New York: Oxford University Press, 2011), 236–63.

——and Zakaras, A. (eds.), *J. S. Mill's Political Thought, A Bicentennial Reassessment* (Cambridge: Cambridge University Press, 2007).

Van Holthoon, F. L., *The Road to Utopia, A Study of John Stuart Mill's Social Thought* (Assen: Van Gorcum & Co., 1971).

Varouxakis, G., 'National Character in John Stuart Mill's Thought', *History of European Ideas*, 24 (1998), 375–91.

——*Mill on Nationality* (London and New York: Routledge, 2002a).

——*Victorian Political Thought on France and the French* (Basingstoke: Palgrave, 2002b).

——'Empire, Race, Eurocentrism: John Stuart Mill and His Critics', in B. Schultz and G. Varouxakis (eds.), *Utilitarianism and Empire* (Lanham, Md.: Lexington Books, 2005), 137–53.

——'Cosmopolitan Patriotism in J. S. Mill's Political Thought and Activism', in N. Urbinati and A. Zakaras (eds.), *J. S. Mill's Political Thought, A Bicentennial Reassessment* (Cambridge: Cambridge University Press, 2007), 277–97.

——and Kelly, P. (eds.), *John Stuart Mill–Thought and Influence. The Saint of Rationalism* (London and New York: Routledge, 2010).

Vernon, R., 'J. S. Mill and the Religion of Humanity', in J. Crimmins (ed.), *Religion, Secularization and Political Thought, Thomas Hobbes to J. S. Mill* (London and New York: Routledge, 1989), 167–82.

Viner, J., 'Bentham and J. S. Mill: The Utilitarian Background', in *Essays on the Intellectual History of Economics* (Princeton: Princeton University Press, 1991), 154–75.

Vlastos, G., *Socratic Studies* (Cambridge: Cambridge University Press, 1994).

Vogeler, M., 'Comte and Mill: The Early Publishing History of their Correspondence', *Mill Newsletter*, 11 (1976), 17–22.

Vogler, C., *John Stuart Mill's Deliberative Landscape, An Essay in Moral Psychology* (New York and London: Garland, 2001).

Waldron, J., 'Mill on Liberty and on the Contagious Diseases Acts', in N. Urbinati and A. Zakaras (eds.), *J. S. Mill's Political Thought, A Bicentennial Reassessment* (Cambridge: Cambridge University Press, 2007), 11–42.

Weinberg, A., *Theodor Gomperz and John Stuart Mill* (Geneva: Librairie Droz, 1963).

——*The Influence of Auguste Comte on the Economics of John Stuart Mill* (London: E. G. Weinberg, 1982).

Weinstein, D., 'Interpreting Mill', in B. Eggleston, D. Miller, and D. Weinstein (eds.), *John Stuart Mill and the Art of Life* (Oxford and New York: Oxford University Press, 2011), 44–70.

Welch, C., *De Tocqueville* (Oxford: Oxford University Press, 2001).

Wernick, A., *Auguste Comte and the Religion of Humanity, The Post-Theistic Program of French Social Theory* (Cambridge: Cambridge University Press, 2001).

West, H., *An Introduction to Mill's Utilitarian Ethics* (Cambridge: Cambridge University Press, 2004).

Wiener, P., *Evolution and the Founders of Pragmatism* (Cambridge, Mass.: Harvard University Press, 1949).

Williams, B., *Truth and Truthfulness, An Essay in Genealogy* (Princeton: Princeton University Press, 2002).

Williams, G., 'J. S. Mill and Political Violence', *Utilitas*, 1 (1989), 102–11.

Williams, R., *Culture and Society: 1780–1950* (London: Chatto & Windus, 1958).

Wilson, C., *Epicureanism at the Origins of Modernity* (Oxford: Clarendon Press, 2008).

Wilson, F., *Psychological Analysis and the Philosophy of John Stuart Mill* (Toronto, Buffalo, NY, and London: University of Toronto Press, 1990).

Winch, D., *Wealth and Life, Essays on the Intellectual History of Political Economy in Britain, 1848–1914* (Cambridge: Cambridge University Press, 2009).

——'Wild Natural Beauty and the Religion of Humanity, Mill's Green Credentials', in G. Varouxakis and P. Kelly (eds.) *John Stuart Mill–Thought and Influence. The Saint of Rationalism* (London and New York: Routledge, 2010), 57–66.

Wright, T. R., *The Religion of Humanity: The Impact of Comtean Positivism on Victorian Britain* (Cambridge: Cambridge University Press, 1986).

Zerilli, L., *Signifying Woman, Culture and Chaos in Rousseau, Burke, and Mill* (Ithaca, NY, and London: Cornell University Press, 1994).

——*Feminism and the Abyss of Freedom* (Chicago and London: University of Chicago Press, 2005).

Zunz, O., 'Tocqueville and the Americans, *Democracy in America* as Read in Nineteenth-Century America', in C. Welch (ed.), *The Cambridge Companion to Tocqueville* (Cambridge: Cambridge University Press, 2006), 359–96.

Index

Parekh, B. 285n.22
patriarchalism 283n.8; *see* despotism
Pattison, M. 265n.7
pedantocracy 9, 45–6, 217, 262nn.8–9
Pericles 40–2, 46, 161, 262n.7
philosophic radicalism 10, 50–2, 70, 263n.2
Philp, M. 267n.17
phrenology 85, 103, 104, 105, 110, 114, 240, 253, 268n.2 270n.6
physiology 268n.2
Pickering, M. 12, 105, 106, 107, 116, 118, 229–30, 262nn.8–9, 268n.6, 271n.1, 272nn.3–5, 273n.7, 274n.14
Plato 9, 26, 40, 53, 259, 282n.4
  and forms of government 45, 72
  Gorgias and *Republic* 36, 262n.5
  Mill–Comte correspondence as a Platonic dialogue 7–8, 12, 97, 113
  and motivation of rulers in *Republic* 194
  Protagoras and utilitarianism 249
  Republic and Thrasymachus 22, 235; *see* Socrates
pleasure(s) and pain(s) 2, 3, 24, 50, 248, 249, 269n.6
  and ennui 80–1, 285n.15
  and intellectual pleasures 265n.10, 285n.15
  self-regarding, social, and dissocial 80
  sensual v. intellectual 80–1; *see* Epicureanism; happiness
polarities 57, 61, 65; *see* contraries and contradictories
political economy 101–5, 268n.4
  based on desire of wealth 102
  and Benthamism 104, 106, 113, 269n.6
  and Comte 101, 113, 123, 270n.6
  and truth 274n.12
political science 10–11, 75, 88–94, 181
  analogy with medicine 73, 75
  no separate science 72–3
  and 'regime change' 25

and theory of government 65–71, 93–4; *see* government; social science
population 16, 170, 184, 190
Portugal 167
positivism 12, 13, 101–2, 104, 108–9, 112, 219, 229–30, 266n.12, 268n.2, 270n.6, 271n.6, 272–3n.6
  defined by Mill 119
  positive dimension to Comte's sociology 120–1
  and religion 214; *see* Comte
prevention (of crime), and liberty 148, 149
Price, R. 131
Priestley, J. 82
progress 4, 26, 44, 111, 112, 132, 158, 164–5, 184, 205, 218, 231, 244, 248, 255–8
  and Christianity 242
  and Coleridge 67–8
  and competition 178–9
  and role of intellect 64, 285n.19
  and progressiveness of the human race 62–3
  and security 137–8, 182; *see* improvement
property 18, 136, 180–99, 278n.3
  and 'natural rights' 19
  private property and class conflict 169, 182, 205
  and security 137–41, 145, 182; *see* justice
Protestantism 64; *see* Christianity; religion
psychology 3, 5, 6, 10, 20, 32, 59, 63, 73–4, 78, 83, 110, 181, 206–7, 209, 210, 235, 253, 268n.2, 279n.6
  associationist psychology 74, 81–2, 84, 104, 193
  and motivation 193, 198; *see* ethology
public and private 9, 41–2, 60, 157–8, 161 183–4; *see* property
public moralist 11, 20, 26, 79, 211, 232